Eileen Agar

'I see myself as a sort of metaphysical serpent who sloughs her painter's skin now and again and comes up with a different idea and works on painting from a different angle'

'The studio: my life-long box of dreams'

(from Eileen Agar's notebooks, undated)

Eileen Agar

Dreaming oneself awake

Michel Remy

REAKTION BOOKS

For Susie

Published by Reaktion Books Ltd
Unit 32, Waterside
44–48 Wharf Road
London N1 7UX, UK
www.reaktionbooks.co.uk

First published 2017

Book design: Carroll Associates

Supported by the Paul Mellon Centre for Studies in British Art

PAUL MELLON CENTRE
for Studies in British Art

Printed and bound in China

A catalogue record for this book is available from the British Library

ISBN 978 1 78023 727 5

Contents

Preface

This book is the story of three encounters in one: the encounter of a young independent-minded woman with the plastic arts in the 1920s and '30s, the encounter of that artist with the secret workings of her own subconscious, and finally the encounter of an English painter – and indeed, of English art at large – with the Surrealist movement. Intrinsic to that story, at the locus of those encounters, the reader is almost naturally confronted with the growing realization not so much of an artist's phenomenal output of paintings, collages, photographs and objects, but of a consummate aesthetic coherence and 'stylistic' consistency in an eighty-year-long career at the service of the marvellous, involving the poeticization of reality and the revelation of myth-making forces which unswervingly link man to nature.

Undeniably, Eileen Agar's work has never been granted proper attention. Only the art critic and author Andrew Lambirth helped bring to public notice the facts of Agar's life through writing with her own autobiography, *A Look at My Life* (1988). He also contributed to exhibition catalogues on Agar, especially two of them: the remarkably informative catalogue published by the Scottish National Gallery of Modern Art in 1999, *Eileen Agar, 1899–1991*, with articles by Ann Simpson, David Gascoyne and Andrew Lambirth, and the *An Eye for Collage* exhibition catalogue published by Pallant House Gallery in Chichester in 2009. That is about all, and it is time that a critical study brought together on the one hand the facts and details scattered throughout those documents and, on the other, systematic analyses of her work in relation to the social and intellectual context in which she lived.

The itinerary followed by Agar was so progressive and gradual that it could easily be compared to what is called in literature a *Bildungsroman*, a novel outlining personal growth, in which the evolution of a young man or woman is retraced from adolescence to maturity and adulthood, ending in the person's full realization of what and who he or she is, and of the complex, ambiguous and fundamentally mysterious quality of life. Similarly with Agar, we can follow the succession of remarkable experiences and chance encounters in her life.

The chapters in this book hinge on the main landmarks of her career, but from one landmark to the next there is no mutation or significant leap, no sharp contrast, no real change of direction – rather a process of deepening and of refinement. The chapters here correspond to the main moments, to the turning points in her personal history. It soon becomes evident that her response to her immediate environment never meant any radical reorientation in her approach to reality and art. In the catalogue of the *An Eye for Collage* exhibition which he organized at Pallant House Gallery, Andrew Lambirth unwittingly emphasized this when he simply chose to divide her life into decades (the 1920s, the '30s, the '40s and so on). In no way does this impair the prevailing sense of coherence in Agar's work. In whatever way one chooses to divide her life and career, the reader follows the same thread, tenuous at first but gathering force and solidity as it unfolds.

This book, then, will try to give a comprehensive vision of Eileen Agar's life *and* work, inseparably, as a kind of ever-widening process of cross-fertilization. Her life *was* her work, her work *was* her life. Ultimately, her legacy is a poetics based on universal themes and symbols – archetypes, one could almost say, ever revisited and ever renewed, the past begetting the present and the future through the objects and images it bequeaths us. This poetics, needless to say, requires the participation of the reader or viewer and the suspension of his beliefs and disbeliefs because it involves him in a descent into the hidden territories where the construction of myths originates.

Fascinated as she was at an early age by the way modern art made onslaughts on traditional values and ventured into unknown spaces, Agar first flirted with Cubism and abstraction, thus moving away from school-taught art as straightforward illustration, only to encounter, on the occasion of avant-garde art exhibitions in London or Paris, the poetic and iconoclastic works of the French Surrealists, whose revolt appealed to her rebelliousness. This gradual step-by-step discovery played a determining part in her conception of painting and acquainted her with the creativity one develops when gaining independence. Once definitively estranged from any direct tutelary influence and attracted by the ever-widening gates of artistic and mental, if not moral, freedom opening in front of her, her work became a hymn to the imagination and a joyful celebration of the secret operations of the subconscious.

Eileen Agar: Dreaming Oneself Awake makes a point of emphasizing the imaginative freedom Agar's mind gained, the way she subverted and derealized the real by breaking through, and overriding, dualities, and by almost naturally releasing the powerful myth-making drive which underlies her works. These qualities partake of the spirit of Surrealism to which she never ceased to pay homage and to which she gave endless shapes, thus exemplifying the quest for what Breton called the 'supreme point'. Now, many are those who would disagree with her possible affiliation with the Surrealists. They would naturally refer to her declaration of surprise when Herbert Read and Roland Penrose labelled her 'surrealist' on their visit to her studio in order to choose some of her works to be represented in the 'International Surrealist Exhibition' in London in 1936. 'They declared me surrealist . . . So I became a surrealist almost overnight' – a jocular, tongue-in-cheek, naive-sounding declaration probably uttered with a smile in her eyes and a slightly ironic tone in her voice. But, as evidence was to prove, in 1936 she had been more or less associated with Surrealism for at least seven years, as many signs go to show: her encounter with Breton in 1929, her friendship with Éluard almost at the same time, her love in 1935 for Paul Nash – with whom she would scour beaches for pebbles, driftwood and sea-shells to create 'monster' objects – not to mention her readings of books on Surrealism, such as David Gascoyne's translation of Breton's *What is Surrealism?* or Gascoyne's own *A Short Survey of Surrealism*, both from 1935, and, last but not least, the kind of objects and paintings which she made prior to 1936. We are convinced that, for Agar, Read and Penrose's decision to invite her to show in the Surrealist exhibition sounded like an immediate and pleasurable recognition of what she had been painstakingly working towards.

If, in the making of this book, I am obviously heavily indebted to her autobiography (*A Look at My Life*) for most of the details, anecdotes and facts of her life, completed by notes culled from interviews which I conducted with her on several meetings at her home, and from other various fragmentary testimonies, nonetheless, most crucial and determining have been her own diaries and notebooks deposited in the Tate Gallery Archives, as well as documents deposited at the V&A. Curiously enough, they haven't been exploited much so far, but referring to them has become indispensable: when carefully read, they throw a completely new light on Agar's own ideas and worldviews – elements which help revise many conceptions and preconceptions concerning her work. The result is the presentation, here, of a fresh outlook on her life and work, a new and original perspective which, I hope, will reveal an artist immensely gifted for disturbing and subverting reality, in the manner of Paul Klee and Joan Miró; that is, in a most subtle and poetic, almost musical, way. Like them, Agar is a card player who holds a deck of cards, asking us to play with her. Her cards are butterflies, fish, birds, sea-shells, leaves and flowers, and she shuffles them and deals them to us, with audacity, provocativeness and vivaciousness, in a kind of *orphic* – in the literal sense – homage to the versatility and inexhaustibility of creation.

1 Unknown photographer, Eileen Agar and Joseph Bard, *1930s.*

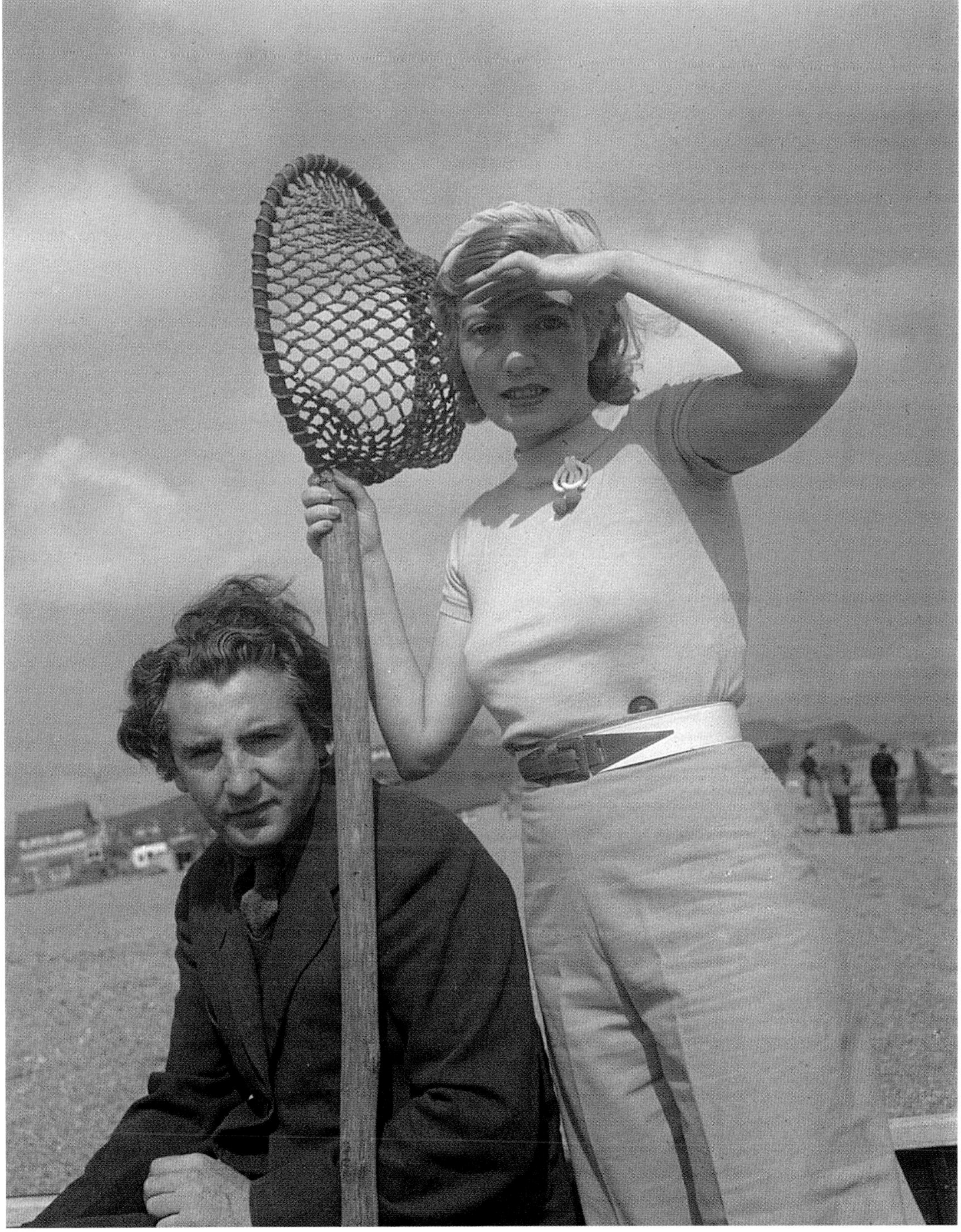

1 Leaving the terrain of representation, 1899–1931

'Curiouser and curiouser,' cried Alice. 'Now I am opening out like the largest telescope that ever was! Good-bye, feet!'

Lewis Carroll, *Alice's Adventures in Wonderland* (1865)

Buenos Aires, 1 December 1899. The British business community in Flores, a fashionable suburb of the Argentinian capital, would have been most surprised to learn that day that one of their number had just given birth to a baby girl who was to become one of the most prominent British women Surrealists and painters of the twentieth century. Such a cosmopolitan, affluent and refined background, with its wide opening onto the world, would indeed play a major role in Eileen Agar's education and in the development of her strong belief in the freedom of the mind. Her father, a Scottish businessman, had gone to Argentina a few years before to meet up with an uncle who had settled there and convinced his nephew that the country was an Eldorado. He started a company of his own, called Agar Cross, which set out to develop irrigation systems, especially by introducing and commercializing windmills, which he imported. With his Aermotor windmills, James Agar became a pioneer in, and a well-known provider of, farm equipment. His windmills helped to turn a great part of the desert into fertile estates and his company became so successful that he had offices not only in Buenos Aires but in New York and London.

At the turn of the century, ninety years or so after gaining its independence, Argentina was fast developing. Buenos Aires had officially become the capital in 1826.There was still some social unrest caused by the fierce opposition between the cattle raisers, tradespeople and businessmen on the one hand, and the army on the other, the former being strongly supported by Great Britain for economic reasons. The constitution, which was that of a democratic, presidential and federal regime, was voted in in 1853 and this ensured national consensus and peace. From 1860 onwards

Argentina developed its educational system by declaring schooling public, non-religious and compulsory, and opened its economy to the world at large – so much so that massive waves of immigrants started to flood in, especially after 1870. A hitherto rather unpopulated land for its size, it had no mineral resources, or any financial or commercial elite to manage the business of the country, which explains why it wholeheartedly yielded to the capitalistic economy brought in by Great Britain especially. The development of railways and harbours, of the wood and sugar industries, of refrigerating plants and the accompanying exports, made Argentina a kind of annex and 'subsidiary' of industrialized Europe, and more particularly of Great Britain, which retained great logistic influence, while southern Europe provided the necessary labour force through immigration. It is in this context that James Agar's uncle settled in Argentina and was followed by his nephew.

Agar's mother, the American heiress to a then-famous biscuit firm, saw to her three daughters' proper upper-class education, encouraging them to write and read, especially art books. Agar remembered loving pictures by Edmund Dulac and Arthur Rackham, both similar in their dealing with oneiric and fairy-like – often disquieting – themes inspired by the world of childhood and myths. Agar spent the first five years of her life in their villa, Quinta la Lila, on the river Tigré, in happiness and affluence, albeit under the control of a severe nanny and later a French governess – her mother had insisted on her daughters learning French as a second language. Her links with England were maintained thanks to almost annual trips to visit family and friends. An anecdote is told by A. S. Byatt in her preface to 'An Imaginative Playfulness: Paintings and Works on Paper', an exhibition held at the Redfern Gallery in 2005, in which she mentions that 'as a little girl, Agar travelled from Argentina to Britain – whether once or on certain occasions only, may we add – accompanied by a cow and an orchestra, because her rich and fashionable mother believed that fresh milk and good music were essential to her well-being.' This kind of experience, if true, obviously lies at the origin of her conception of art as, precisely, 'imaginative playfulness' – that is, 'the interpenetrating of a certain degree of reason and a certain degree of unreason'.

Agar's parents were not religious, nor would Agar be, although she once declared she felt a certain elation at the sight of cathedrals as the creations of man. Early on, she got accustomed to a lively social life, her home in Argentina being frequently so full of the English expatriates entertained by her parents that it was known as 'Hurlingham', the name of the local English club. Her mother, as she confides in her unpublished notebooks in 1985 and '86, had a warm heart . . . very large eyes and a rather square jaw which with her determined mouth, proclaimed the autocrat . . . she was gregariously worldly, adored hats and chinchilla fur-coats and loved entertaining and nurtured aristocratic views on society, affirming that 'the poor are poor because they do not work hard enough.'

On the contrary, her father had 'a sneaking sympathy for Socialists though he thought it would take years before they got enough good people to enter Parliament . . . he refused a knighthood because he believed in hereditary titles or none at all.' Interestingly enough, a crucial role was played by her godmother Mita Sewell, from an Irish family who had emigrated to Argentina. She spoilt the little Eileen and struck her by disregarding most conventions. 'She was a natural while my mother was an "original",' Agar later wrote, and proved to be a good companion to the young girl, creating a kind of happy balance between the strictness and class-consciousness of her mother and the relative open-minded laxity of her father. Agar's own words in her notebooks – 'my childhood memories are full of balloons, hoops and St Bernard dogs' – could be an image which sums up the first five years of her life.

When Agar was six she was sent to England to be educated at a private school, Canford Cliffs, near Poole in Dorset. By that time, her family owned a house in Belgrave Square where they settled after leaving Argentina in 1911 with twelve servants – where there was a ballroom and where she met Rudyard Kipling, a family friend, at the age of ten, and once played musical chairs with ex-Prime Minister Herbert Henry Asquith. The family had another property, Alton House, in Nairn, Scotland, where they could entertain friends and play tennis and golf, as Agar recalls in her autobiography. This carefree way of life was given some direction when Lucy Kemp-Welch, her art teacher at the second school she went to, at Heathfield, near Ascot, realized how gifted she was at drawing and encouraged her to pursue further study in art. Lucy Kemp-Welch, an early prodigy in painting – she held her first show at the age of fourteen – became director of the Herkomer Art School in Bushey at the age of 36 and acquired fame with her paintings of wild Exmoor ponies or of ponies galloping at polo matches, but also of flowers and landscapes in the realistic vein. In 1914 she became the first chairwoman of the Society of Animal Painters. When she taught Agar just before the First World War, she was still at the Herkomer School and had just illustrated Anna Sewell's famous bestseller, *Black Beauty*. An early memory of her stay at Heathfield – a determining one, in our opinion – is that of a print of Jean-Baptiste Greuze's painting *La Cruche Cassée* on her bedroom wall. This would conjure up in her a strange confusion of feelings. In a note written in 1978, she saw the print as 'the early erotic dream of a girl, which in my case, was prophetic in more ways than one', an experience which was unconsciously linking art and pleasure and somehow revealed, albeit in a subdued way, the sensual enjoyment of art forms. There is no need at this stage to expatiate on the allegorical, not to say psychoanalytical, meaning of Greuze's Neoclassical work – the allegory of lost innocence, the hesitation between virginal candour and sexual undertones in the demure as well as impish attitude of the girl. But the influence of such a banal but meaningful everyday scene on a teenage girl should not be underestimated.

In 1914, then, at the age of fifteen, Agar was living in London, but, in order to avoid the occasional hazards of wartime life, she was sent to stay at Tudor Hall in Chislehurst in Kent, where the music master Horace Kesteven, confirming Lucy Kemp-Welch's feelings, was struck by her artistic gifts, and introduced her to the artists – be they musicians, writers or painters – whom he invited to his house in London, taking her also to the studio of Charles Sims RA. He himself collected art and it was the first time that Agar was introduced to some of Paul Nash's early works, which hung on Kesteven's walls. 'At last,' she wrote in her autobiography, 'I found myself in a milieu where art was a valued part of daily life.' Before the end of the war, she attended a finishing school in Paris, the Demoiselles Ozanne's, to improve her French – a school which had a very good reputation among the rich and famous and was run by the three unmarried daughters of a Protestant clergyman from Calais. Incidentally, it had also been attended by Nancy Cunard around 1913. Back in London, Agar took weekly lessons in oil painting at the Byam Shaw School of Art in Kensington.

Quite evidently, all of these early experiences reinforced Agar's own inclination towards artistic activities and it needed but little for her to judge the Byam Shaw School of Art as too academic and to look elsewhere, challenging her mother's own warning: 'You don't want to cover yourself with paint all over and be one of these filthy artists who are dirty.' Encouraged by one of her mother's friends who knew Renoir – then in his last years in Cagnes-sur-Mer in France – and who insisted that Agar should be allowed to go, 'because she has definitely got some talent and should learn how to paint', Agar stood up to her mother (whom she called 'the queen bee'), convinced her family after considerable discussion to agree to her choice, and resolved to try to enrol at the Slade School of Art, which she would do in late 1920. Meanwhile, as recounted in her 1978 notebooks, one night, she packed up her bag after a furious quarrel, got up early, had breakfast before her father and her two sisters appeared, and departed from Paddington Station, leaving a note for her parents saying she was on her way to Truro and St Mawes where her family's friends, the De Kays, were staying and would put her up.

In the summer of 1920, the family, who had come back from Argentina when James Agar retired and settled at Balfour Place in London in 1919, spent their holidays in Cap d'Antibes where her mother found a private art teacher, Georges William Thornley. Like Lucy Kemp-Welch, Thornley – a French painter and printmaker – had been a student of two minor Impressionists, Eugène Ciceri and Edmond Yan, and had developed a technique based on bold, firm brushstrokes and thick impasto. His works – most of them taking after Corot, Pissarro and Puvis de Chavannes – capture the fleeting moment of the light through colour effects which actually make the light radiate from the landscape itself and enhance its panoramic quality. From the 1880s onwards he was widely acclaimed among the artistic circles in Paris, especially for his landscapes of the French and Italian Rivieras, which stand halfway between a kind of naturalism and decorativeness – two elements which we will encounter in Agar's works much later on. Moreover, Thornley took the young Agar to Paris to see the murals by Puvis de Chavannes in the Pantheon, and also took her to Rodin's studio. He taught her how to paint landscapes in watercolour in a conventional way, thus helping her to feel the importance of being taught rigorously and to start to move away from representational art. At the end of 1920, she had an interview with Professor Henry Tonks, the head of the Slade, who orientated her towards the newly created Brook Green School in Hammersmith, where, in the classes taught by Leon Underwood, she met and became friends with Cecil Beaton, Rex Whistler, Gertrude Hermes, Henry Moore and Blair Hughes-Stanton. The difference between the Slade and Brook Green School lay in the former institution's refusal of, and in the latter's adherence to, the new forms of modern art, especially those which had recently emerged from the Continent.

This is not the place to retrace the whole history of the introduction of modern art into England. Suffice it to say that the tremors of the new artistic developments in France had filtered through into England and had given birth to various kinds of reaction against the Royal Academy, initiated, among other events, by the creation in 1886 of the New English Art Club with artists like Sargent and Steer. Its first members had studied in Paris, stimulated by the free atmosphere and Bohemian life of the studios and encouraged to paint in the open – *en plein air.* They also discovered the practice of having elected juries in the Salons, instead of the rather closed system of the Royal Academy, which was obviously a more democratic way of having one's work judged and selected. However, due to repetitive motifs and a lack of inspiration, the New English Art Club had not been capable of achieving the revision of values envisaged by its French inspirers in the 1880s. From within the Club's own ranks there emerged a progressive wing which turned its back on Impressionist influences, embraced a more vehement treatment of colour and distanced itself from the credo of representationality. Artists seceded from the Club to create groups such as the Fitzroy Street Group and, more importantly, the Camden Town Group, with Spencer Gore as its president and including artists like Augustus John, Lucien Pissarro, Walter Sickert and Wyndham Lewis. All of these artists were under the influence of French art since most of them had stayed and studied in France. Their predominant concern was with low-life subjects, interiors from the suburbs, scenes from cities and socially oriented portraits, which expressed their love of life, whether it be beautiful or sordid, and, more generally, their attempt at liberating painting from dogmas.

This is why no one can actually imagine the artistic storm that broke over London when the 'Manet and the Post-Impressionists' exhibition was organized by Roger Fry and Clive Bell at the Grafton Galleries from November 1910 to January 1911. The paintings by Gauguin, Van Gogh, Cézanne and many others constituted neither more nor less than a challenge to England's insular artistic conservatism and divided the art world into two camps – the traditionalists and the modernists – a division which would last and re-emerge when Surrealism in its turn broke over the country. An article published by C.R.W. Nevinson in Joseph Bard and Eileen Agar's *The Island* in 1931 evoked the reactions to the Grafton Galleries exhibition, which Nevinson had actually helped organize:

> People literally rocked with laughter before Van Gogh or Gauguin, Matisse's conversation picture was considered excruciatingly funny . . . Imagine the friendships that had to be broken, the abuse to be faced, the supercilious mockery that had to be tolerated by the small band that could feel the structural beauty of Cézanne, the abstract art that he was already inspiring in such men as Braque, Derain and Picasso.

Indeed, the aesthetic upheaval taking place in France and the subsequent domestic debate were seen as 'the evils of cosmopolitanism', the kind of fierce criticism repeated the following year when Fry organized the second post-Impressionist exhibition in the autumn of 1912, which included the emergent British avant-garde, most notably Wyndham Lewis.

It is reported that Tonks told his students not to visit the Grafton Galleries' exhibition for fear they might be attracted by the freedom given to colour, and to the absence of drawing, and by those who 'believed that pictorial art was capable of much besides, or beyond representation', in Nevinson's words. As Paul Nash recalls, Sir Claude Phillips of *The Telegraph*, a most uncompromising critic, threw down his catalogue upon the threshold of the Grafton Galleries and stamped on it. Clearly, England was then 'enveloped in a pall of stagnation' and change was regarded with horror, and that was exactly what Agar would enjoy, feed on and thrive on a couple of years later.

Almost running parallel to the tensions at work in the world of art, the teachings of Henry Tonks at the Slade and of Leon Underwood at Brook Green School also stood apart, but the contrast between the two was in fact formative for Agar. Moving from Brook Street to the Slade, she started to develop and adopt an intermediary, and above all, independent aesthetic approach and position, which would be her own. Interestingly enough, Henry Tonks had come to painting at the rather late age of 26. He had previously studied medicine at the Royal Sussex County Hospital in Brighton and then at the London Hospital in Whitechapel from 1882 to 1888 and had become a surgeon, moving to the Royal Free Hospital that same year and teaching anatomy at the London Hospital medical school from 1892. Parallel to this activity he enrolled at the Westminster School of Art under Frederick Brown in 1888, had his first exhibition with the New English Art Club in 1891, and a year later started to teach at University College, London, and then at the Slade School of Fine Art. His medical training developed in him a kind of strictness as regards respect for detail and a kind of authoritarianism, which made him famous for never being satisfied and always critical of his students' progress. Paul Nash, as well as – among his most famous students – David Bomberg, Mark Gertler, Spencer Gore, Augustus John, Wyndham Lewis, Stanley Spencer and Rex Whistle, all testified to his sarcastic and intransigent attitude. During the First World War he served as a medical orderly and produced many pastel drawings recording cases of facial injury, thus bringing together the circumstantial exactness his medical training had developed in him, and the priority given to fine and strong drawing dependent on a kind of intellectual self-control, a grammar based on the outline more than on the in-line of a subject. Agar first met him a little after he had become Slade Professor of Fine Art in 1918, succeeding Frederick Brown. After interviewing her, Tonks recommended that she should follow Leon Underwood's teaching in Hammersmith.

Brook Green School – the name comes from Brook Green at the end of Girdlers Road where an architect's studio stood, the lease of which he had managed to buy – was the place where Underwood could develop and teach his own ideas after he had finished studying under Tonks at the Slade. There was no rivalry as such between the two men; Tonks had so many applicants at the Slade that he had no hesitation in sending some of them to Brook Green, as he did with Agar. The atmosphere and teaching there were evidently different. In short, even if Underwood was critical of the tendency of art in Europe and the United States, he predominantly believed in the fundamental importance of the subject and its spiritual content. Art, life and the spirit should not be separated. 'No significant artist', he wrote in *Art for Heaven's Sake* (1934), 'can work without a definite idea about the reconstruction of the world he and his fellows live in.' At the time of Roger Fry's theory of the 'significant form', Underwood's teaching appears to be conservative and idealistic, almost untenable in the face of the development of abstract art – which he admired to some extent, one has to say, but all the same rejected. This is why he could not see what Cézanne had actually liberated – the severance of colour from form and vice versa – and that Cézannian geometricality was merely a means and not an end in itself.

However, the year Underwood spent at the Slade under Tonks provided him with firm foundations in life drawing and increased his own need for self-expression, an obvious, understandable reaction to what he thought was dogmatic dryness and sterility in Tonks's technique. Drawing could not be an end in itself, nor the sole end of art. A way to escape was not to use the line for the outline only but above all for the suggestion of mass and volume. Breaks in the linear rhythm, making the line move towards or away from the foreground – this depending on the thickness of the line – conferred a kind of dynamics away from flat representation. These aesthetic principles, as well as the stress he used to lay on primitive art, were elements which helped his students to express their own originality informally and spontaneously. This unorthodox insistence on the necessary search for one's deep capacities through the questioning of forms, mass and direction – once these were firmly established as starting points – was extremely stimulating, and, we would say, particularly determining to Agar, especially as it was open to scathing criticism from conservative circles.

There is a painting by Leon Underwood which, in a way, sums all of this up and establishes a direct, vivid link with Agar, and that is his 1921 painting *Venus in Kensington Gardens* (illus. 2), a highly criticized and debated work on account of the nude figure right at the centre, a provocative exercise looking back to Manet's *Déjeuner sur l'herbe* and to works by Renoir. In this painting, most of Underwood's students and friends are included and among them, Agar, the figure standing at the extreme top right – in the red hat – thus

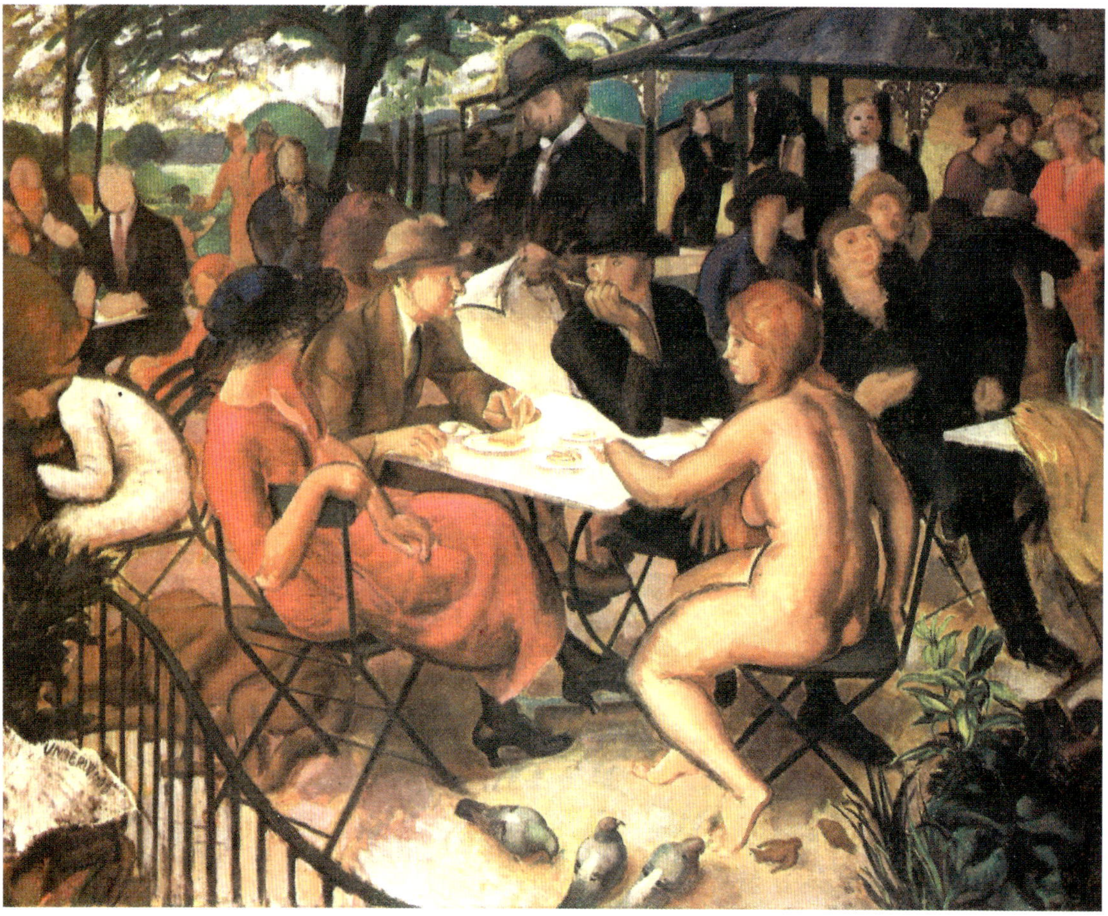

making obvious her participation in the gradual break with convention. For some time, then, she had been spurning the debutante parties and weekends with the Asquiths offered by her family – who were close friends of the famous politician – although, as the anecdote goes, she was often driven to the school in a chauffeured Rolls-Royce.

In the autumn of 1920, Agar's parents took her back to Argentina to celebrate her twenty-first birthday in a quite lavish way, booking the Hurlingham Club outside Buenos Aires for three hundred people. It was an opportunity for her father to check on the situation of the family firm, Agar-Cross, after the war. It was also Agar's farewell to the country where she was born, and which she loved.

Relief from that stimulating, albeit slightly frustrating, artistic atmosphere in London – she confessed that she resented the separation of men and women and the puritanism which hovered over the teaching – came not only when she left home in 1921 to settle in a flat made up of two rooms and a studio in Chelsea, but mainly in 1924 when she set off for Paris with her fellow student and lover, Robin Bartlett. Freedom took the form of a tour of Spain, the two of them visiting Madrid, Toledo, Seville and Granada, seeing the works of Goya and El Greco as well as the Moorish architecture of Andalusian towns. Paris was a revelation to Agar. Her mother had a flat there and Agar was fluent in French – taught her by a French governess when she was a child. Moreover, after she married Bartlett in November 1925, the death of her father the following month left her with £1,000 a year. She could devote herself entirely to painting, living what seemed to be a typical Romantic life. But her hasty marriage to Bartlett proved to be just a pretext to escape from the shackles of her family. They left England to live in a romantic cottage in the midst of an apple orchard in Varengéville, a small village near Dieppe, but the young girl's bucolic dream would not last and one of those ordinary and ludicrous, apparently immaterial, episodes in life opened her eyes. As she clearly remembers in some notes written in 1978, it was an episode which happened at a party given by her brother-in-law Hugh Mackintosh, when Bartlett was violently sick after drinking – and disgustingly so. The spell was broken: 'The tie between us was for me – uninitiated as I was in the mysteries of sex – only an exploration, though being young I had just cast a romantic glamour on the liaison.' Her marriage collapsed a year or so later when, on a chance visit to see Warren J. Vinton – who was a friend of Robin Bartlett, a fellow American student at the Slade, and who also featured incidentally in Underwood's painting *Venus in Kensington* – she was introduced to Joseph Bard, who happened to be there. Moreover, Vinton's wife had gone to Berlin to visit Bard's wife.

2 Leon Underwood, Venus in Kensington Gardens, *1921, oil on canvas.*

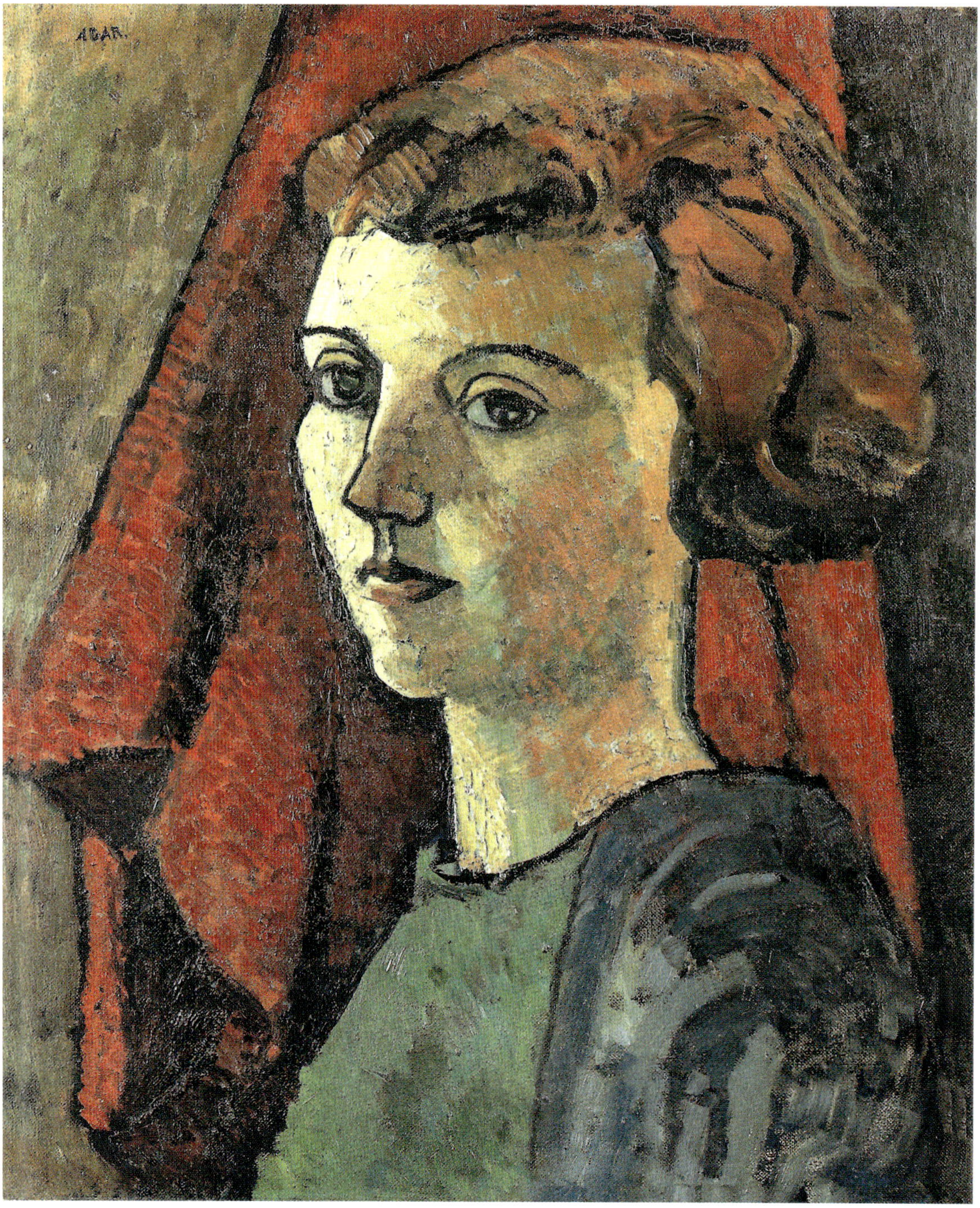

This was a decisive encounter, which meant for her the definitive step into the world of art, and, beyond, into the dynamics of European culture at large. In Ann Simpson's words, 'she thrived on the intellectual stimulation of the literary world to which he [Bard] introduced her and found new confidence and fluency in her painting.' This actually shows in her *Self-portrait* of 1927 (illus. 3), 'a rather thick impasto [painted] straight onto the canvas, which gives it a fresh sunlit look', as she recalls in her autobiography. The portrait is based on the sharp tension between two complementary colours, green and red, forming a kind of background on which her face stands out with strength and aplomb, almost in a Matissian light, a restrained but vivid construction, which also appears in the portrait she made of Rodney Thomas the same year. It is obviously a way to make a statement about herself, in a newly gained assertiveness.

The contrast between the two men, Robin Bartlett and Joseph Bard, was huge in the sense that Bard, who was a Hungarian expatriate – his real name was József Diamant – was a more mature and experienced personality. He was seven years older than Agar and was already an established linguist who had studied at the Sorbonne in Paris and was a correspondent of Reuters, of the Associated Press of America and of a few English papers. He had already had two children with Jolan Weinberger in 1911 and 1913, had left Hungary in 1922, had then married the famous American journalist and writer Dorothy Thompson in 1923 in Vienna, had befriended artists like the painter Oskar Kokoschka and the architect Adolf Loos and had met Sigmund Freud as well as Cosima and Siegfried Wagner – a rather busy early life! At the time, he had also embarked on an ambitious philosophical work on the 'mind of Europe', the present state of its culture in the light of its past – a work he never completed, although he published *Shipwreck in Europe* in 1928. Quite an internationalist, concerned with the threat hovering over the fate of European culture, Bard had followed his wife to Berlin, and then, bored by her own commitments as a world-famous journalist, left for London in 1926, where he met Agar. His cosmopolitan culture, the scope of his intellectual powers, his special brand of humour, the blending of his Jewish origins and his multiple experiences all created a new world of stimulation and exciting sophistication for the young Agar. Later, in her 1979 notebooks, she described him in the way she always saw and loved him, saying he was then 'a foreign visitor from outer space with his courtly manners and outrageous ideas, good-looks and so-called bad intentions, indolent yet energetic, an observant, humorous and talkative intellectual who gave spice and wit to any conversation'.

3 Eileen Agar, Self-portrait, *1927, oil on canvas.*

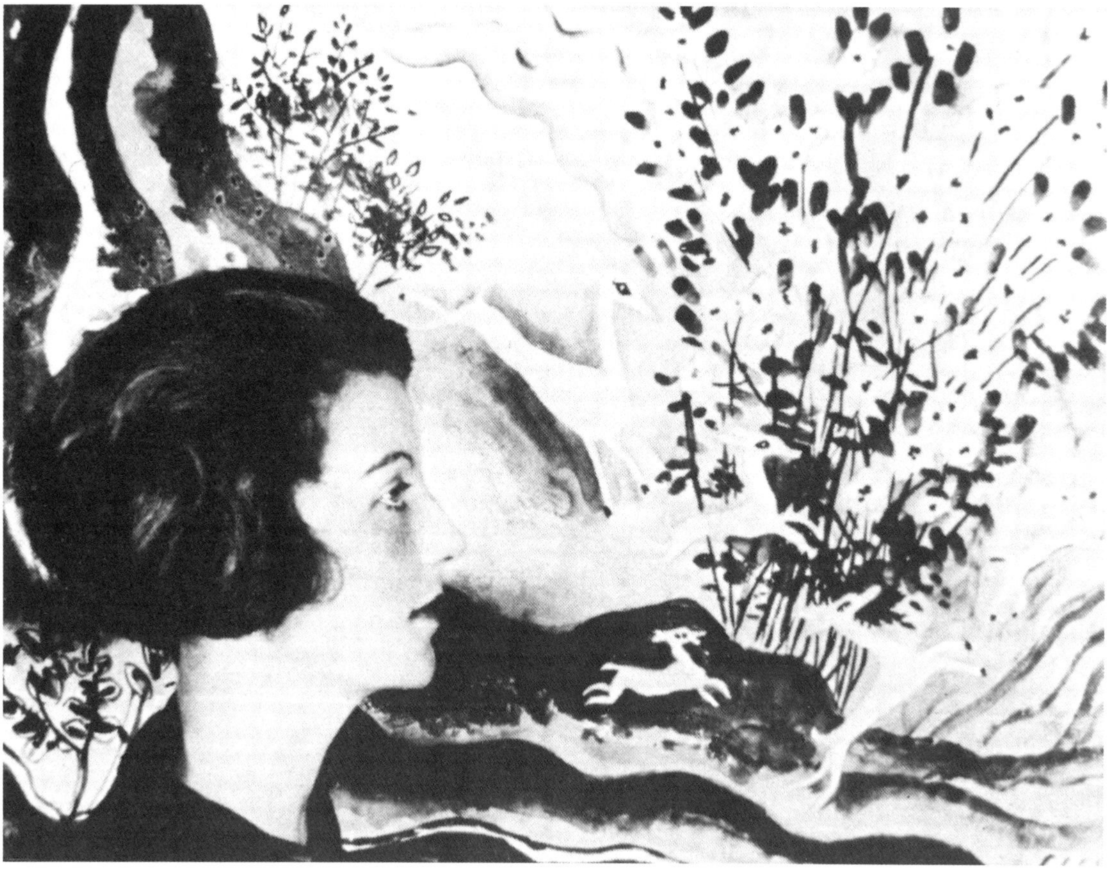

Joseph Bard's break with his wife did not take long and in 1927 he and Agar took a flat in Fitzroy Square. In an emblematic move, prompted by Bard, Agar painted the self-portrait mentioned above. As another unconscious sign of the new turn she was taking, she sat that same year for Cecil Beaton, a friend of the family who was starting in society as a photographer of celebrities (illus. 4). The portrait has something both poetical and oneiric, physical and aerial, with her profile apparently gazing at an explosion of flowery designs, emerging from waves from another world, while a horse-like creature gallops away from her. Entrance into a dream-like world is definitely hinted at, as if Agar were standing at a threshold, wondering, as in a trance, at what she sees – is it a vision or a waking dream?

Agar had evidently acquired more self-assurance and self-confidence, as well as fluidity in her way of painting, realizing that all she had done so far had been academic and tentative whereas the horizon was open before her. Well, it was broadened later that year, when she rented with Bard a small villa at Portofino on the Italian Riviera coast for the winter. They used to go to nearby Rapallo where they came across Ezra Pound in a café – the beginning of a long friendship. When Pound was taken to hospital years later, Bard was among the only ones to visit him. Pound's place was at that time the haunt of many intellectuals and poets from all over Europe and it was the occasion for Agar to meet, and take part in, discussions, often while taking walks in the countryside, with people like Max Beerbohm, William Butler Yeats, Basil Bunting, the art critic Adrian Stokes, and Osbert Sitwell – quite a stimulating series of encounters.

Back in London, Agar made the acquaintance of Boris Anrep, a Russian artist, at the Warren Gallery in Maddox Street, who pressed her to go to Paris in order to broaden the scope of her inspiration, since the art scene in England was definitely diffident, if not hostile, towards the new artistic tendencies from France. After having studied in Italy, Boris Anrep had enrolled at the Académie Julian and the Académie de la Grande Chaumière in Paris, then had crossed to England where he developed an interest and amazing skill in mosaic. He had become a prominent figure of the social and intellectual milieu in London, especially the Bloomsbury circle, and was to lay two mosaic pavements in the vestibule of the main hall of the National Gallery in 1933.

So, in 1928, Bard and Agar settled in Paris for a while. She took a studio at 11 rue Schoelcher where, as she loved to say, she was 'reborn'. In her autobiography, she records how fascinated she became in Paris with the Jardin des Plantes and the fossils and bones of prehistoric creatures displayed there, learning about the complexity of animal structures and sensing

4 Cecil Beaton, Eileen Agar, *1927, photograph.*

the links which can be established with the remotest past of humanity, a fascination which was to re-emerge in her collages of the 1930s and even later. These grew into the first signs of a pervading and growing sense of atemporality in her works. In her diary, which she started when living in the rue Schoelcher in 1928, one of the first entries reads: 'I must realize that I have to start from the very beginning. The earliest forms of Nature to a painter are studies in pure abstract design. I must go back to these forms and create design out of what the scientist tells us,' and there follows an astoundingly premonitory scribbled note which reads like a programme for the whole of her career and which we will encounter again later:

> The Trinity
> Nature: Prehistory, Jurassic, archeozoique
> Man: intellect – Jewish – Egyptian
> Woman: imagination – Christian – Greek

And one word, added in the margin in an attempt to bracket the three concepts together, is 'Europe'.

This is when another decisive meeting took place, when the Austrian architect Adolf Loos suggested through Bard, who was one of his contacts in Paris, that Agar should meet the painter František Foltýn, who had the reputation of being an excellent teacher. Born in Austria-Hungary, he had come to Paris in 1924, attracted by the persistent influence of Cubism, which was for him the perfect way to break away from academicism and realism. He went to the Académie Julian and the Académie de la Grande Chaumière, the antagonists of the Académie des Beaux-Arts, and visited his compatriot František Kupka, who gave lessons in his workshop in Puteaux outside Paris. All this explains why Foltýn soon joined the Cercle et Carré group and then the Abstraction-Création group before leaving to go back to Brno in 1934. Attending Foltýn's classes, one may well guess, introduced Agar to a greater, deeper concern with the geometrization of space, the use of planes and angles and the disruption of conventional perspective in order to lay the emphasis on a kind of 'mental perspective' and the playful treatment of forms. There is no doubt that we can see in these coincidental influences of the secret patterns bequeathed by prehistoric creatures and of the secret life of forms arising from playing with them one of the two most determining factors in Agar's development. The other one will be Surrealism, a movement rejected by Foltýn but formative in Agar's growing independence of any given artistic dogma. For the time being she was learning and gradually gathering weapons in order to forge an entirely personal style.

5 Eileen Agar, Mrs Roger Eckersley, *1930, pencil and watercolour.*

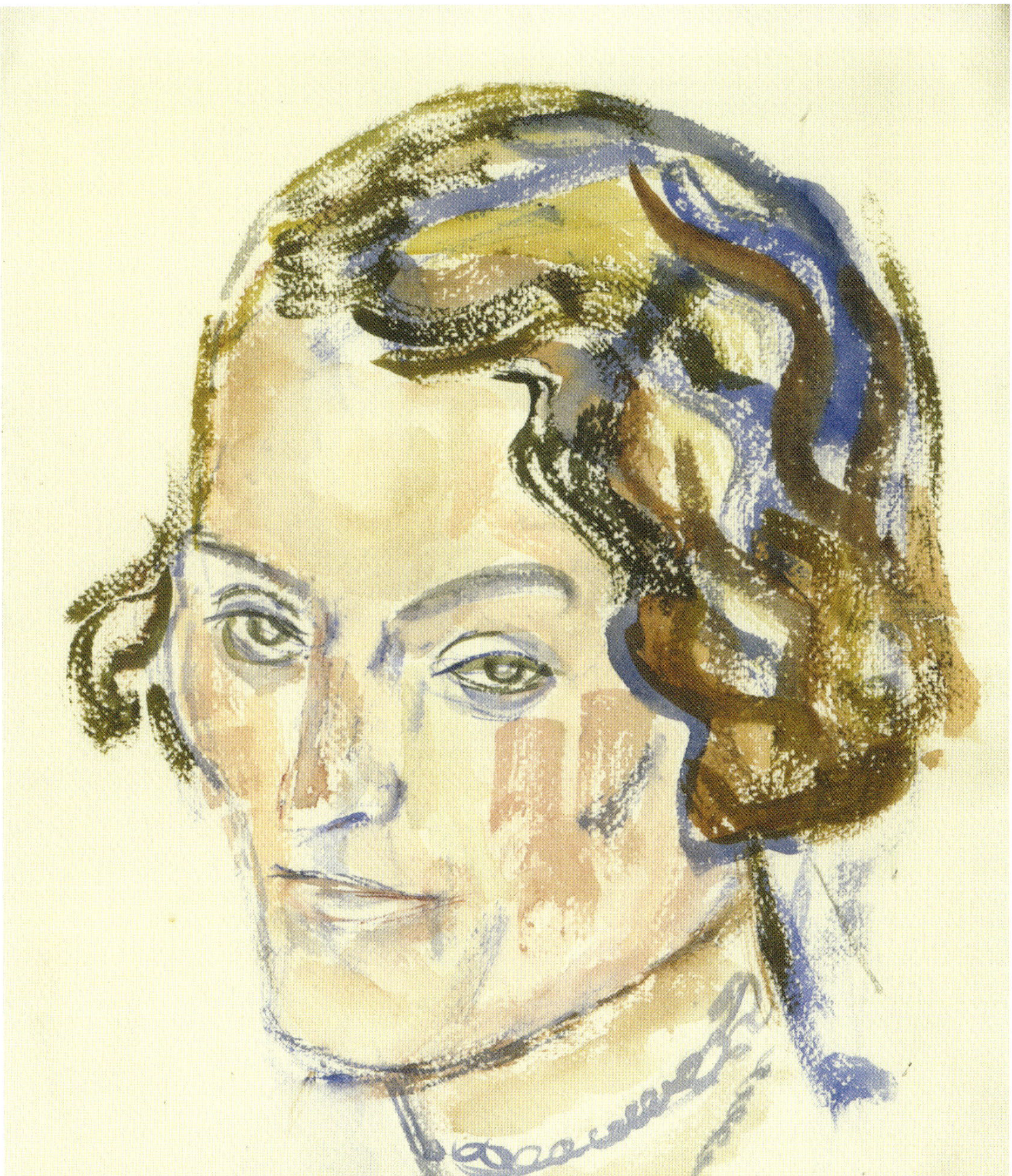
AGAR 1930

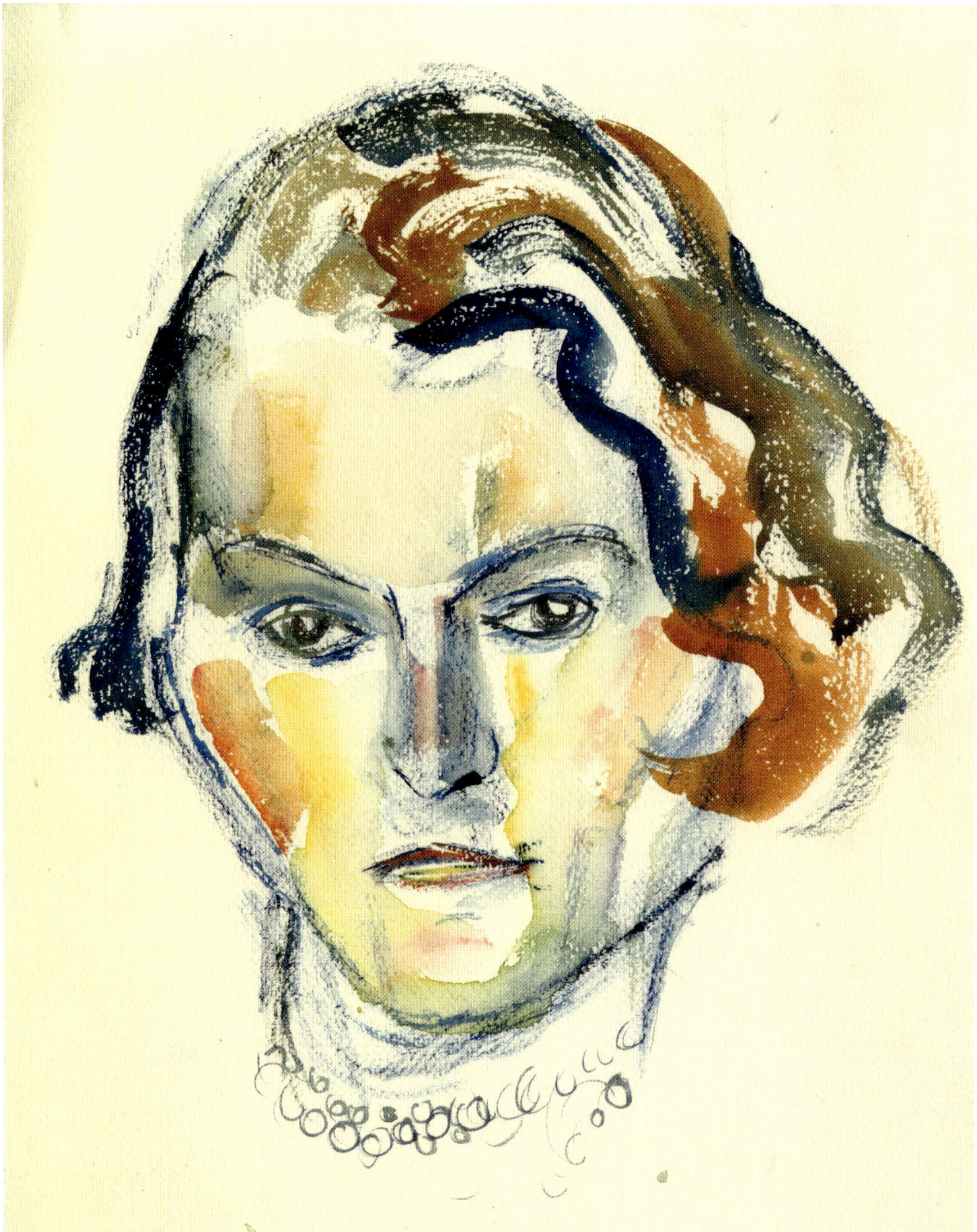
AGAR 1930

When in Paris, it did seem that all gates were opening for Agar's own artistic and intellectual progress. Ezra Pound, on one of his visits to the French capital, took Agar and Bard to visit Brancusi's studio and gave her letters of introduction to Marcoussis and André Breton, and through him, she met Paul Éluard – an encounter which would gather meaning some eight years later. Several trips to Paris ensued, with two excursions: one to Bandol, a little seaside town on the French Riviera – where they became acquainted with D. H. Lawrence – and, upon Foltýn's advice, one to Menton, in January 1930, where they rented a villa at Cap Martin for some six months – a villa they rechristened Casa Allegra, after the pet name Bard had given Agar. There, Agar explored the possibilities of abstraction and Cubism, especially struggling with, on the one hand, the treatment of colour, which tends to be more muted and nuanced in her abstract compositions, and on the other, the use of more or less geometrical shapes, which require sharpness and deliberateness. These, of course, in her own mind, were at odds with her previous predilection for the representational. The point was, then, for her to liberate herself from figurativism – and Foltýn's lessons helped her in this – while not abandoning a vaguely referential content. In this, as she confesses in her autobiography, she was particularly influenced by Juan Gris' paintings.

The leap was achieved and came to fruition, so to speak, through the gradual yielding to the imagination – a way to bypass the demands of Cubism and the relatively greater laxity of abstraction. Halfway between the two, she sometimes yielded to the alluring quality of expressionist colours, as when she painted *Mrs Roger Eckersley* in 1930 (illus. 5, 6), an echo of her earlier *Self-portrait* and reminiscent of Matisse's use of large, flat tints of vivid complementary colours, especially to create shadows. Obviously, the answer to this dilemma was to come from Surrealism a little later, and it is precisely the first manifestations of Surrealism which inspired her to paint *The Flying Pillar* (1930). As she herself wrote: 'It was my first attempt at an imaginative approach to painting, and although the result was in some way surreal, it was not done with that intention.' But, of course, who can say that the resulting work does not short-circuit the original intention? That is the whole point about Surrealism. Agar continues her declaration, saying, 'Surrealism was in the air in France and poets in France, later in England, were kissing that sleeping beauty troubled by nightmares, and it was the kiss of life that they gave.' Doesn't the kiss of life wake someone up from near death, near unconsciousness, revealing him or her to another, hitherto unsuspected state of consciousness? This is the way Surrealism worked on Agar who, at this stage of her life, was unconsciously ready to adopt a more or less definitive direction.

6 Eileen Agar, Mrs Roger Eckersley II, *1930, pencil and watercolour.*

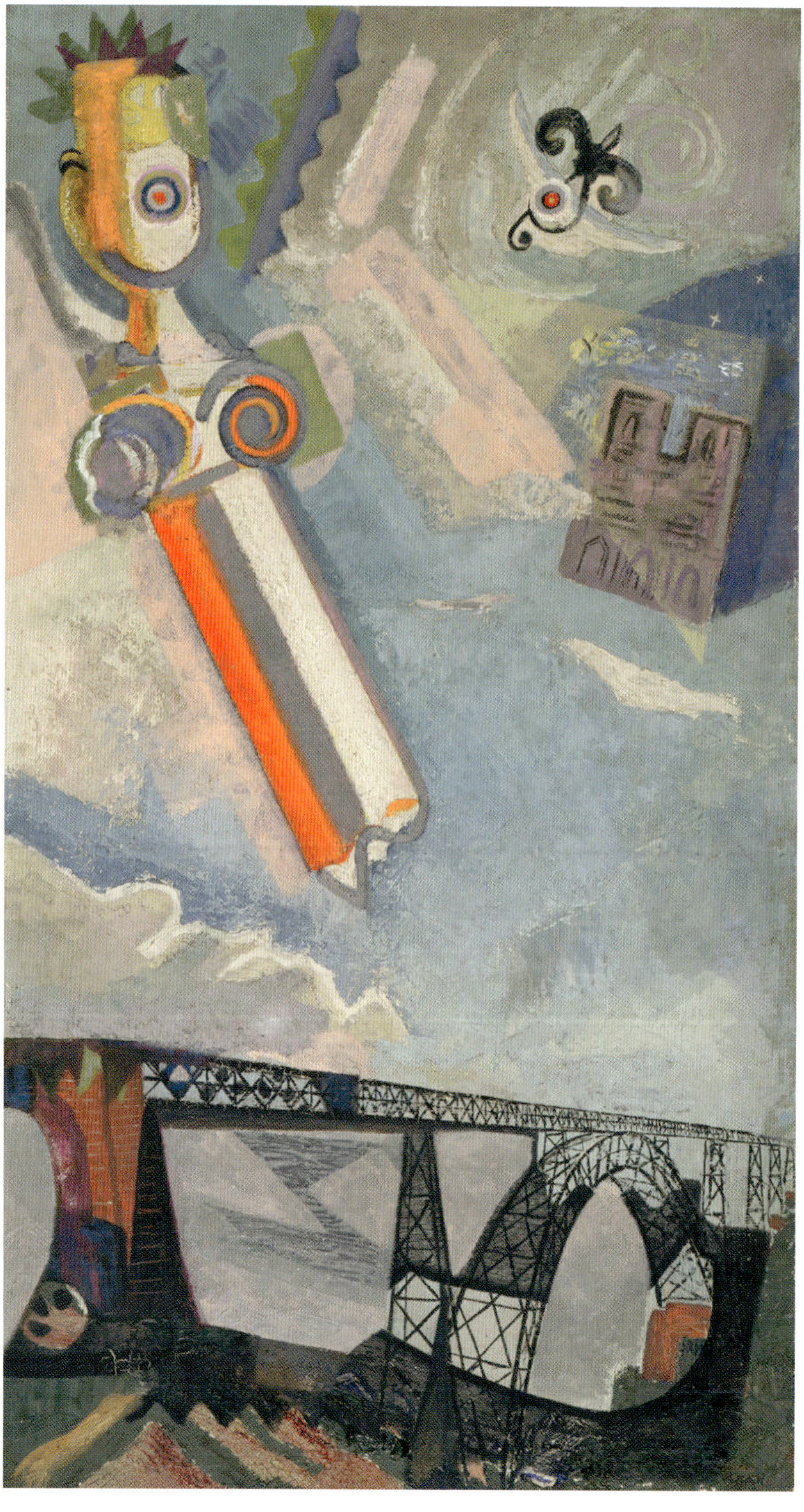

The Flying Pillar, later renamed *Three Symbols* (illus. 7), is the epitome of Agar's situation at that moment, a kind of crossroads in time. As she herself described the work, the pillar – a reference to Greek art with its vaguely ionic pediment – is flying off, away from a metallic bridge – a reference to Gustave Eiffel, the bridge builder, and to his famous tower, the symbol of modernity – and from Notre Dame cathedral, a reference to medieval Christian art. A vague representation of a fleur-de-lis balances the flight of the pillar on the right-hand side. Here, as was to be the case in many of her works, time rules supreme in a kind of affirmation *and* erasure of time – past, present and future haunting the imaginative space simultaneously. But more than that, let us not ignore that the bridge connotes firm solidity as well as the opening to the future; it is the emblem of the passage from, and the establishment of links between, the past and the future, bridging the chasm of the present: a self-projection in an elsewhere still to be defined. Of course, we are miles away from Surrealist subversiveness, but the direction is given, especially as Agar's own comments on the painting in her diary point to a deeper level of interpretation than simple symbolism. From her own words, it is clear that the Greek pillar plays a central role in the painting. In that entry, dated December 1928 – two years before she completed the painting – she writes in a more or less rambling way: 'Greece, the meeting place of Judaeo-Egyptian and Graeco-Christian' followed by the words 'the Judaeo-Graeco pillar' as if it were a note to bear in mind and to be later developed. Three years later, in *The Island*, C.R.W. Nevinson – coincidentally? – emphasizes the same idea, saying that 'the heavy weight of Judaeo-Christian and Graeco-Roman symbolism settled over the indigenous European imagination', and adding that 'the cultural inheritance of Palestine, Greece and Rome stifled the native imaginative life of the European population,' words which echo Agar's notes, no doubt the result of discussion between Bard, Agar and Nevinson. Couldn't we see, then, in *The Flying Pillar*, the wished-for liberation of the energy of the imagination from the fossilized past, the determination to retrieve 'a happy relationship between individual imagination and social existence', in Nevinson's words? In the light of the statements made by Agar and evidently supported and reinforced by Nevinson, one cannot but see *Three Symbols* – the definitive title – as the attempt to go beyond time towards myth, beyond material reality towards a kind of spiritual rebirth, that of 'an energy tapped from the original source of pre-Christian imagination'. All this, indeed, delineates Agar's strong and staunch beliefs as they were when the year 1931 came to a close, the shape which her mind had taken after a continuous personal self-questioning fostered by teachings and influences from various mentors, however transient or deep, superficial or decisive, these influences might have been.

7 Eileen Agar, The Flying Pillar, *1930, oil on canvas.*

2 Approaching the shores of objective chance, 1931–6

'I should think you could draw treacle out of a treacle well, eh, stupid?'

Lewis Carroll, *Alice's Adventures in Wonderland* (1865)

In 1931 Eileen Agar painted *Movement in Space* (illus. 8), a kind of farewell to pure abstraction – with traces of Cubism whose lesson she seems to have integrated perfectly – and a kind of lifting and opening of planes seen through transparent surfaces, a subtle variation on brown and ochre, only animated by two intersecting red crescents which counterbalance and counteract the general movement of slipping surfaces from black to light yellow when one looks from left to right. Movement is here arrested, although intimated – poised, so to speak, thus creating some visual destabilization, especially as this movement seems to liberate a round, organic shape towards the right. She also left an untitled drawing from 1931 (illus. 9), a sketch which shows in a rather conceptual way the basic components of lines sufficient to create movement *and* space with simple 'purified' means. Together with *Compotier and Still-life* – a homage to what she had learnt from Gris's and Marcoussis' works – *Movement in Space* is probably the last oil painting she produced in the Cubist-abstractionist vein. The same effect is achieved in her photographs of the early 1930s, such as the one of foldable chairs and shadows (illus. 10). There, she begins to find a formal quality in shadows, which will develop into a symbolic dimension in her collages later on.

The year 1931 was especially marked with the attempt undertaken by Joseph Bard to launch a magazine firmly geared towards modernity and devoted to art, poetry and the imagination. The title was *The Island*. The idea came from Bard in discussions with Leon Underwood. Indeed, Bard's internationalist mind placed him at the forefront of manifestations of European culture. Agar financed the magazine while Underwood acted as art director and Bard as literary director. The objective was to defend

8 Eileen Agar, Movement in Space, *1931, oil on canvas.*

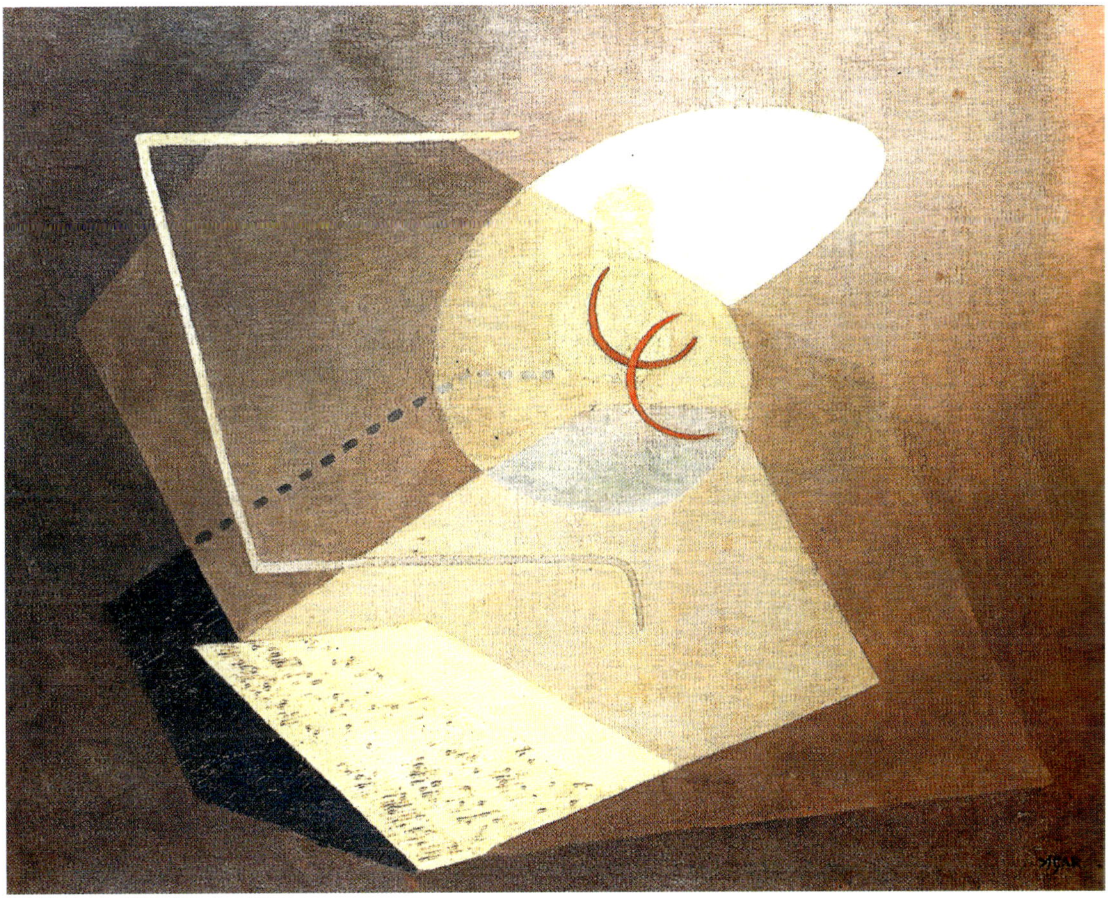

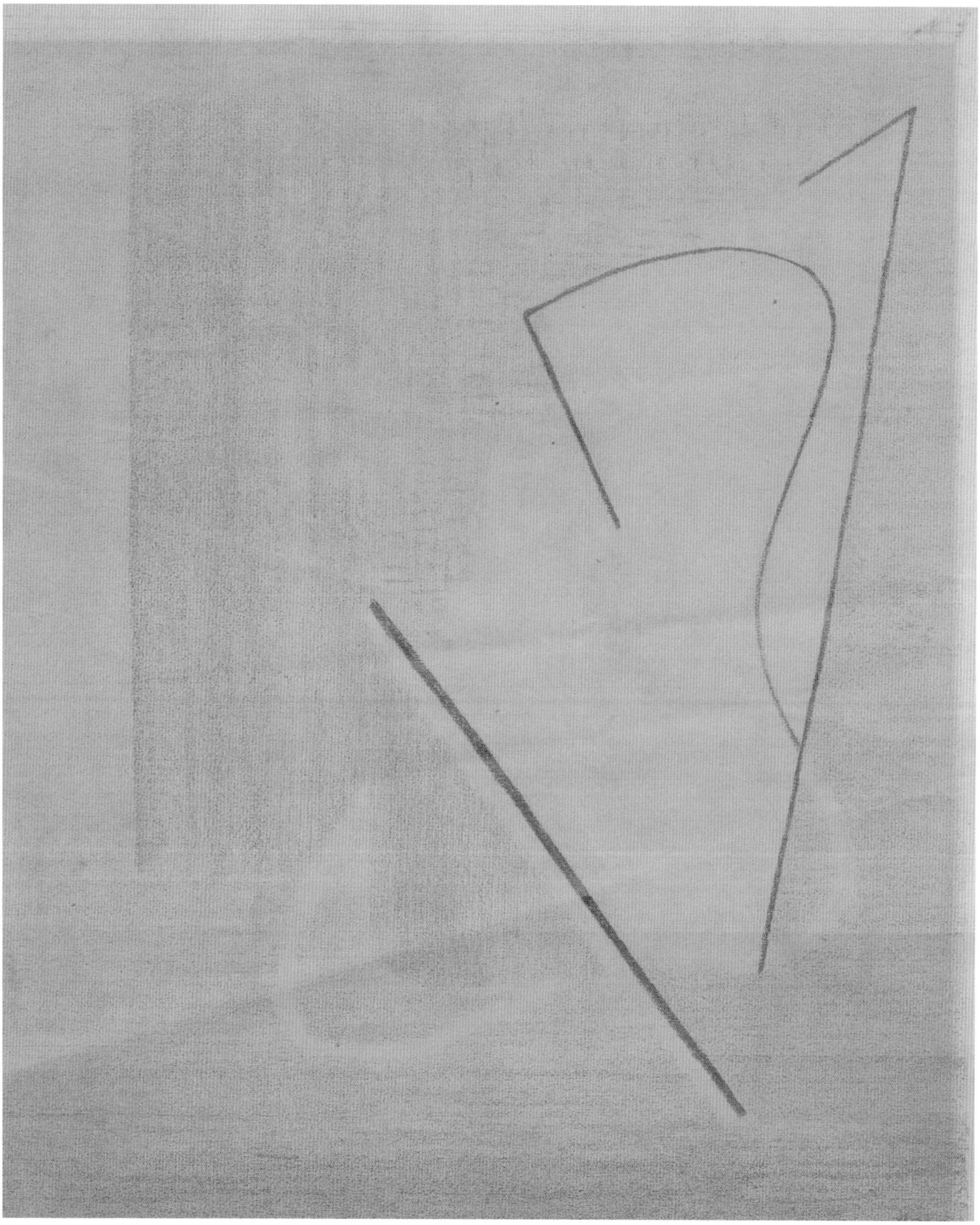

modern ideas and 'resistance to commercialized art', in Bard's words in the editorial of the first issue, and to rally high-quality contributors at this dramatic moment in the history of Europe. As often happens, unfortunately, the venture collapsed after the third issue due to lack of funds and editorial disagreement. Underwood was in favour of a less intellectual, 'theoretical' stance, contrary to Bard, who saw *The Island* as the place to test and develop his ideas on 'the mind of Europe', the fate of Western civilization and the aesthetic and moral zeitgeist.

The subtitle of the review read: 'a vehicle of expression for valuable living contemporary thought and imagination', and the review's profession of faith read:

> Its purpose is to strengthen the creative life of the individual struggling under the weight of the industrialized and standardized spirit of the age. It is endeavouring to form a centre of artistic and literary activity that shall represent a line of continuity with the past and at the same time, build from contemporary poetic imagination immune from post-war disillusion and fatigue.

Every issue featured drawings or engravings, like Agar's *The Bird, or Two Lovers* (I/1, p. 13), *Family Trio* (I/2–3, p. 63) and *Vivos Voco* (II/2–3, p. 39), next to illustrations by Gertrude Hermes, Henry Moore and Laurence Bradshaw. Bard wrote an article on a book by Raymond Aron and A. Dandieu, *Décadence de la nation française*, which shows the international *vision* of the review and in which he says 'France has to return to a real, emotional, anti-rational, individual will or she will be submerged by the commercial colossi of the new world.' In another article on the sublime, he explains that,

> the scope and ideals of rationalism (following the mysticism of the Middle-Ages) deprive human beings of their sentient reality and consider them only as particles in a machinery for a supposed human happiness and consider them, that is, as functional and not as ideal realities.

Sharing the same perspective, Mahatma Gandhi's contribution proclaims that,

> both religion and art have to serve the identical aims of moral and spiritual elevation . . . In this relationship of man to God, it is the mysterious forces which matter, and not the meagre texts expressed in words.

9 Eileen Agar, Untitled, *1931, pencil on paper.*

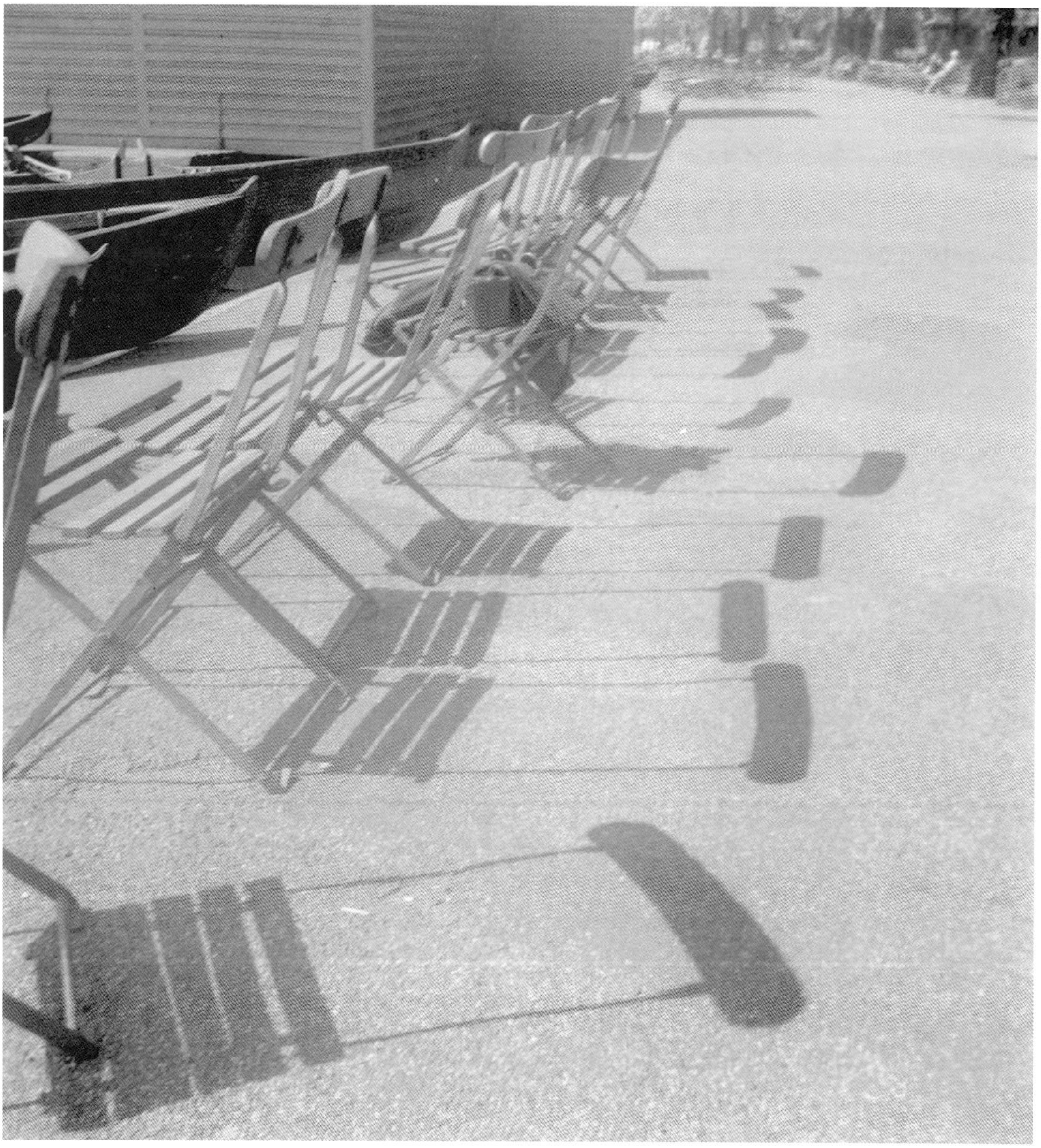

10 Eileen Agar, foldable chairs and shadows, early 1930s, photograph.

It was unavoidable that all these statements should have profoundly imprinted themselves on Agar's mind. We shall actually come across the same concepts and words when quoting from her notebooks and diaries, and in the last issue of *The Island* (I/4, p. 102) she sums up her own beliefs, which, as we shall see, remained consistent throughout her life and hardly varied from the way she expounded them in 1931 in the only article she ever wrote, 'Religion and the Artistic Imagination' – an article which can be seen as fulfilling a necessary stage before she fully adhered to the tenets of Surrealism.

Her introduction clearly defines her standpoint as essentially spiritual rather than religious:

> As an artist, the Earth, the Sun and the Moon have a greater significance for me than the highly rarefied idea of the Holy Trinity. For natural symbolism has a greater emotional appeal to the woman than has religious mysticism. Measured by the artist's sensitiveness, Christianity appears to undergo profound changes resulting in a new and more naturalistic mythology in Europe, Russia and America.

Her refusal to adhere to a rational system of thought is here blatant. She then goes on to analyse what is presently developing in Europe. 'In Europe', she writes,

> the importance of the subconscious in all forms of Literature and Art establishes the dominance of a feminine type of imagination over the classical and more masculine order. Apart from rampant and hysterical militarism, there is no male element left in Europe for the intellectual and rational conception of life has given way to a more miraculous creative interpretation, and artistic and imaginative life is under the sway of womb-magic.

The sun is an increasingly important symbol in the new mythology of Europe. Here are the living, solid fundaments of what will guide her throughout her life – the belief in the infinite opening to reality of the mind of the artist, and the need to tap the springs of creativeness unrestrainedly.

In Russia, the second source of change for her, she sees signs of a new approach, linked not to the sun but to the earth:

> The new Russian form of life is already near to earth. They are the only people in the world to build up images tied directly to the earth, pictures of fertility and fecund life, no sharp-shadowed moon-like landscapes as in America, for under the hammer and sickle grow wavy seas of corn.

Bearing the message that Bard was undoubtedly embodying, she adds: 'The Jewish race alone has this same quality of virile earth-nearness, expressed not in terms of the peasant but in terms of the intellectual . . . The centre of energy in Russian life will be essentially Jewish.'

Finally, as regards America, the third term of her world trinity, she predicts that, 'only in the child-like emotional veracity of the negro can America find its creative fulfilment, for, excepting the Indian tradition, there is no other cultural background to the present-day amorphous civilization of America.' She sees 'the negro's emotional life' as 'moon-hit, in him life is the most primeval . . . Negro music is at present but a note in the desert, a plaintive, new-born cry, a note nevertheless taken up by the whole of America, distorted into a syncopated, savage, sexless roar.'

These words come from a singular visionary power, a capacity to launch bridges from one continent to another, from one culture, one mind-set, to another, and reach a bold, daring and convincing synthesis which opens onto a complex combination and interaction of mythical forces. At 32 years of age, Agar may well be compared with the most perceptive philosophers and anthropologists of her time, as her conclusion vibrantly states:

> For only by reaching back to the deepest and simplest emotional sources native to a particular life-form can a creative harmony be projected into the world. Expressed in the symbolism of the Earth, the Sun and the Moon, the Holy Trinity of Christianity is realized and surpassed by these three emergent cultures in Russia, Europe and America.

Jotted down three years before this article, she had summed up her worldview in her diary in an entry dated 1 December 1928 under the title 'My Trinities':

Moon	Earth	Sun
Sea	Land	Sky
Fish	Flesh	Bird
Negro	Jew	Christian

As it appears, the main categories resulting from the division of reality are blending into each other. Under cover of a dialectical, ternary classification, the world is recomposed by Agar as a series of forces, first at a cosmic level, then at a terrestrial level, then at the level of all created creatures and finally at the level of the human race in the Western world. However unexplained this remains, the horizontal and vertical readings of this classification are in themselves challenging, in the sense that they

11 Eileen Agar, Family Trio, *1931, pen and ink on paper.*

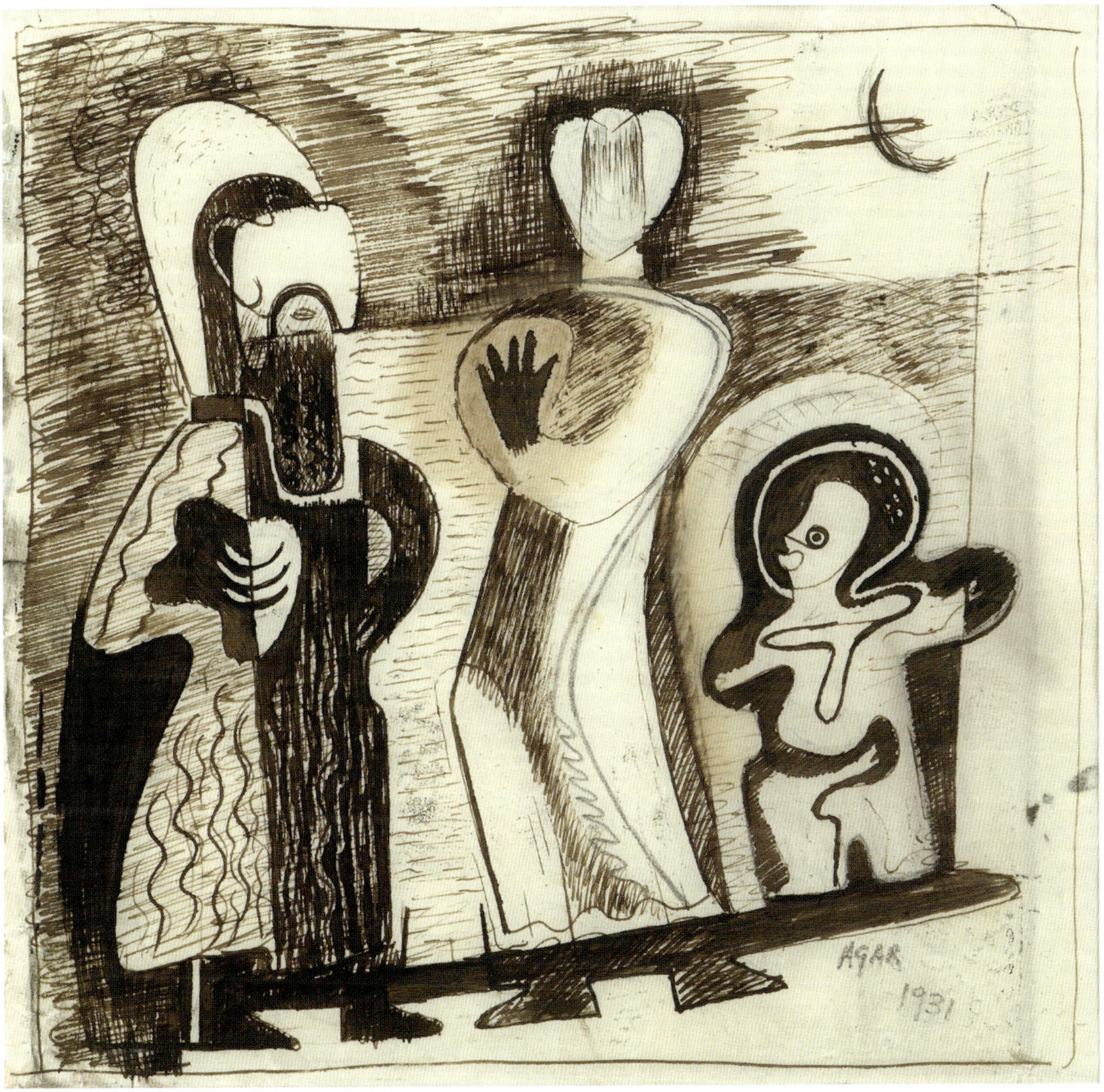
AGAR
1931

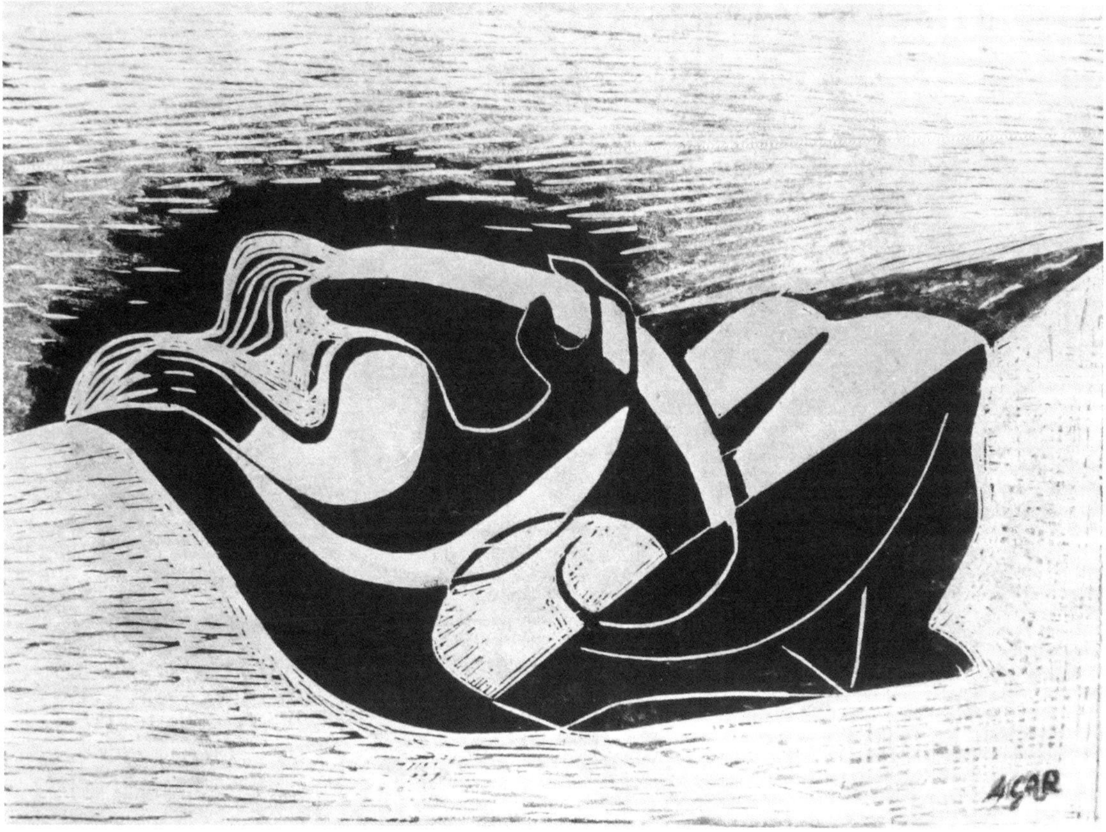
AGAR

propose an imaginative system, a series of criss-crossing dialectics without a synthesis. This is exactly what Agar was to find in the special kind of Hegelianism underlying the Surrealist approach at that very moment. These constitute the founding elements of her own Surrealism, which she was never to abandon.

It is indispensable that these statements should be quoted here, for the first time. Agar had, no doubt, through the influence of, and through her closeness to, Joseph Bard, reached an undeniably mature vision of art, of what orientation her own art should take and of what deep values it should rest upon. This was to lend her work a profound seriousness and thoroughgoing commitment to both the magical and organic values of art, which was never to abate or slacken.

In *The Island*, Agar published three engravings illustrative of what she called 'womb magic' and of her gradual departure from pure abstraction into symbolism. The woodcut entitled *Family Trio* (illus. 11) is the figurative echo of the ideas expounded in her article in *The Island*, with three figures, representing Judaism as the robed, bearded figure on the left, Christianity as the more feminine figure in the centre with her arms in the shape of a cradle, and on the right, the Child of Time, the African spirit now inhabiting the New World. Spanning centuries and continents, Agar's 'artistic imagination' found a kind of new coalescence. The same impression arises from *The Bird* (illus. 12), another woodcut alternatively titled 'Two Lovers', since the shape of a sitting, roosting bird is the result of the intertwining of other shapes, arms and legs and faces, whose arrested embrace is conjured up by the contrast between black and white forms and the tension between flatness and depth. Here the natural, animal and human kingdoms coalesce in the name of a universal process of organicity – something she also found at the same time in the works of Miró, Max Ernst and Picasso, to which she introduced herself. In fact, that same year, she painted two watercolours which bear the title *Surrealist Composition*.

In 1930, after a brief summer stay at her sister Winifred's on the isle of Sark, Bard and Agar had moved into two flats at 47 Bramham Gardens in London. In an unwittingly Surrealist move, she asked Rodney Thomas, her one-time fellow student at Leon Underwood's studio – now an interior decorator and designer, and at the time a supporter of Le Corbusier's 'purist' style – to redecorate her new flat, and more specifically her bathroom. The result turned out to bear a certain similarity to something Edward James designed a little later on in his mansion at West Dean, Chichester, following Dalí's advice. As she recalls in her autobiography, the front door, seen from inside, looked like a huge face,

12 Eileen Agar, The Bird, *or* Two Lovers, *1931, woodcut on paper.*

with the letter-box forming a mouth, a plaster hand the nose and twisted ironwork eyes and hair . . . A chromium dish-clock . . . [had] a frosted glass back-plate, pierced with the hours of the day, electric light [shining] through the apertures of Father Time. Around the clock, I made a huge collage of images . . . Other objects were constantly changing, drapes and sculptured plaster heads, textures, fabrics . . . (illus. 13)

Art coalescing with life! But the *pièce de resistance* was the bathroom, 'decked out with rope, propeller, chart and lifebelt', with 'the curtains made of fine fishing net' and 'a toy swan mounted on a Bath Oliver biscuit' – a photograph of the bathroom would even be published in the *Birmingham Post* on 9 June 1936. Unwittingly, Surrealism was slowly making its way into Agar's consciousness. Emblematic of this was Paul Nash's declaration in his article on Giorgio de Chirico in *The Listener* in April 1931 – an article which Agar must have seen: 'One of the most important contributions of Surrealism to modern painting is what might be called the extension of liberty on the subject. The tyrannical reign of Nature Morte is, at last, over. Apples have had their day.'

In March 1932 Agar exhibited with the National Society of Painters, Sculptors, Engravers and Potters at the Royal Institute Galleries in Piccadilly. It was the first time she had been the target of quite a lot of critical reviews, some negative, some laudatory, which comforted her in the direction her art was taking. *Descent into Paradise*, a painting, is 'a figure seen through

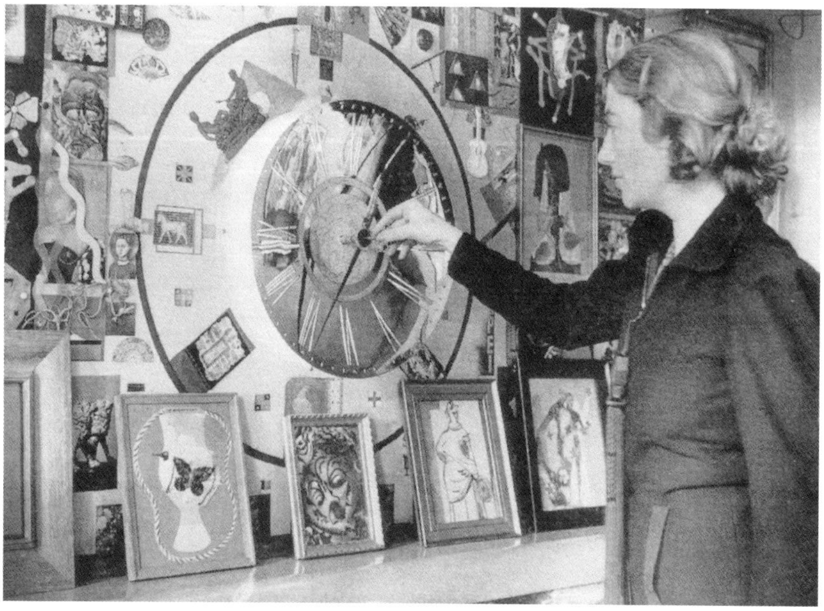

Right: 13 Clock designed by Rodney Thomas in Agar's flat, photograph.

Opposite: 14 Eileen Agar, The Egyptian Family, *1932, oil on canvas.*

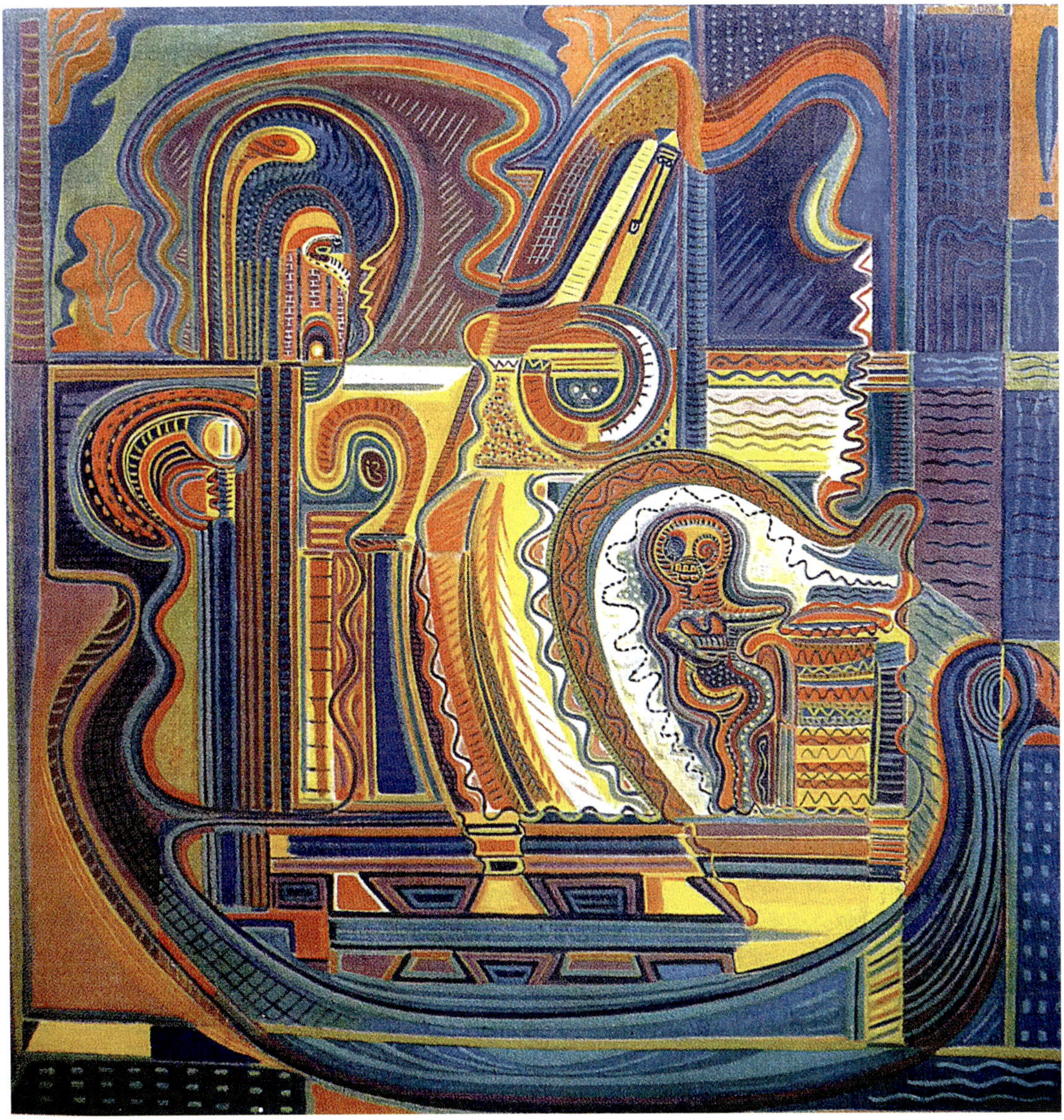

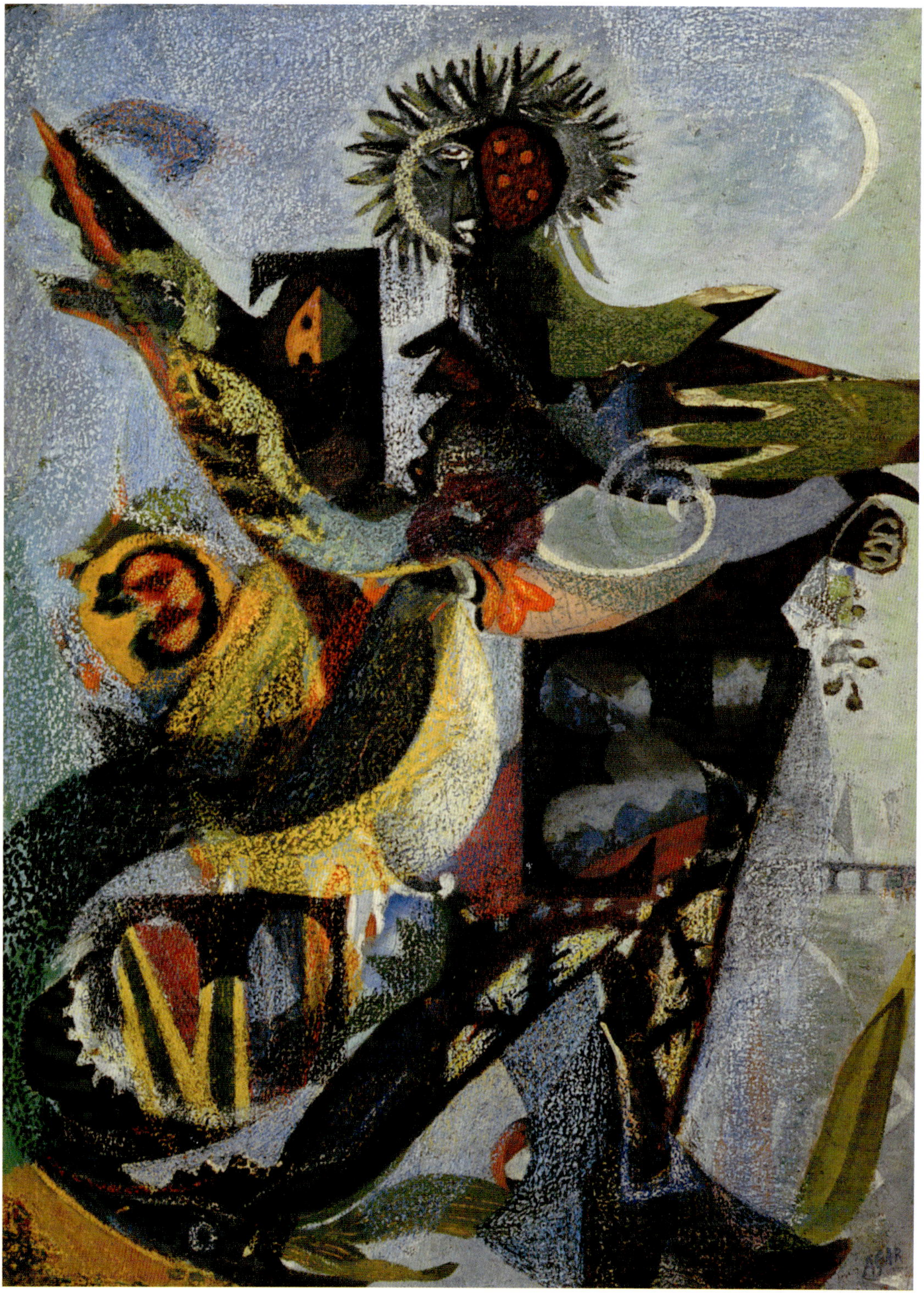

the spectrum of an aura', said the *Guardian*, while the *Observer* published a long, positive appreciation, calling her works 'compositions of sur-realistic inventions' – the first mention of her 'style' – and *Apollo* thought that 'her ambitious *Descent into Paradise* is nonsense.' P. G. Konody in the *Sunday Times* wrote that 'it is a pretentious but apparently meaningless' work. At 33 years of age, Agar was acquiring the status of a prominent, since controversial, artist. The exhibition was also a stepping stone for her to accepting Henry Moore's suggestion that she should join the London Group – which she did in 1933. At this time she had her first one-woman show at the Bloomsbury Gallery in Bloomsbury Street, displaying her work of the past seven years. This was another instance of her own conviction that she had reached a decisive stage and that she had to reflect upon what she had done up until then. This clearly corresponded to her profound determination to step beyond her past achievements and open up new vistas.

The Egyptian Family (1932, illus. 14) may well be seen as both the sign of this achievement and the harbinger of the amazing production of works two years later. Symbolizing the aesthetic unity she had reached, this painting builds a bridge between the mythological past and the present, where we see her gradually developing a style of her own based on the proliferation of organic and geometrical forms within a womb-like shape. Actually, the all-containing but also liberating shape in the painting is that of a vessel – the famous boat of Egyptian mythology which links the world of the living and the world of the dead, the terrestrial and the spiritual worlds; it can also be seen as a huge bird with a Horus-like head – letting feminine and masculine forms and a foetus-like child, reminiscent of *Family Trio,* soar up into space. The whole of the painting is carefully framed, and the family is made complete, watched over by a huge, central Horus eye. The same complexity of this work, stressed by the entanglement of colours and forms, was to be found in the 1934 paintings.

Another case in point is *The Wandering Minstrel* (c. 1932, illus. 15), which also exemplifies the transitional quality of these years. A host of the land and the sea, his sun-like head rising high in the moonlit sky, the minstrel builds musical bridges between all sorts of nascent shapes and colours, uncoiling them from under his cosmic, Harlequin-like mantle. Telling us stories from distant places, which he brings in the folds of his cloak, he belongs to no place and to all places. At a distance from both abstraction and representation, the painting features a grammar of rhythmical lyricism, halfway between. Isn't the minstrel the artist's alter ego, performing for his or her viewers?

15 Eileen Agar, The Wandering Minstrel, *c. 1932, oil on board.*

Two works from 1932, *Rooster and Hen* (illus. 16) and *Child's Head into Profile*, are typically seen as transition pieces: the former is a composition essentially based on the rhythm of lines and forms, inherited from Cubism, which creates a beautifully balanced centrifugal movement echoing the 'panache' of the bird, replete with musical and sexual connotations, while the latter clearly announces the use of profile hidden in the face and vice versa. The dynamism of overlapping colour areas which was to be Agar's trademark later and the figurativeness of these two paintings constitute turning points in her work.

Two photographs she took in 1934 indicate this twofold source of inspiration. One, of a street lamp (illus. 18), echoes her interest in the geometrical rhythm of forms, with the added fascination with shadows, as in the photography of folding chairs and shadows – shadows hold the living secrets of forms and distance them from reality. The other, of a figurehead and wheel (illus. 17), indicates her Surrealist orientation, by playing on the absurd disproportion of the juxtaposition, thus precipitating the viewer into a parallel world.

Socially speaking, Agar and Bard were becoming more and more a part of the artistic milieu. A. R. Orage became a friend they could rely on. Orage was a British intellectual, in 1907 the brilliant wayward editor of *The New Age*, a weekly journal devoted to the defence of modernist culture and socialist politics; he was one of the theoreticians of Social Credit. Then, from 1931 to 1934 (the year he died), he edited the *New English Weekly*, in which Dylan Thomas and David Gascoyne published their very first poems. He actually prompted Bard to publish short stories but their relationship faded away when, convinced of the necessity of reforming man's mind, he joined the mystic Gurdjieff's group for a while. Henry Moore was also a faithful friend who was always ready to give advice, just like Alec and Evelyn Waugh, Eddy Sackville-West and the painter C.R.W. Nevinson, a Royal Academician rather critical of the self-complacency pervading English art and an anti-conformist contributor to *The Island*. There were also the artists Jacob Epstein and Alexander Calder, whom Agar met in Ben Nicholson's studio. On another memorable occasion, Rosalind Wade, whose novel *Children be Happy!*, published in 1931, had created a furore for involving real-life characters in sexually risky situations, came one evening with David Gascoyne and Dylan Thomas to a party hosted by Bard and Agar. Wade was a friend of both Agar and Gascoyne and was a regular visitor to the Parton Street Bookshop where she had heard David Archer talk enthusiastically about Dylan Thomas. Gascoyne was then a promising young poet who had published an autobiographical novel, *Opening Day*, as well as a slim volume of poetry, *Roman Balcony*, in 1933, and was about to start working on his epoch-making *A Short Survey*

16 Eileen Agar, Rooster and Hen, *1932, ink and gouache on oil-soaked paper.*

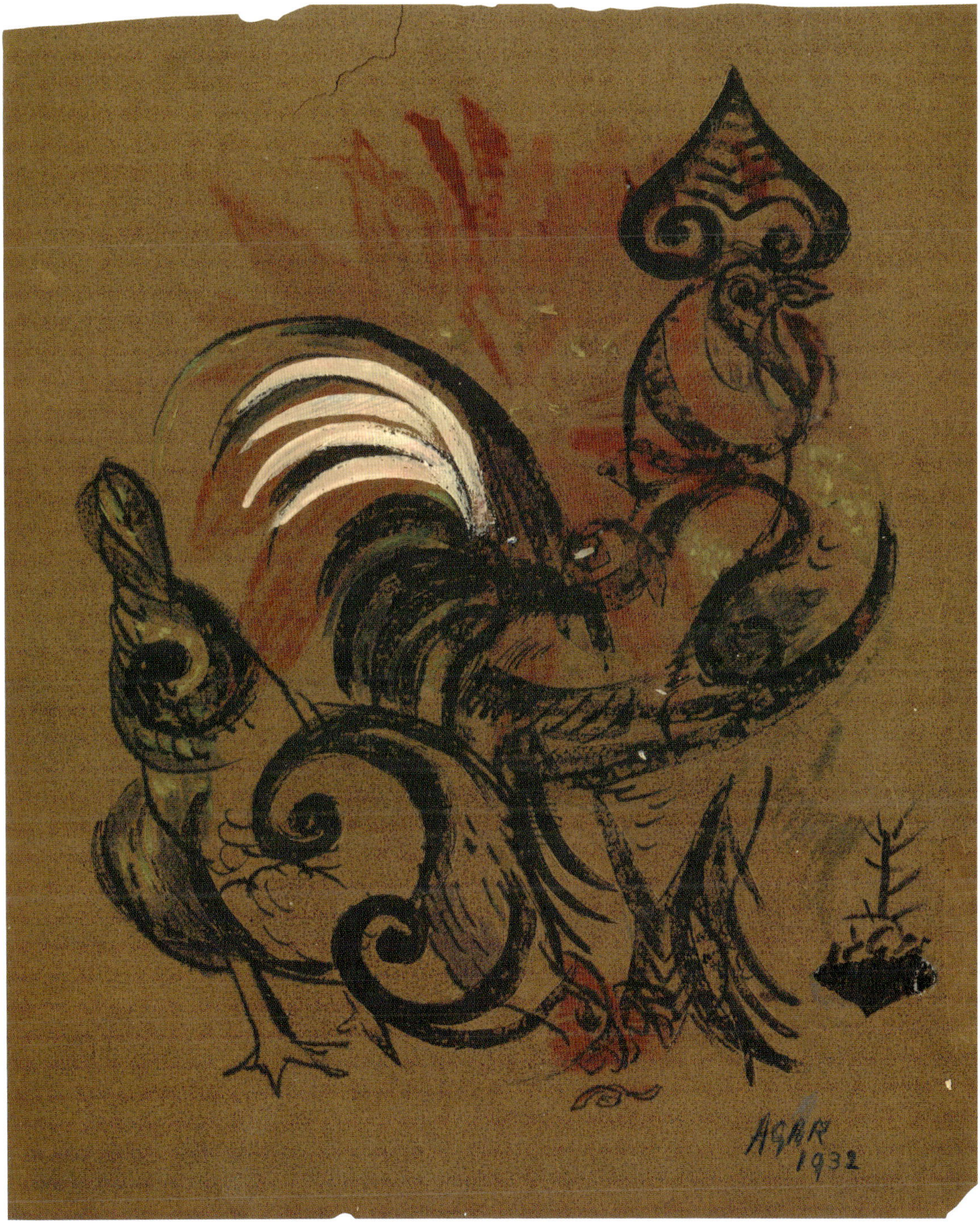
AGAR
1932

of Surrealism. Before going to the party, Wade and Gascoyne were sitting in Café Royal off Piccadilly when Dylan Thomas came in. Wade suggested he should accompany them to Agar's place. This is how Dylan Thomas's close friend, Daniel Jones, describes the evening:

> Most of the guests were in evening dress. Dylan Thomas in contrast had a very grubby jersey of the kind worn by Wolf Cubs and he sat cross-legged on a small pouffe, all red in the face like a 'malignant gnome'. He attacked everything and everybody, employing swearwords in his vocabulary. But the sophisticated company merely laughed good-humouredly and urged him to cheer up and grow up.

This is a lively testimony to the atmosphere of the 'Bohemian' literary and artistic scene in London at the time and of the widening circle of their acquaintances; such an encounter could only strengthen Agar's self-

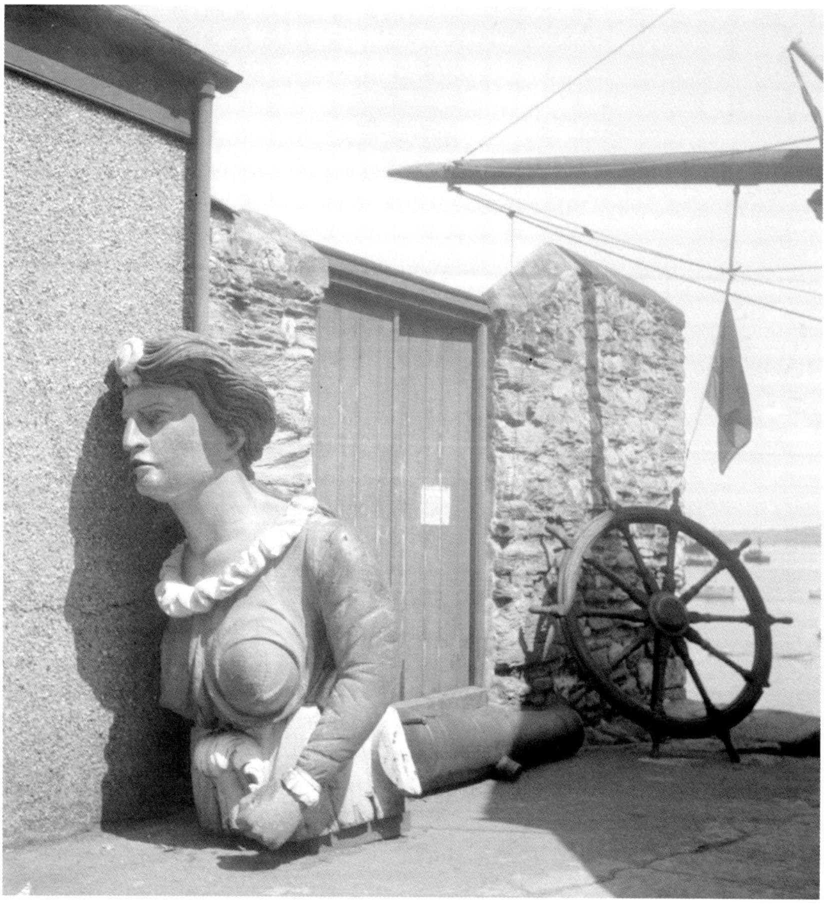

Right: 17 Eileen Agar, figurehead and wheel, 1934, photograph.

Opposite: 18 Eileen Agar, street lamp, 1934, photograph.

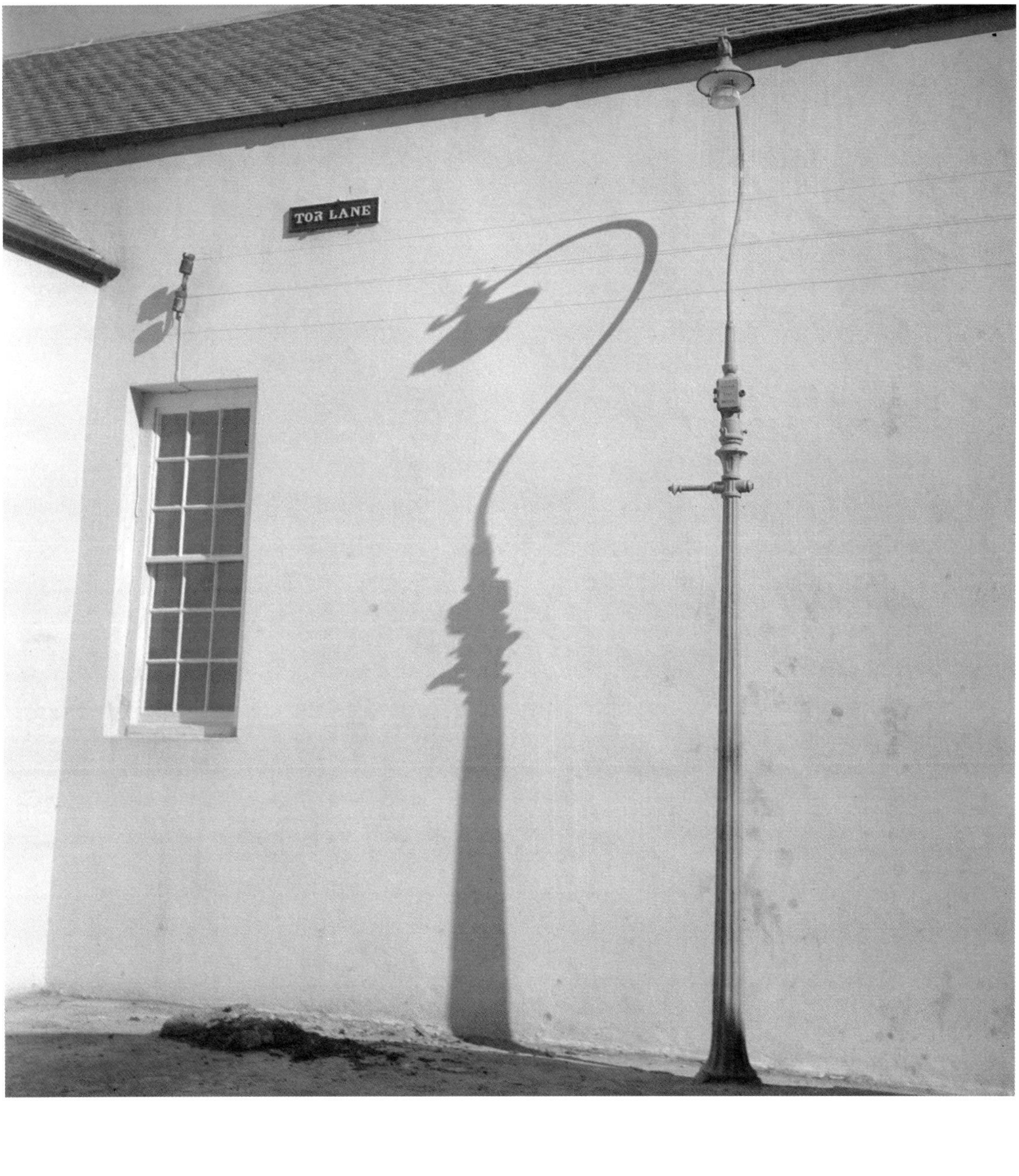
TOR LANE

confidence. Her individualism and sense of independence could not but be flattered and encouraged in such a stimulating atmosphere she felt so much attuned to. This also reveals how both Bard and herself situated themselves at the margin of conventionality.

The year 1934 was most prolific, with the first groundbreaking and self-assertive works that created a personal style heralding a brilliant career. Four very important works were produced, which established Agar at a very original and unique place in a milieu dominated by Nicholsonian abstraction or Duncan Grant-esque still-lifes and landscape paintings. Interestingly enough, these four seminal works, *The Autobiography of an Embryo*, *The Unnatural Child*, *The Modern Muse* and *Madonna with Cat's Cradle*, are concerned with the process of creation and procreation. Obviously femininity imbues them all and it would be easy to reach hasty conclusions claiming that Agar was from the very start of her career the proponent of a feminist art. This is too rash. The four paintings are all given a complexity which projects them beyond such reductive meaning into a wider world of the imagination. *The Autobiography of an Embryo* (illus. 19), for one, is a radical, systematic, all-comprehensive opening up of the subconscious, exploring irrationality, proliferation and unsuspected symbolism – a work to be read and deciphered over and over again, a hymn to unbounded creativity, a fabulous fable of the workings of what Agar called 'womb magic'.

The painting requires our reading from left to right, as if it were a story, but a story told *un-narratively*. Each chapter in the story, each 'panel' in this quadriptych, tells its own story of shapes and rhythms, and carries us forcefully on to the next one – and back to the beginning once we have reached the end, if we choose this way of reading – thanks to the wheel-like circles, a motif which recurs in all 'panels' and reminds one simultaneously of the wheel of life, the womb, the egg, the entrance into the inner world and the notion of perfection and the infinite. In the foreword to the catalogue of an exhibition of Agar's paintings and works on paper held at the Redfern Gallery at the end of 2004, the novelist A. S. Byatt, who frequently mentions her deep interest in Surrealism, describes the painting in this way:

> The round black holes contain various forms which are ambiguously embryos or eggs or birds – a hawk-like white form is bursting through the shell of one egg. There are repeated small circles – the dividing cells, the eye in the dark of the unborn human, a seaweedy lump that might be a placenta, surrounded by a rainbow palette . . . the embryo she carries is an eye which makes colour, and is also a pinhole opening on the dark . . .

This is an attempt to give a description which does not preclude a host of other attempts, so inexhaustible is Agar's world of awakening forms.

Through these echoes and cross-references, the embryo tells us about its life-before-birth, the dark forces and obscure energy which precede the coming into the world and the forming of cells into a child – the cells which will shape and haunt his mind throughout his forthcoming life. We are given an insight into the prehistory of forms in the making, blending evocations of shells, birds, plants, hands, eyes, faces – a world of anarchic disorder which, in its turn, calls upon the viewer's own inner anarchic mind and imagination to be permanently deconstructed and reconstructed. Aren't we all heirs to these primitive shapes and forces? There is nothing abstract in this, everything is alive and concrete – like a Baudelairian forest of signs and correspondences we are invited to roam through. Intuition rather than reason gives birth to this 2-m-long mindscape of a developing artist.

That same year, Agar took up the motif of *The Island*'s linocut of *Family Trio* produced in 1931, to paint a watercolour on paper and an oil with a similar, frontal but less intricate, and more stylized, almost abstract, arrangement of foetal and embryonic forms, bearing the same title (illus. 20, 21). In this work, the forms are, in the words of Louisa Buck, 'fluid shapes floating over the surface like wandering thoughts, to be trapped in a net of geometric planes . . . a subtle locking of diagonals, horizontals and verticals', which re-emphasize the discipline inherited from her Cubist lessons but balance it with organic forms. The symbols are the same as in the linocut, a reference to the three cultures which haunt the Western world. Jewishness is represented by the upright hieratic form on the left; Christianity is denoted by the glow emanating from the pale-coloured shapes, 'the rays of light which symbolize faith'; the foetal 'Negro' shape to the right inside a womb-like oval, 'an amniotic bubble' says Andrew Lambirth, stands for African art and the magic it has introduced into the Western mind. Ovals, circles, crescents, solid forms or transparent planes all metaphorically lead to the progressive entrance into the subconscious of man.

It is important, in order to fully understand the stage which Agar had arrived at, to explore the subtext of *Family Trio*. This triple representation of an archetypal family can be seen as the emblematization of the ideas she was at the very same time expounding in her article in *The Island*. Proof is given in early 1928 when in her diary she developed this philosophical, transcontinental vision of the deep workings of man's mind, which dovetails femininity and masculinity, intuition and emotion on the one hand, and reason and the intellect on the other:

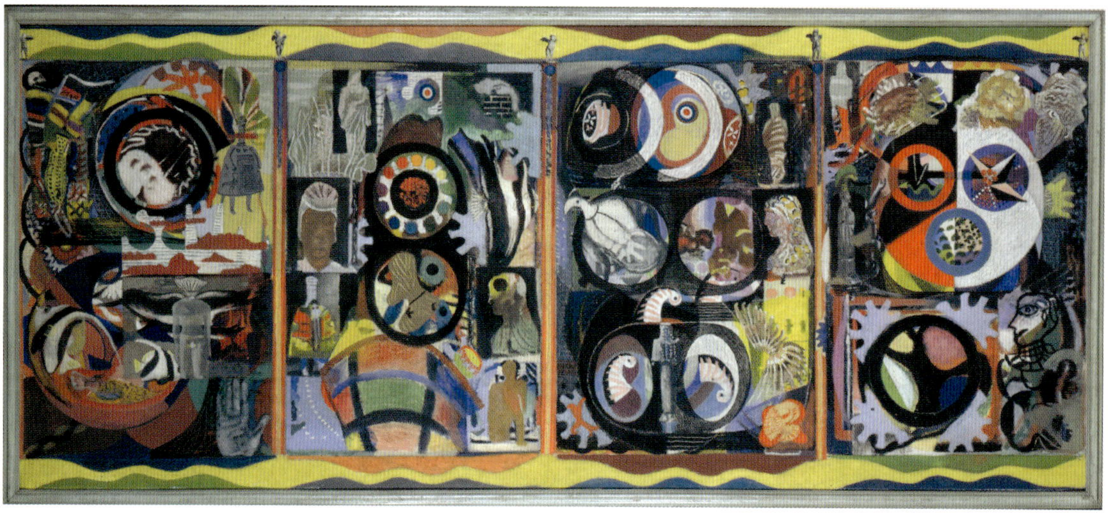

> The history of rationalism in Europe might be likened to a male child with such a strong fixation on the mother (irrational or unconscious) that whatever he does in later life off his own bat is not only deeply coloured or distorted by this fixation, he can only repeat himself to a certain point and break. Christ the man is the child who could never free himself from the mother, the Unconscious (therefore proving that no intellect or male ideal *can* do so) and whose life is a tragedy played by a *Poet* in order to show the impossibility of the reign of the intellect over the unconscious. The unconscious must reign *through* the intellect.

Then, in her diary, she turns to the third person in the *Trio*, the male Jewish father, whom she detects behind Nietzsche's 'cry of Anti-Christ':

> Christ as a Rationalist must die, because he can never be a true rationalist. This ties up with the Jewish refusal to recognize him as Messiah, for the Jewish intellect knows the falseness of that type of rationalist. For he alone has the true rationalist mind-type. When the Christian mind-type can produce an emotional imaginative soul, a mind-mate in fact which can play content with the Jewish form (intellect), then will he recognize and worship the true Messiah.

It is this series of philosophical preoccupations which have to be read into the successive works of that period, all related to the child and mother, gestation and parturition. These three agents, which she sees as haunting the Western conscience – Christian, Jew and Negro – could easily be supplemented with another three factors: emotion, reason and imagination. Trinities and vernary rhythms do seem to haunt these exploratory years.

Is *The Unnatural Child* the embryo after it has grown? (illus. 22) A child, the result of the superimposition of circular shapes and flames of colour, begotten not of nature but of an interior world, begotten out of wedlock and 'civilized' prejudices, is here growing from huge cells, one of which is that of the star-studded night of time, emerging from the blood-coloured fire of love and held in the eternal movement of the wheel of life whose still centre lies in the palm of a symbolic hand, that of the maker – whoever that may be, the mystery will for ever remain undisclosed. But we know where it comes from. It comes from the mother figure which dominates that period, *The Modern Muse*, the epitome of what creation means for Agar (illus. 23). Her orange and yellow heart-shaped face beats with all the fertility of linear and soft curving shapes, a face never

Opposite: 19
Eileen Agar, The Autobiography of an Embryo, *1933–4, oil on board.*

Overleaf left: 20
Eileen Agar, Family Trio, *1931, watercolour and pen and ink on paper.*

Overleaf right: 21
Eileen Agar, Family Trio, *1934, oil on canvas.*

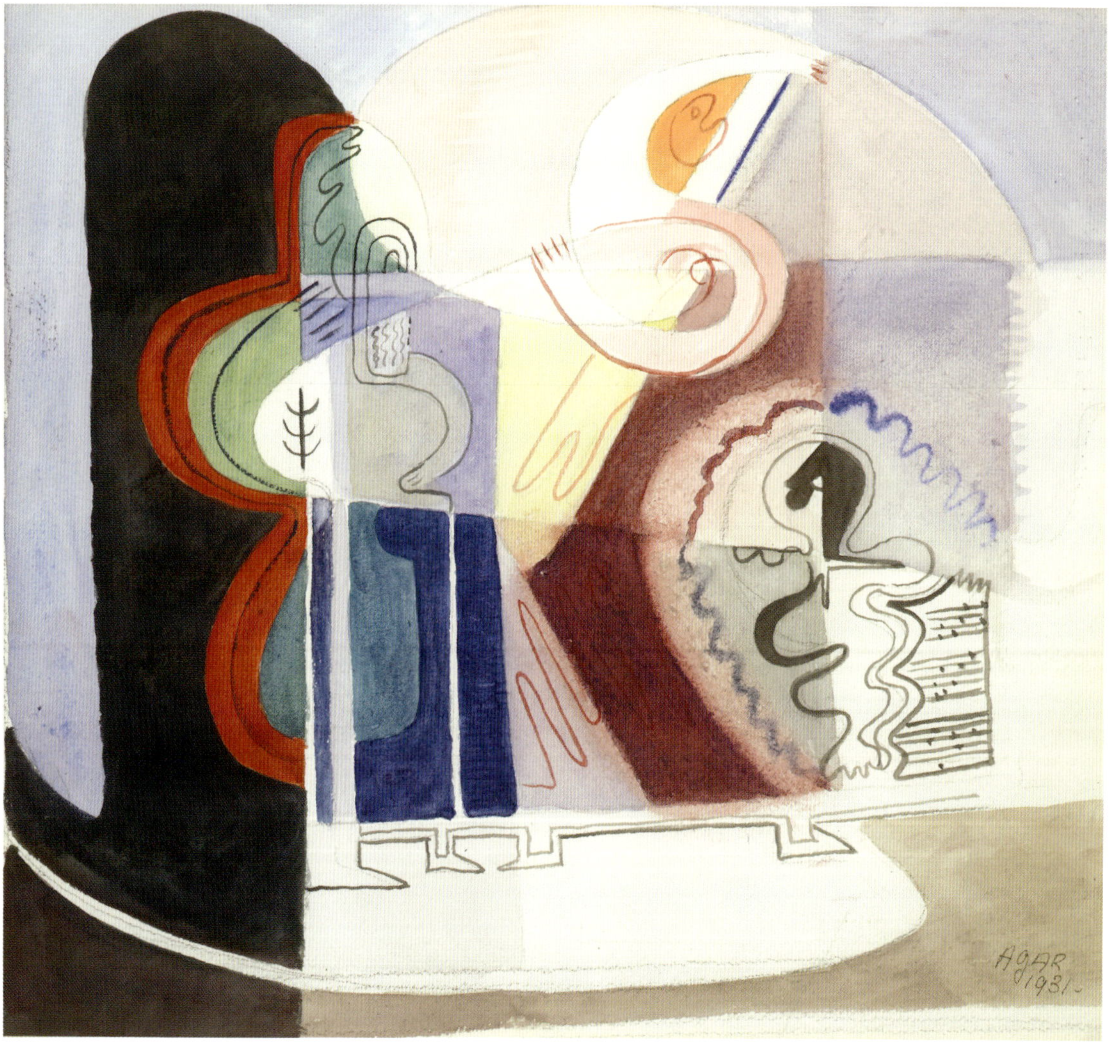
AGAR
1931

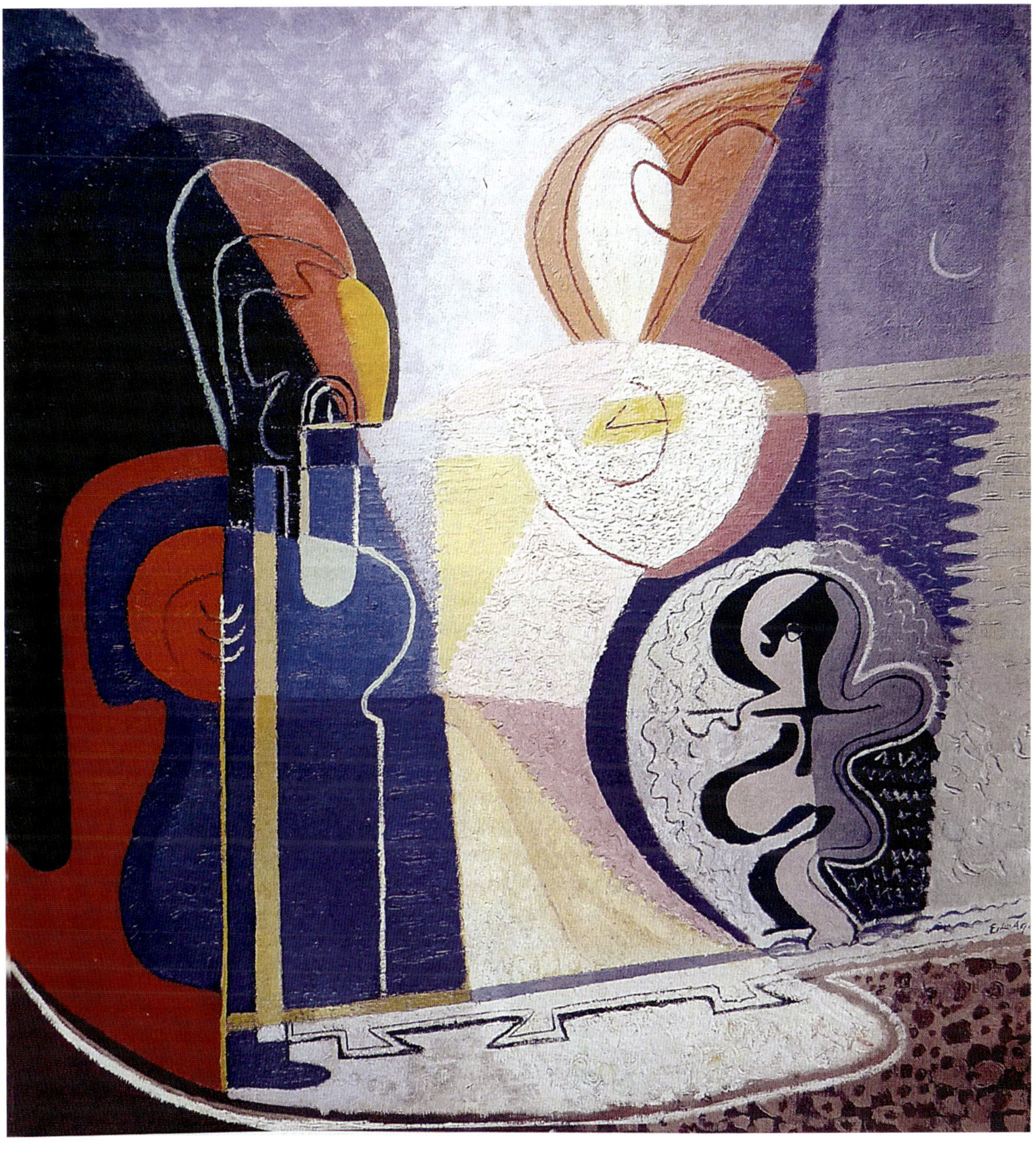

complete, both feminine and masculine, always being transformed, the source of a never-ending movement, as is indicated by the whirling rhythm of lines around the face on a blue background. The Muse is modern, in the sense that it provides the artist with renewed sources of inspiration, derived from primitive mask-like or fluid, dynamic forms, which one also finds in Picasso's faces, like that of Marie-Thérèse Walter, in *La Femme Fleur*, painted in 1932.

But there is more. In his perceptive analysis of the painting, Andrew Lambirth wonders if there is not a hidden reference to Agar's intimate life at the time, a possible reference to a thwarted wish for children, or to some accident or mishap in her life as a woman. The painting would thus become a kind of exorcization or disculpation. Indeed, a note written in her diary and dated November 1928 reads:

> What song should women sing if not a love-song? Every child she bears should be a paean in praise of him who fructified her. There is no other story than that of love and creation and birth. It is a woman who should answer Solomon's cry. For it was written that through Love should the world be born anew.

Whatever the explanation – if one is deemed necessary – this will turn into, and will definitely *found*, Agar's own constant celebration of femininity and her use of all those natural elements which, at her touch, are likely to become symbols of woman.

This is also echoed in *Madonna with a Cat's Cradle* (illus. 24). The drawing itself reminds us of the same serpentine forms seen in the previous paintings as well as in Picasso's. The title, together with its humorous reference – a divine figure playing a child's game – emphasizes the profoundly feminine and secular quality of the universal mother figure who cradles creation in her hands. The shape of a horse's head prefigures the horse's heads of *Quadriga* (1935) but may also be that of a sleeping child or a cat resting in the Madonna's hands. The whole figure is here again framed both by a line *and* flame-like lines – the emblem of the Holy Spirit in the Christian tradition? – and refers, although in a slightly irreverent way, to the central figure of Christianity, Mary, whom Agar, let us remember, sees as the unconscious. The whole composition is thus made intellectually active, starting with the title; isn't the cradle the evocation of the womb, or of the birth of Christ? Following on from this, isn't *playing* a way of *praying* to the imaginative forces of the unconscious? Isn't it what hands are made for?

Opposite: 22
Eileen Agar, The Unnatural Child, *1934, oil on canvas.*

Overleaf left: 23
Eileen Agar, The Modern Muse, *1934, oil on canvas.*

Overleaf right: 24
Eileen Agar, Madonna with a Cat's Cradle, *1934, oil on canvas.*

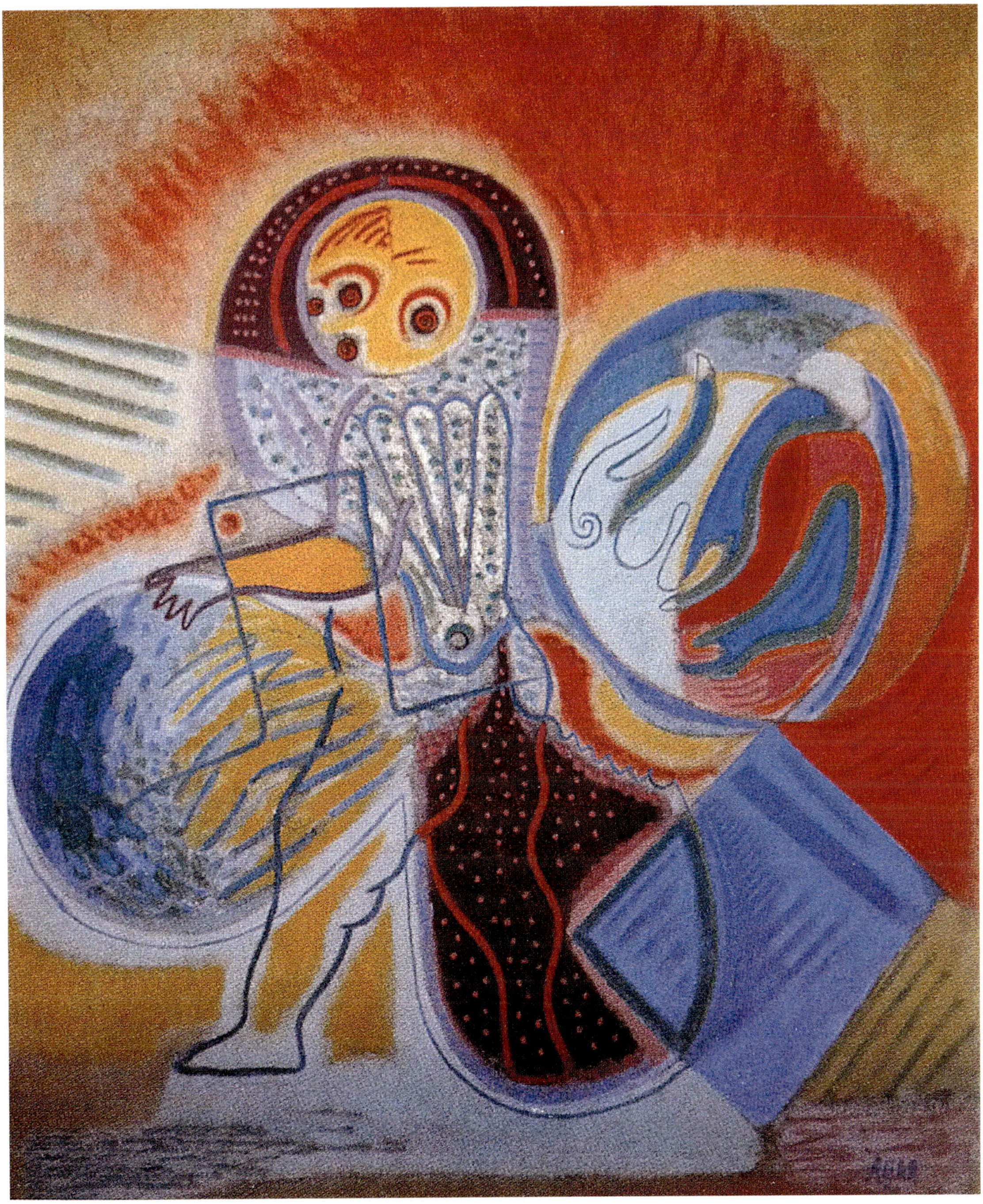

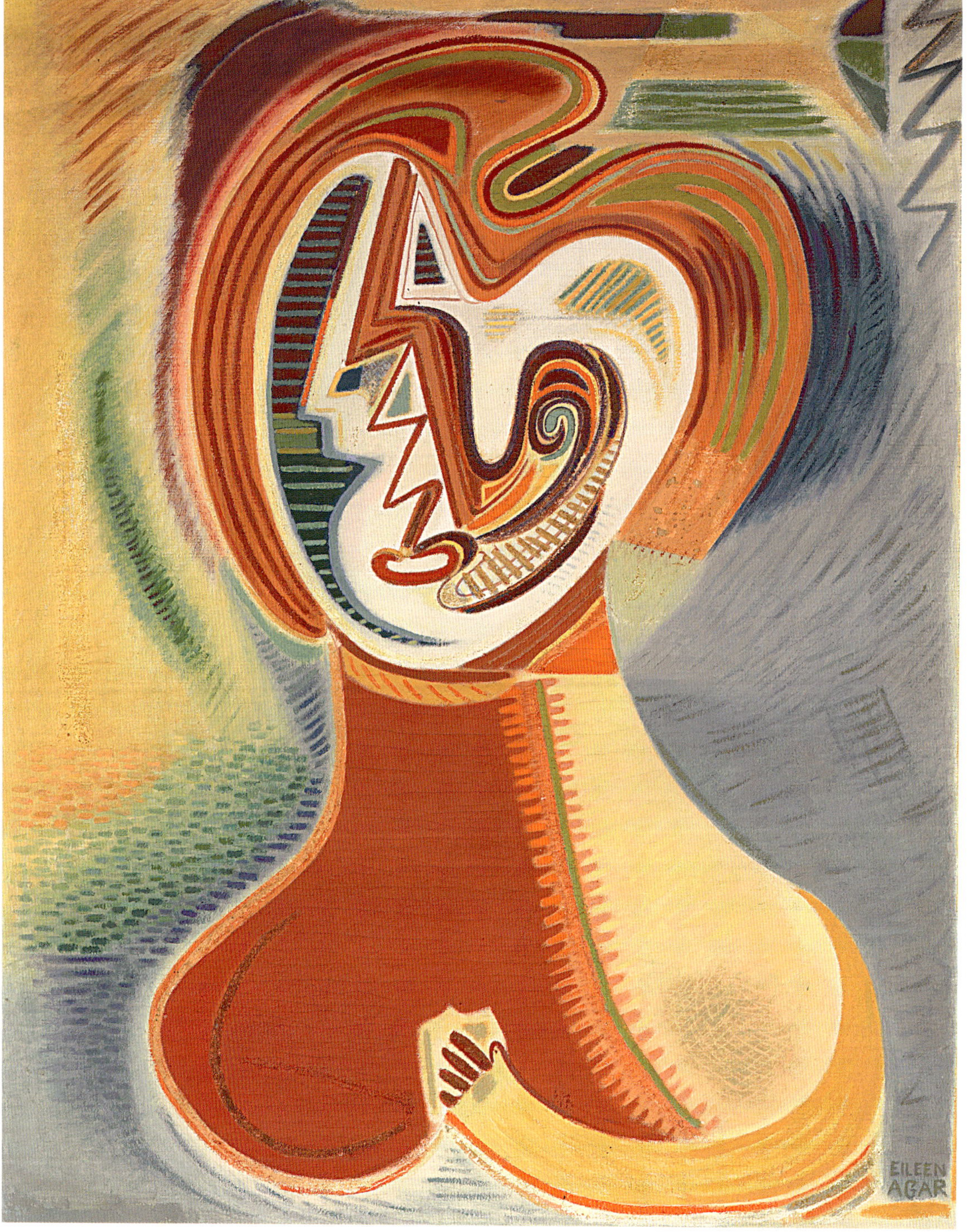
EILEEN
AGAR

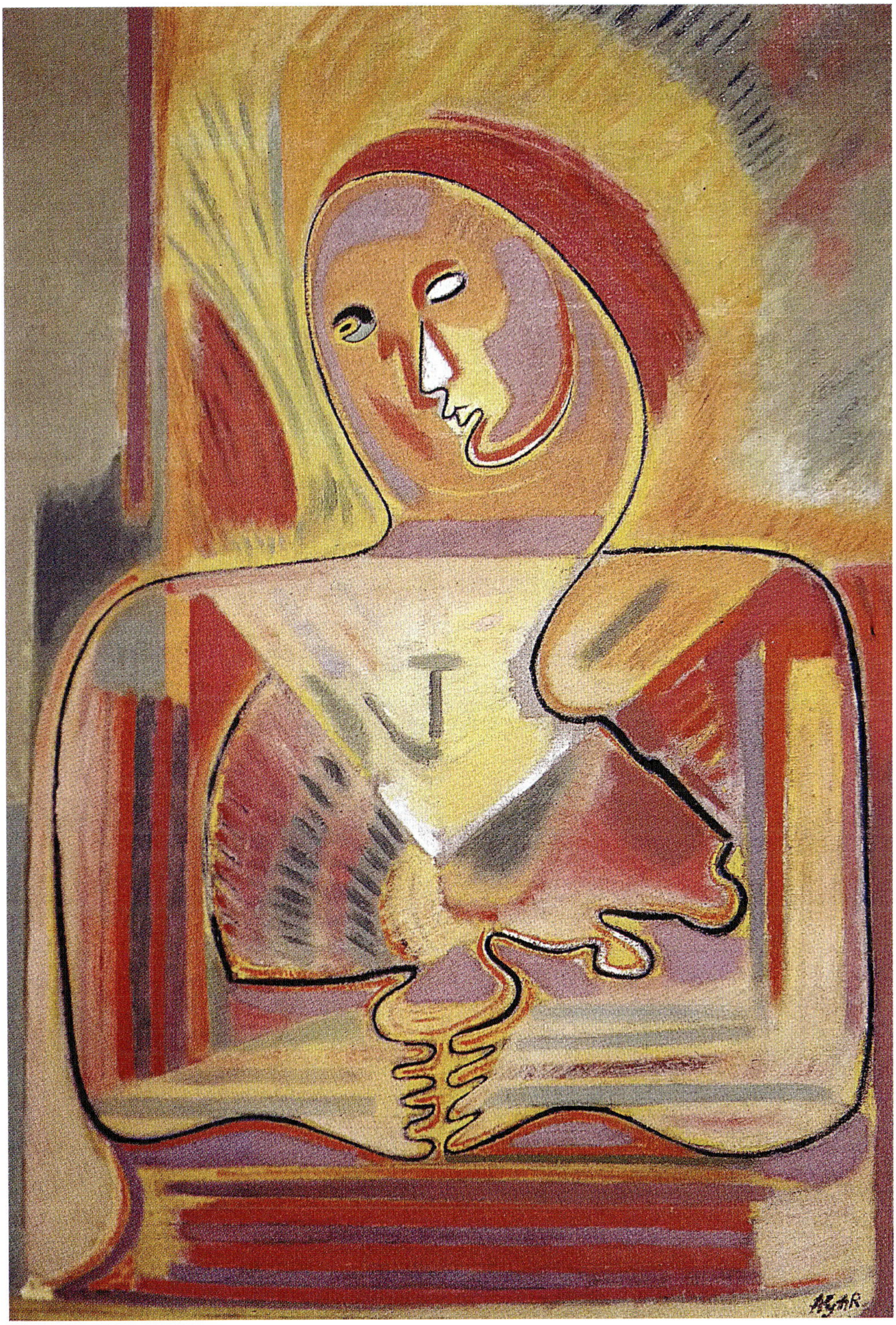
AGAR

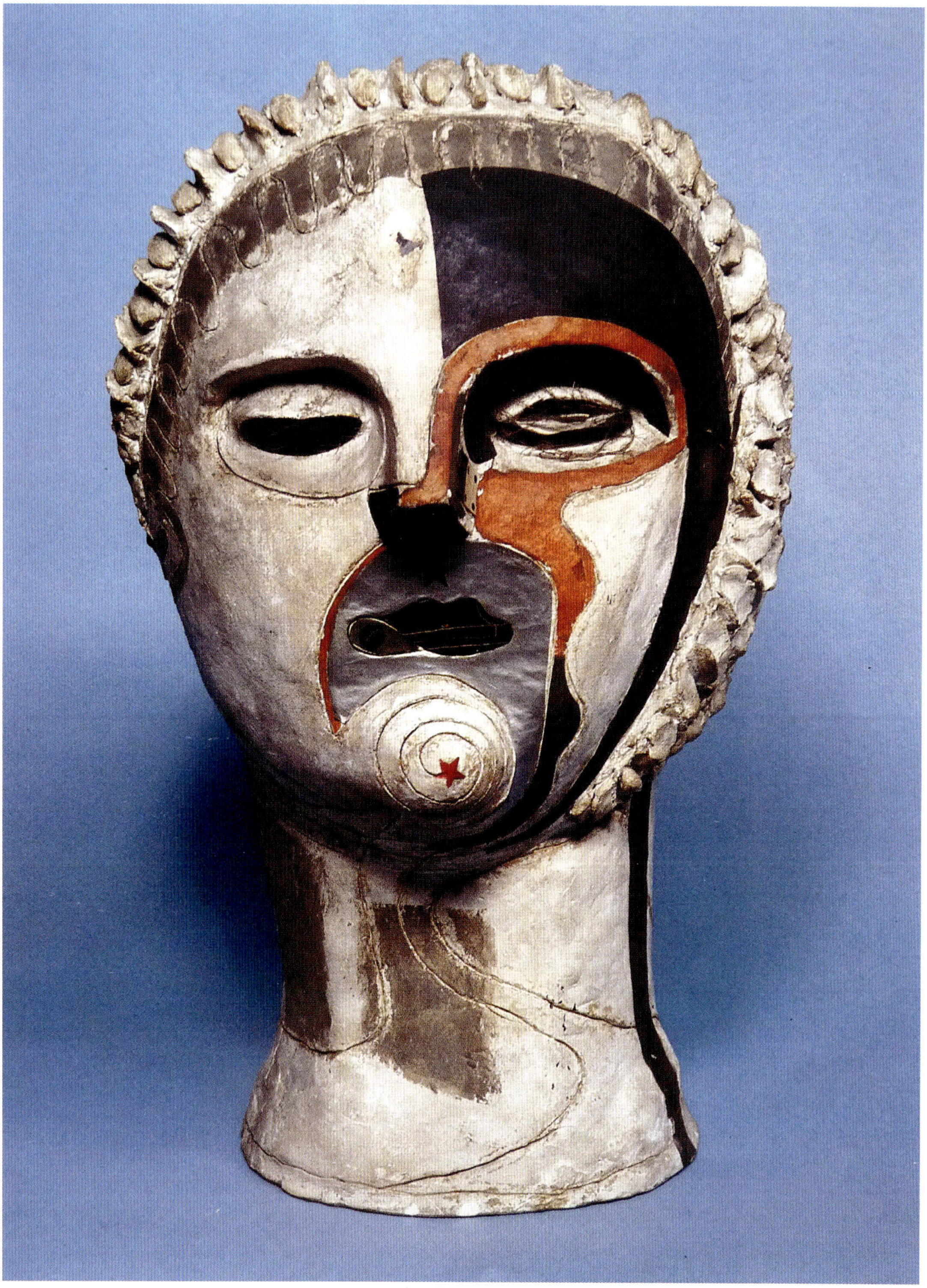

That same year, *Woman Clad with Leaves* was probably one of Agar's very first collages, especially collages made with actual leaves – earlier on, she had chanced upon a book containing dried leaves. The link is clearly established then between woman and nature. The collage, framed with a winding line, presents us with a kind of bird-like form, which watches lines unrolling from the leaves and covering what appears to be a spread-eagled feminine shape. In *The Shell*, an oil painting from the same year of a less fanciful and more stern figure holding a shell, one is reminded of Picasso's strong women painted with angular breasts, legs and arms – and the interaction of curving and straight lines endows the painting with a grave balance. Here again the shell is the image of the female sex but also of the source of creation and of the process of emergence from the vastness of nature.

> I had modelled the head in wet clay and my ambition was attempting a portrait head of Joseph Bard. When it came back from the plasterer, not being able to afford bronze, I was dismayed by its white sepulchral unpleasant look . . . I decided to turn it into something more poetic and imaginative, this left me free to do as I liked with it. So, having always collected scraps of ill-considered trifles, I proceeded to cover it with green feathers, bits of D'Oyley's [*sic*] black astrakhan fur and coloured paper, letting the white of the plaster cast show through.

Bard was both a modernist and a classicist, and here one aspect vies with, and balances, the other, as day vies with, and balances, night – while his blind eyes look inside the mind, the symbol of profound meditation and wisdom. The crenellated crown of plaster increases the solemnity of the whole attitude and of its arrested upward movement – a serene balance is thus achieved, inspiring and suffusing mercy. The die used for the nose, the lines drawn on the neck and forming a spiral on the chin, the diamond shape on the forehead, and the stars – one black, one ochre – which echo the two colours used on the face, all add mystery to the possible meanings the viewer may detect.

In the summer of 1934, Agar and Bard visited A. R. Orage and Henry and Irina Moore in Yorkshire, two renewed encounters which could only encourage further Agar's opening up to the manifestations of the spirit of modernity and freedom of inspiration, as is anecdotally but pointedly emblematized by a curious, humorous oil painting, *Bernard Shaw Feeding the Birds* (illus. 27). In a cave-like setting, that of a recluse, the whitish, ghost-like figure of the great man on the right extends its arm towards two white birds while in the distance, in a kind of opening, a plant, with all its roots hanging

25 Eileen Agar, Angel of Mercy, *1934, plaster with collage and watercolour.*

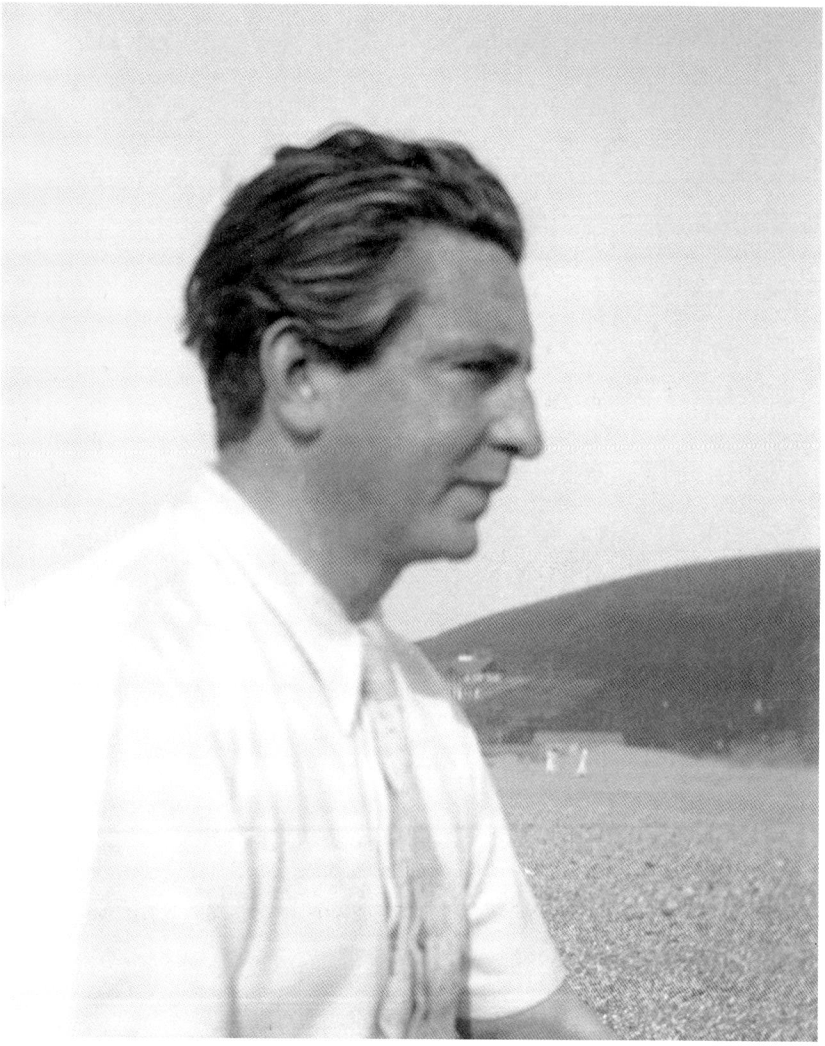

Above: 26 *Eileen Agar,* Joseph Bard, *1934, photograph.*

Opposite: 27 Eileen Agar, Bernard Shaw Feeding the Birds, *1934, oil on canvas.*

down, is suspended in the air. The lightness of the three realistic presences contrasts with the darkness of the background, the recognizable quality of the former with the confusion and thick pigmentation of the latter, as if all this were an apparition, reminding us of St Anthony at the entrance of his cave.

The year 1935 was determining. It witnessed a gradual coming together of factors which were to launch Surrealism as a movement in England. Indeed, a number of young artists were returning from France between late 1934 and early 1936 – artists such as John Banting, Humphrey Jennings, Julian Trevelyan, David Gascoyne and Roland Penrose, all of whom had befriended some of the French Surrealists and most of whom Agar had already been acquainted with earlier on. In 1935 she also made a most

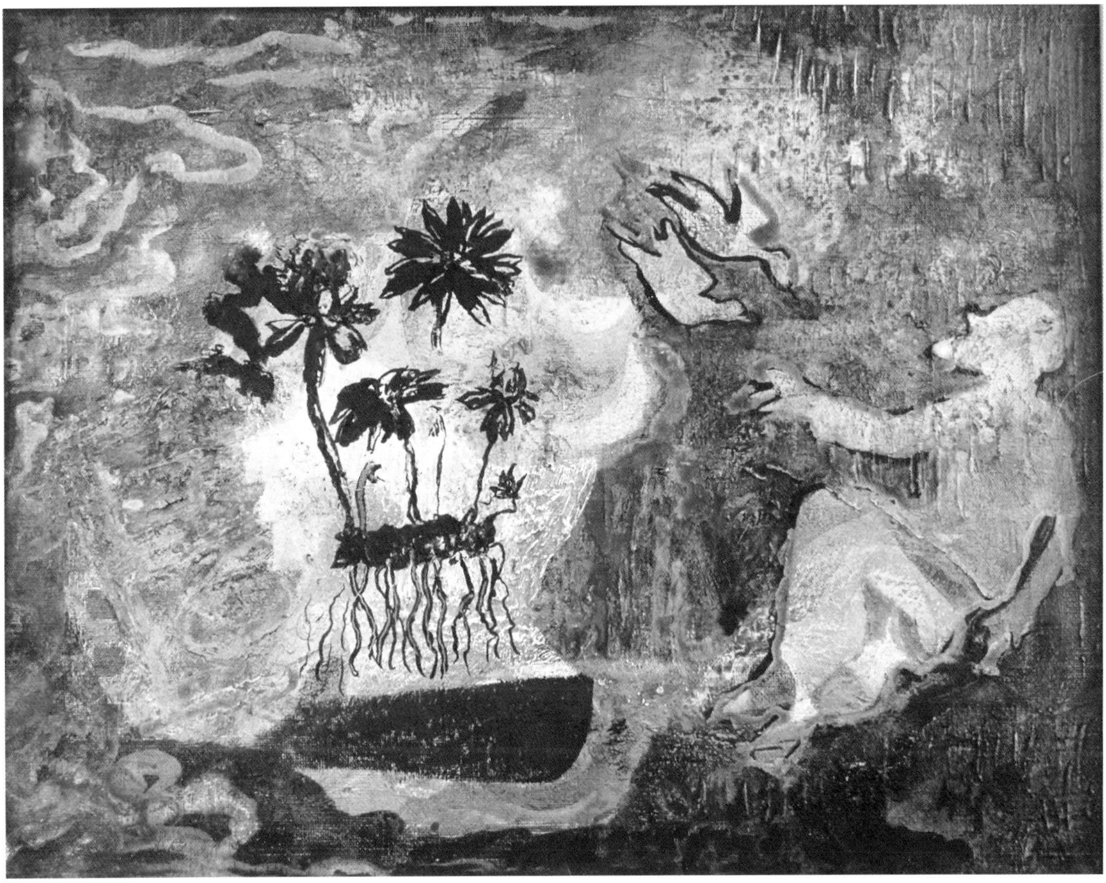

influential visit to Paul Nash in Swanage on the south coast of England. Agar and Bard were introduced to Nash by Ashley Havinden, the famous poster designer, whom Bard had met before, and they rented a place – Clarence Cottage. This meeting, as I have pointed out, introduced Agar to a whole new imaginative universe, that of found objects, an incentive to leave the doors of the subconscious wide open so that the interaction between the outer and the inner worlds could be freed from all preconceptions. Moreover, Nash, besides being a painter obsessed both with the construction of landscapes – whether imaginative or not (see his *Northern Adventure* (1929) and his *Mansions of the Dead* (1934)) – and with nature's manifestations, was a prominent photographer who could turn his hand to teaching how to structure and organize a snapshot. In September 1933, Nash had visited Avebury and its circle of megaliths which was for him 'an affirmation of man's desire to make a structure which mirrors the providential use of a God who orders days and nights'. At the end of the year, he had gone to France, staying in Nice where he met Matisse, and in Cagnes-sur-Mer through the winter, taking many photographs of beaches and returning to London in June 1934.

From April to December 1935, Nash had worked in Swanage on the Dorset Shell Guide, a commission initiated by John Betjeman which gave him the freedom to break with the traditional guides – under, to a certain extent, the influence of Max Ernst's 'forest' paintings, frottages and decalcomanias (Ernst's Mayor Gallery show in 1933 had created a stir in the art world). Nash exploited in his text and in his photographs of Dorset the mythical dimension of fields and forests, leading the reader into remote corners where nature was at its rawest and especially stressing the unsuspected richness of its geological formation – chalk, limestone, Kimmeridge Clay, shale and coolites – a guide which Agar couldn't but be guided by. Nash thus ignored many all too obvious places and the resulting book was a personal rendering of what Dorset was like far from the beaten track. It is exactly at that time that Agar and Bard met him – an encounter of like minds. Needless to say, this conjunction of the rigour of rationality and the acceptance of the irrational was in perfect harmony with what Agar was exploring and one understands why Nash and Agar became inseparable, and even lovers. Of course, this did make Bard suffer considerably – but there never was any threat to the couple's mutual understanding and deep complicity.

In Swanage they met Helen Muspratt, a photographer friend of Nash's, who lived in Cliff Cottage in Shore Road, not far from were Agar and Bard had rented a place. Born in India, Muspratt was living with her recently reunited family at Cliff Cottage. She had opened a studio in Swanage before moving to Cambridge with a friend, Lettice Ramsey, leaving her studio in the care of her

28 Eileen Agar, untitled box, 1935, coral, seahorse, feathers, eye of Horus.

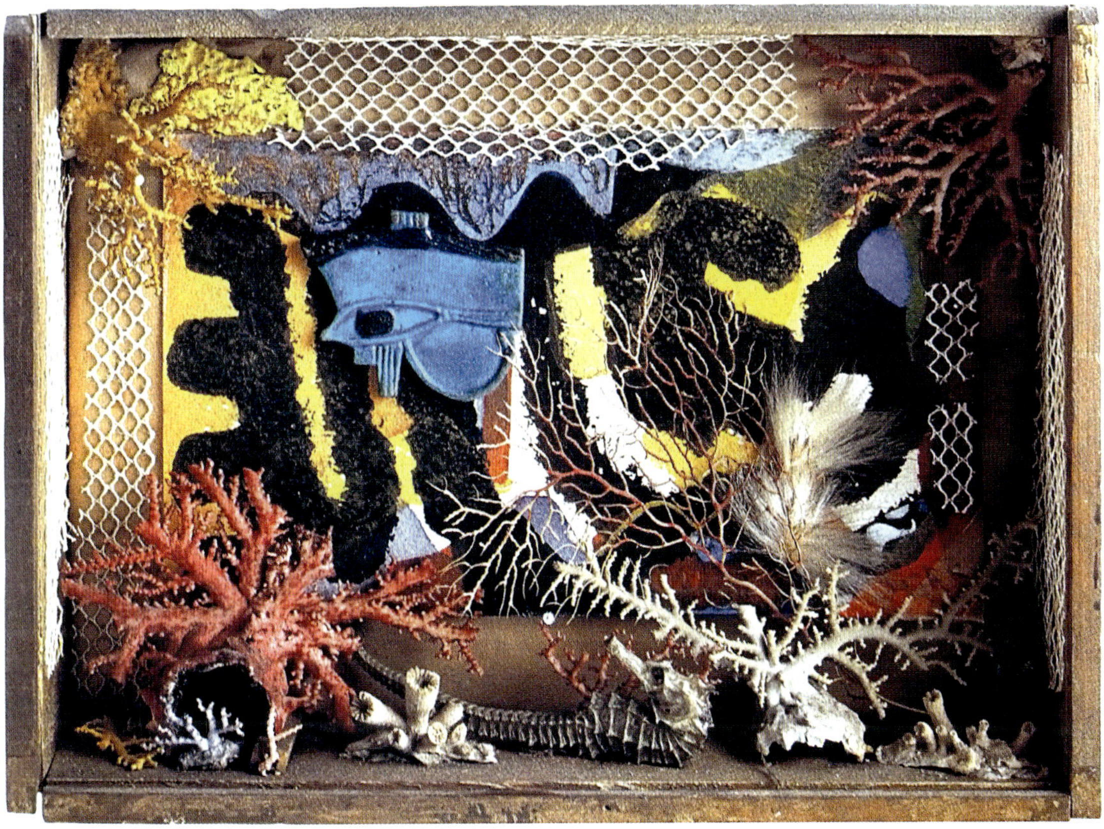

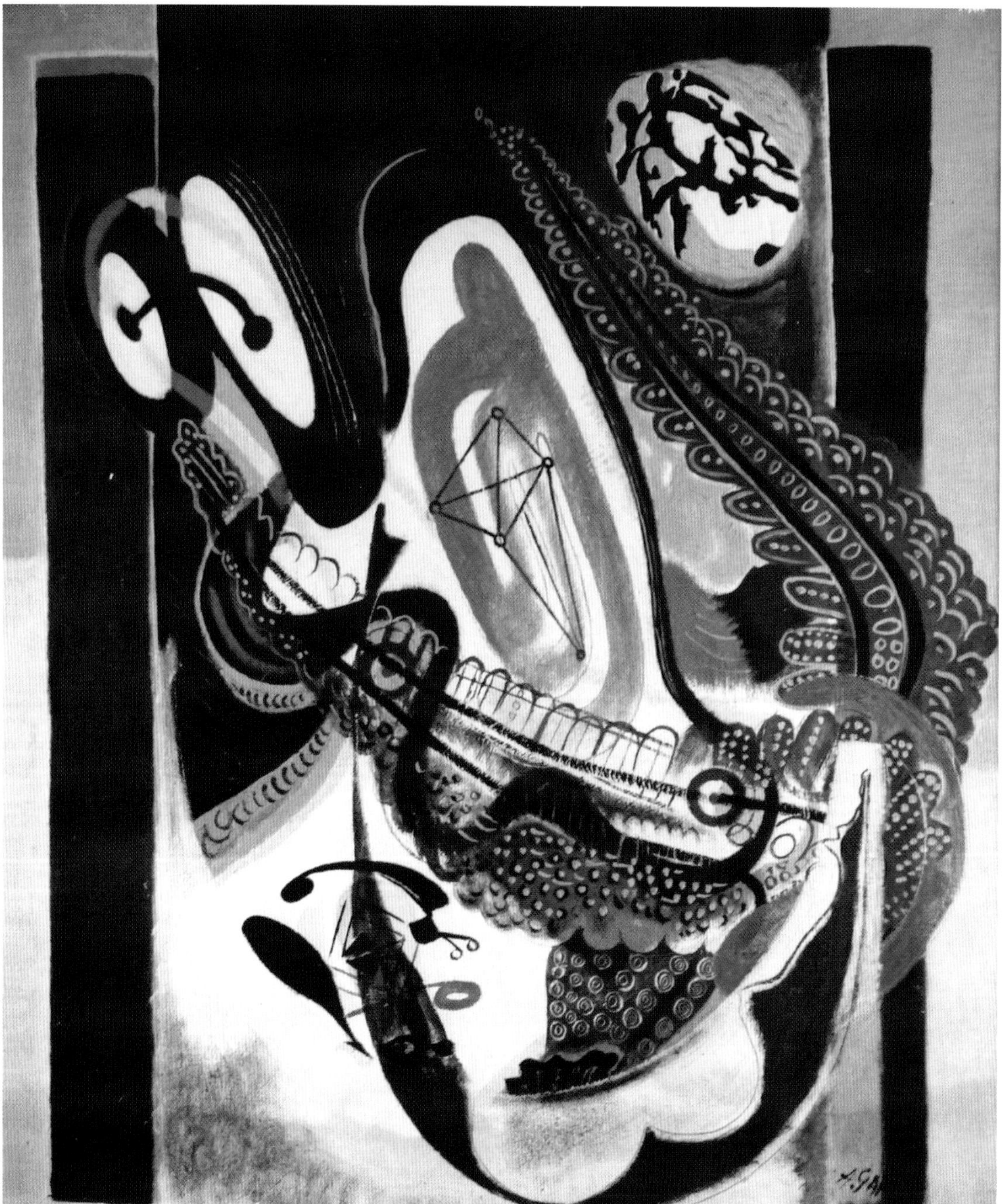

younger sister, Joan. Influenced by Man Ray, whose solarization techniques she regularly employed, she had started her professional career in the late 1920s, specializing in portraiture. On one of her visits to her home town, she took a wonderfully poetical solarized photograph of Agar, a dynamic shot which 'emphasizes a mass of sculptured, silvered hair cascading from a head thrown back', the solarization liberating a most unreal, unearthly aura from Agar, an attempt at grasping the essence of her magical personality (illus. 31).

In 1935 Agar made quite a few Nash-like photographs, like *Seashore Monster* (thus named by Nash), a long anchor chain 'clothed in stones, shells and all sorts of other marine accretions . . . metamorphosed by the sea into a new creation, a bird-snake' – a telescoping of animal categories which will often recur in her work. Her untitled box (illus. 28), made in the same year, gathers together coral, a dry sea horse turned on its back, stone concretions, shells, feathers, paper and one Horus eye in the middle, with fish net all around – a composition addressing the viewer from the bottom of an imaginary sea – a veritable theatre-like microcosm of the marvellous, a deep-sea diving into her subconscious world which manages to bring dry, dead creatures back to life through the imagination. That same year, *Hiver* (illus. 29) is a veritable epitome, if not a forerunner, of the canvases which had brought together, and would continue to do so, the organic and the inorganic in the blending of huge fern leaves and snake-like winding arabesques being hatched out of egg-like receptacles, especially as here an egg is being born while two ovoid shapes on the left, echoing the egg on the right, are made to look like eyes. Is the general egg structure liberating shapes to come or protecting them, thus denying winter its negative quality and stressing its fecundating role? Indeed, the shapes of flowers and leaves can be seen both as memories of the other three past seasons and as promises of future germination secured by the sleep of winter. Notes in Agar's diary dated November 1928 actually announce this *vitalist* conception of Nature: 'In gaining Power over Nature, Man without realizing it, is gaining Power over Death. Harnessing the forces and energies of the Dead and making them work for him.' Going further and referring to the artist's work, she continues: 'He achieves this by the sacrifice of himself, i.e. by giving himself up to the dead, the mechanistic conception in which he turns himself into a machine in order to rule the machine.' Couldn't we see in these words a reference to herself, especially if, under the adjective 'mechanistic', we read her own use of Cubist forms which she had succeeded in taming and in fully integrating into her own 'style'? As is clear, *Hiver*, in 1935, was firmly announcing Agar's commitment to her own brand of Surrealism: the clashing of forms within a liberating structure, together with a mythic dimension related to a sense of time *and* timelessness.

Opposite: 29 Eileen Agar, Hiver, *1935, oil on canvas.*

Overleaf left: 30 Helen Muspratt, Eileen Agar, *1935, photograph.*

Overleaf right: 31 Helen Muspratt, Eileen Agar, *1935, photograph.*

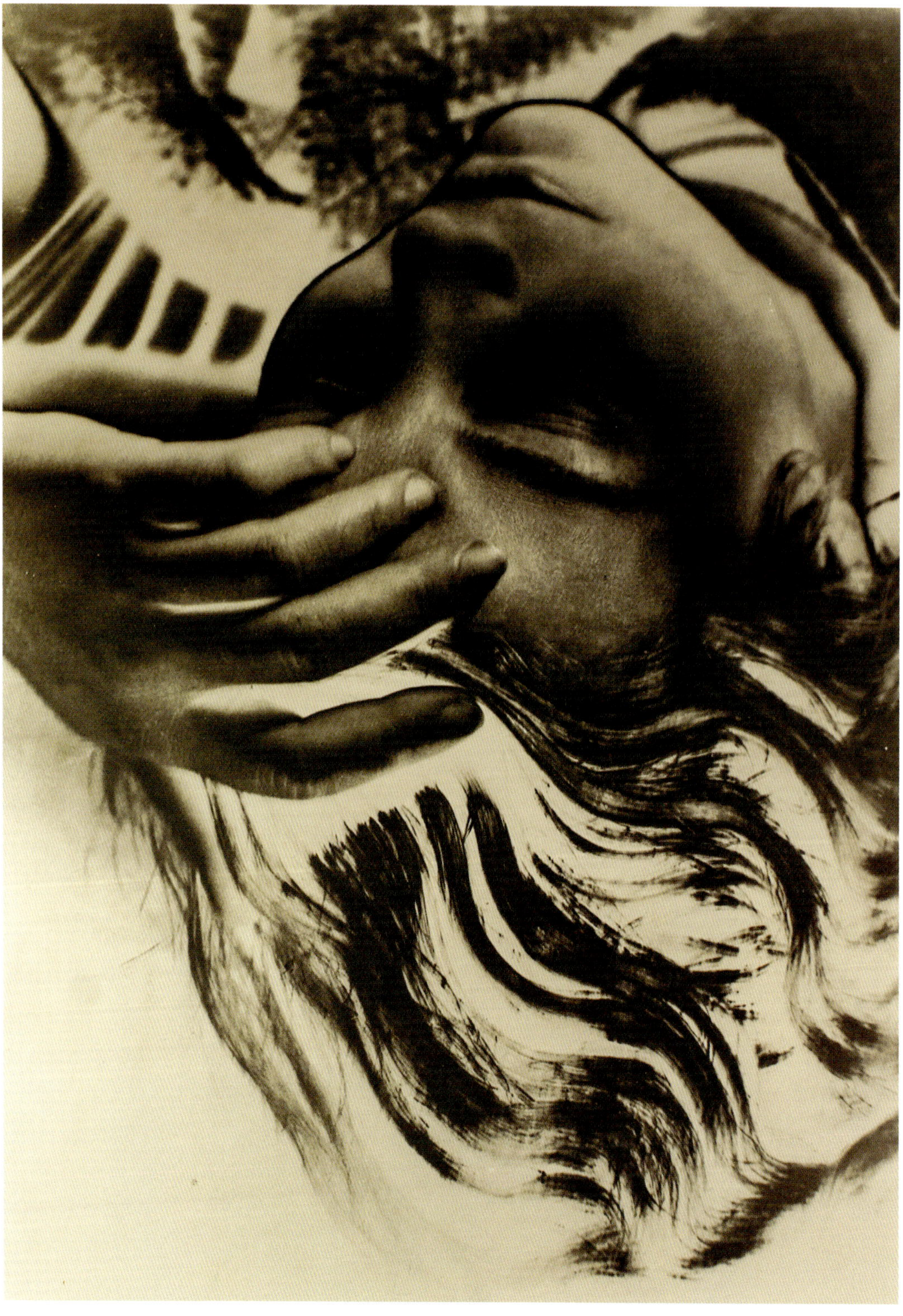

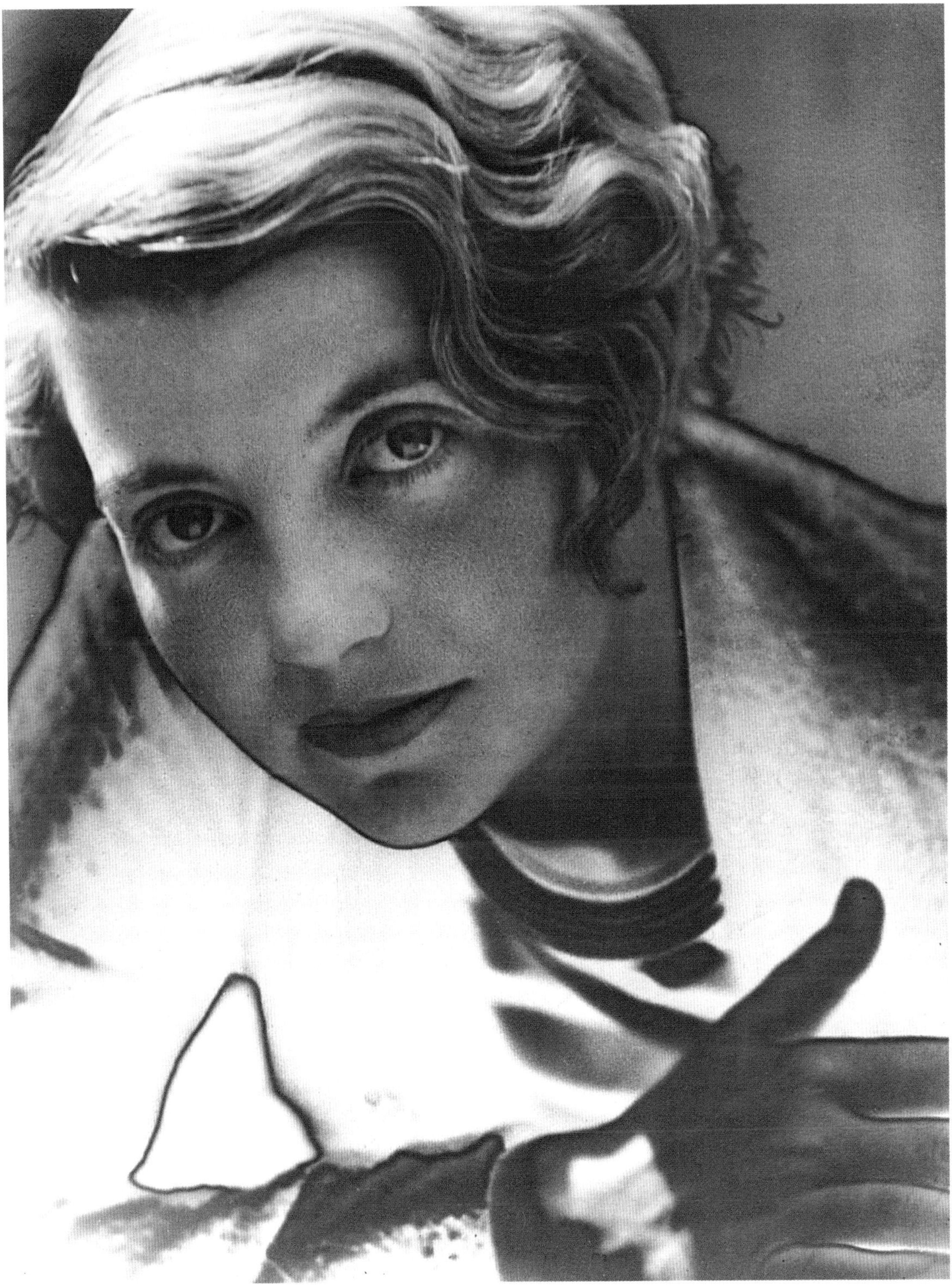

But of course, the masterpiece of that period is *Quadriga*, which became one of the centres of interest of the 1936 Surrealist exhibition in London (so much so that Roland Penrose bought it immediately) (illus. 32). As is recorded in many places, the starting point was a photograph of a horse's head on a frieze at the Parthenon. Agar painted it into four different aspects, transforming it, as she reveals in her autobiography, into 'four ghost heads, agitated, beating rhythm, cabalistic convoluted signs expressing movement and anxiety, each square a different mood. Were they the four horsemen of the Apocalypse?' As in *The Autobiography of an Embryo*, a story seems to develop, between order and disorder, symmetry and asymmetry, along fluid lines and echoing symbols, which tend to erase the compartmentalization at work. This urges us to read another narrative – or rather narratives – hidden and gradually emerging, based on mythological references, such as the Muses' sacred fountain, the Helicon in Boeotia, which gushed when the winged horse Pegasus struck the ground with his hooves, or Selene who was given horses to drive across the sky – a multi-layered vision of the mythical, archetypal 'arch-horse', carrying us off wherever our eyes alight, in a frenzied, unbridled race from one square to the next and back again, thus fundamentally expressing the energy of creation in the artist as well as in the viewer.

On the eve of realizing the direction in which her painting and her vision of the world were taking her – towards Surrealism – she gave some clue to her mindset. In her 1928 diary, she wrote a short, extraordinarily lucid text which projects her on to what appears to be a threshold:

> It would be strange to discover that we are going through (in embryo or sublimated form) in this age the forms of life that the world has been through since the beginning. How else can I explain the likeness in build of the giant reptiles and the modern trains, the modern aeroplanes and immense dragon flies that existed in Paleozoic and Jurassic times. This becomes a certainty for I could develop these connections endlessly. This is a completely magic world for me, it is this quality of magic that I must reveal to this world of sleepers. The magic and the dramatic elements.

In a sublimated and harmless way we still live with all these strange and wonderful creatures around us, among us, beautiful because death has removed their poison fangs and left us the miracle of their memory. Death has sublimated them and yet not a leaf of their tree is lost, any more than a leaf of the coal forests, for in us is Eternity.

32 Eileen Agar, Quadriga, *1935, oil on canvas.*

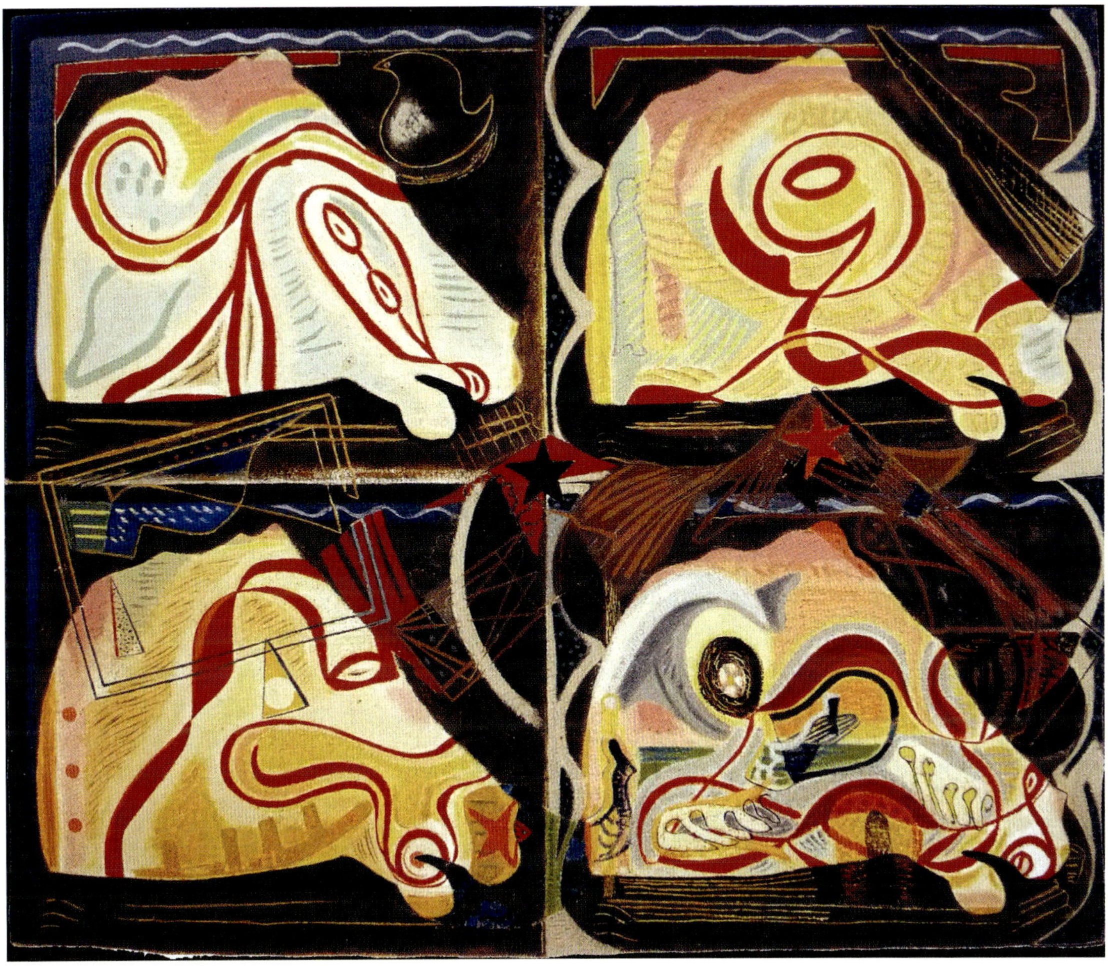

3 Facing the crisis of the object, 1936–45

**– 'Would you kindly tell me the meaning of the poem called "Jabberwocky"'?
– 'Let's hear it,' said Humpty Dumpty. 'I can explain all the poems that ever were invented, and a good many that haven't been invented yet.'**

Lewis Carroll, *Alice's Adventures in Wonderland* (1865)

33 Poster of the 'International Surrealist Exhibition', designed by Max Ernst, 1936, photograph.

Two factors prepared the ground for the outburst of Surrealism over London. Nash had played a long-standing role in the development of the interest in Continental avant-garde art. In June 1933 he had launched Unit One in an article published in the Readers' column of *The Times*, the official birth certificate of the movement – a group who gathered to promote, defend and illustrate the expression 'a truly contemporary spirit'. They received the help of Freddy Mayor, the young, buoyant director of the Mayor Gallery, where they held their first (and only) exhibition in April 1934. The group was constituted by the painters Paul Nash, John Armstrong, Edward Burra, John Selby Bigge, Edward Wadsworth, Ben Nicholson and Tristram Hillier (who came in after Frances Hodgkins's resignation), most of whom painted in the 'magic realist' vein – a kind of satellite of Surrealism. There also were the sculptors Henry Moore and Barbara Hepworth and the architects Wells Coates and Colin Lucas. Unit One was seeking a new synthesis between aesthetics, materials and purpose, a new coherence free from the dogmas of fidelity to nature and an emphasis on structural and formal research. A few weeks before the *Times* article, in the spring of 1933, Henry Moore introduced to the group a neighbour from the same street where he lived in Hampstead and a fellow Yorkshireman, the poet and critic Herbert Read, who soon became their champion and almost their spokesman, editing the book *Unit One*, which secured the group's place in art history. The year after, Roland Penrose rented a flat in Rossmore Court and a little later settled at 21 Downshire Hill in 1936, not far away. This later gave critics the impression that a 'Hampstead Group' had existed from 1934, which is not entirely wrong, even if this gathering had nothing formal about it.

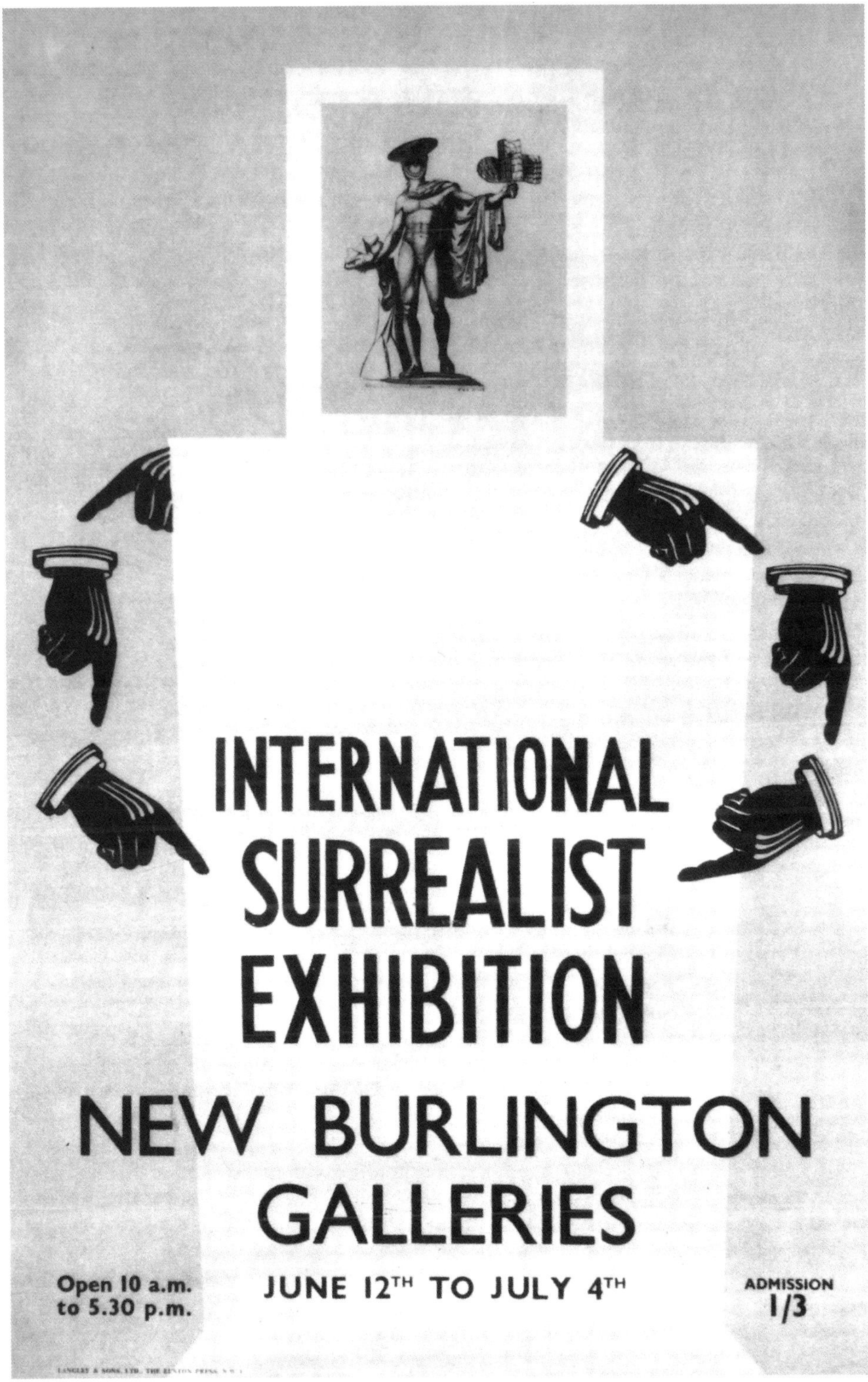
INTERNATIONAL
SURREALIST
EXHIBITION
NEW BURLINGTON
GALLERIES
Open 10 a.m.
to 5.30 p.m.
JUNE 12TH TO JULY 4TH
ADMISSION
1/3

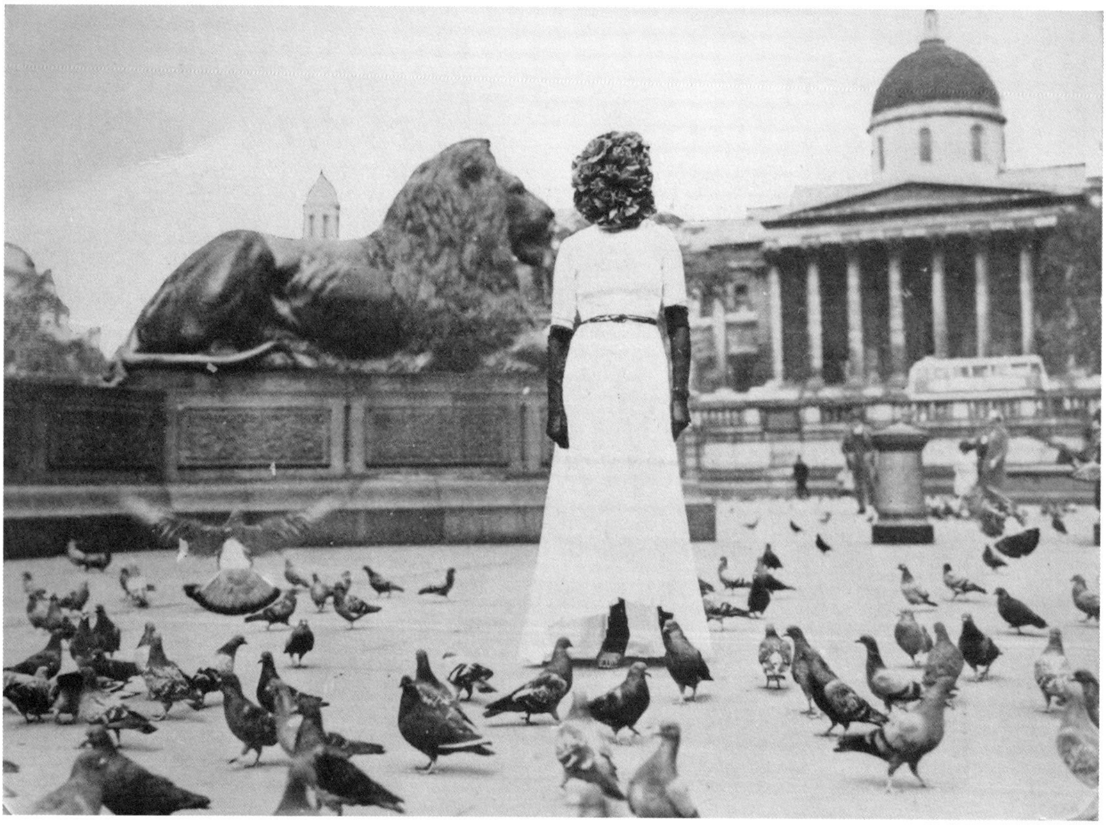

On the other hand, it is now well known that the inception of Surrealism in England is due to a chance encounter in the streets of Paris between David Gascoyne and Roland Penrose – not surprisingly for a movement which made chance one of its cornerstones. Strangely enough, they had never met before but on that day of July 1935, Gascoyne met Paul Éluard, whom he knew well, quite by chance at the corner of the rue de Tournon, and Éluard was accompanied by Penrose. Éluard introduced the two men to one another. 'It was the encounter of two explorers who had discovered independently the same glittering treasure', remembered Penrose. Gascoyne had exclaimed: 'Why do we know nothing of this in England?' and both men there and then decided to 'do something' in their country, a resolve which led to the 1936 'International Surrealist Exhibition' in London.

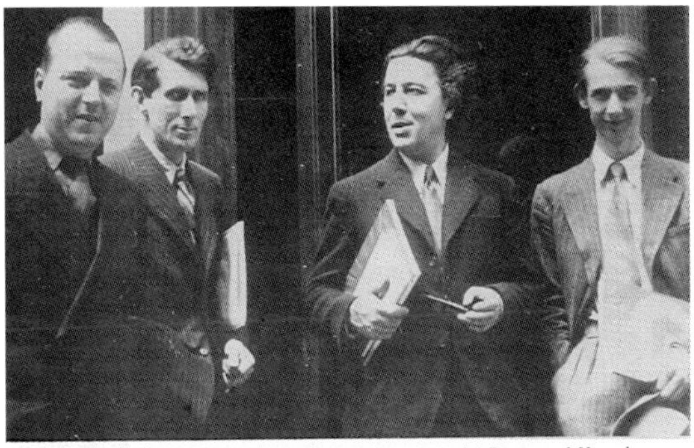

From left to right:– E. L. T. Mesens. Roland Penrose. André Breton and Humphrey Jennings outside the New Burlington Galleries. 1936.

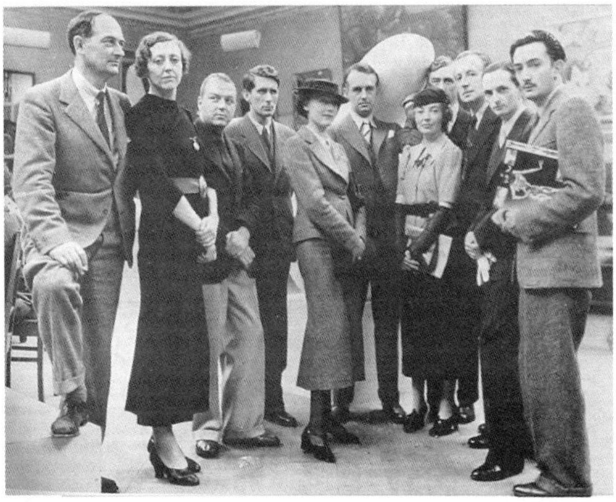

Group photograph at The International Surrealist Exhibition. 1936. Left to right: Rupert Lee (Chairman). Diana Brinton Lee (Secretary) E. L. T. Mesens. Roland Penrose (Hon. Treasurer) Nusch Eluard. Stellan Mörner. Herbert Read behind Eileen Agar. Paul Eluard, Edward James. Salvador Dali.

Needless to say, then, this series of encounters explains why Nash urged Read and Penrose, who set about selecting artists for the exhibition, to go and visit several studios, including Agar's in Bramham Gardens in Earl's Court. Seeing her many found and Surrealist objects, and her paintings, including *Quadriga*, the decision was easily made. 'Both of us', recalls Penrose, 'were at once enchanted by the rare qualities of her talent, the product of a highly sensitive imagination and feminine clairvoyance.' Moreover, the proximity between Joseph Bard and the organizers of the exhibition is evidenced by the fact that at one of the preparatory meetings of the organizing committee on 2 May, it was planned to produce a volume of essays, to which Bard was supposed to contribute, with an essay on 'Surrealism and Psychology'. The publication, however, never saw the light of day. Nineteen thirty-six was thus the year of Agar's consecration as a Surrealist, even if she tended to make fun of this sudden recruitment! Three oil paintings and five objects were selected – some of which now exist only as photographs – and exhibited at the New Burlington Galleries from 11 June to 4 July.

The scandal the exhibition created in London (illus. 33) fed all the headlines of the dailies and weeklies, especially with the oft-cited spectacle of Sheila Legge on Trafalgar Square, dressed as 'the Surrealist phantom' in a

Opposite: 34 Sheila Legge, 'the Surrealist phantom', on Trafalgar Square, 1936.

Above: 35 E.L.T. Mesens, André Breton, Roland Penrose and Humphrey Jennings at the New Burlington Galleries, 1936, and another photograph of the group.

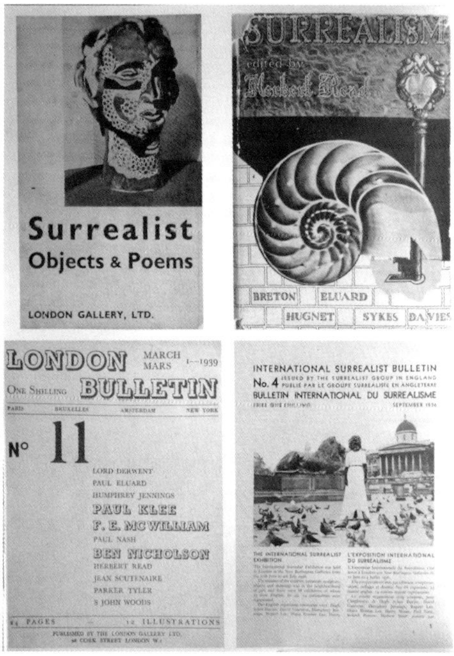

tight white satin gown, her face shrouded in a mass of roses, and carrying, in certain photographs, a dummy leg, or a pork chop, according to some of the press (illus. 34). At the opening, Dylan Thomas circulated among the visitors with teacups full of boiled string, politely enquiring 'Do you want it weak or strong?' In the *Daily Telegraph,* Agar's objects were said to come 'from the flotsam and jetsam one associates usually with a dustbin', while three other comments from the press will suffice to echo the critics' discomfiture: the *Daily Telegraph* with 'Poor jokes, pointless indelicacies and relics of an outworn romanticism'; the *Daily Express* with 'Blotches on the face of space are surreal'; and the *Evening News* with 'It is not worth looking at. I don't mind it being meaningless but it is horribly clumsy as well.' The success was overwhelming, with more than 25,000 visitors over the three weeks it lasted, the result being, generally speaking, a reorientation and an opening of the modernist spirit in art in England. More concretely, it led to the constitution of a Surrealist group in England, a bulletin reporting on the exhibition and its various events, poetry readings by David Gascoyne, Humphrey Jennings, George Reavey, Paul Éluard and André Breton, lectures by Hugh Sykes Davies (on biology and Surrealism) and Herbert Read (standing on a sprung sofa and interrupted every minute

Above: 36 Surrealist publications, 1936–8.

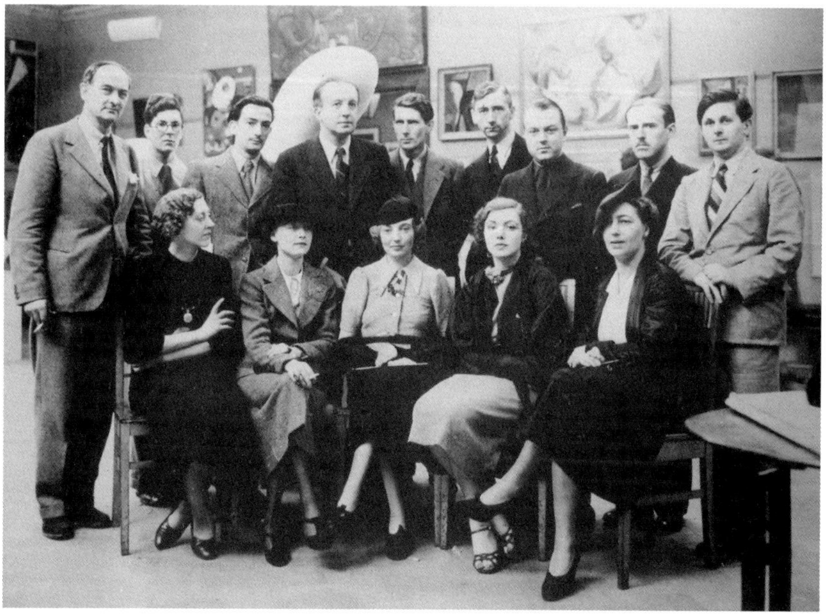

Right: 37 The Surrealist group at the New Burlington Galleries, 1936, photograph. Back row, left to right: Rupert Lee (chairman), Ruthven Todd, Salvador Dalí, Paul Éluard, Roland Penrose (Hon. Treasurer), Herbert Read, E.L.T. Mesens, George Reavey, Hugh Sykes Davies. Front row: Diana Brinton Lee (secretary), Nusch Éluard, Eileen Agar, Sheila Legge and a friend of Dalí.

or so by the ringing of a bell) and a famous talk by Salvador Dalí who spoke from inside a deep-sea diving suit but, suffocating, had to be delivered from his helmet by Edward James and David Gascoyne who managed to unscrew it with great difficulty. Agar, in her notebook, recalls:

> I was in a huge room on a sizzling hot day with a thousand people who had come to see a gathering of astonishment in which the mad beast of convention was to be hunted down. The hubbub was terrific, the artists and writers were the surrealists and I was proud to be among them. (illus. 35)

The newly formed group decided to act in a revolutionary way through publications, exhibitions, public demonstrations and collaboration with Surrealist groups abroad (illus. 36). Strong, friendly links were established with France, especially as Breton was seeing the advent of Surrealism in England as 'the highest point in the graph of influence of our movement'. He added that

> the demonstration and internationalization of surrealist ideas . . . reached their critical point here . . . Searching as we were and are, now more than ever, for a European consciousness, if not a world consciousness, it is towards England that we surrealists have turned.

A photograph taken at the opening of the exhibition shows Agar at the very centre of the group between, on her right-hand side, Diana Brinton Lee and Nusch Éluard and, on her left-hand side, Sheila Legge and an unidentified friend of Dalí. Behind them in the photograph can be seen some of the main participants in, and guests at, the exhibition: Salvador Dalí, Roland Penrose, Herbert Read, Paul Éluard, Hugh Sykes Davies, E.L.T. Mesens, George Reavey and Ruthven Todd (illus. 37).

In May 1936, the first issue of a poetry review entitled *Contemporary Poetry and Prose* had appeared as the unofficial organ of the expression of Surrealism in England. It was edited by nineteen-year-old poet Roger Roughton, a close friend of David Gascoyne and Dylan Thomas. The second

Soluble Noughts and Crosses; *or*, California, Here I Come

(to E.A.) *by* Roger Roughton

In a small theodolite of paper
I could see the eyelash of a girl,
The most beautiful young girl of all,
Who was only dressed in cellophane,
Who was speaking from a stone
And saying this to me:
" Look out for the red and written triangle,
And enclose a penny-halfpenny stamp;
For I must go at ten to one,
Ten to one it's guineas time,
Ten to one will be too many,
Ten to one you'll come in last.
Yes, did you hear:
My fingers hang like pictures,
And my breasts are pointing to the North? "

So I made an expedition to the Pole,
While thin birds flew off sideways with a sob;
There I heard a ringing at the door,
Where some gongs were waiting in a queue;
I played them all in turn
And presently she stepped out from a handbag,
Saying this to me:
" The happy compass is decided,
I must come at ten to one,
Ten to one's beginner's time,
Ten to one won't be enough,
Ten to one we'll get there first.
Please take this down,
Yes take this down, for purple trees will sing the answer,
For rhyming trains are meeting at a foxtrot,
For string is floating on the water,
For we are opening a parcel meant for both;
Yes please take this down, for living words are played together,
For love has grown up like a hair."

Above: 38 Roger Roughton's poem to Agar, in Contemporary Poetry and Prose, *3 (July 1936).*

Right: 39 Eileen Agar, David and Jonathan, *1936 (subsequently destroyed).*

Below: 40 Eileen Agar, Mate in Two Moods, *1936 (subsequently destroyed).*

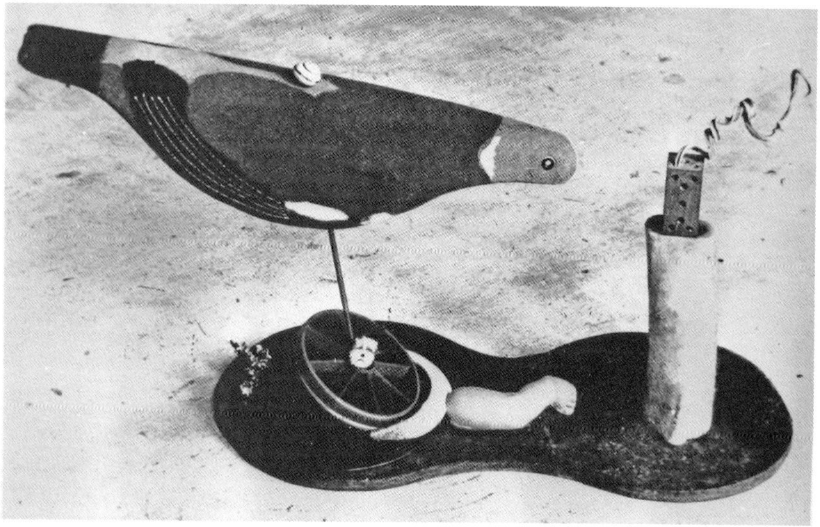

issue, in June 1936, was devoted to French Surrealist poetry translated by Gascoyne, Jennings, Reavey and Samuel Beckett, and to English Surrealist poetry and prose by Jennings, Gascoyne and Davies. In the third issue, in July, Roger Roughton published a poem dedicated to E[ileen] A[gar], 'Soluble Noughts and Crosses; or, California, Here I Come', the dislocated images of which proliferate to sing of love, desire and beauty, a half-hidden homage to his young addressee and now a companion in Surrealism (illus. 38).

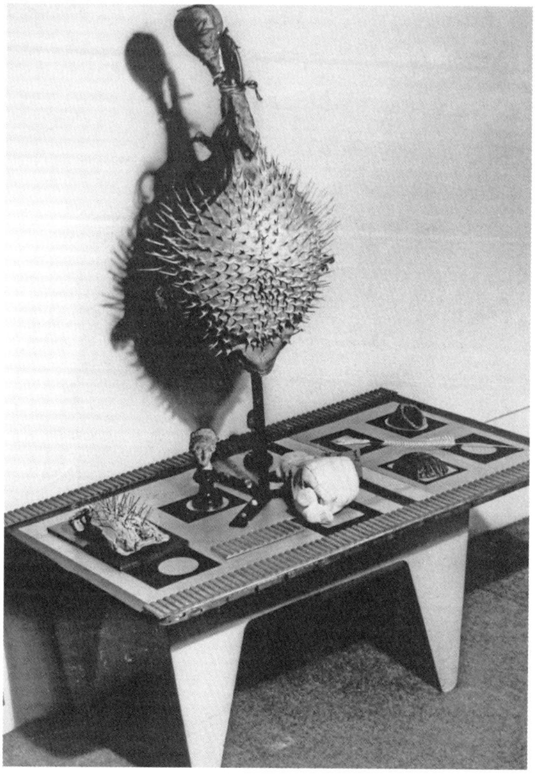

Amid this whirling activity, Agar kept her own place, not wanting to risk having to relinquish her freedom of mind through her participation in politically engaged commitments. This is why her name does not appear as a signatory of the solemn declarations made by the group in 1936, such as the 'Declaration on Spain' in September in which most of the English Surrealists protested against the British Government's non-intervention policy in Spain, or the 'Artists Help Spain' in December the same year. In no way is her attitude to be seen as indifference to or criticism of the commitment to this or that cause; rather, it should be seen as a desire to secure her independence. The feeling that such involvement might threaten her creativeness overcame, most of the time, the feeling that it was necessary to step forward publicly and take sides. Actually, her attitude was never criticized by her friends, not even by Nash or Moore, who were deeply committed, but it is true that this encouraged critics, rightly or wrongly, to consider her later on as isolated from the movement.

Only the broadside 'We Ask Your Attention', published on the occasion of the enormous Marxist-inspired AIA's exhibition in March–April 1937, received her signature. The exhibition displayed, among almost five hundred works of different styles, 118 Surrealist works, 43 of them by British artists, and the broadside itself called for a 'United Front against Fascism', a long and clear indictment of the British Government's Spanish policy printed on the background of a drawing by Henry Moore. The protest ended with these words: 'Intervene as poets, artists and intellectuals by violent or subtle subversion and by stimulating desire' – a typical Surrealist claim reconciling the public and the private, conscious, revolutionary and deep subconscious forces.

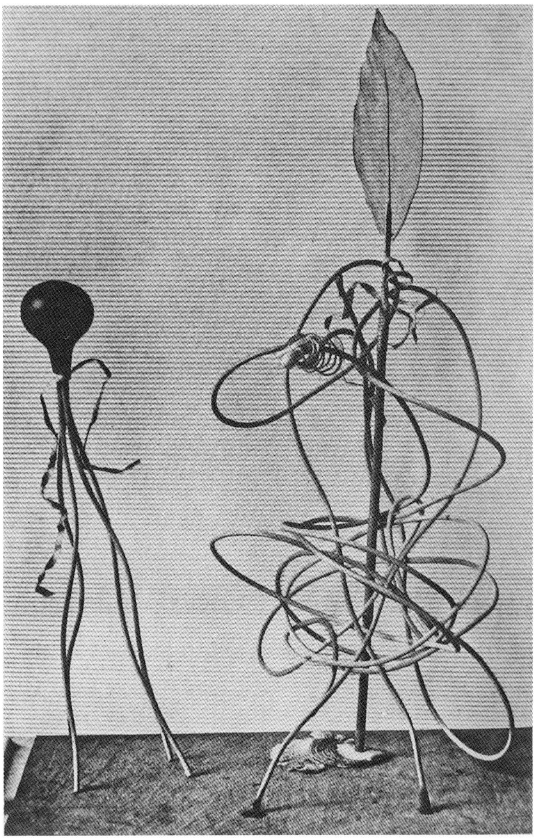

Her output of objects and collages that year was remarkable and they considerably outnumbered her paintings. Four objects stand out. *David and Jonathan* (illus. 39) – now destroyed but photographs remain – suggests the inseparable, complementary quality of totally different, separable objects, stressing, *beyond their differences*, their identical capacity to challenge rationality. The biblical story of eternal friendship is turned here into a closed circuit of basically unexplainable relationships, reiterating the mystery of life and death; the fragments of a celluloid doll (Jonathan) contrast with the 'explosive' quality of the link between the metallic decoy pigeon and the marrowbone with a fuse (Agar calls the marrowbone a watch tower) – a confrontation which suspends the unity of our vision. In between all the possibilities of interpretation – who is David? who is Jonathan? – the circularity between them is endless. They resemble each other in that they resemble themselves in being both unlinkable to any referent. Through the title, they are made to belong to the biblical subtext, which associates them with notions of friendship and inseparability but *sideways*, if one may say, by force almost. The objects are faithful to each

Above: 41 Eileen Agar, Untitled, *1936, wire construction (subsequently destroyed).*

Overleaf Left: 42 Eileen Agar, Rock Form – Two Faces, *1936–7, ink, pastel and watercolour.*

Overleaf Right: 43 Eileen Agar, Face Form, *1936–7, ink, pastel and watercolour.*

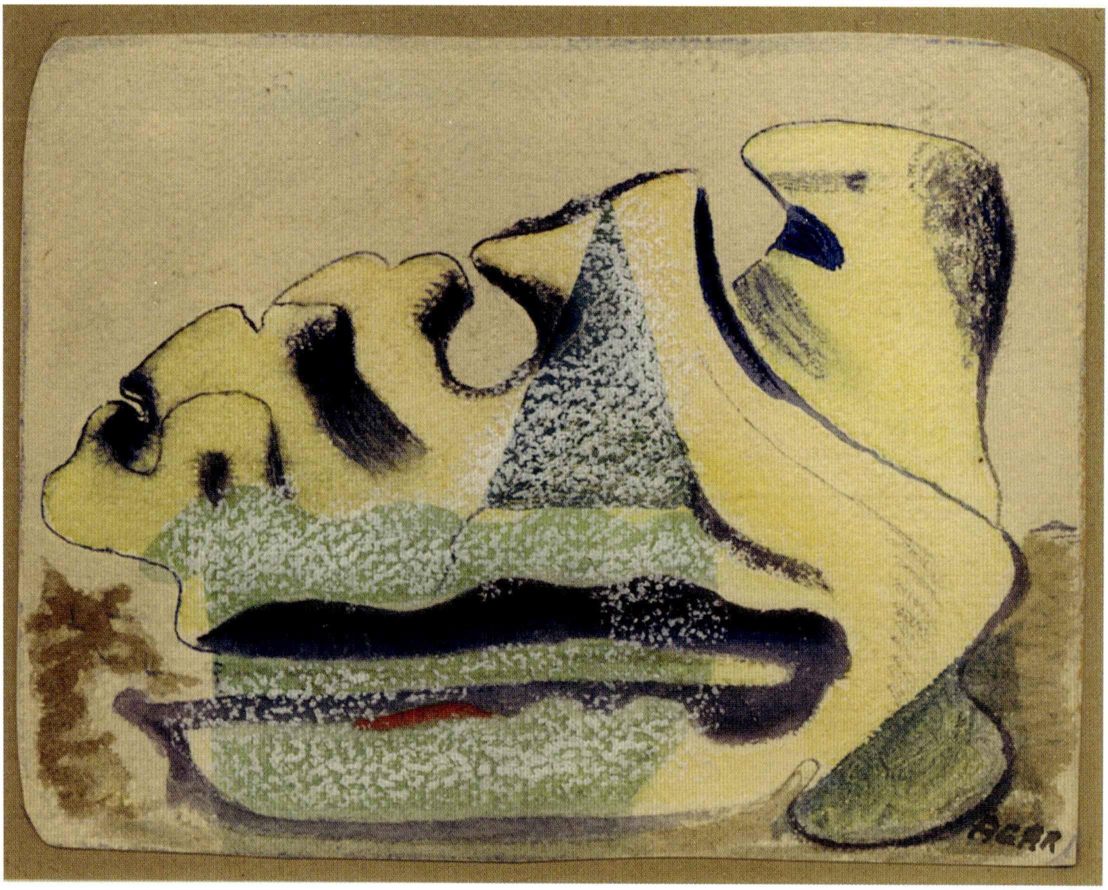

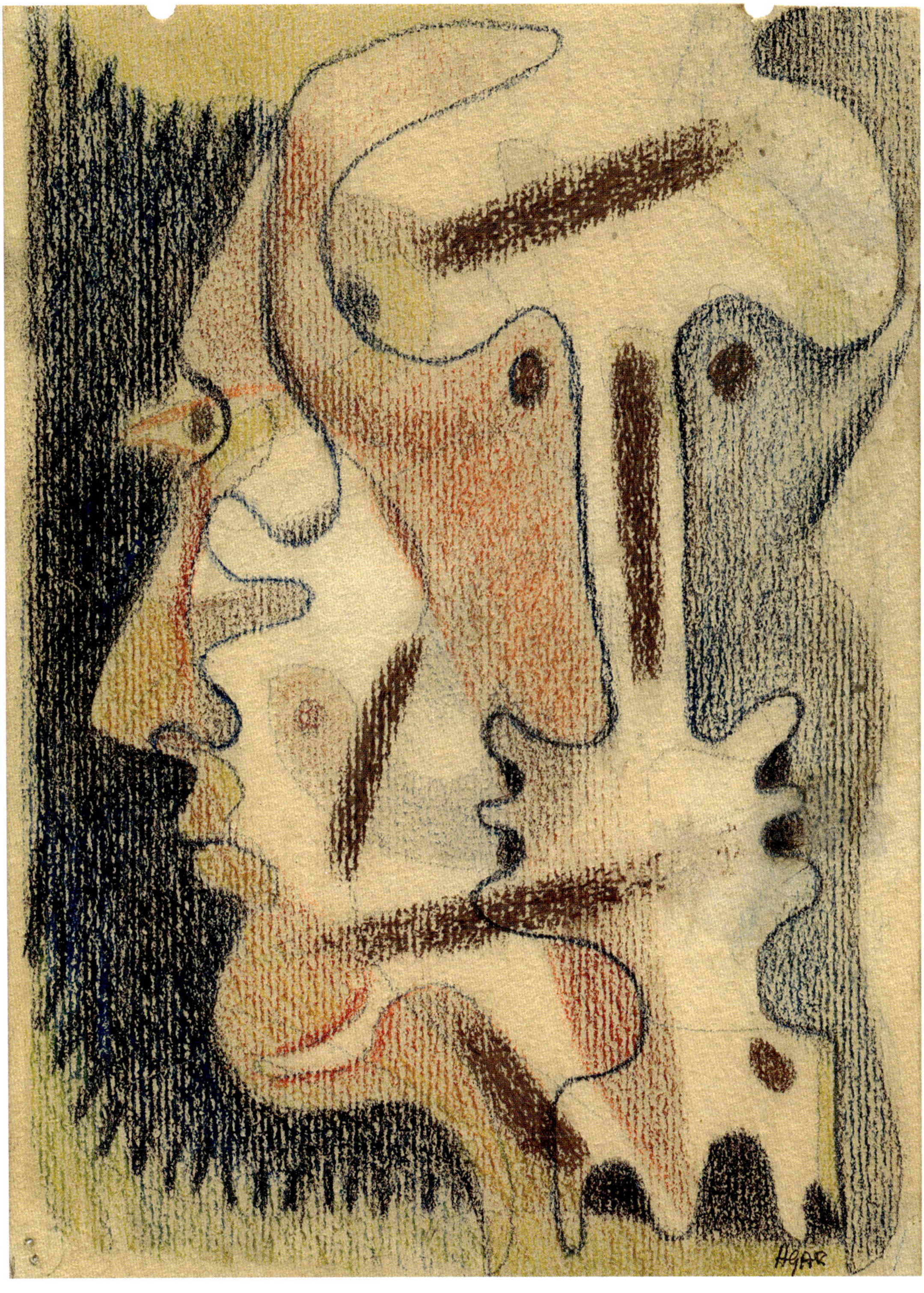

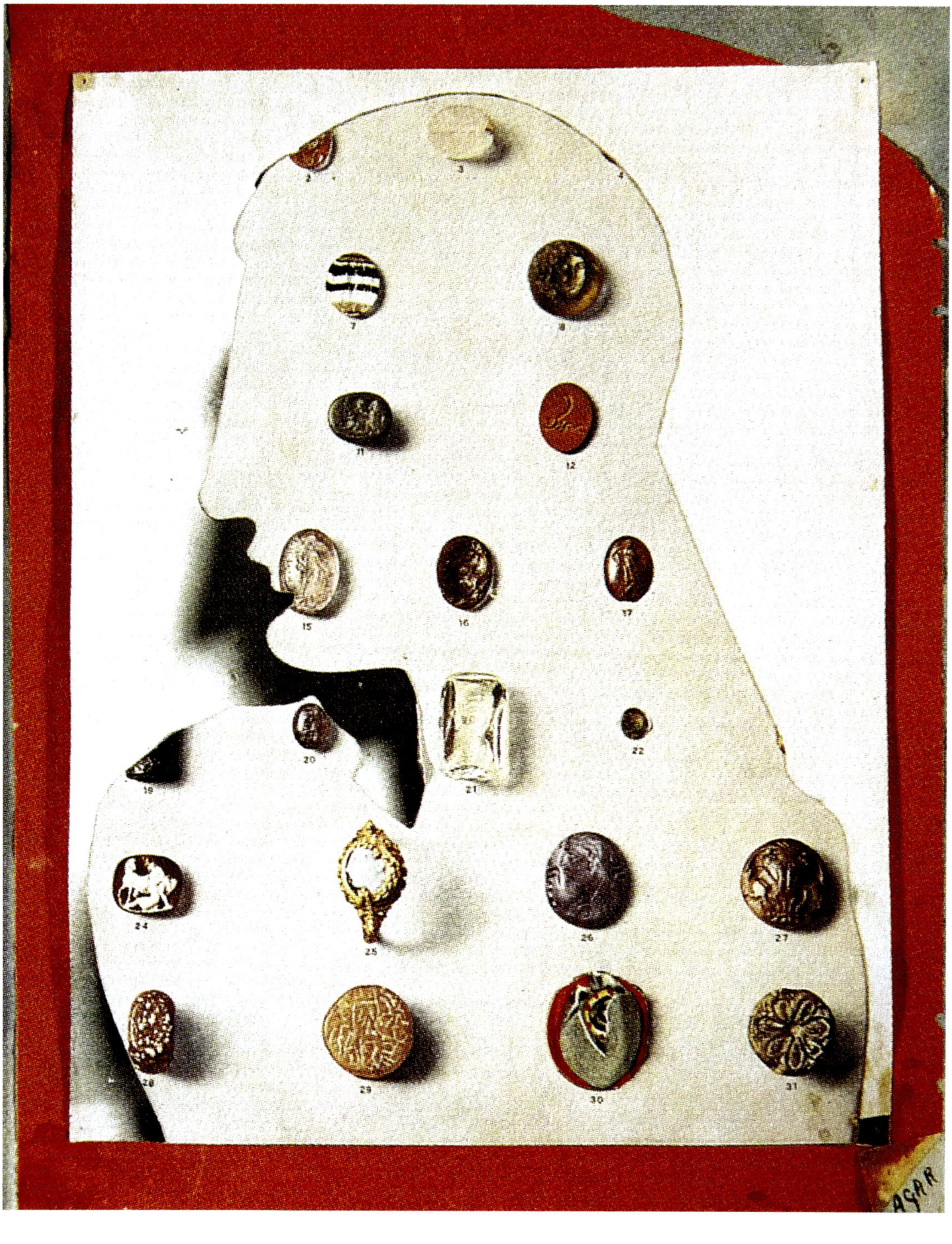
AGAR

other in a kind of extra-ordinary, subversive world (according to 2 Samuel 1:25, the love between David and Jonathan was 'beyond the love of a woman'); so much so that their reason for being there is simply contained in the 'and' of the title. Trying to understand, the observer flounders helplessly: should he stop at the slow-moving (or immobile?) snail on the pigeon's back or wait for the marrowbone charge to explode?

In the same way, *Mate in Two Moods* (illus. 40) is a playful reference to chess-playing: spread out, on a drawing board covered with white circles on black squares and black circles on white squares, figure the plaster cast of a hand, a fishbone (the diagonal of the bishop), a little Tanagra head (the queen), a prickly marine object and a bloated sunfish (the king). Agar had specified that the construction had to be placed against a wall so as to play with its own shadow. This increases the ambivalence of the title, the general duality at work and the playfulness which in a way projects these objects into a kind of desubstantialized space. Another object, *Untitled* (illus. 41), also exhibited at the New Burlington Galleries, establishes the typical relationship between two objects which is so central to the Surrealist operation. Two 'anthropomorphic' 'creatures' made of wire look at each other, one with the head the shape of an electric bulb, the other with the head of a feather. They are engaged in a kind of conversation – or so we are made to believe – a relationship without a relationship, a dialogue reduced to its simplest form, which necessarily takes place in our imagination, inseparable from its own fragility and ephemerality. A drawing combining ink, pastel and watercolour, *Rock Form – Two Faces* (illus. 42, 43), emblematizes Agar's deep fascination with doubleness and inclusiveness, which she betrays in her objects, one form being *also* another one, in an almost indistinguishable way. It is a 'rock form' (unless it is a bone form reminiscent of Henry Moore's hollowed-out reclining figures), a monstrous deformed head, a dent in the rock as its grinning mouth, a multi-eyed, multi-mouthed, multi-nosed pebble, poised as it is on the shores of reality like an embarkation taking the viewer into the fertile, fantastic world of natural creation.

It is easy now to realize the far-reaching significance of Surrealist objects – and collages. Clearly, they assert the continuity and coalescence of chance, coincidences and dreams, creating a constant flux, an exchange between the world outside and the world inside, the very manifestation of 'objective chance'. What actually happens, deep down, is the encounter between an object, or an image given by reality – the result of a series of external causalities – and the subconscious – the repository of internal finalities – call them correspondences, similarities, sympathies or analogies. In other words, man is given his place at the heart of the universe.

44 Eileen Agar, Precious Stones, *1936, collage on paper.*

Nineteen thirty-six is indeed the year of Agar's most stunning collages, most of them based on the use of the profile of a face. *Precious Stones* and *Woman Reading* are cases in point. The former (illus. 44) has the silhouette of a bust – a face and its neck? It is simply cut out from a book on precious stones, in the shape of a male head, no doubt a reference to Joseph Bard, who collected gems. What is striking is the contrast between the strict arrangement of the stones – as in all classificatory books – printed with their numbers, and the almost arbitrary outline of the face which cuts into the established, orderly arrangement of the stones, five stones being reduced to fragments by the scissors. A kind of reciprocal defiance thus emerges between the laws of order and the laws of the body, between the inorganic and the mineral on the one hand and the organic and the human on the other hand. In *Woman Reading* (illus. 45), the double superimposition, one very exact – the fragment of the printed page and the silhouette of the face – and the other inexact – the flower and its leaves which exceed the face itself – creates, here too, a tension between what is inorganic (the paper and the text) and organic (the flower), between death (the cut-out page comes from a kind of encyclopaedia narrating the dramatic events following the 1870 Franco-Prussian war) and life (the flower). *Reading* is thus an operation of suspension of oneself from oneself. This is why the use of the profile is so appropriate: the surface reality of the face is abolished, the surface opens and the interior becomes the exterior – one of the very principles underlying Breton's definition of surreality.

Two untitled collages (illus. 46, 47) give free rein to the imagination by constructing the semblance of a figure – or two figures? – sitting at a table with a plate, and by dividing our vision: we both see the different parts – head and hands, similar in their texture – separately and also link them to build an impossibly unified picture. The parallel between the 'plate' on the table and the ellipse of the hat-wearing head is baffling, while the lack of a title conveys the total freedom given to us by what is nonetheless a carefully structured collage.

The same operation of superimposition found in *Precious Stones* and *Woman Reading* takes place in two other collages: *Food of Love* and *Le Charmeur de Serpents*, both haunted by what lies outside the limits of reality – music. In the former (illus. 48), the superimposition of several leaves, one from a spiral notebook, another the result of a frottage and another from some wallpaper with the drawing of a guitar, the addition of a tower, a hand planted in the ground, two hooks stuck together, a wax seal and flower designs all hint at the unfinishedness of the process of accretion. The face, which appears as formed by the side of the guitar, blends them together, as if the face were kissing the guitar or vice versa, an echo of which is provided by the two hooks stuck together, their coupling being sealed by the wax seal. The title obviously refers to the first line of Shakespeare's *Twelfth Night*, bringing together the notions of love, music and excess. Everything in the collage is *insatiable*. In *Le Charmeur de serpents* (illus. 48), the silhouette of a standing man is cut out from the pages of an encyclopaedia on the history of India and China – the provenance of the snake which covers the collage from

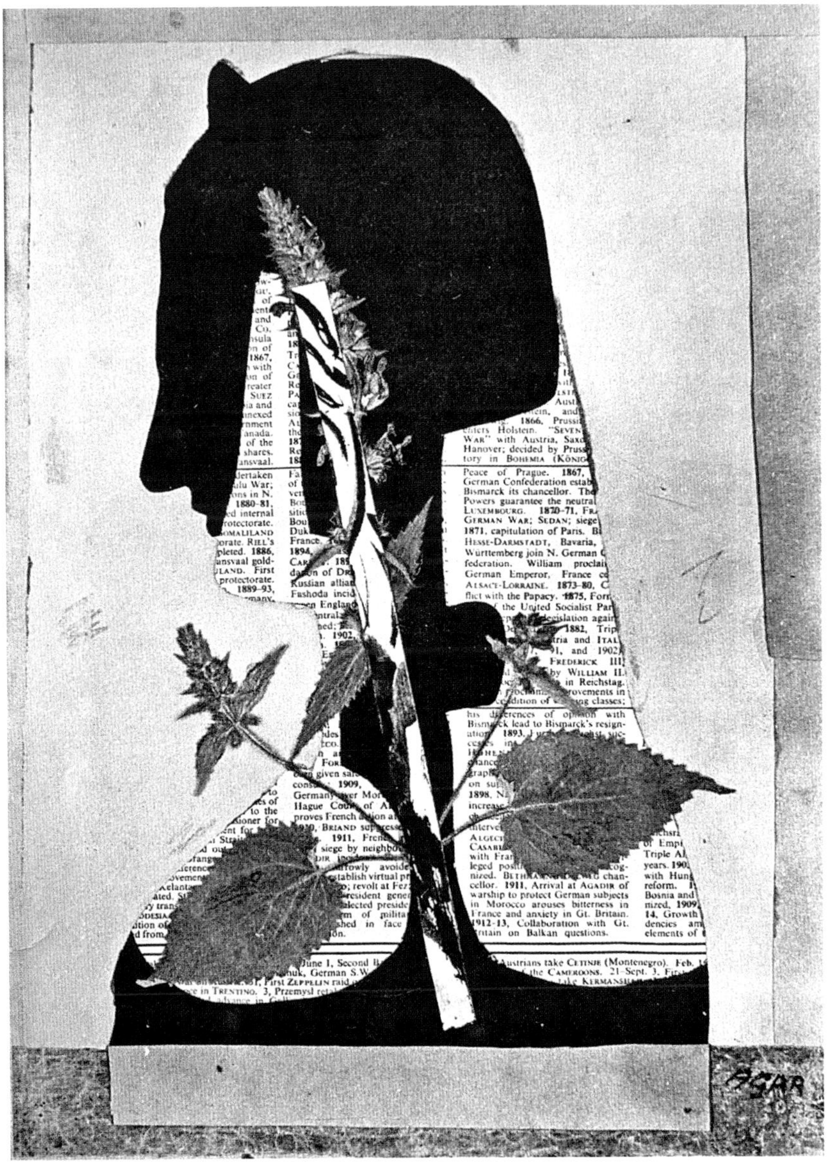

Left: 45 Eileen Agar, Woman Reading, *1936, collage on paper.*

Overleaf left: 46 Eileen Agar, Untitled, *c. 1936, mixed media collage on paper.*

Overleaf right: 47 Eileen Agar, Untitled, *1936, collage of paper, celluloid, feather, string with watercolour on paper.*

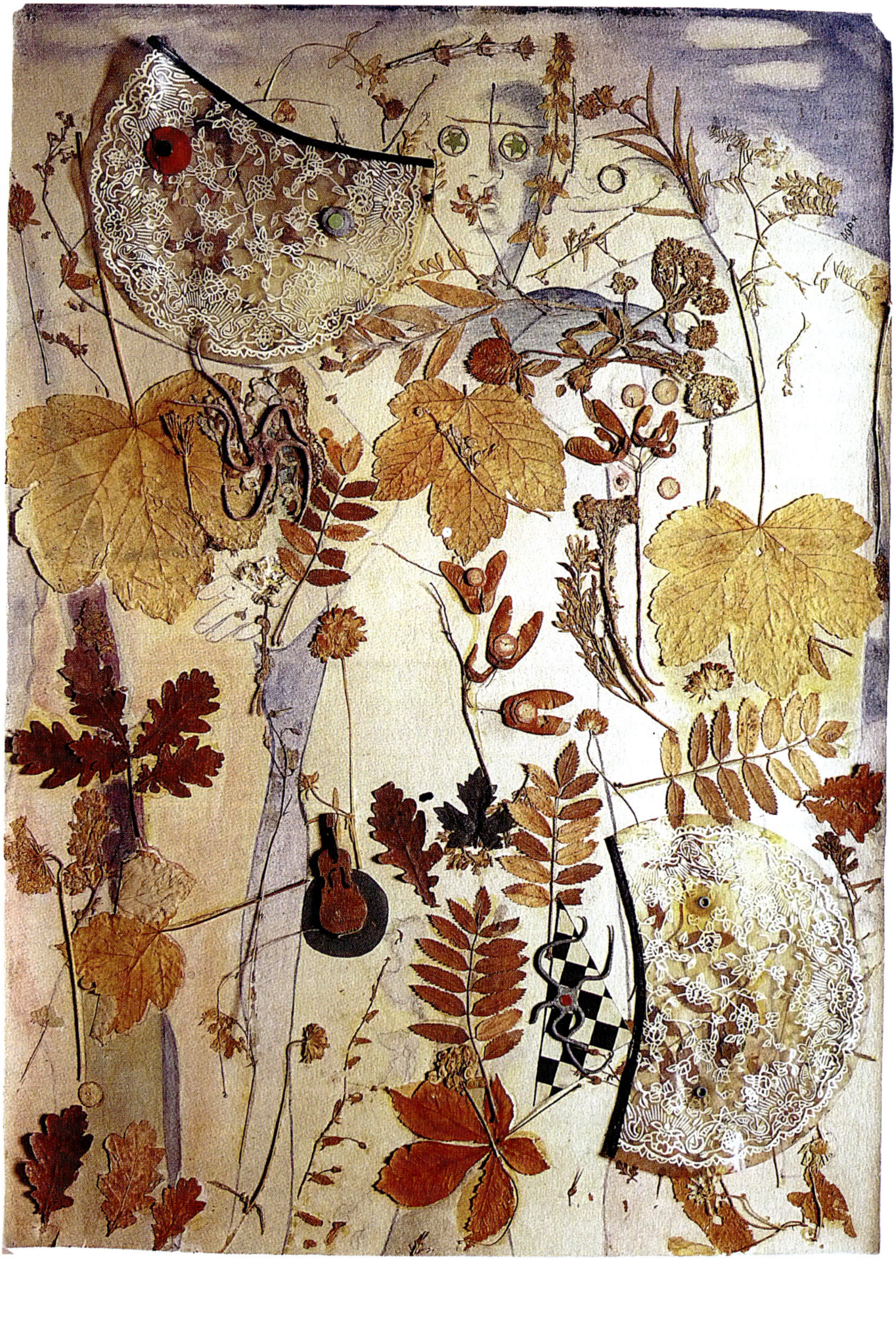

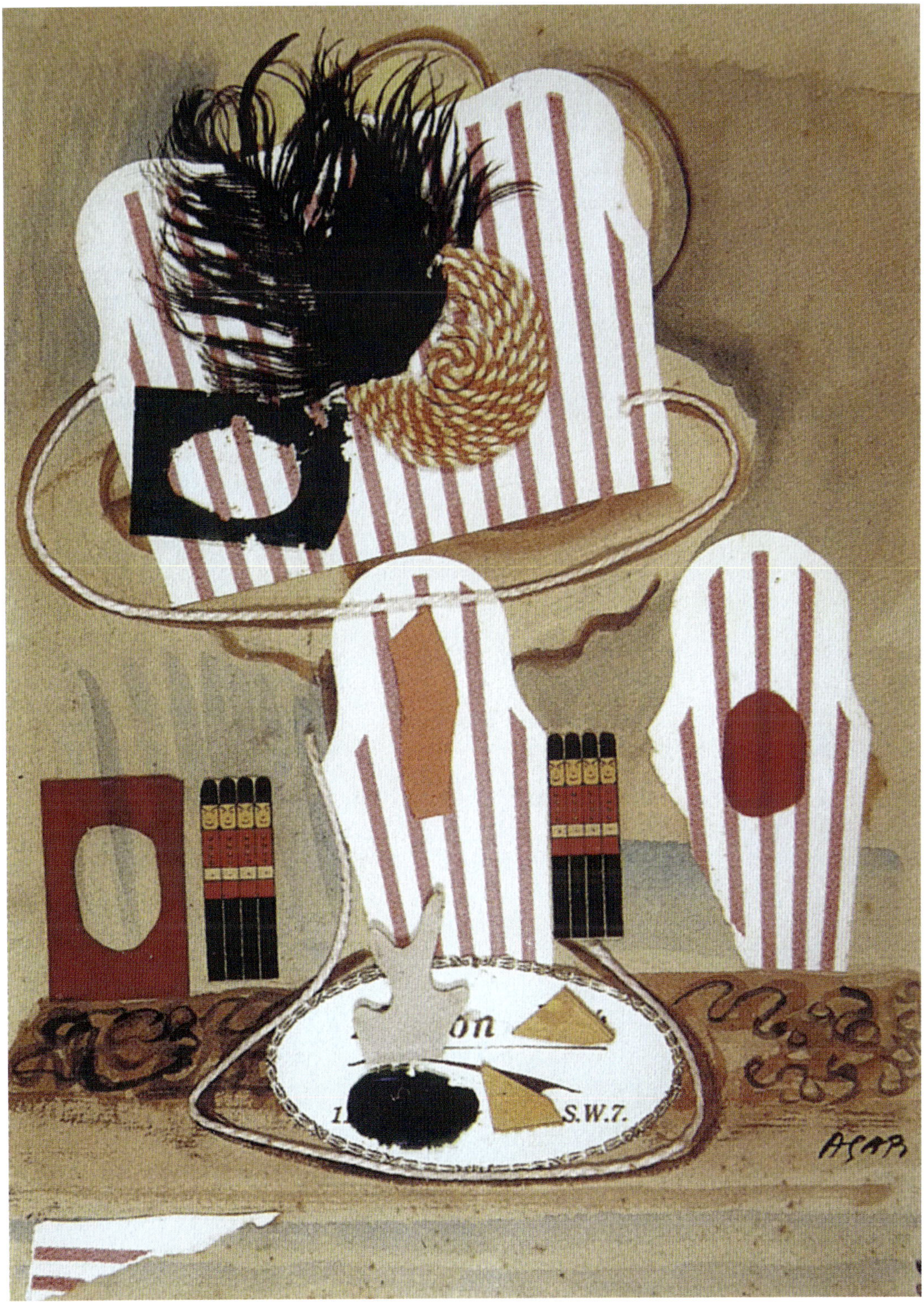
on
S.W.7.

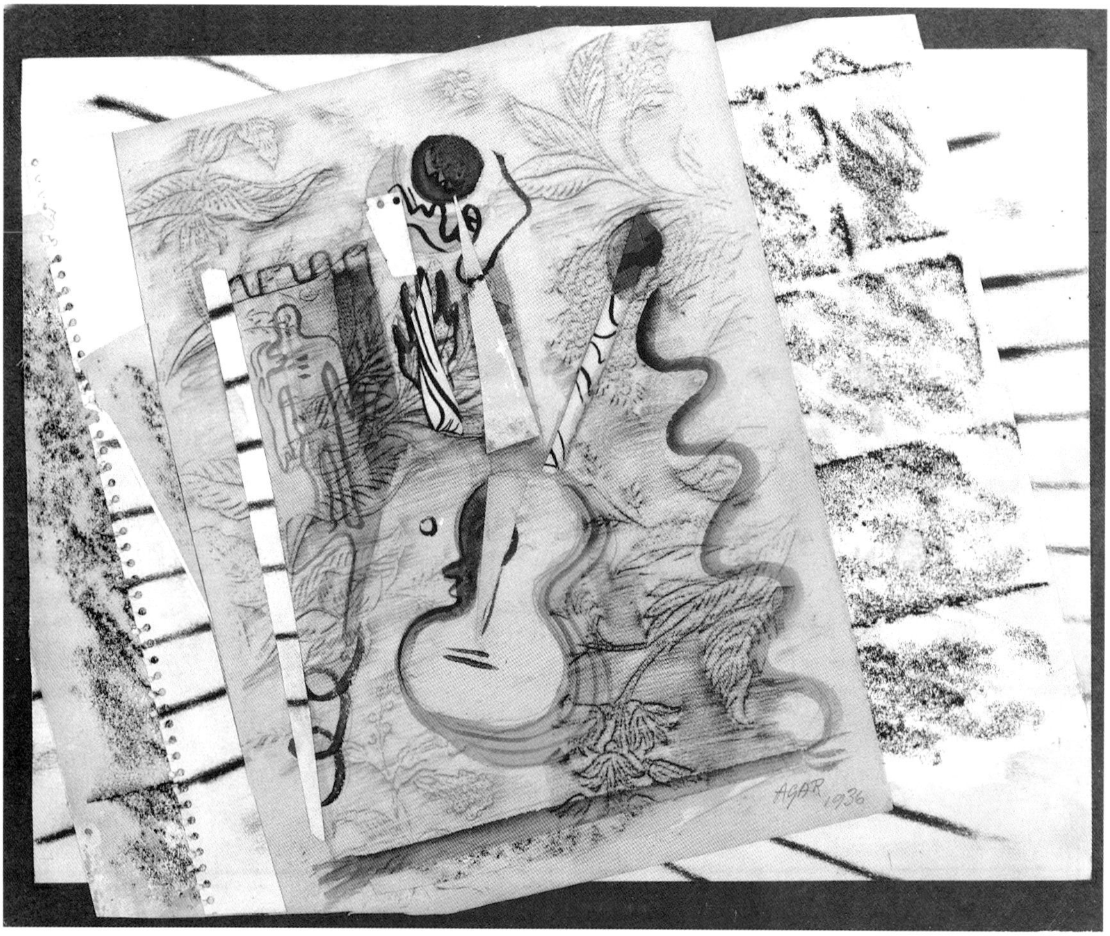

top to bottom and next to which there is a glove, a guitar shape with a butterfly and a Hilliard miniature. Here again the construction of the collage is precise, and urges us to seek the links behind it, charming us into their never-ending rhythms. *Ma Muse* (illus. 50), in a similar way, is both a butterfly and a machine, a rectangular body flanked by two identical circles, a body which looks like a paint tube out of which paint seems to have trickled. The Muse is complex: the source of inspiration, it also requires order and reason. Indeed, the two palettes on each side give birth to the butterfly, a reference to Mnemosyne, the mother of the nine Muses. A classical and Romantic, noble and 'savage' collage, it is also playful. The Muse is no longer a general, external principle; it is Agar's own. It is hers and no one else's, as in Romanticism. It is a dynamic internal principle of play. The title is in French and also sounds like 'je m'amuse' ('I am enjoying it' or 'it amuses me' or 'I am playing with it')

– pleasure being here expressed by the blobs of paint which mark the inception of the artistic gesture, often philosophically considered as play. These collages are all places of a joyful dislocation, of an inexhaustible musicality – that of the 'displacement of the banal by the fertile intervention of chance or coincidence', as she herself stated.

One of only a few paintings from 1936, *Keyholes of the Sea* (illus. 51), pictures the pleasurable surrendering of the self to automatism, as if one could peep into the subconscious from the other side of Nerval's 'gates of horn and ivory'. The wealth of different organic shapes, all of them unidentifiable, is here inseparable from a lavishness of vivid colours, seen as it is in and through a profile cut out from a neutral background, corresponding

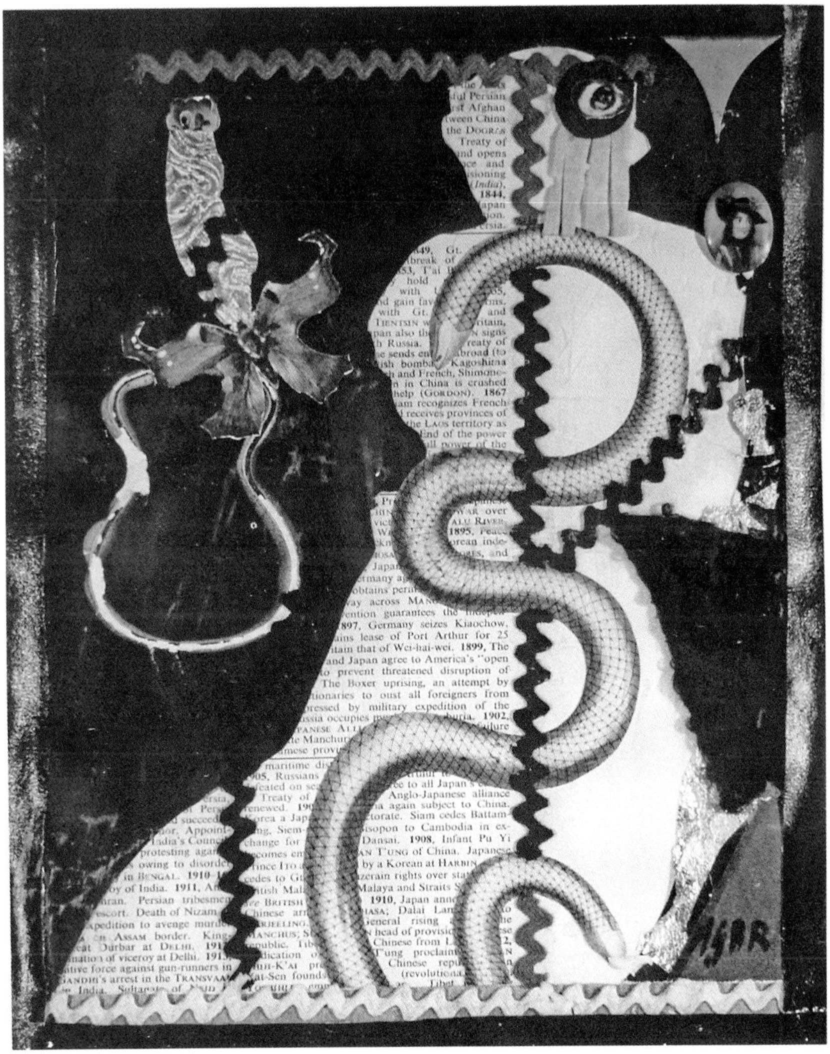

Opposite: 48 Eileen Agar, Food of Love, *1936, collage.*

Left: 49 Eileen Agar, Le Charmeur de serpents, *1936, collage.*

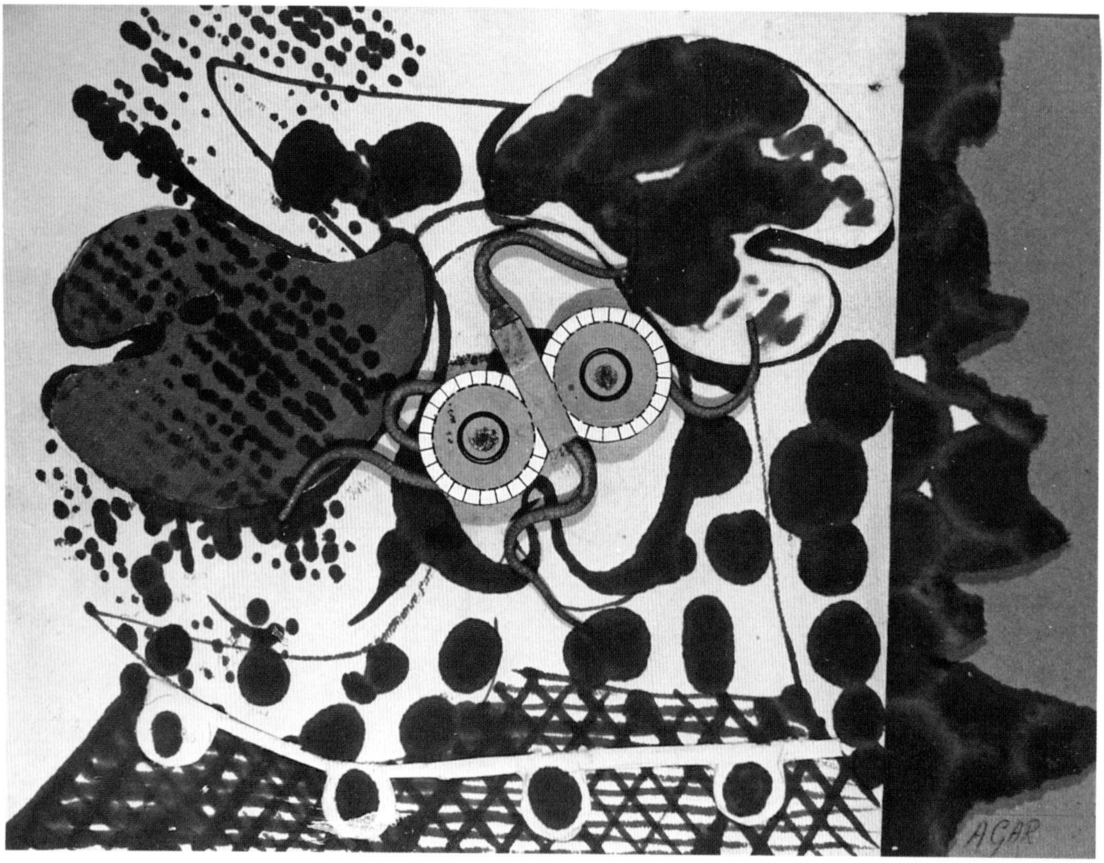

50 *Eileen Agar,* Ma Muse, *1936, collage.*

Opposite: 51 *Eileen Agar,* Keyholes of the Sea, *1936, oil on canvas.*

to the wealth issuing forth from the subconscious. The cut-out face holds the keys to access the depths of the mind and its secret workings which escape rationality – here symbolized by a plunge into a world of half vegetable, half animal shapes emerging from the depths of the sea to which the artist's introspective imagination gives us access. This work eventually confirms the analogy between the psyche and the sea and can be seen as the harbinger of the works produced in the 1970s and '80s.

In the summer of 1936, Agar and Joseph Bard went to Brittany in France. Travelling on the train, they caught sight of the fantastic rock formations of Ploumanac'h near Perros-Guirec and decided to stay there for a while. Agar bought a Rolleiflex camera and took many photographs of the rocks:

> Before us were the most fantastic rocks. They lay like enormous prehistoric monsters sleeping on the turf above the sea, a great buttock ending in a huge thumb, or a gigantic head tuned with organ pipes, a crowd, or a foot rearing up like a dolmen, all sculpted by the sea.

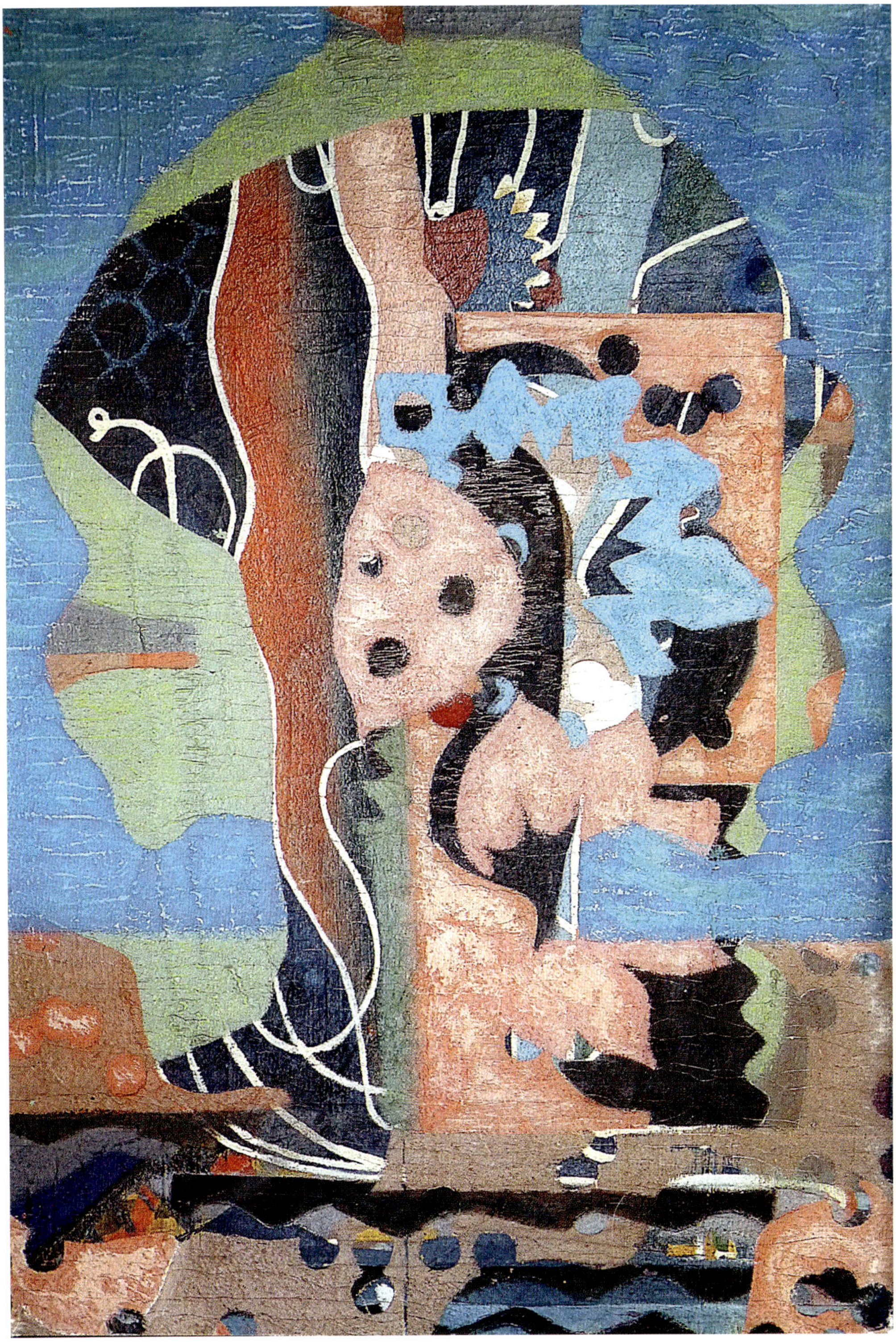

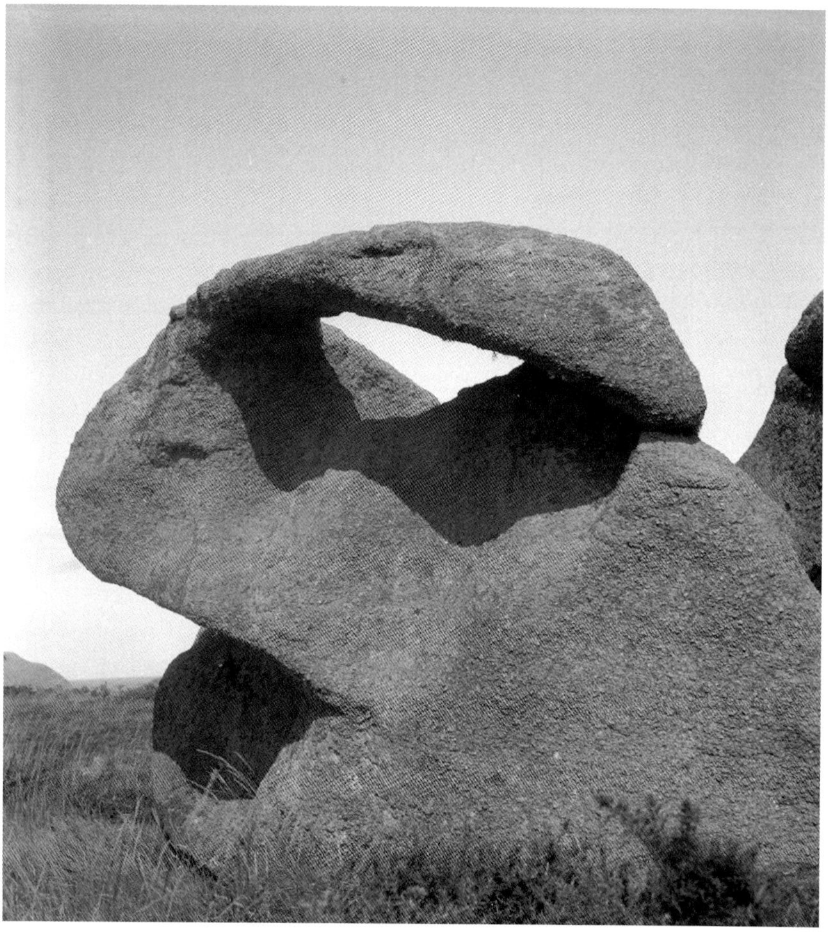

This, as Ian Walker has it, 'came as a bonus after the excitement of the exhibition in London ... as if nature had arranged a show of sculpture in the open air, just to prove that she too was keeping her hand in.' But for Agar this was a decisive encounter with the geological time of man, the past before his past, and in the astonishing work of nature – which had fascinated Henry Moore and Paul Nash alike – she found natural objects, but oversized! In an isolated entry from her notebook in 1979, she remembers:

Above: 52 Eileen Agar, 'le lapin', Ploumanac'h rocks, 1936, photograph.

Opposite: 53 Eileen Agar, Ploumanac'h rocks, 1936, photograph.

> When I saw them, they seemed alive with a pre-existent animal quality . . . some with a benevolent air, some more malign and even devilish. It was as if some aesthetic deity with a canning and original eye had scattered the landscape with these primeval objects of immense size and weight.

All these rocks were anthropomorphizable objects, if one may say – the dormant agents of the dialectics propounded by Surrealism as the solution to dualities. This was also for her the realization that photography could reveal more than the reality it is supposed to record, that it was another key to the vast field of the dovetailing of objectivity and subjectivity (illus. 52–4). The fact that she gave names to some of them – like 'le lapin' – increases the rock's, and the viewer's eye's, power of metamorphosis.

As in Paul Nash's photographs, inseparable from the notion of found object and chance encounter which extracts and dislocates the object from its natural milieu and projects it into another space, the photographed object is an object retrieved from the place it is found in, whose constitutive difference is suddenly revealed. The integration it seemed to achieve is suddenly fractured and its otherness comes to light. The photographed object is dis-identified, de-finalized. Difference is liberated, the object is reinvested, especially through the angle of the shot; the lesson Nash taught to

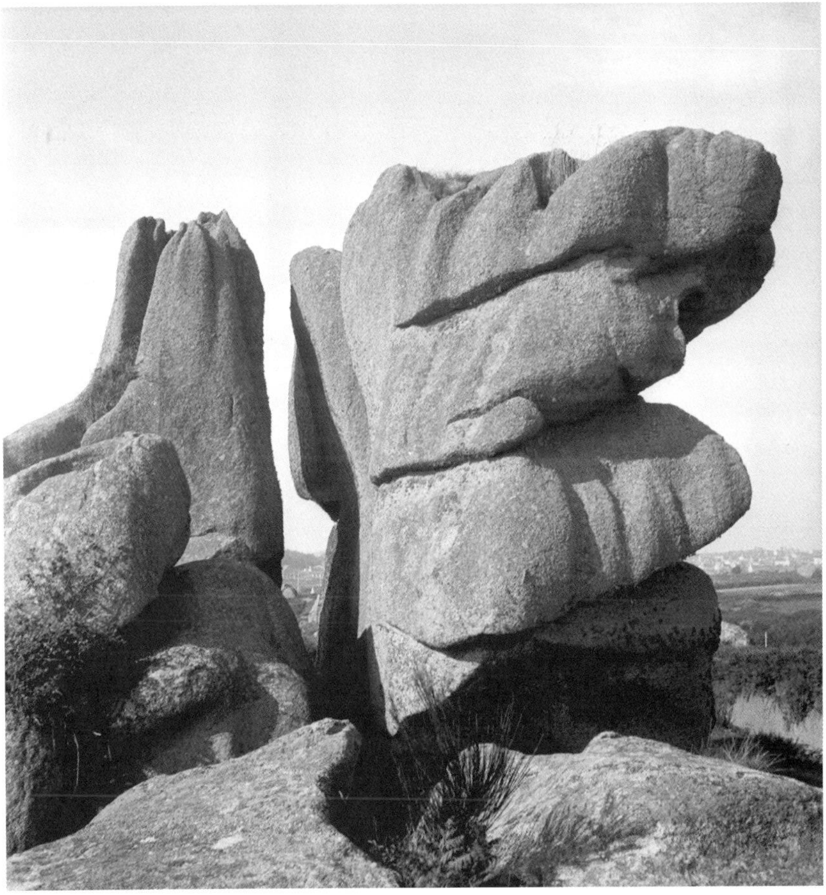

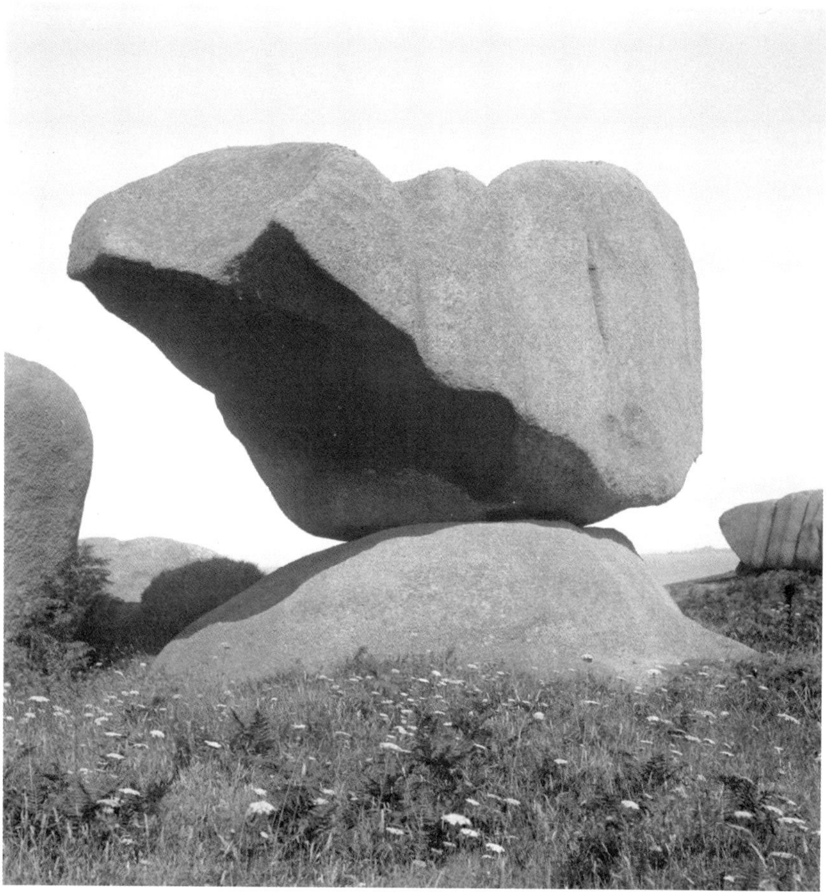

Agar is a lesson in the interiorization of the photograph's vanishing point. This is powerfully echoed in a photograph she took on a beach in Perros-Guirec in Brittany, of a beached tree, another Nash-like 'monster on the shore', its monstrosity being mainly due to the angle of the shot (illus. 55).

Collages and objects form the main and most characteristic output of Agar's during those years, as well as right into the 1940s and '50s. This is indeed the case with all Surrealists, including those whose main activity was writing poetry, since the Surrealist object represents neither more nor less than the criticism of the *usefulness* of an object and the corresponding process of the metaphorization of given reality. At the 1936 exhibition, David Gascoyne, Sheila Legge, Hugh Sykes Davies, Roger Roughton and Rupert Lee had indulged in the making of objects, and Agar and Roland Penrose made regular visits to the Caledonian Market in London. This clearly ties in with André Breton's own declarations concerning the 'surrealist object'. In his article published in *Cahiers d'art* in 1936, Breton wrote that the aim of all

Above: 54 Eileen Agar, Ploumanac'h rocks, 1936, photograph.

Opposite: 55 Eileen Agar, Beached Tree, *1936, photograph.*

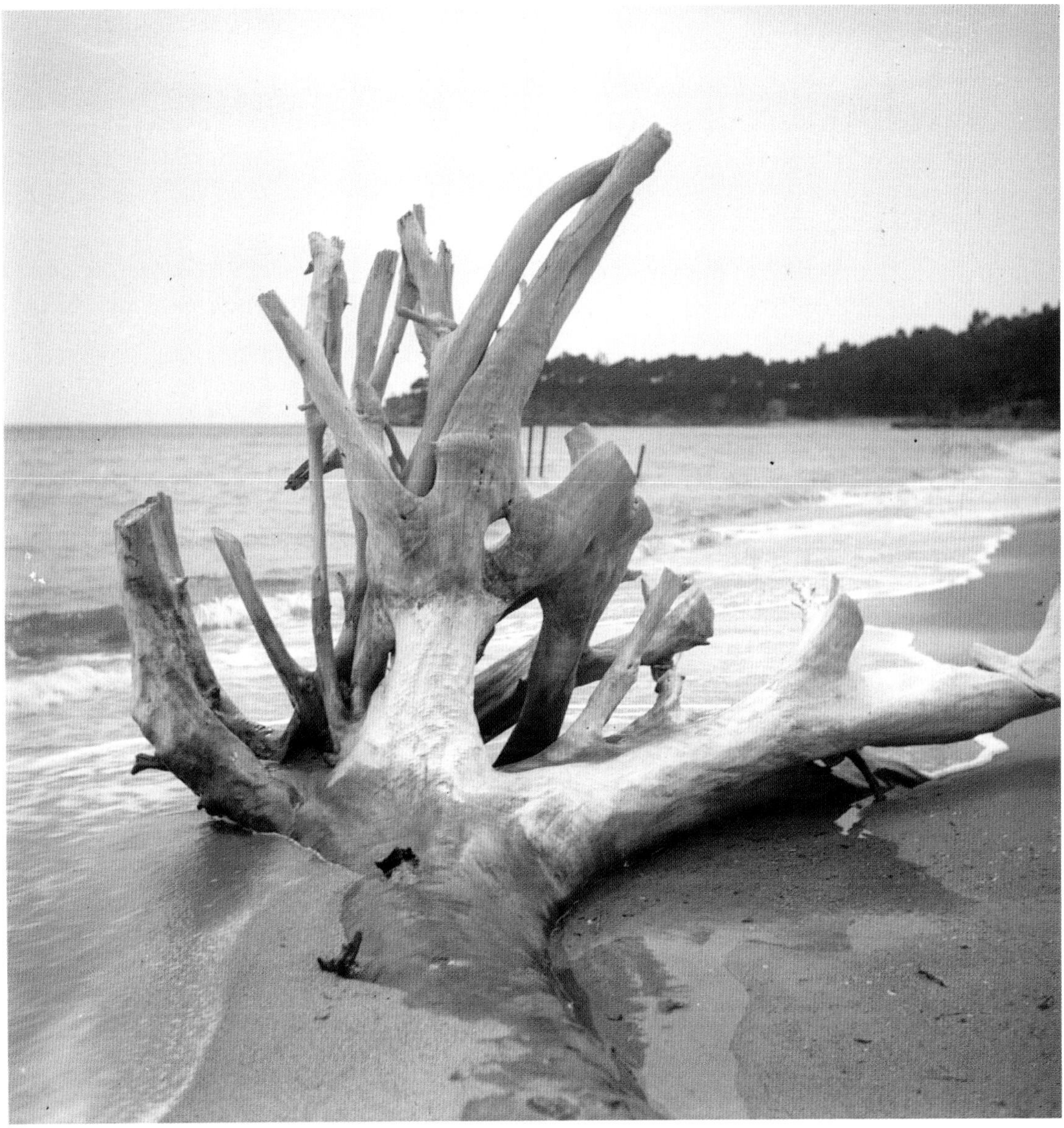

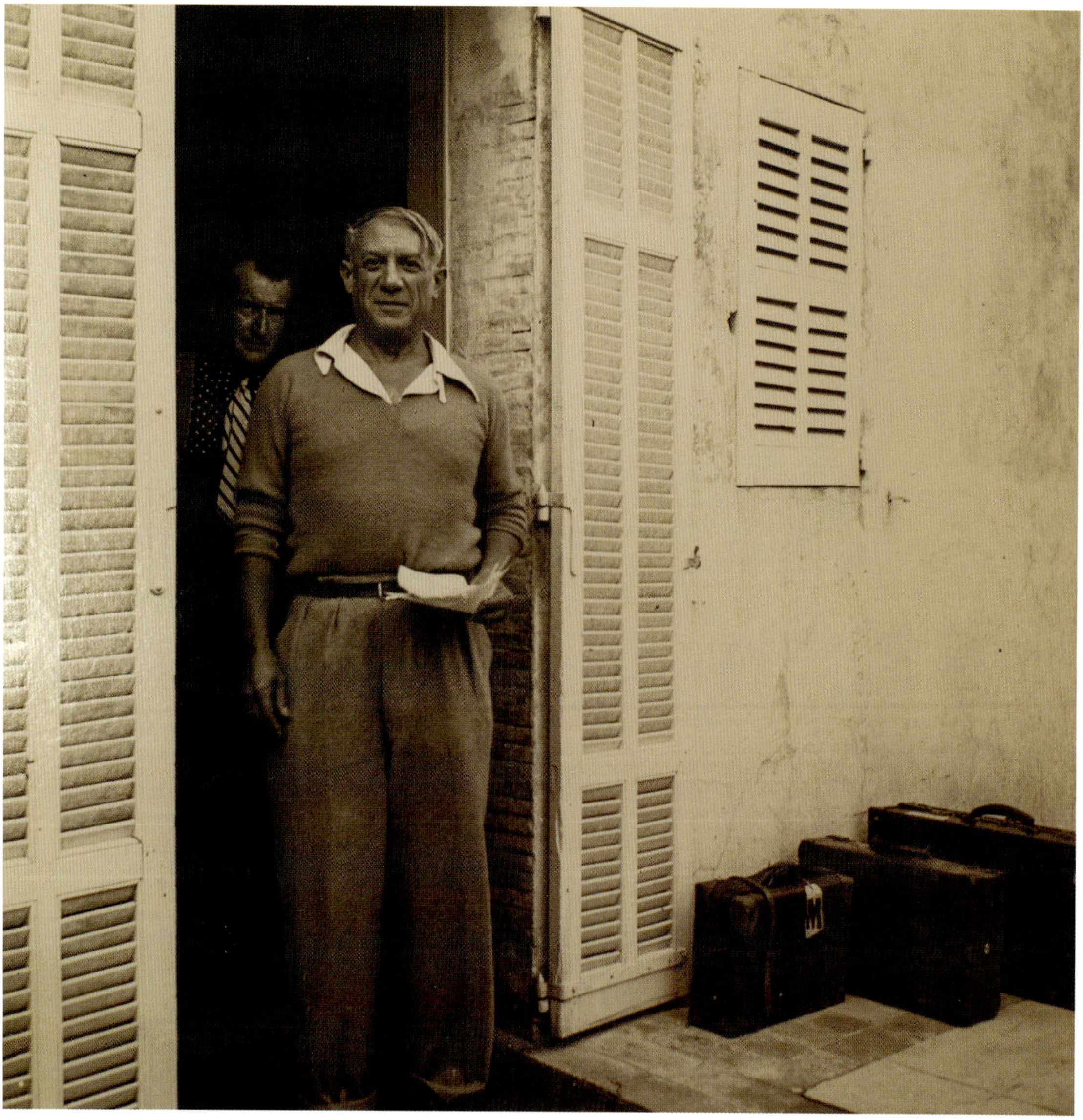

Surrealist objects, whatever the process they trigger, is 'the objectivization of the dream activity, its passage into reality'. And it is true that seeing any of those objects is similar to the act of dreaming: displacement and condensation are both at work at the service of a kind of anamnesis, by which the objects we see are the results of a grafting of different objects onto each other, each one thus losing its bare, common identity. In other words, the repressed is unwittingly made to resurface through a whole network of metaphors – each object being jostled and shaken out of its habitual identity. Its banality is transformed into a sacred, hieratically conceived mind-reality. It no longer has a proper function; it proves to be endowed with magical virtue. The Surrealist object 'stages' a synthesis of dream and reality. It manifests itself as a communicating vessel engineered, so to speak, by the power of desire which it reveals and unleashes. Such a fundamentally Surrealist process was never abandoned by Agar.

Towards the end of 1936, Agar was asked to participate in the 'Fantastic Art, Dada and Surrealism' exhibition organized from December 1936 to January 1937 by Alfred H. Barr Jr, the director of the Museum of Modern Art in New York. *Quadriga* was especially requested and this signified Agar's accession to the status of one of the only prominent women Surrealists in the world. In November 1937 a photograph of her was published in *The Evening News* to illustrate an article entitled 'Women in the News'.

In July 1937, after her participation in the AIA's mammoth exhibition 'For Peace, Democracy and Cultural Development', in which she exhibited three oil paintings, *The Ringleader*, *Hommage à Madame* and *Genoblast* – unfindable pictures at the moment of writing – she was invited by Roland Penrose and his recently met lover, the Surrealist photographer Lee Miller, to spend a few days in the beautiful Georgian house belonging to Beacus, Roland Penrose's brother, at Lambe Creek on the Truro River in Cornwall. Penrose had also invited Paul and Nusch Éluard, Man Ray and his girlfriend Ady, Henry Moore and his wife Irina as well as Max Ernst who came with Leonora Carrington. 'It was', Agar records, 'a delightful surrealist party with Roland taking the lead, ready to turn the slightest encounter into an orgy. I remember going off to watch Lee taking a bubble bath, but there was not quite enough room in the tub for us all.' Apparently, as is recounted by Whitney Chadwick in her *Women Artists and the Surrealist Movement* but with no evidence given, 'Eileen Agar, Nusch Éluard and Leonora Carrington all danced naked round the disconcerted figure of Herbert Read, illuminated by the glare of a car's headlamps.'

Opposite: 56 Eileen Agar, Picasso and his chauffeur at Mougins, 1937.

Before separating, the party promised they would meet again, at Éluard's suggestion, at Picasso's place in Mougins, France. This indeed took place on 19 August, when Picasso and Dora Maar entertained Paul and Nusch Éluard, Man Ray and Ady, Penrose and Miller, and Agar and Bard, who were picked up at Cannes station by Penrose and Miller. As Agar recalls, parties were merry affairs and at one of them, they decided to swap their first names. Eileen Agar became Dora Agar, Pablo Picasso became Don José Picasso, Joseph Bard became Pablo Bard, Man Ray became Roland Ray, 'and if one forgot one's new name, one was fined one or two francs.' This was apparently pushed further – if one goes by oral testimonies – with the exchange of partners, Agar falling into Paul Éluard's arms and bed ('a living Eros', she called him), Ady into Penrose's and probably Nusch into Picasso's. An anecdote which Agar narrates in her diaries refers to her flirting with Penrose, which was noticed by Miller 'who seized hold of a siphon standing on the table in front of her and squirted soda all over me'. She continues: 'She should have squirted it over Roland! However I brushed the water off and I asked him if he couldn't control his girlfriend.' Actually, the point of these gossipy stories is to emphasize the friendly atmosphere of complicity which prevailed among the group and which she sums up in this joke: 'In Mougins, Surrealism was on the horizon, Stravinsky was in the air and Freud was under the bed.' Elsewhere in her diaries, a 1980 entry reports that she had told Annette Armstrong, a close friend of hers, 'how at Mougins I had said that I didn't like Kandinsky and to my surprise Picasso said he didn't either' (illus. 56–8). At that time, as Antony Penrose says, Picasso had surrounded himself with a huge number of objects found by chance on the beach in Antibes and Juan-les-Pins: strange stones, shells and broken shards, which couldn't but fascinate and inspire Agar. At that gathering, too, Agar took several photographs of Picasso, Penrose, Éluard and others and a wonderful photograph of Miller, one of the most poetical, with spiritual overtones.

A photograph of Agar dancing on a roof at Mougins in 1937 (illus. 59) also epitomizes the atmosphere of those happy days in the South of France. It was taken by Joseph Bard, no doubt on the roof terrace of the Hotel Vaste Horizon at the entrance to the village of Mougins. The explicitness and frankness of the photograph is in keeping with Agar's own spirit of independence and affirmed – and affirmative – femininity. However provocatively exhibitionist her nudity might be considered, it still ties in with her general desire to reveal and uncover the deep nature of reality. The flimsy, see-through 'dress' she is wearing is to be compared with the opening of surfaces onto an inner reality we see in most of her collages and paintings. In *Ladybird* (1937), the same intention prevails: thick black and white swirling lines in gouache and ink are added to an almost similar photograph, probably taken at the same time by Bard, of

57 Eileen Agar, Dora Maar, Nusch Éluard, Picasso and Paul Éluard at Juan-les-Pins, 1937.

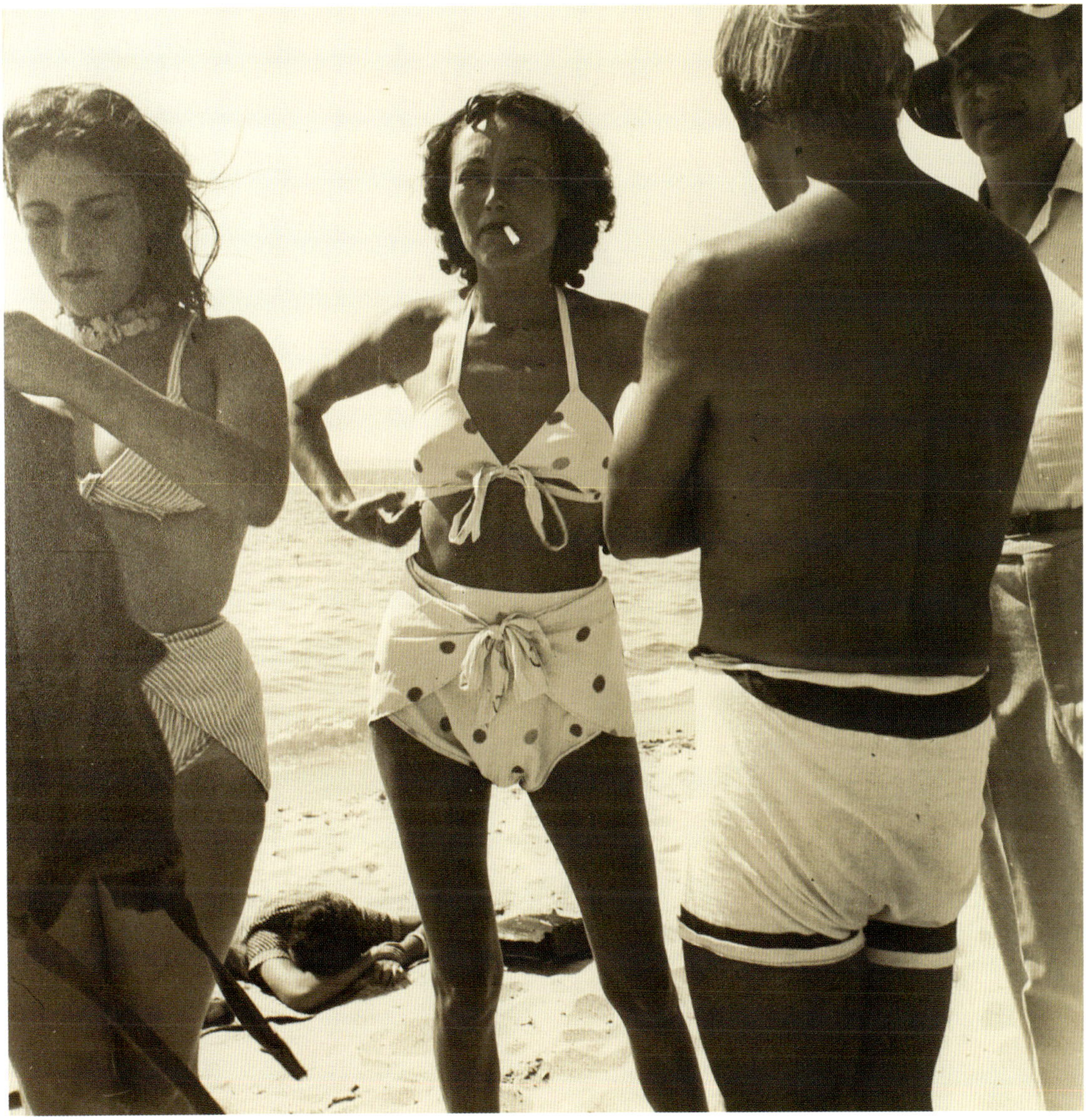

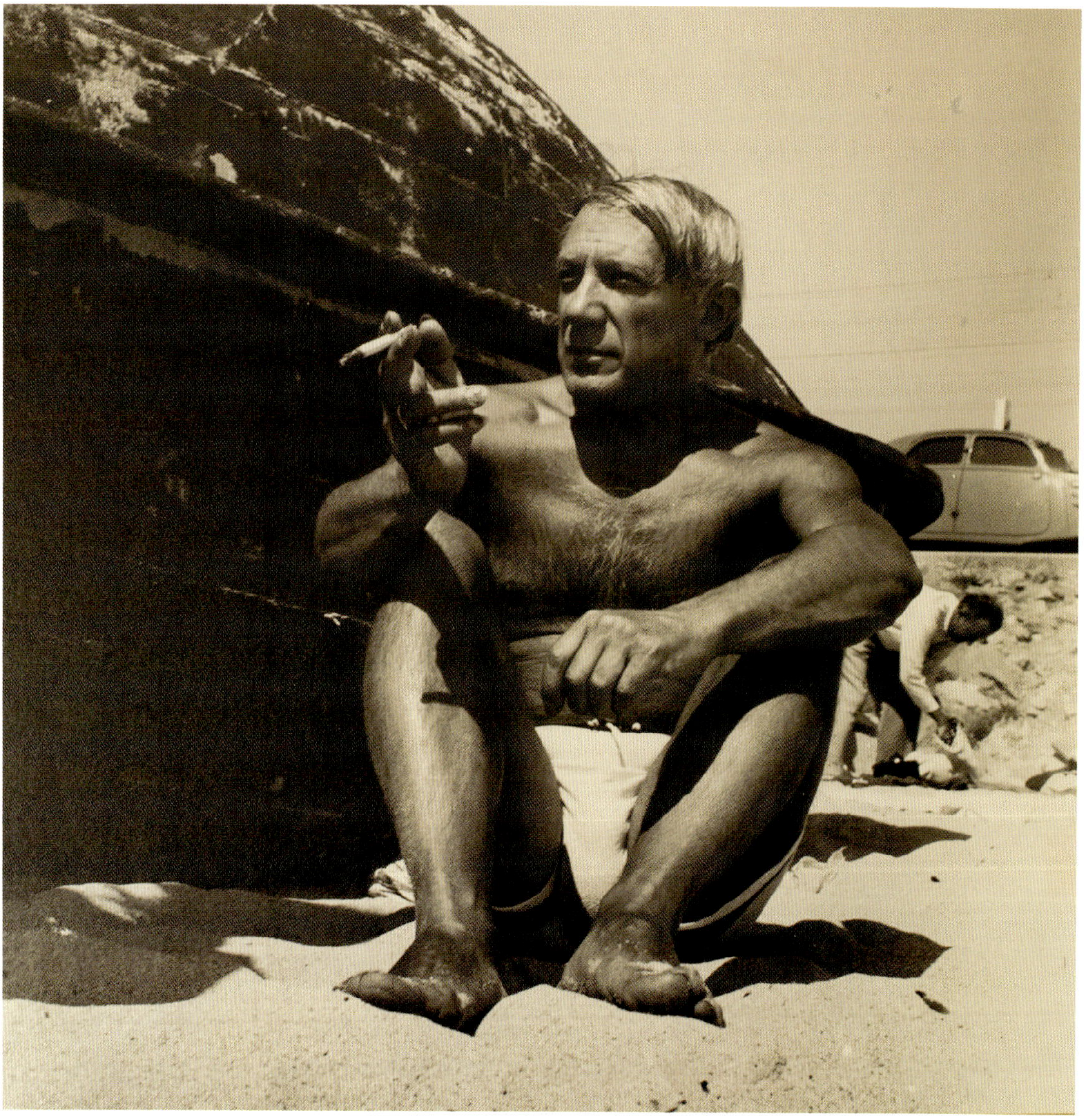

her dancing in the same outfit – a means to go further and emphasize the rhythm of the body and deconstruct it. The telephone dials and starfish shapes dispersed at its surface superimpose another rhythm and create other references to the outside world, as if the dance involved the whole of reality. The eroticism of the body, veiled or unveiled, is seen as from behind a fuzzy windowpane, revealing the lines of the body in their almost magical quality in contrast to the world around. All this forces a double reading upon the observer between revelation and unreachability.

The same could be said of another photograph taken by Lee Miller on the occasion of a party at Brighton Pavilion in 1937 – a photo of Agar's shadow on a column (illus. 60). The shadow, deformed by the undulations of the fluting and fillets of the column, reveals a non-existent pregnancy, while the excrescence at the level of her womb – the shadow cast by the camera she herself was carrying around her – looks no less than a non-existent penis, turning her into a kind of ambiguous, supernatural being, 'pregnant with a camera, transformed by Rolleiflex', as she describes herself in her autobiography, or a witch, as the pointed hat seems to imply, revealing the other in her, a projection, if not an unconscious denial, of her deep dark secret – her refusal of pregnancy which she had avowedly and consciously decided on. To this we can only add that Lee Miller managed to catch the deep link between Agar and the magic behind objects, especially objects from primitive beliefs and lore. She further proves it with another portrait, a photograph also taken in 1937, in which the wooden statue she is seen embracing is, apparently, that of a prophet or deity, found in a junk shop in Menton, where Agar and Bard were staying with Foltýn back in 1929. The garments of the wooden carving were then painted blue and to them was added a starfish, a reminder of the place where they had found it.

Another work of that year, *Double Head* (illus. 62) – body colour and coloured chalk on paper – is also worth mentioning. It certainly reminds us of *Double Take* of the year before, and reiterates Agar's fascination with doubleness – in other words, with the paradoxical repetition of the same which, because it is repeated, cannot be the same and thus unavoidably reveals difference, identity being made to slip from itself and vary from itself in this *passage over*. This is exactly what happens with her resorting to profiles and shadows (as in *Woman Reading* and *Precious Stones*): the otherness in the same, the other side of the same, is hinted at and made to surface. In *Double Take* (illus. 63), as the title implies, the doily used as a centrepiece makes us wonder about the links – conflicting or associative – between the two faces, and dramatizes their similarity. In *Double Head*, the reference to Janus,

58 Eileen Agar, Picasso on beach at Juan-les-Pins, 1937.

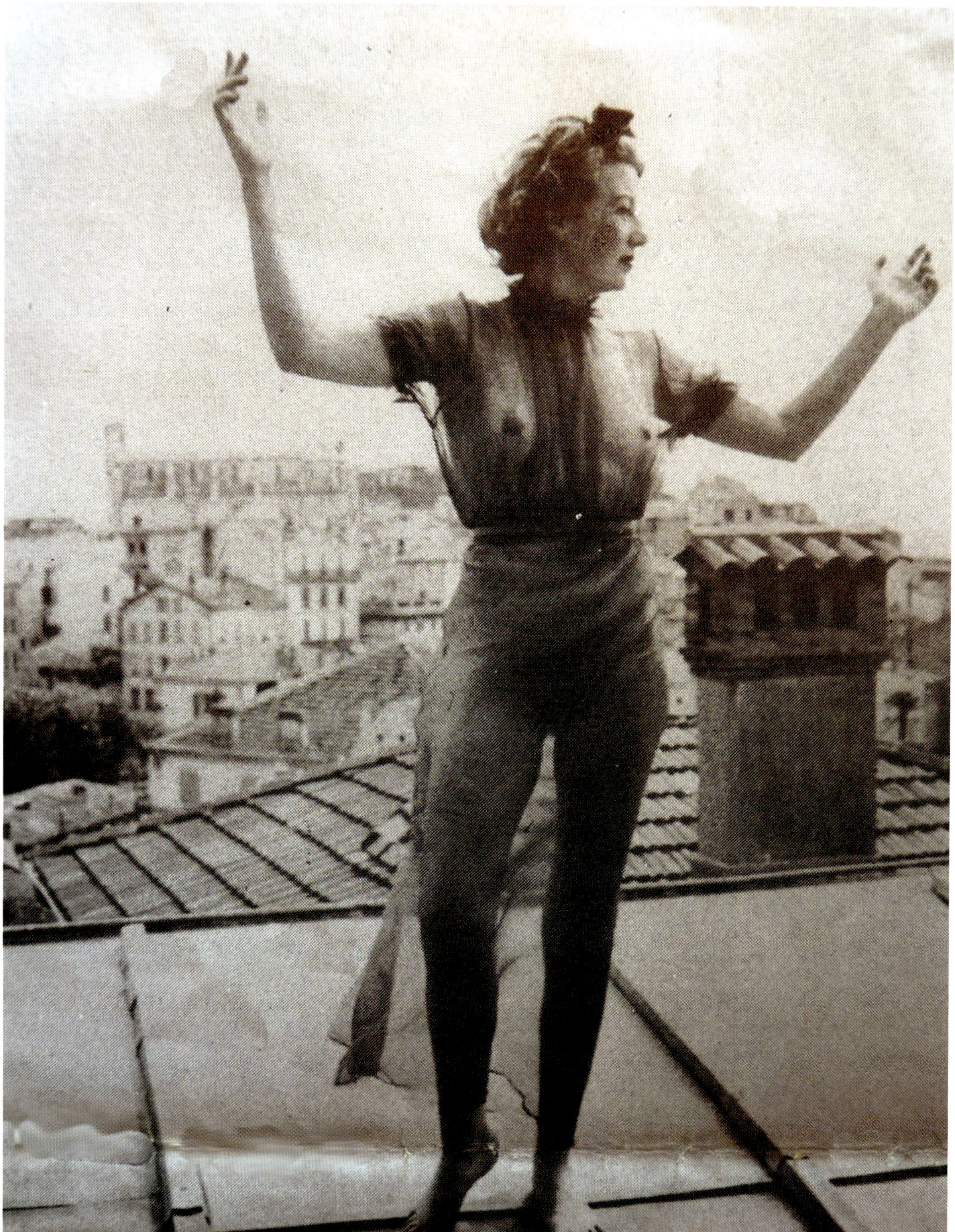

the god of peace *and* war, takes us back to the ambivalence at the core of man's being, the conscious and the subconscious, as is hinted at by the tribal, primitive designs on the two profiles which appear on two different coloured backgrounds.

From 4 to 19 June 1937, eight British Surrealists were invited by the Japanese Surrealist Shuzo Takiguchi to take part in a large international exhibition in Tokyo, in which Agar exhibited one oil painting, *The Return of the Native*. This apart, probably the most seminal event of that year was the 'Surrealist Objects and Poems Exhibition' opened at the newly inaugurated London Gallery, by Herbert Read, E.L.T. Mesens and Roland Penrose on 27 November 'on the thirteenth stroke of midnight'. Julian Trevelyan opened it, disguised as a blind explorer, the symbol of the unidentifiable and inaccessible quality of the subconscious and of one's inner visions of reality. Altogether 138 items were exhibited, 88 of them by British artists. All of these objects were carefully classified into categories, such as 'surrealist objects', 'interpreted objects', objects for everyday use (as Roland Penrose's

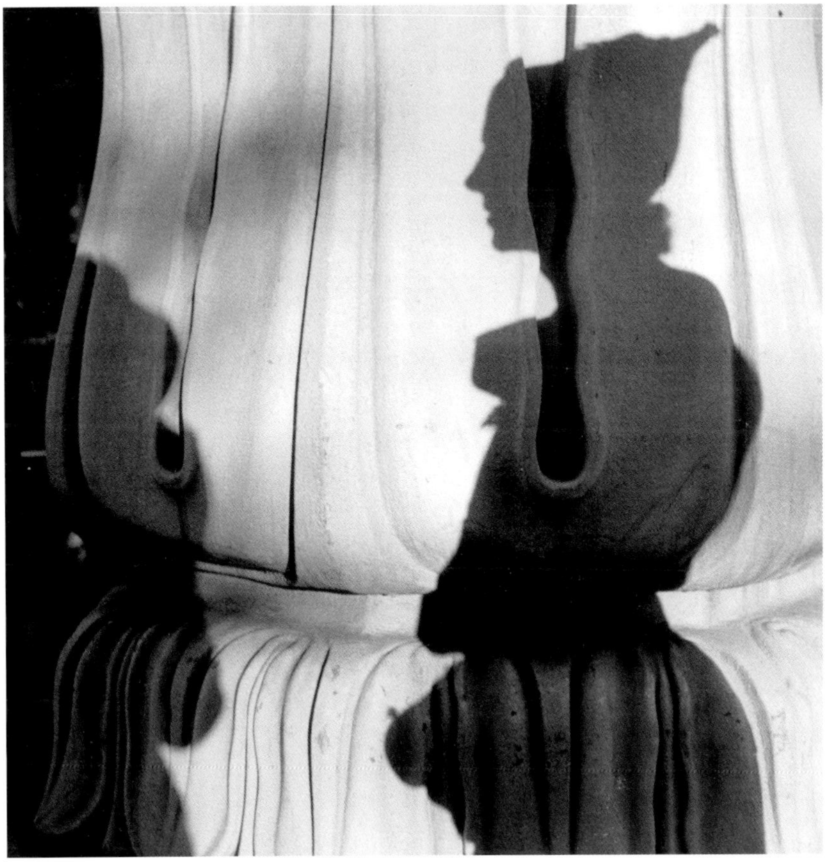

Opposite: 59 Eileen Agar dancing on a roof at Mougins, 1937, photograph.

Left: 60 Lee Miller, Eileen Agar, *photograph taken at Brighton, 1937.*

Below: 61 Roland Penrose, Group at Lambe Creeke, Truro, Cornwall (from left to right: Lee Miller, Nusch Éluard, Joseph Bard, Eileen Agar and Paul Éluard), 1937, photograph.

Opposite: 62 Eileen Agar, Double Head, *1937, body colour and coloured chalk.*

Guaranteed Fine Weather Suitcase or Trevelyan's *Machine for Making Clouds)*, mobile objects, poem objects, perturbed objects, constructed objects, photo collages. The most memorable one was certainly Agar's *Angel of Anarchy* (illus. 64) – the first version, which got lost a little later on its way back from a show in Amsterdam, the Galerie Robert's 'Surrealist Exhibition' in March–June 1938. Agar then made another version in 1940, using the same plaster cast of Joseph Bard's head, and gave it the same title. As photographs of the time show, the surface of Bard's bust was divided into two parts, one with black fur, the other white, but the whole of it was covered with doilies and green osprey and ostrich feathers obtained from her mother, who used to wear them in headdresses – again the same process of accretion which makes surfaces variable and turns the object into a place of anarchy – 'a combination of Heaven and Hell' – and the artist into an anarchist. Of course, we also know that it might well be a reference to the Spanish anarchists engaged in fighting against Franco, but also to Herbert Read, who had just published articles and books on anarchism (*Poetry and Anarchism*, 1937) as well as an echo of what Agar, as she recounts in her autobiography, had heard from carpenters working outside her studio and talking about 'Archangel pine' (letter to the Tate Gallery, 18 May 1984). Let us not forget either that 'Angel' had been used three years before for her first plaster cast of Bard's head for *Angel of Mercy*.

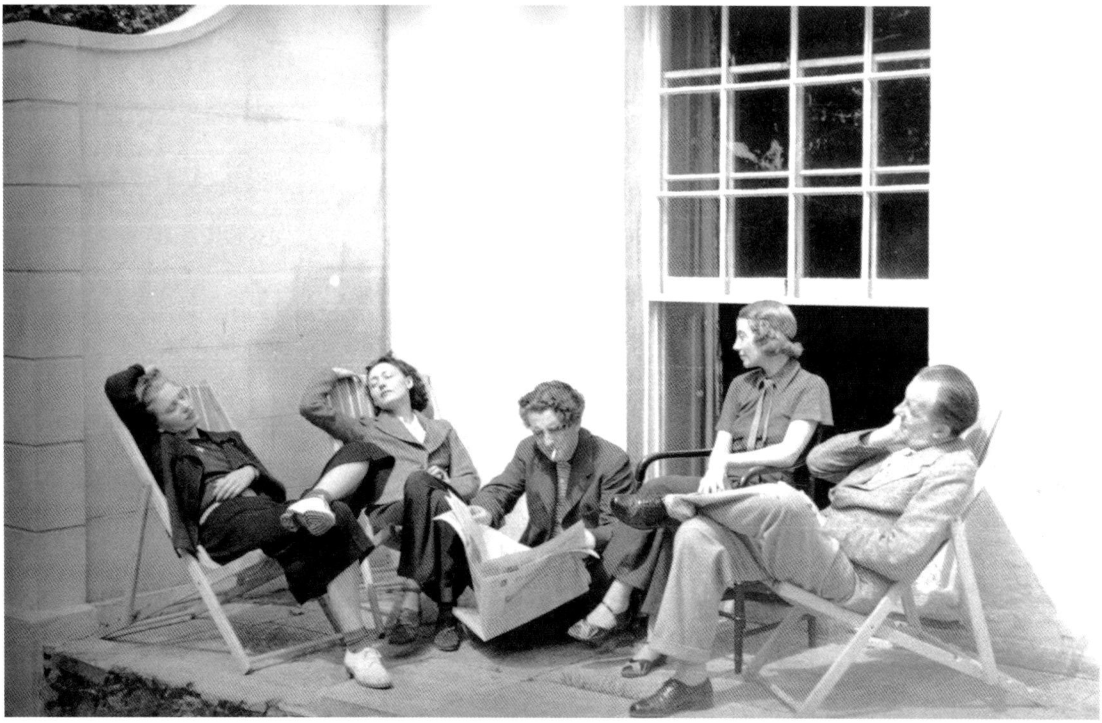

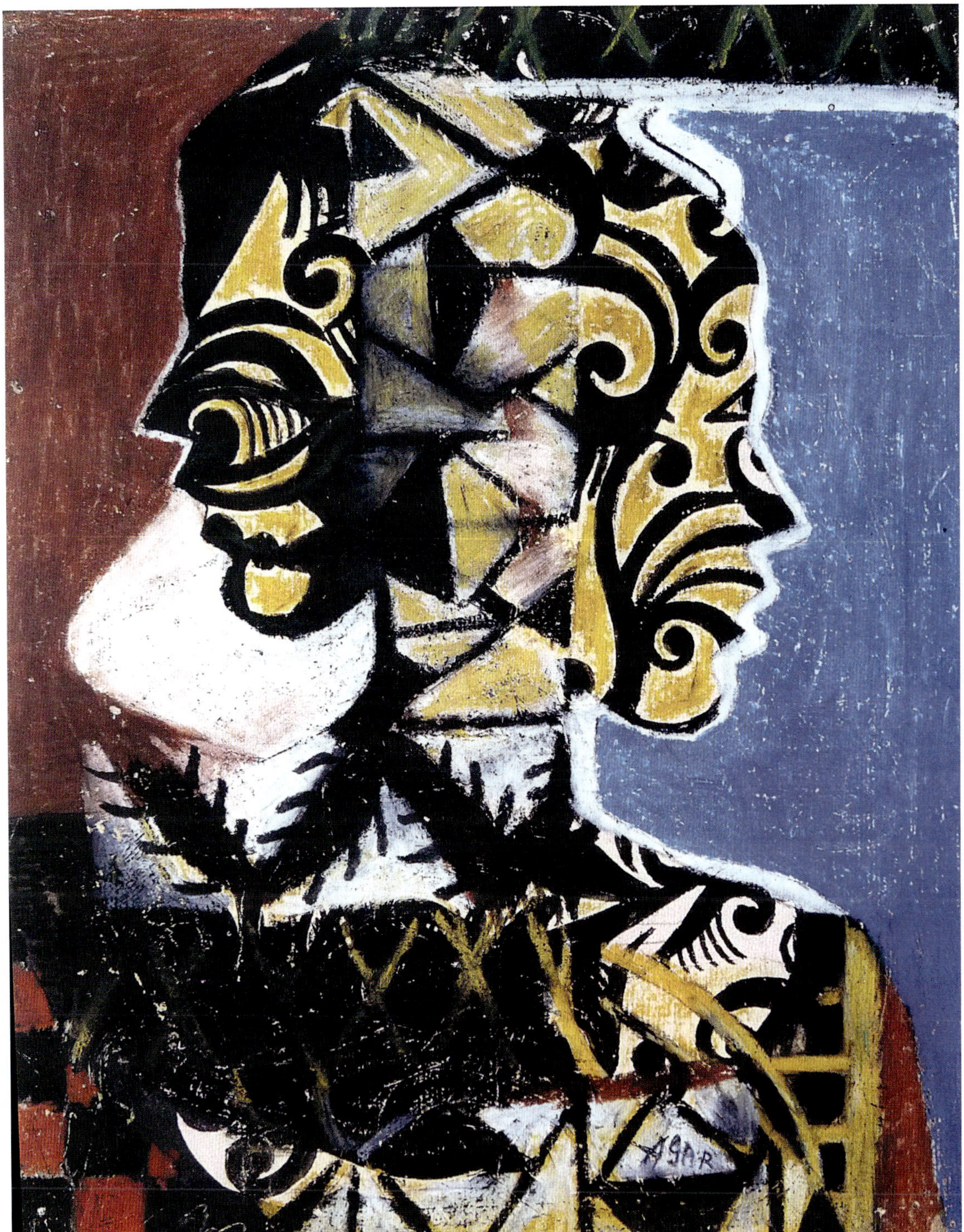

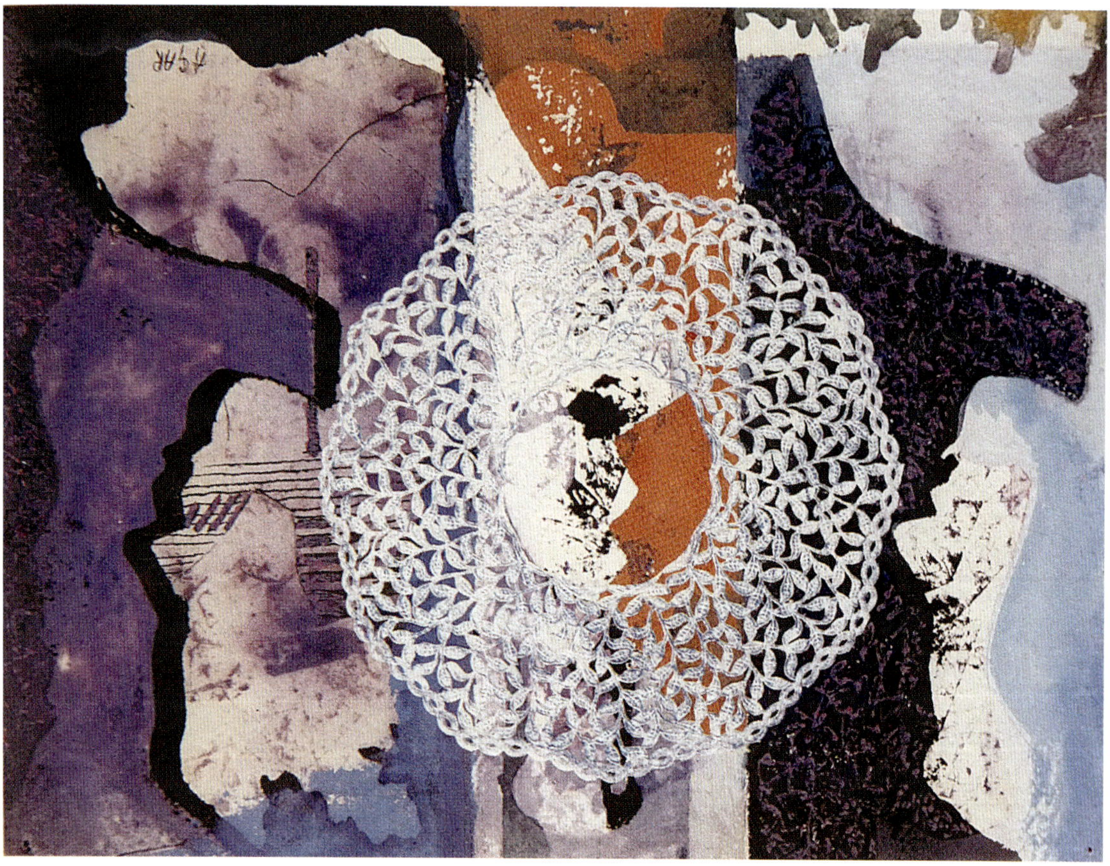

Finally, this might also half-consciously correspond to her own personal brand of anarchism, given her reluctance to adopt any kind of political commitment. But again, more than anything else, the work shows how Surrealist it is as the result of a precipitation and interaction of external influences.

Next to the angel, Agar also showed *Rococo Cocotte* (illus. 65). Using the same kind of plaster cast, she stuck on top of it a dishevelled mop of black hair – a heap of string actually – adding a dented piece of cloth as a moustache and four identical brooch-like objects, one as a goatee, another two as eyes and the fourth one surmounting the head like a small statue on the mop of hair. The face is rather forbidding, with the vacant eyes looking like sunglasses – reminding us of Marcel Jean's 1936 object *Le Spectre du gardénia*, with the mouth a zip fastening. The whole object resembles that of a frowning prophet or guru of modern times – unless it hints at a transvestite, as it might in view of the title, as *cocotte* is a French word for prostitute or for a homosexual and 'rococo' a reference to its outrageous ornamentation. The alliteration in the title, precisely re-establishes the humour which the construction of this Surrealist object communicates and helps put the seriousness one might feel at first sight at a distance.

Three collages were also exhibited together with the *Angel of Anarchy* but no trace has been found of them so far: *The Mosquito Minotaure*, *Visitation* and *Aerial Combat*. On the evening of the opening, Agar wore 'cream gloves with scarlet cloth finger tips' – the appearance conveyed by her gloves telling us more about her than about the reality of her bare hands and implying that appearances replace or even exceed reality. Two photographs achieve the same effect. In *Hat Still-life* (illus. 66, 1937), the hat is endowed with added existence beyond its utilitarian meaning thanks to its emergence from an entanglement of verticals and horizontals. In *Industrial Still-life* (illus. 67, 1937), a conversation seems to take place between two huge mouths about a plant in a pot. Two still-lifes far from being still…

By April 1937, E.L.T. Mesens had become, almost naturally, the leader of the Surrealist group in England and had taken over the London Gallery at 28 Cork Street, as its manager. The lease was definitively signed on 27 February 1938 with the financial help of Roland Penrose, who had raised three-quarters of the capital by selling the farms he had inherited in Suffolk and Norfolk, and Anton Zwemmer, the Dutch proprietor of Zwemmers bookshop, the first bookseller in London to sell Surrealist magazines from the middle of the 1920s on. The group had thus a place where they could meet and exhibit, and Mesens had added to his gallery activity the publication of a magazine, the *London Bulletin*, from April 1938 to June 1940, producing twenty issues, which printed articles on painters and sculptors, and gave

63 Eileen Agar, Double Take, *1937, gouache and collage on paper.*

news of Surrealist activities and the catalogues of Surrealist exhibitions in London. The gallery became the centre of resistance to obscurantism, making Surrealism a pivot of living avant-garde art and the proponent of the artists' struggle against the rise of fascism and European dictatorships and in favour of cultural development in a period of unrest and anxiety. The year 1938 was to be one of intense activity for the now fully-fledged group, with many meetings and exhibitions in England and abroad. In January and February 1938, André Breton organized the 'International Surrealist Exhibition' at the Galerie des Beaux-Arts in Paris with works by Agar – the famous *Quadriga*, lent for the occasion by Roland Penrose, an object entitled *Valise pour Maris*, and a few collages. From March to June, Kristians Tonny organized the already mentioned 'International Surrealist Exhibition' in Amsterdam, where Agar exhibited *Angel of Anarchy* – lost on the way back, as we have already mentioned – and an object entitled *Vierge*, and in the summer a Surrealist exhibition took place in São Paulo. In May and June the group took part in a debate, 'Realism and Surrealism', at Gloucester's Guildhall together with an accompanying exhibition, to which Agar contributed, along with John Banting, Sam Haile, S. W. Hayter, Reuben Mednikoff, Roland Penrose, F. E. McWilliam, Grace W. Pailthorpe, Ceri Richards and Julian Trevelyan, a militant gathering. The preface to the catalogue was written by Herbert Read.

From July to September, the 'Canadian National Exhibition' comprised 21 British Surrealists, creating a veritable 'upheaval' in Canada, as the press generally emphasized. In late autumn, the Cambridge University Arts society organized an exhibition of 61 French and English Surrealist works arranged by Roland Penrose on the premises of the Gordon Fraser Gallery in Portugal Place, off Bridge Street. Benjamin Péret wrote, as a preface, a typically 'automatic' narrative in which he telescopes all the productions of the artists displayed into a constantly rebounding metaphor, seeing the exhibition as 'an asbestos flag flaming with a fire of its own creation, [a] standard which the creatures of Eileen Agar brandish in their desperate course . . . a standard clothed with reliefs by Arp' in 'this world of bleached bones and warrens of bones'. Agar exhibited an object, *Le Père Ubu*, and two works, *Inexplicable* and *Le solitaire*, the description or details of which have been lost. Finally, in October and November, the '64th Autumn Exhibition' at the Walker Art Gallery in Liverpool invited seventeen British Surrealists to participate. Agar exhibited two works there, *The Yellow House* and *Winter*. Except for the São Paulo exhibition, Agar had works included in every one of these shows. This being said, it was a time felt by Agar as a one of political uncertainty and apprehension, dismay and despair. On 1 May, the Surrealist group demonstrated in the streets of London with the people and the workers; four

Opposite: 64
Eileen Agar, Angel of Anarchy, *1936, plaster cast with mixed media (subsequently destroyed).*

Overleaf left: 65
Eileen Agar, Rococo Cocotte, *1937 (subsequently destroyed).*

Overleaf right: 66
Eileen Agar, Hat Still-life, *1937, photograph.*

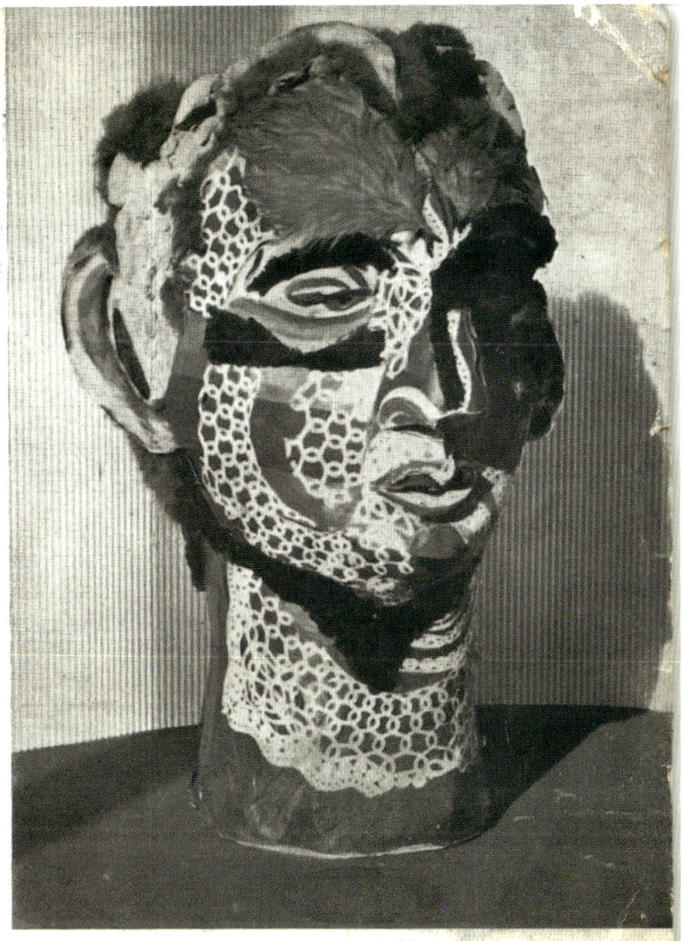

Surrealist
Objects & Poems

LONDON GALLERY, LTD.

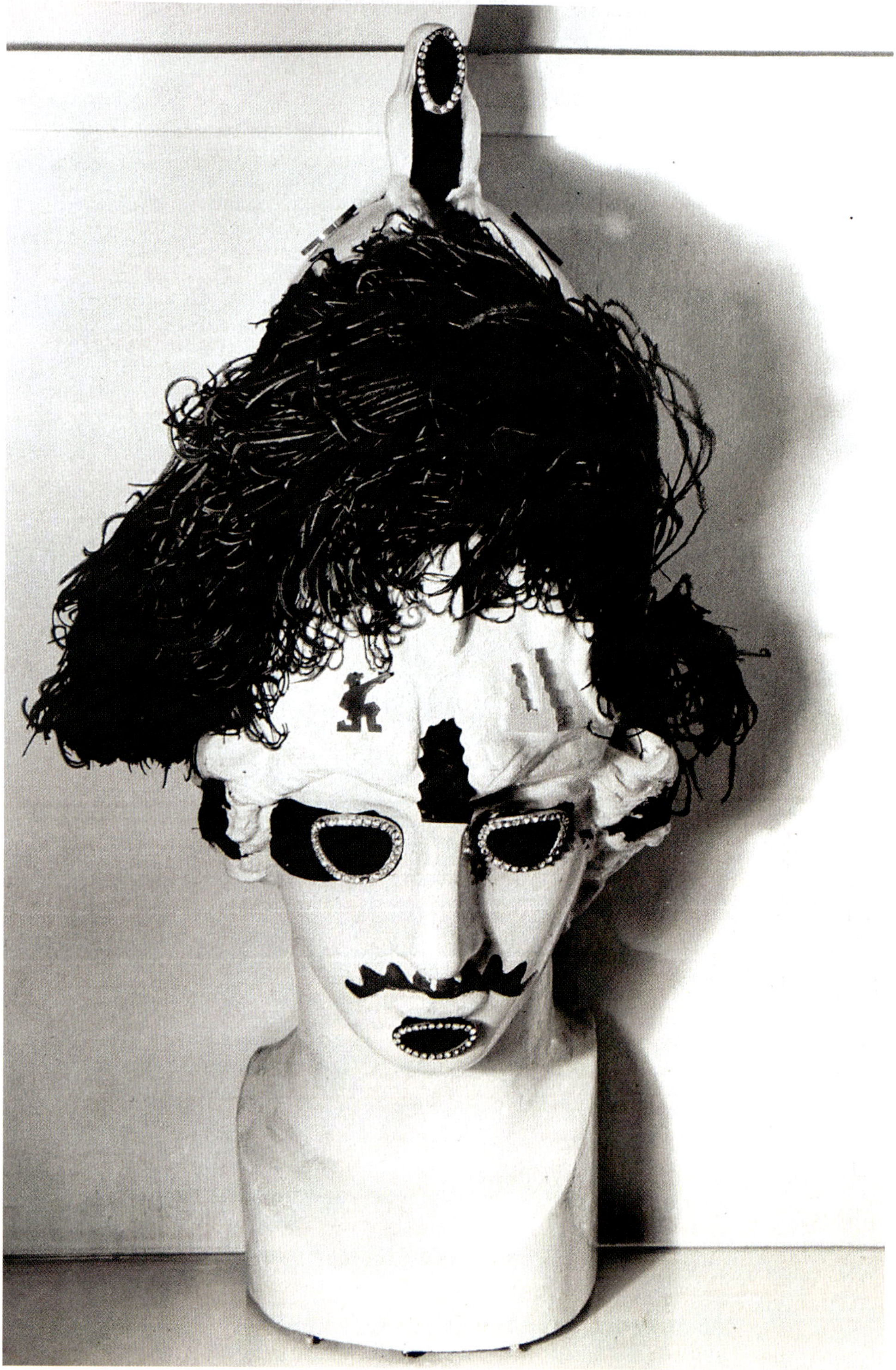

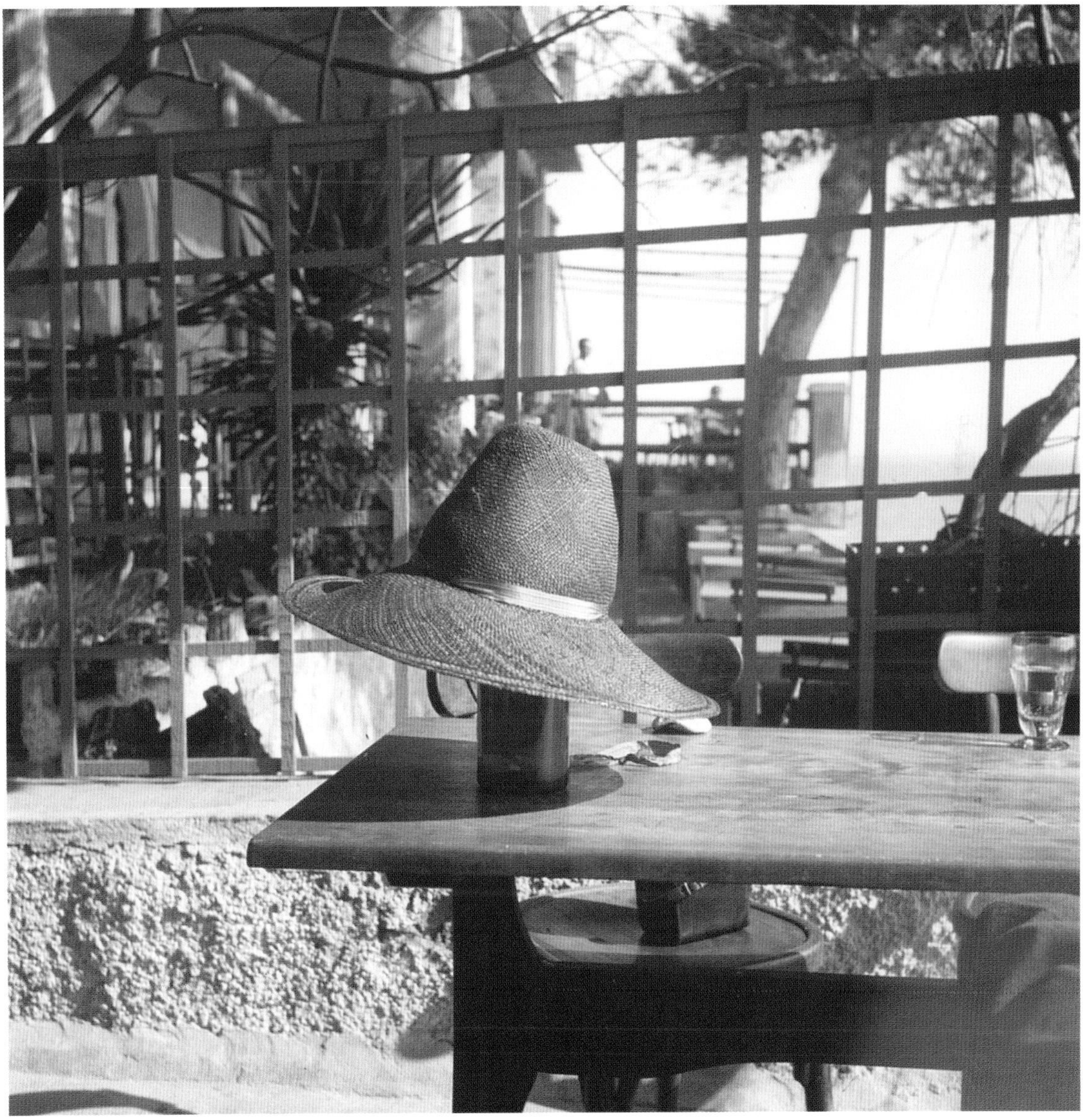

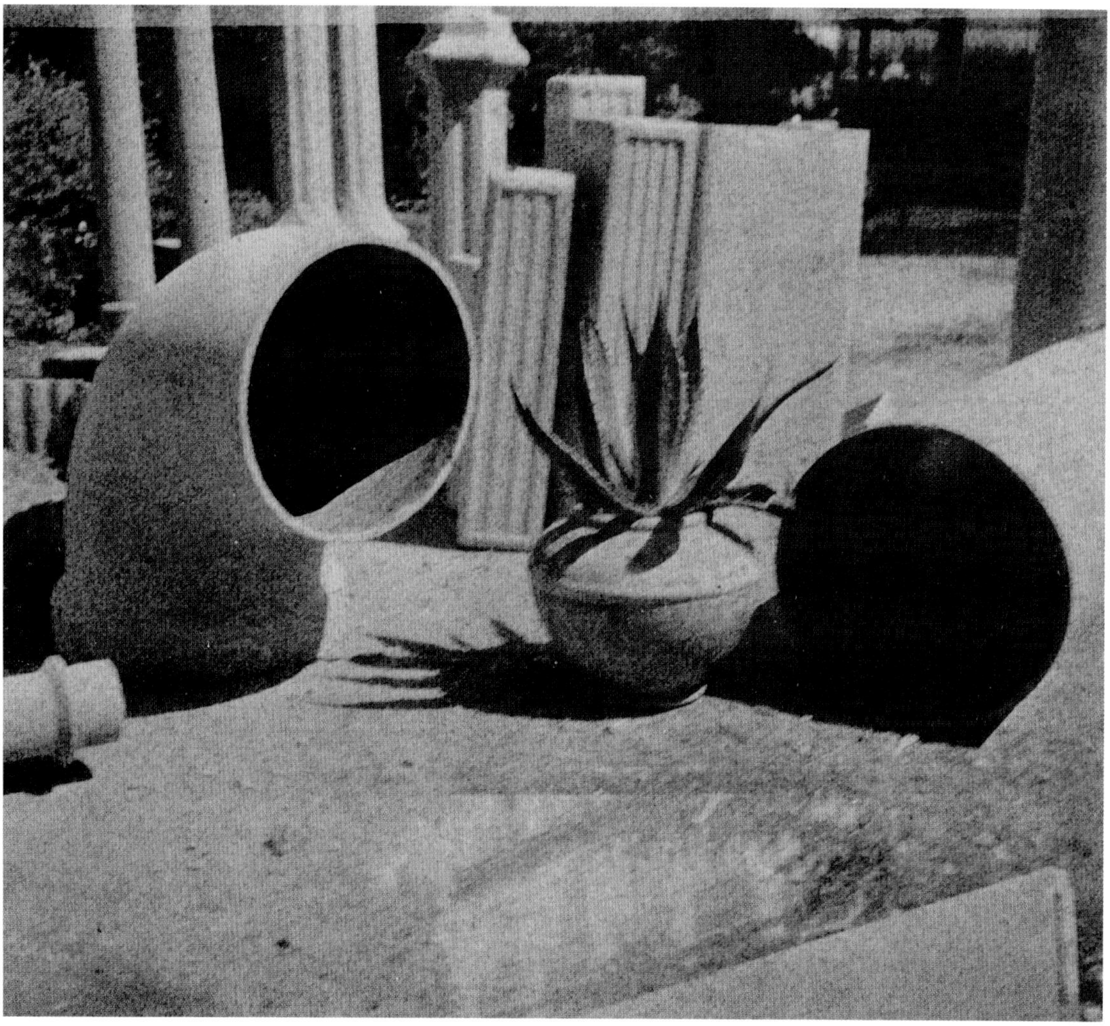

of them, Roland Penrose, Julian Trevelyan, Geoffrey Graham and James Cant, wore masks resembling Chamberlain (made by F. E. McWilliam), and made the Nazi salute all the way down the streets as a take-off of the destructively pacifist policy of the British government, making Chamberlain behave and present himself like a Nazi. Let us remember that the Daladier-Chamberlain-Hitler meeting was to take place on 29 September that year, followed by the 'Peace with honour' speech upon Chamberlain's return from Berchtesgaden.

The year 1938 was not a prolific one for Agar. Time was spent travelling a lot, to Somerset in the summer and to Belgium in the autumn. Two works from that year have to be mentioned. *The Reaper* (illus. 68), a gouache on paper with mixed media, is interesting in its beautifully balanced, almost Kandinskian rhythm which may be seen as that of the reaper's scythe, the leaf stuck on the paper reminding one of the way Agar is keen on introducing the vegetable world into her works and on balancing it with geometrical lines, an ominous piece when one thinks of what was to happen the year after. Indeed, the large, thick, black semi-circles hint at the ample movement of the mower's scythe – the Grim Reaper – echoed in the descending rhythm of the four dark circles from top right to bottom left – the death of the sun. *Butterfly Bride* (illus. 69) echoes *Precious Stones* and, more similarly, *Woman Reading*, by using the same negative head (negative in the photographic sense) glued on a page torn from an encyclopaedia, the page referring to dates from the history of British colonies. In the collage, two butterflies seem to indicate the flight of the profile's conscience away from the materialistic concern with politics and history into the dark territories of the mind, hidden from sight while a 'real' vegetal leaf introduces a pun by the contrast it establishes with the *printed* leaf. *Possessed* (illus. 70), is an assemblage on canvas whose painted shapes remind one of Aztec birds and in which the smiling face is actually made of a kind of ambivalent dancing puppet, its hands being its own eyes, its body its own nose and its open legs its own smiling mouth. Forms haunt forms, literally, 'possessing' him who looks and inevitably hesitates to define what he sees, also haunted by the serpentine rhythm of the band of colourful triangles at the back; the return of Quetzalcoatl?

In November 1938, an appeal had been sent to influential artists and art critics in Britain to form a committee, essentially through Roland Penrose's efforts and with the aid of the AIA, to raise funds for the immediate maintenance of the refugee artists from Central Europe and to find the employment and host families required before an entry visa would be issued to them. The committee mounted a United Front exhibition with a selection of three hundred works. In London alone it attracted forty thousand visitors. The idea was to demystify the concept of exhibitions and bring art to the

67 Eileen Agar, Industrial Still-life, *1937, photograph.*

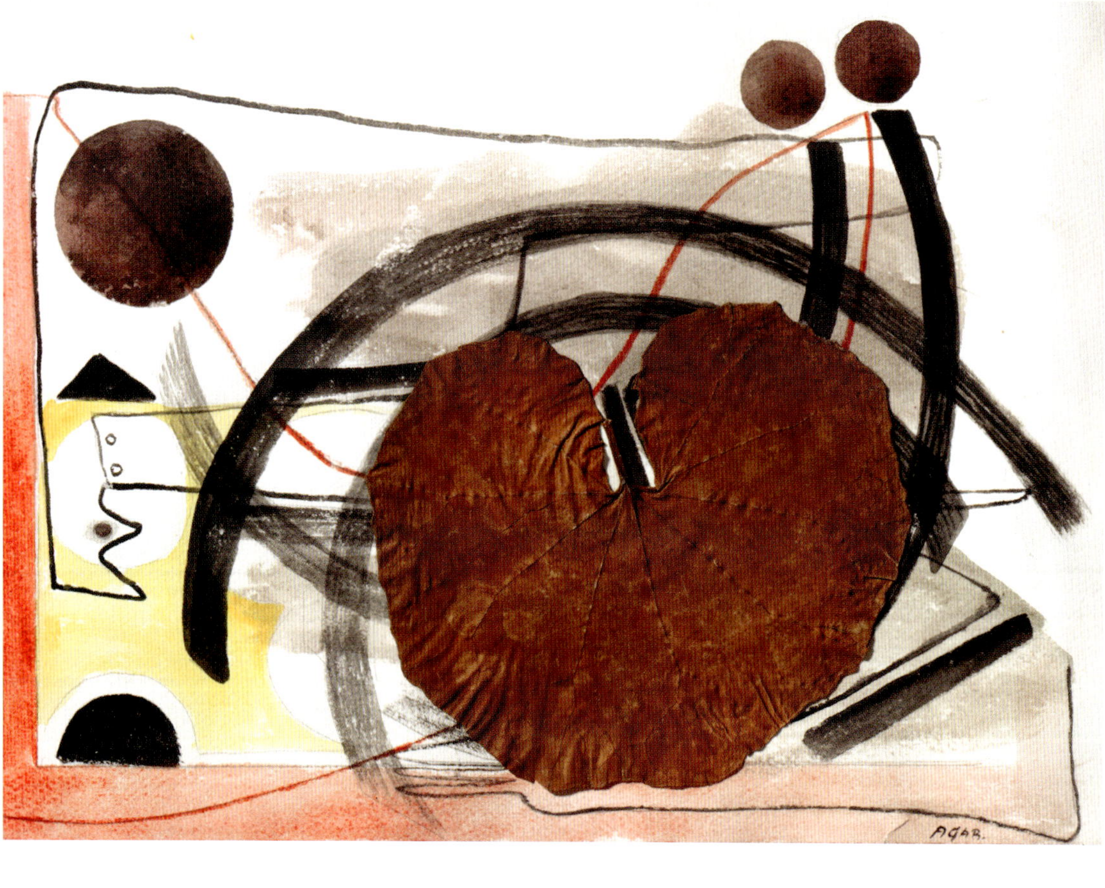
AGAR.

people. An unemployed worker was selected at random from the street to open the exhibition officially and the artists were required to be present as much as they could to discuss their work with the visitors. It was very eclectic: next to Duncan Grant, Graham Bell, William Coldstream and Ben Nicholson, there were Roland Penrose, F. E. McWilliam, Julian Trevelyan and Eileen Agar. The exhibition toured thirteen English towns, such as Bradford, York, Carlisle and Kidderminster, with great success.

In contrast to what appears as unity and group coherence, a violent debate broke out in June 1939 between E.L.T. Mesens, the leader of the Surrealist group, and Herbert Read, in which Agar had to take sides. Peggy Guggenheim, who had opened a gallery at 30 Cork Street next to the London Gallery, had approached Read and Kenneth Clark, the then director of the Tate Gallery, to help her create a Museum of Modern Art in London. Read was to be the director of the museum. Guggenheim and Mesens had collaborated on the shows they had each organized and Mesens's *London Bulletin* advertised the Guggenheim Jeune exhibitions in its pages. There had even been an intimate relationship between Guggenheim and Mesens. But this move made Mesens furious. He saw Guggenheim's initiative as a means of legislating over the world of art thanks to her immense wealth and for purely mercenary ends, and Read's acceptance as treason to him. In a letter dated August 1939 and written to Penrose, whom he feared would join Read and Guggenheim, Mesens summed up all the testimonies of support he had obtained from Surrealist friends. He wrote that 'Nash hated her [Peggy Guggenheim] and found Read a weakling', that Jennings considered 'any business which associates the names of Herbert Read and Kenneth Clark to be doomed from the start as a smutty dirty trick' and that Agar and Joseph Bard asked him: 'What are you waiting for to attack all these people in the *London Bulletin*?' Moral intransigence and intellectual rigour were Mesens's hallmark. Penrose accepted Mesens's arguments and welcomed the idea of the creation of a counter-museum with their own various collections and the contribution of many artist friends from overseas. The declaration of the Second World War put a stop to the feud.

In 1939, the fatal year for peace in Europe, Agar and Bard went to France, 'determined, "as she says", to have a last fling on the Mediterranean coast'. They rented a two-room flat outside Toulon, and eager as her eyes were to catch sight of any 'marvellous' object – in Breton's sense – she happened to find on one of their walks in the nearby Carqueiranne harbour fragments of a Greek amphora brought up from the seabed by a fisherman in one of his nets – something which Picasso would often experience when he stayed in Antibes after the war. The broken top part and the bottom part of the amphora, on

Opposite: 68 Eileen Agar, The Reaper, *1938, gouache, mixed media on paper.*

Overleaf left: 69 Eileen Agar, Butterfly Bride, *1938, gouache, collage and mixed media on paper.*

Overleaf right: 70 Eileen Agar, Possessed, *1938, assemblage on canvas.*

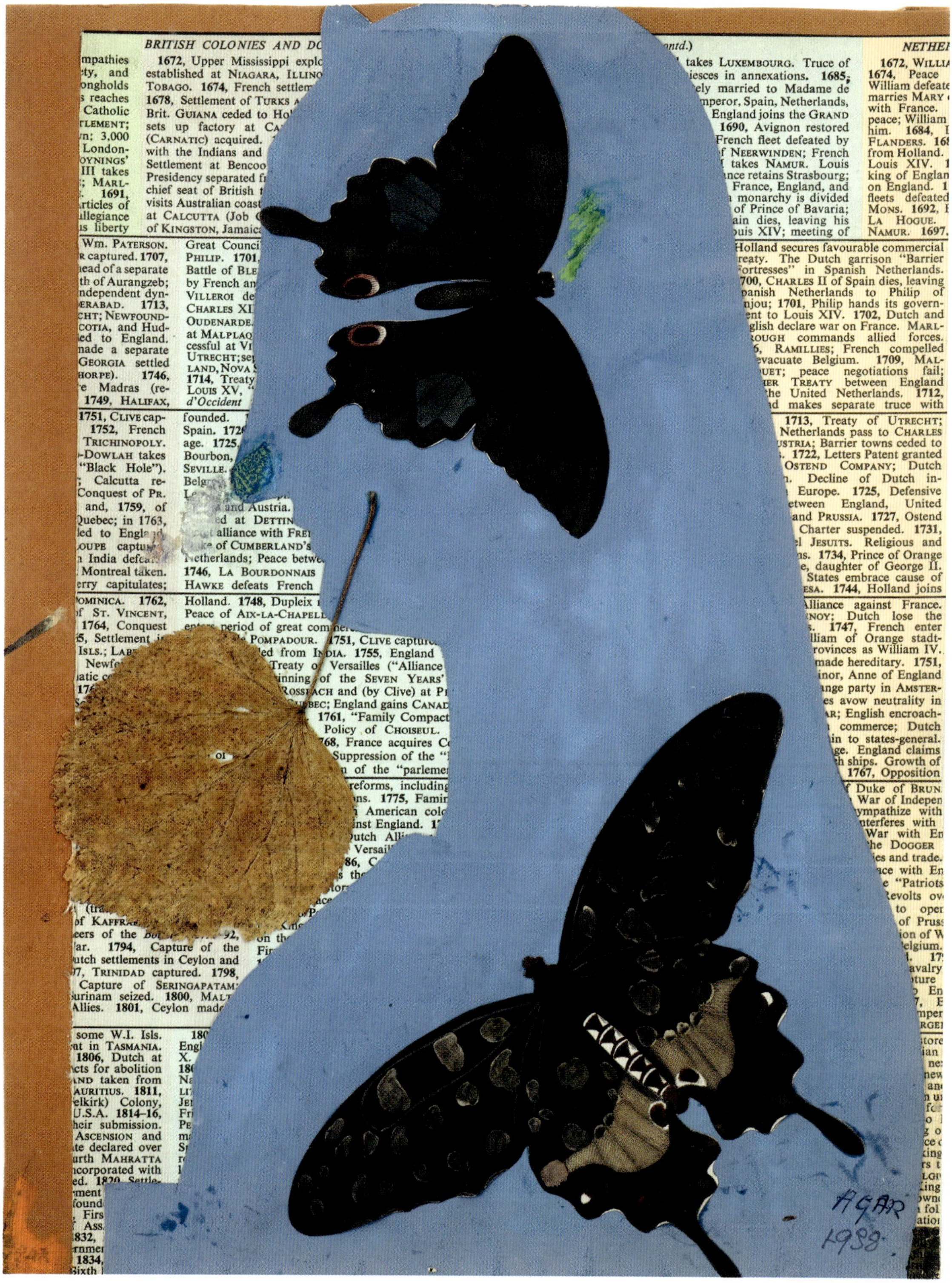
BRITISH COLONIES AND DO
NETHE
AGAR
1938

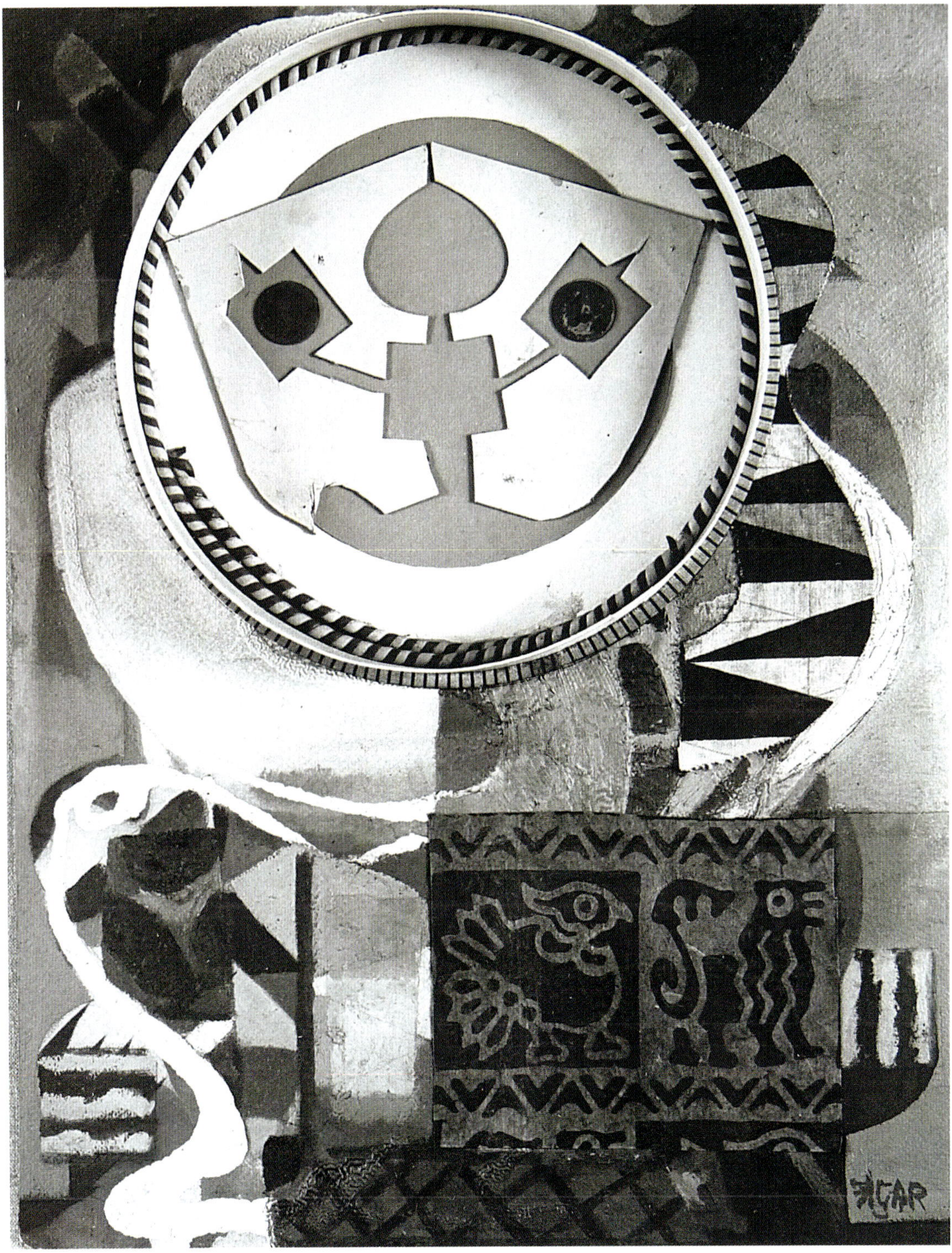

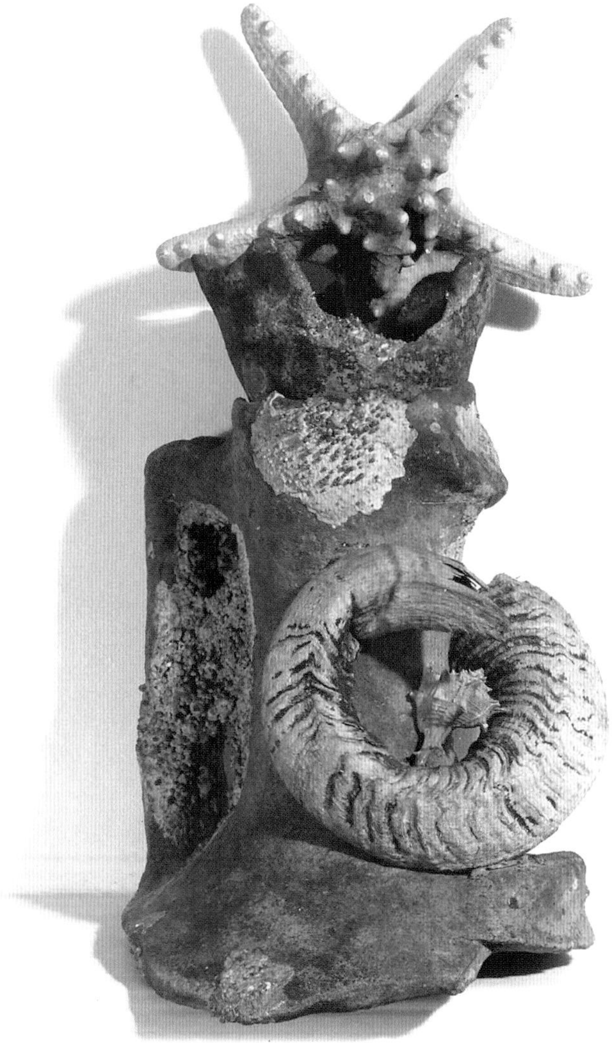

Right: 71 Eileen Agar, Marine Object, *1936, mixed media.*

Opposite: 72 Eileen Agar, Marine Collage, *1939, collage.*

Overleaf left: 73 Eileen Agar, 'secret writing' *photograph of rock in Port Cros, 1939.*

Overleaf right: 74 Eileen Agar, The Muse of Construction, *1939, oil on canvas.*

which there still clung tiny barnacles and sea-shells, were fitted together; a little later she added a shell and a dried starfish, simply poised at the top, so that all these parts could be separated when the object was moved or when one wanted to remove them playfully – a variable object, then, whose unity lies in the fact it can be played with. This assemblage, called *Marine Object* (illus. 71), exhibited at the Zwemmer Gallery in June 1940, was added to when Agar chanced upon a ram's horn, picked up when at Mougins, increasing the variability at work, evoking the marine and animal worlds beyond time, since the actual origin of the object is Greek. No final definitive unity can be achieved in a Surrealist object, especially as the viewer's eye is, in any case, never at rest.

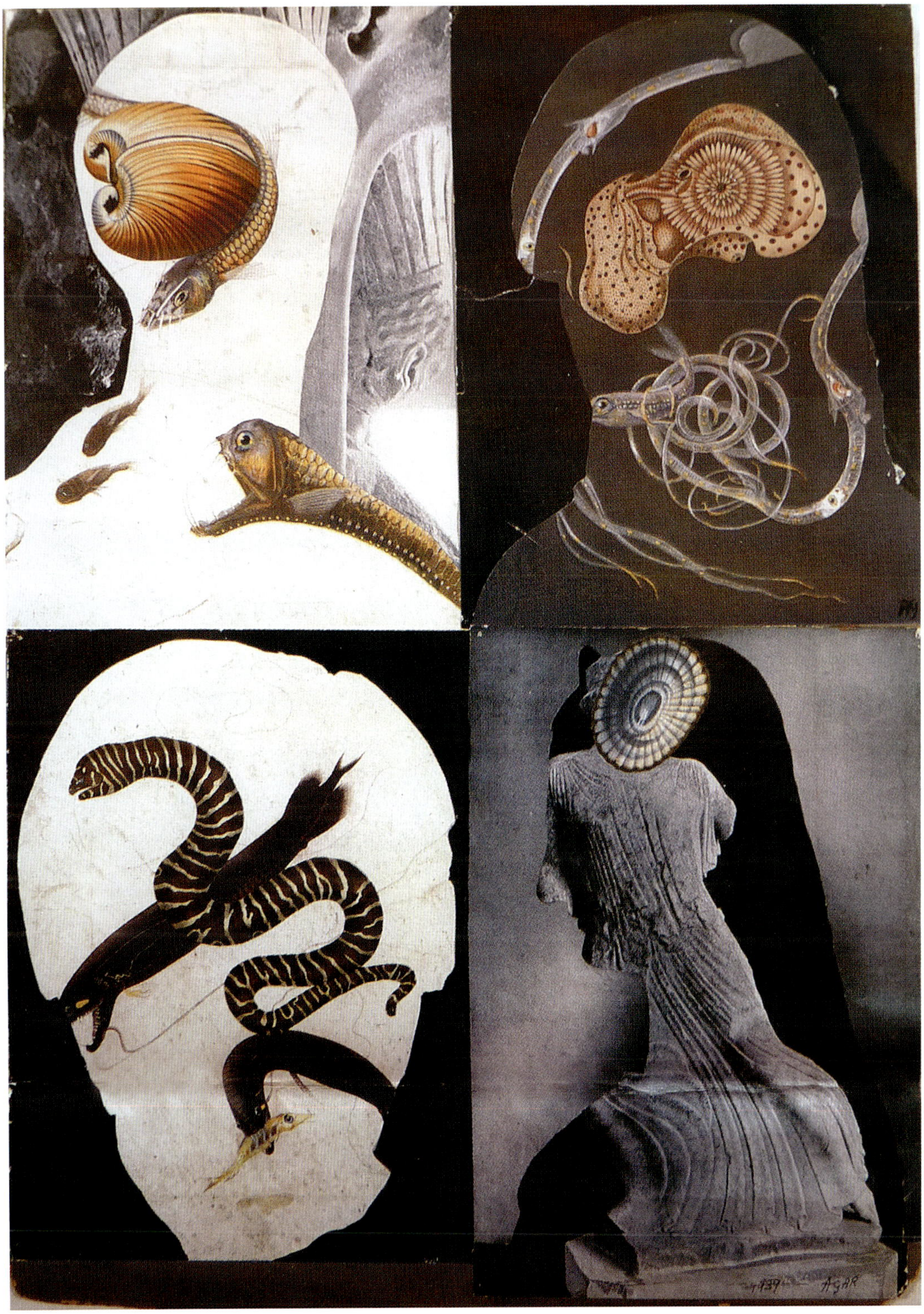

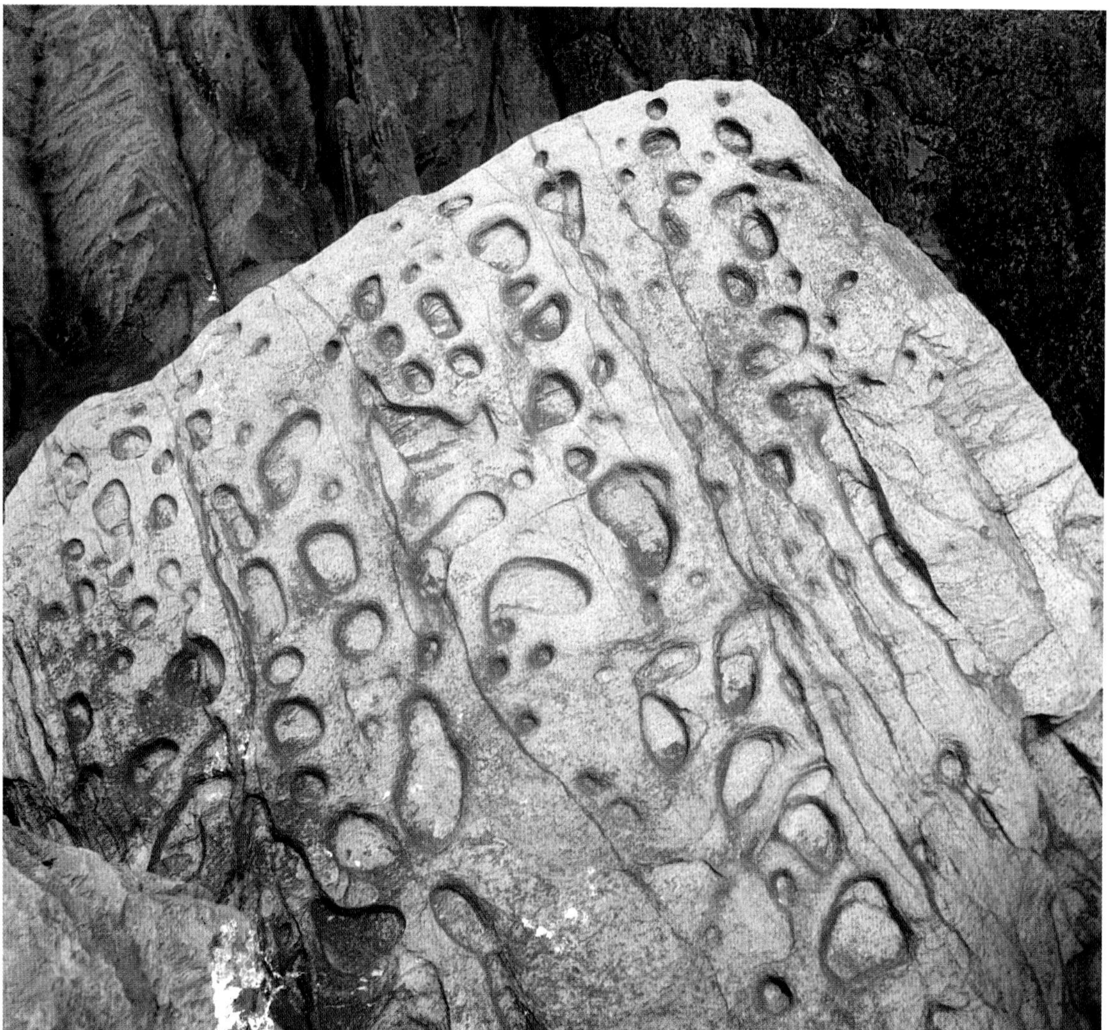

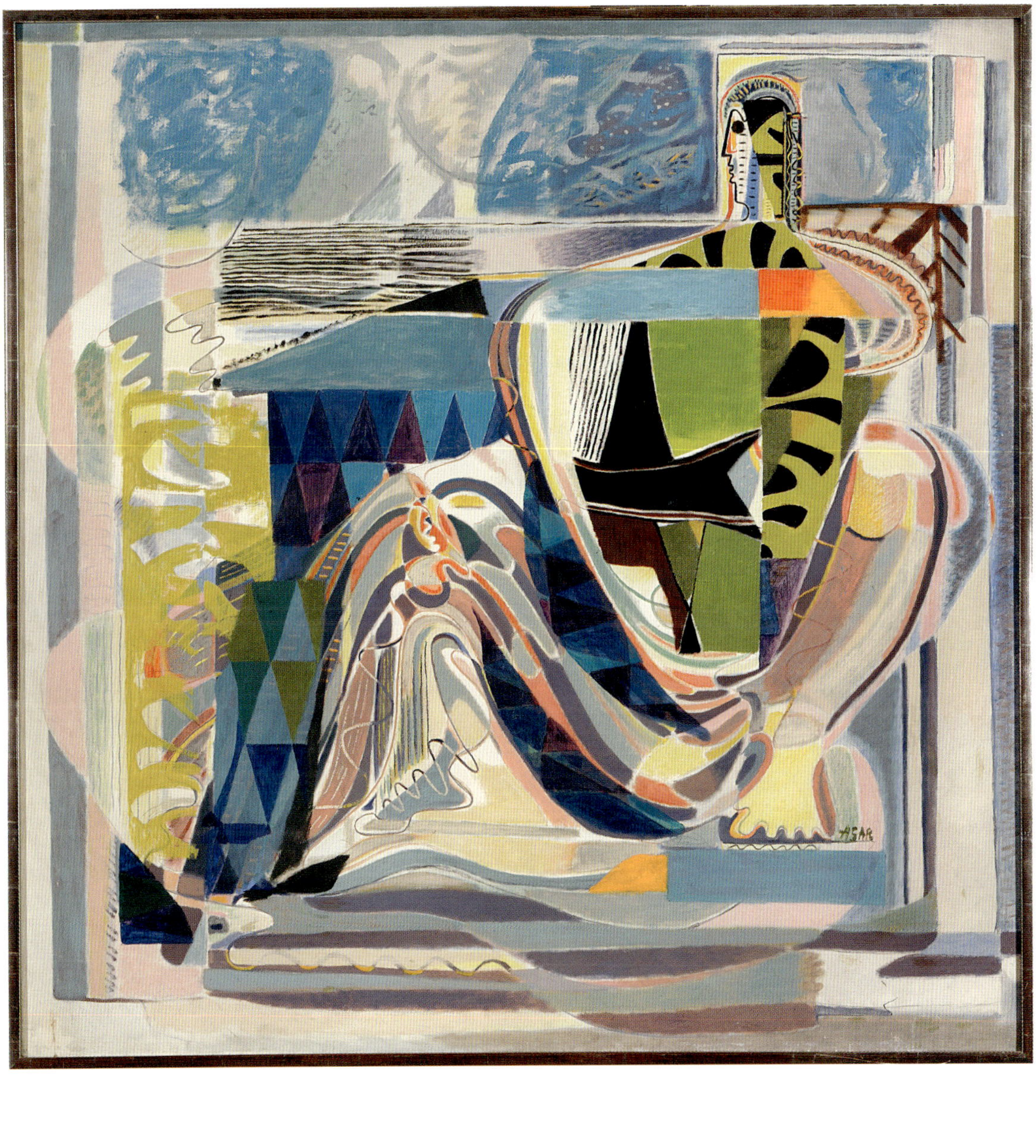
ASAR

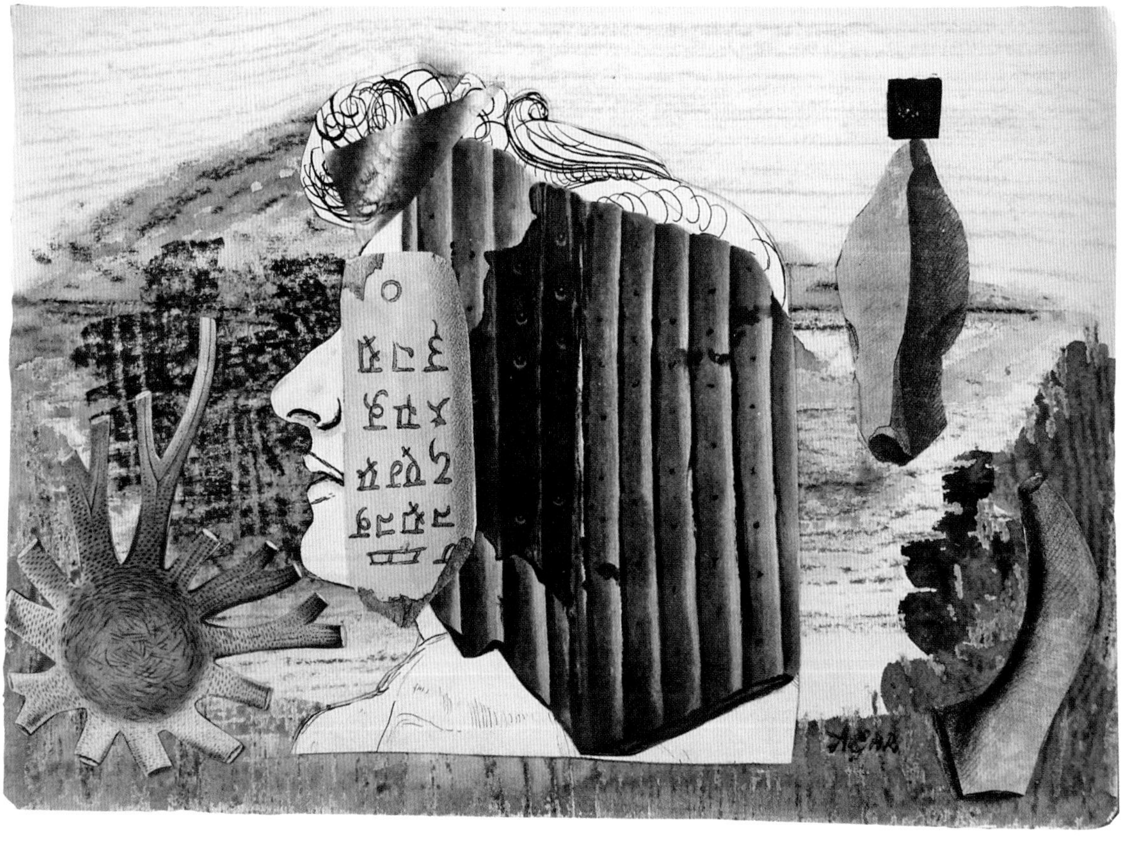
AGAR

Almost corresponding to *Marine Object*, *Marine Collage* (illus. 72) is based on the same principle as *Quadriga* and *The Autobiography of an Embryo*; that is, the deconstruction of the eye by making its visual process plural, multilayered and impossible to arrest. Divided into four equal squares, this juxtaposition of textbook plates of strange sea creatures with cropped illustrations of ancient statuary, leads the eye from one square to the next ceaselessly – with no beginning or end – taking in, as it proceeds, fishes, shells, water amoebae and swimming cells, lampreys and leeches. These animal forms are all 'included' in cut-out silhouette heads and profiles, 'heads made transparent as if they were revealed from the inside of a mind'. From the square at the top left to the last one at the bottom right, the head grows more and more realistic as if it were the result of a gradual surfacing from the depths of the mind, or the sea – the subconscious being traditionally compared to the ocean. The collage is thus a way to establish relationships but at different levels and depths, and following an endless operation of displacement and replacement, or rather a slipping from one identity to another, a move which eventually prioritizes what happens in-between, in the mind of the beholder.

At the end of July, frightened at the news of imminent war, Agar and Bard travelled back to England, after a last trip to the South of France, where she took photos of Port Cros, an island off Hyères. In London, they held a party for artist friends from Europe – refugees coming to find shelter in England, most of them Jewish artists, before leaving for the United States. For this last farewell dinner, Agar and Bard had devised a Surrealist table, topped by a 'pedal-operated fretsaw as a centrepiece hung with fruit and flowers and crackers', and covered with coloured dishes, which pleased their guests Walter Gropius, Marcel Breuer, László Moholy-Nagy and Oskar Kokoschka. These artists had arrived in England some six months before and it was to celebrate them that E.L.T. Mesens had organized at the London Gallery an ecumenical gathering of Surrealists, Constructivists and abstractionists in the flamboyant 'Living Art in England' exhibition. Mesens's idea was to draw the public's attention to the fate of art and democracy in Europe and highlight the presence of those refugee artists who couldn't but provide a leaven for British art. Works by Agar (*The Light Years*, and later *Battle Years*), Humphrey Jennings, Ithell Colquhoun, Grace Pailthorpe and Roland Penrose and others from the group were exhibited alongside works by Piet Mondrian, Oskar Kokoschka and Naum Gabo, as a testimony to the living progressive forces which resisted fascism and denounced, again, London's complacent atmosphere. The presence of Surrealists next to abstractionists must have filled Agar with joy and hope. Over the following months, in February and March, she participated in the United Front exhibition at the Whitechapel Gallery under the theme

75 Eileen Agar, Collage of Pamela Travers, *1939, watercolour and collage.*

'For Peace, Democracy and Cultural Development' – an unusual move for her, indicative of her state of mind. The show, organized under the aegis of the Marxist-inspired AIA, had selected three hundred works and attracted over forty thousand visitors, a kind of gathering call to all artists – realist or Surrealist. Agar exhibited with Henry Moore, Roland Penrose, Julian Trevelyan and F. E. McWilliam. The exhibition toured thirteen English cities until autumn 1940. In Bradford alone, 32,500 visitors are said to have attended.

However, we do know that all these efforts and campaigning could in no way stop the storm that was to strike Europe, and the war broke out on 3 September 1939. In her determined way, Agar still produced quite a few very important works. One of them is almost a self-portrait, or at least has an autobiographical flavour. It is entitled *The Muse of Construction* (illus. 74), a kind of assessment of her own techniques and of her fascination with the generation of forms and the consequent assault on the stability of given reality. On the whole, the painting sums up her main aesthetic preoccupations. It is a hymn to the birth of the image. Triangles, lozenges and rectangles, along with human forms – a leg, a foot, a face – emerge from an entanglement of lines and colours, making the observer witness the birth of a hieratic figure out of angular and fluid rhythms, a goddess of forms and colours; the initial title was *The Urn Goddess*, a reference to the womb-like, feminine image of woman often used by Agar. As the eye moves from the centre outwards, more and more vivid and light colours are liberated in a profusion which fecundates, so to speak, the substitution of linearity for curves, so that no real unity, no totality, can be established. All this is reinforced by the egg-like shape of the body, an egg held as in a kind of crucible, another analogy of the womb, that of the seated figure. The Muse, from under the semblance of ample robes, liberates that primeval energy, a diffuse, centreless, self-generating energy, which, from the spring of Helicon, brings and welds together the universe of forms and the universe of colours. In her autobiography, Agar comments on her painting:

> When I called the painting *The Muse of Construction*, I wanted to emphasize the fact that although the word construction is usually associated with building, architecture and things mechanical, I wished to associate it with the human form which is a marvellous construction, built and assembled over millions of years, adaptable and flexible. Although its skeleton is worn inside and the software outside, it goes through many changes and holds a lot of secrets in its trunk. At one time I thought of calling the painting the 'Urn Goddess' as I have always been interested in the shape of a vessel but somehow *The Muse of Construction* seemed more mysterious and poetic.

76 Eileen Agar, The Garden, *1939, gouache and pencil on paper.*

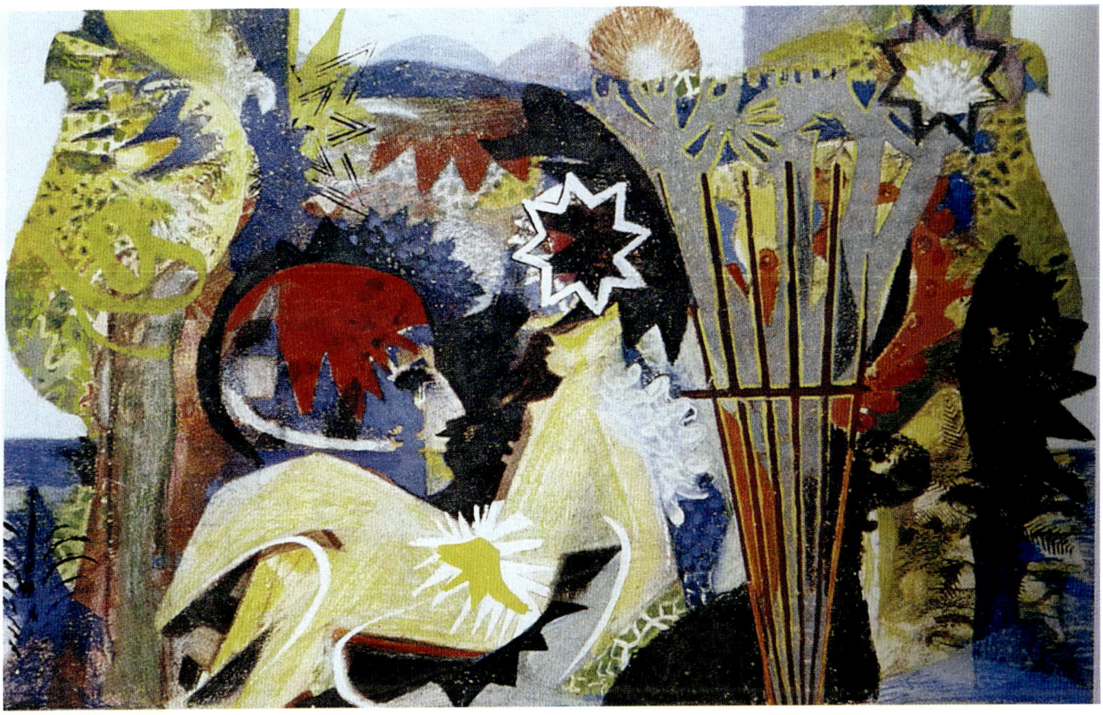

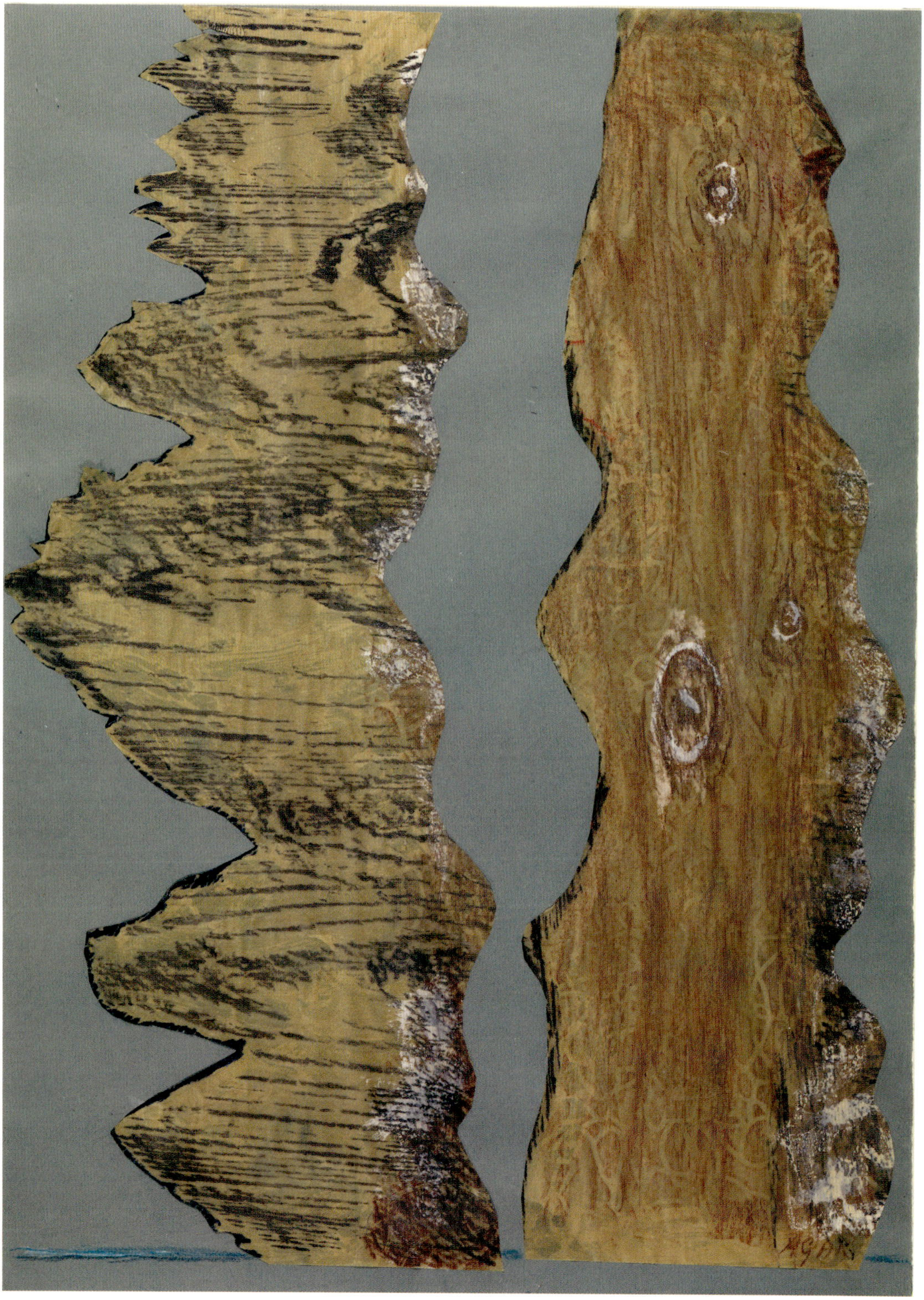

The same kind of construction endowed with a plurality of meanings is found in *Collage of Pamela Travers* (illus. 75), a watercolour and collage celebrating one of Agar's friends, the famous author of *Mary Poppins*, who had struck up an acquaintance with Agar especially through her interest in myth and magic. From left to right, the various elements – a watercolour, a photograph, a pencil drawing and a collage – all refer back to a kind of archaic background, blending past and present, ancient writing and geological items. Pamela Travers's personality is thus opened up and condensed and this juxtaposition of forms – a profile, hieroglyphics, an anatomical body part, a pipe of Pan, a flint stone and a fossilized horn – reveals the play of references which may define her personality and requires, in its turn, the observers' attempt to solve the enigma it harbours, an enigma hinted at and emblematized by the apparently runic signs in the middle.

A more playful and serene collage of this period is *Fish Circus* (see cover), a definitely musical composition on account of the many almost symmetrically arranged echoes of forms. Around a starfish pinned at the very centre, flanked with its shadow, there revolve two round sole-like fish, a coral branch and two chessboard-like plaques, one horizontal and the other vertical, linked by more or less identical grids, to get a clockwise movement started. Nothing is telescoped as in many of her other collages, but all items create a circular play on round and fluid and geometrical forms, as in a number performed in a circus ring.

The Lotus Eater is based on the contrast between the objects drawn in ink which lie behind the Oceanian-like mask. More than a reference to Tennyson's *The Lotus Eaters*, it is, as Agar herself pointed out in a note written for the National Scottish Gallery of Modern Art in Edinburgh (which acquired the collage), the picture of one of those lotophagi, who, by absorbing the lotus fruit, would be able to 'forget his own country and desire to live in a land of his own choosing'. The objects behind the mask are about to be abandoned when the owner of the demented face enters his other world. Seeing another of her collages of the same period, one is tempted to ask the question: is this other world the one she lavishly painted in *The Garden* (illus. 76)? A colourful vegetable forest-world haunted by human faces, bodies and stars, a festival of bright colours, night and day brought together as we read from left to right, almost reliving what the Garden of Eden could have imaginatively been. Here Agar almost reaches a mythical dimension in her approach of a pristine vision of an unadulterated nature and expresses her belief in the permanently precious value of natural growth, and a hope beyond reason at a time when the war was becoming a serious threat.

77 Eileen Agar, Philemon and Baucis, *1939, collage and frottage on paper.*

Evidence of this profound belief in the timeless operation of the imagination is also found in the collage *Philemon and Baucis* (illus. 77), in which the use of frottage to represent the two famous lovers is appropriate, since the impression of a wooden surface which it gives fits in perfectly with Ovid's story. Ovid, in his *Metamorphoses*, recounts how the faithful old Phrygian couple gave shelter in their humble cabin to Mercury and Jupiter who had been refused hospitality everywhere else. When the gods departed, their cabin was turned into a temple in which they lived and worshipped until they died. Then they were transformed into a linden and an oak growing side by side and interlacing their foliage – the archetypal blending of the vegetable and the human, which Surrealism retrieves from the primitive mind as a way to fuse categories, and causes a metamorphosis to work in our eyes and, thus, in our minds. Similarly, the story is retrieved from, and made to escape, time, and to take on a universal value which is no longer religious. As in *Philemon and Baucis*, a photograph from that year, of a rock in Port-Cros (illus. 73), a small harbour on the Mediterranean coast, confronts the viewer with the manifold forms given by the joint workings of chance and nature. As the subtitle to the photo says, nature has spelt out a mysterious 'secret writing', reminding us of immemorial runic inscriptions and the timeless energy of nature's own cryptic message.

In *Head and Bird* (illus. 78), the famous Agar profile – the shadow of Being, the ghost of Life, the matrix of the Imagination – functions as a *tabula rasa*, almost 'abstracted' from time and from itself, in order to liberate what it holds and thus offer itself to new inscriptions arising from its deep inner life and subconscious. These are emblematized by the *real* bird flying towards it from the world outside, the symbol of the flight of the Muse-like imagination now returning, an aerial being which contrasts with the earthly materiality of the human body and yet embodies its secret wishes. The leaves flying around tell of the perennial presence of nature, so much so that they pervade the figure itself – obviously cut out from some decorated paper. Here again the limit between inside and outside is erased and our eyes pass from one to the other with irresistible de-categorizing fluidity – a most delicate poetical statement which turns the face, if one may dare to say, into a place of *sur-facing*.

Following the declaration of war on 3 September, Agar brought together the different threads she had been weaving all those years: the concept of doubleness, the reference to Greek mythology, the dislocation of forms, the use of various surfaces, materials and techniques and the refusal to leave the eye at rest. This is emphasized by *Bacchus and Ariadne* (illus. 79), a quite original work from 1939. The title refers to Ovid and Catullus' story of the rape of Ariadne by Bacchus, the story of the loss of civilized manners induced by drunkenness and the subsequent rowdy violence, a theme not

78 Eileen Agar, Head and Bird, *1939, collage on paper.*

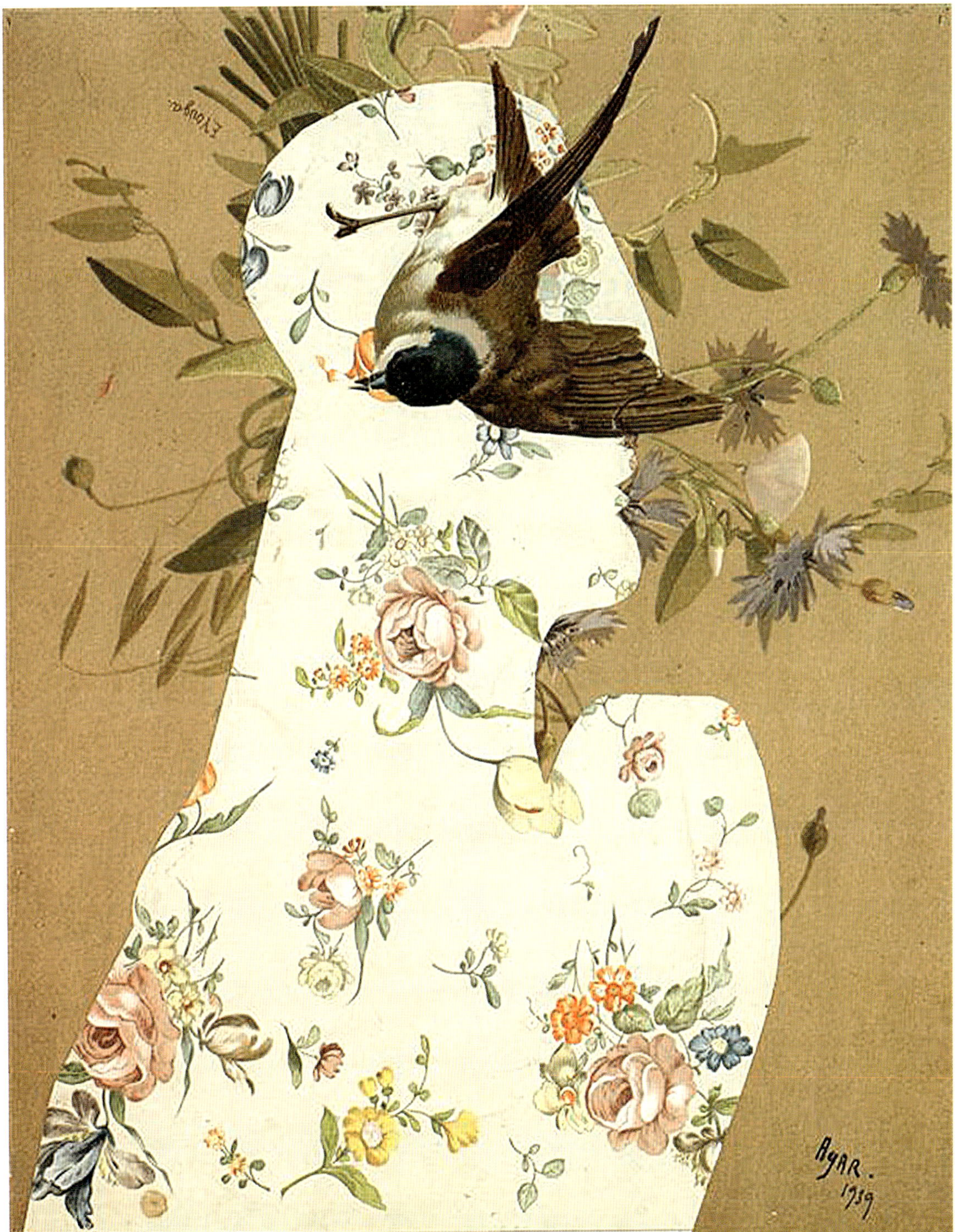
AGAR.
1939

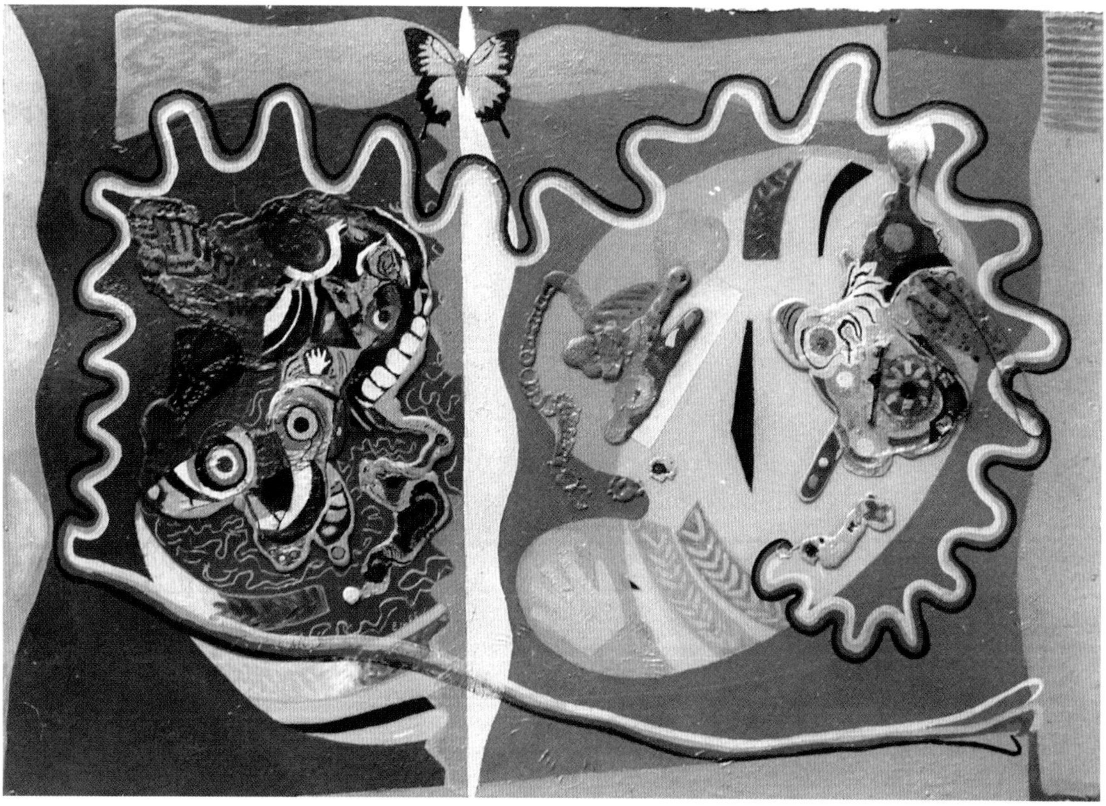

altogether inappropriate at the time. The work is divided into two parts, symmetrically arranged, one a gathering of bodily fragments – eyes, mouth, teeth and nose forming a face – the other a splintering of the facial features, both linked by a kind of umbilical cord which reinforces, by contrast, the destructive violence at work. The support is a sheet of tin, and various paints and materials cover it, including plaster and molten lead. Commenting on the work, Agar declared:

> I covered parts of a tin tray with melted lead, which I had heated easily over a small burner, and let the fluid form its own shapes. I watched, fascinated, but when it had cooled, and fixed itself, I began to criticize the result, and decided that I should improve upon it. I juxtaposed various disjointed images with the lead shapes, using paint and plaster to try to catch some of the atmosphere of those years. A face, an eye and some teeth, hands and a sword, a small skull and a star. The end result was a mixture I found satisfying.

The process here is very clear and typically Surrealist: starting with automatism, as with decalcomania or automatic drawing – the chance shapes of molten lead – the artist then rebalances and controls it with the intervention of intuition, emotion and the intellect in order to create a whole universe to be deciphered at the cost of a 'battle' with oneself – never forget the part which has to be played by the viewer in Surrealism. It is a work which significantly underscores the violence and irrationality of the time together with the corresponding hope in the possibilities of rational control which prevailed in 1939. Indeed, the disintegration of traditional means and media is reinforced by the different titles which it bore. After the mythological reference it had as its first title, it was retitled *The Light Years* when it was exhibited in January 1939 at the 'Living Art in England' exhibition at the London Gallery – a rather daring understatement. Then it was given another title when it was exhibited at the Zwemmer Gallery's 'Surrealism Today' exhibition in June 1940, when the war had already been going on for about seven months, and that title was *Painting Battle Cry/Bullet-proof Painting*, a rather sarcastic expression of the resistance of art and premonitory of the September and October blitz, a prophecy made by the same painting when it was titled *Bacchus and Ariadne*. The butterfly, the only glimpse of hope and purity, is both the materialization of a resisting mind and, possibly, a reference to the metamorphosis of Ariadne into a constellation, two poetical agents of an other wished-for world.

79 Eileen Agar, Bacchus and Ariadne/ The Light Years/ Bullet-proof Painting, *1939, sheet of tin, plaster, molten lead, various paints.*

4 Welcoming the eternal return of magic, 1940–53

'The next moment soldiers came running through the wood, at first in twos and threes . . . and at last in such crowds that they seemed to fill the whole forest . . . The confusion got worse at every moment and Alice was very glad to get out of the wood into an open place.'

Lewis Carroll, *Through the Looking-Glass, and What Alice Found There* (1871)

At the inception of the war, every British citizen was required to do his or her duty and Agar abided by this call to national efforts. After the first attacks on London by the Germans, she and Joseph Bard thought it was the best time to get married, as a way to affirm love in the face of the destructive forces around, holding a party at her Chelsea flat and honeymooning in a Sussex cottage lent to them by Pamela Travers. Her new patriotic activities, obviously, meant reducing her artistic work. Through a friend, she was enlisted as a canteen assistant in Savile Row, 'peeling potatoes, scrubbing floors, washing up . . . pushing trolleys' and serving dishes, which allowed her to stay in London rather than being 'called up and sent to drills in the countryside'. Like most people, she served as a fire watcher on night duty while Bard served as an air raid warden. Some of the other Surrealists, like Roland Penrose, Julian Trevelyan, John Buckland Wright and Stanley William Hayter, served in the Camouflage Research Unit created by Penrose and Hayter, the premises of the Unit being the house of the architect Ernö Goldfinger, a great Surrealist sympathizer who had participated in the 1937 and 1938 AIA exhibitions along with the Surrealist group, and whose portrait Agar had drawn in 1938. The unit taught camouflage techniques and built fake plaster trees, dummies in rubber tanks, pillboxes camouflaged as houses-on-wheels, houses in ruins, sham haystacks, sham thatched cottages and sham wayside cafés to make the German planes erroneously believe there was activity on the ground when it actually took place elsewhere. When the Blitz hit London in December 1940, all the documents and paintings which the London Gallery had moved to, and stored in, the buildings of Van Oppen & Co. on the Thameside, were destroyed by the bombs: twenty-five Magrittes, forty Ernsts, six Delvaux and

80, 81 Catalogue for the Zwemmer Gallery 'Surrealism Today' exhibition, 1940, and postcards of the group.

two Brauners, among others, went up in flames, not to mention archives, books and documents.

Before the group was, by force, disbanded, E.L.T. Mesens, who had by then received a permanent permit to stay in England, where he worked for the Belgian services of the BBC, had the time to rally the English Surrealists at a meeting at the Barcelona Restaurant in Beak Street. On Thursday 11 April 1940, Mesens insisted on dispelling any ideological confusion by laying down a number of guidelines to which everyone had to swear. Among these, he asked the Surrealists to pledge not to exhibit with other groups, not to participate in non-Surrealist reviews and to reiterate their adherence to the proletarian revolution. Agar – just like Henry Moore – could not accept all the recommendations since she regularly exhibited with the London Group. As a consequence, she was 'suspended' for a while. But she was accepted back soon after – just like Herbert Read. Two months later, on 13 June, Mesens organized the 'Surrealism Today' exhibition at the Zwemmer Gallery in an attempt to revitalize the group (illus. 80–82). Eighteen British Surrealists and seven 'fellow travellers' – refugees from France like Hayter, Gordon Onslow Ford and Esteban Francés – displayed their works for three weeks. The gallery window had been designed by Agar and Penrose. Agar had found an armchair in an antique shop in Chelsea, which she upholstered into a fat 'Negro' woman with her wide lap forming the seat, her white cuffed hands the arms, her grinning face surmounting the back. Next to her, a miniature bed with rumpled sheets was transfixed with a dagger. Apart from *Battle Years*, Agar also showed three oil paintings, *Seraglio* (1938), *Romeo and Juliet* (1940) and *Double Vision* (1940), and a couple of objects. Few were the critics who realized then how 'the surrealists instinctively sensed whither the European society in which they lived was tending', as an article in *The Studio* pointed out, but more just did not see the point of such art – that culture could only be a violent cry of protest then – and found it shocking in such emotional times. But the resilience of the movement was further revealed in the Surrealist exhibitions which Mesens and Penrose organized at the Oxford University Art Society, in the collaboration they had started with Dartington

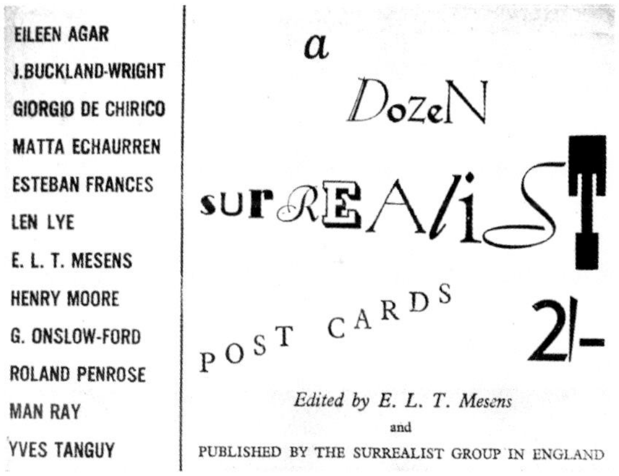

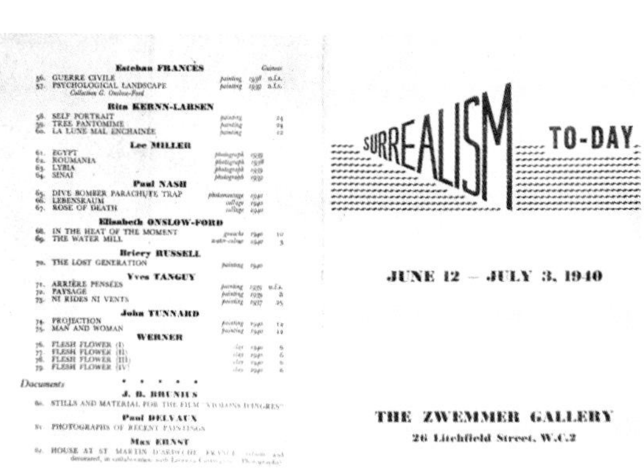

College in South Devon, and in the lectures he and Penrose delivered in Birmingham and Hereford in the last week of July 1940.

It was around that time that, having no news of *The Angel of Anarchy* which had been lent to Amsterdam for the Galerie Robert 1938 'International Exhibition of Surrealism' and got lost on the way back, Agar decided to make another one which would bear the same title. This is how she recounts the way she did it in a note dated 18 May 1986 to the Tate Gallery when they acquired the object:

> So, in 1940, I started covering the second plaster head. This one, I decided, should be totally different, more astonishing, powerful (and forgetting about a portrait) more malign. Although the same base it has ostrich feathers for the hair, a Chinese silk blindfold, a piece of bark cloth round the neck and African beads at the back of the head, as well as occasional osprey feathers and a diamanté nose.

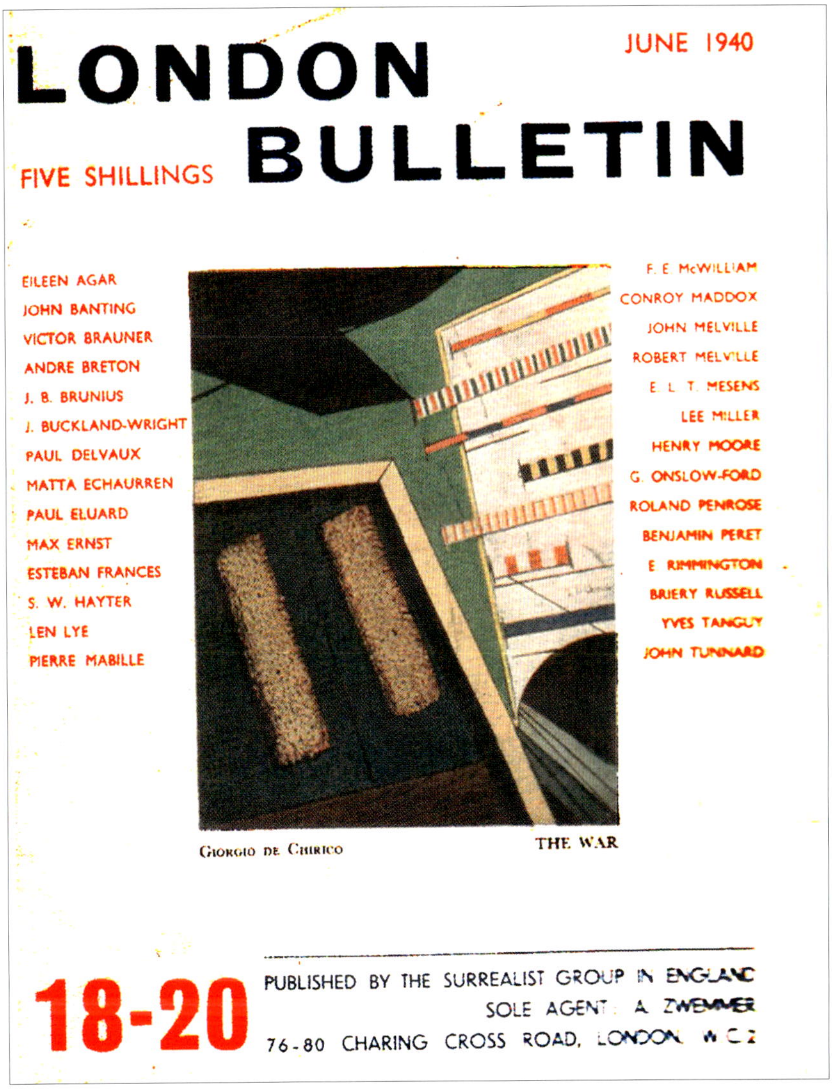

Opposite: 82 Window of the Zwemmer Gallery during the 'Surrealism Today' exhibition, June 1940.

Left: 83 Cover of London Bulletin, *18–20, 1940, photograph.*

Overleaf left: 84 Eileen Agar, Angel of Anarchy, *1936 (re-made 1940), plaster cast with mixed media.*

Overleaf right: 85 Eileen Agar, Object Lesson, *1940, construction with painting of woman's head, basket, lay figure and champagne cork.*

The process of accretion here reaches a kind of climax, opening itself to infinite additions.

In June 1940, Mesens's *London Bulletin* published a triple issue (illus. 83), no doubt the outcome of Mesens's rallying call at the Barcelona Restaurant. It printed a declaration against Hitler's ideology, poems translated from French Surrealists, and articles and reproduced works by eighteen artists, making it a kind of operational platform for further Surrealist activity. Simultaneously, a series of twenty Surrealist postcards were published, one of them by Agar. There was the reproduction too of one of her collages entitled *Object Lesson* (illus. 85), which could be

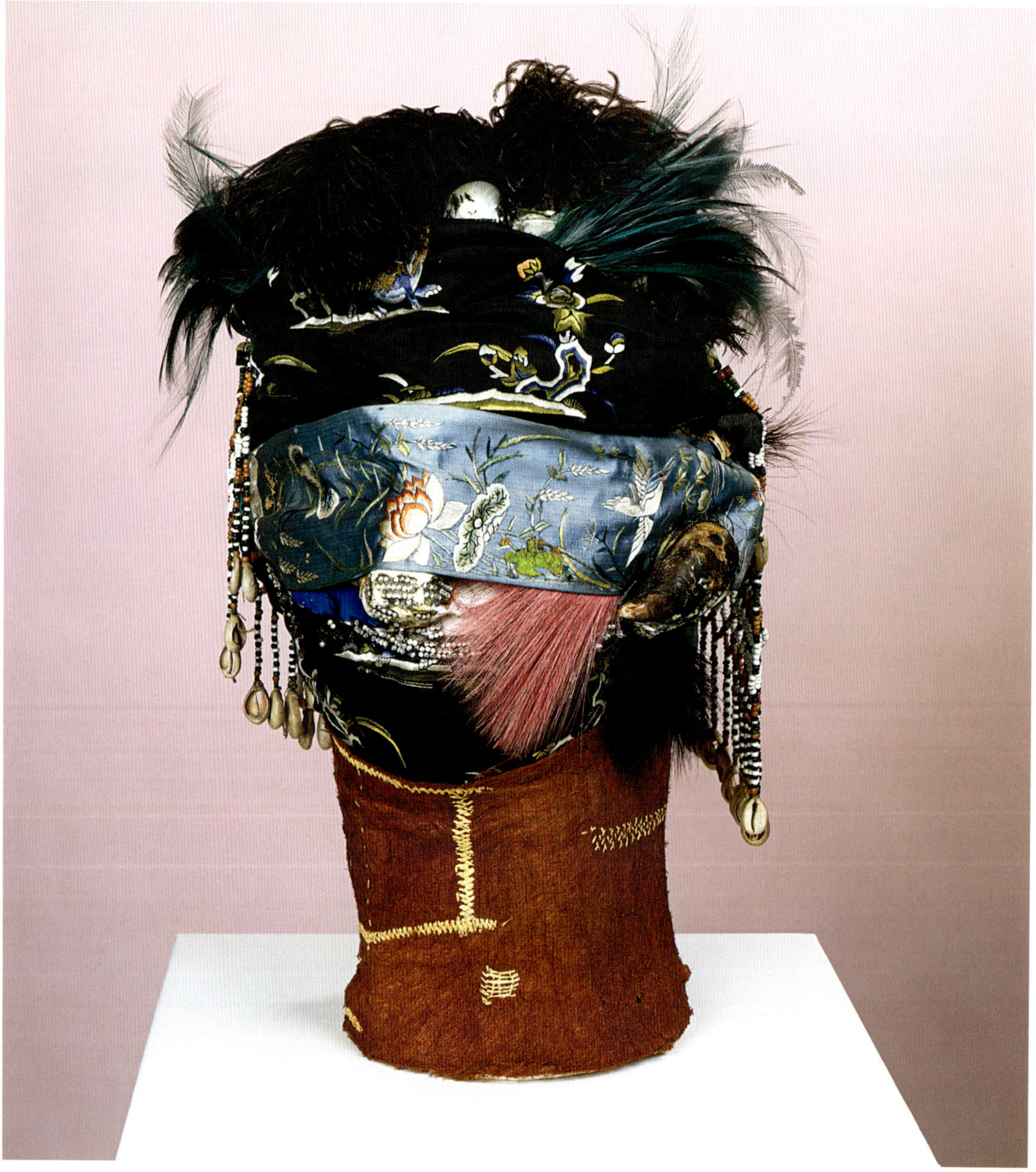

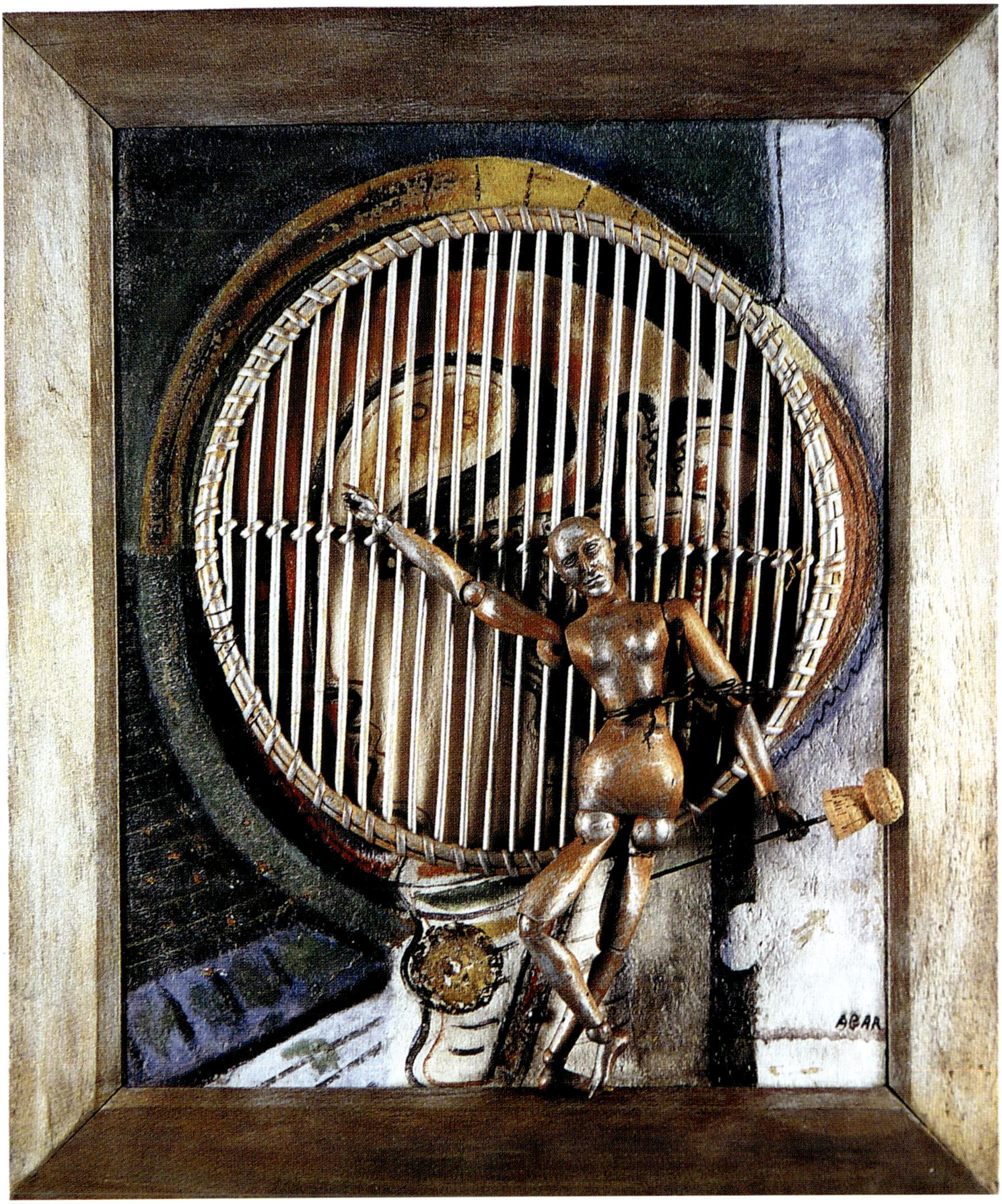
ABAR

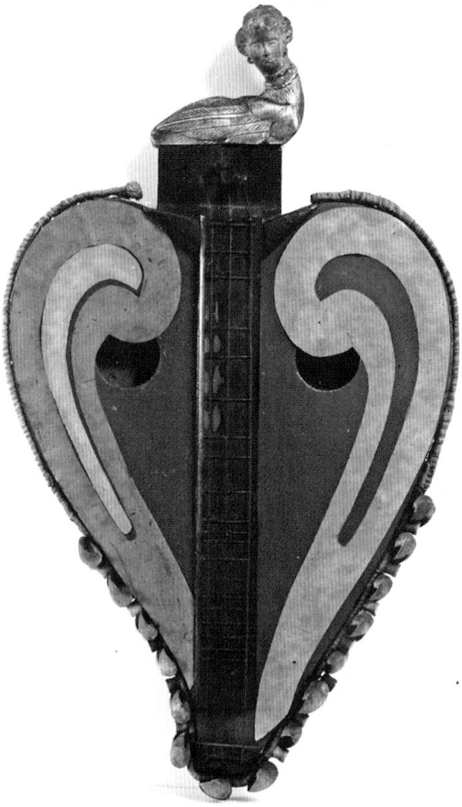

seen to illustrate Conroy Maddox's seminal article on the object, printed next to it. It was a construction made up of a lay figure, a cane platter for handing cheese or bread around, a champagne cork stuck at the end of a brush – the cork given to her by Picasso in Mougins back in 1937 – and the painting of a woman's head. Clearly, the lesson given here is that the manipulation of objects is hardly separable from the manipulation of man. The cane platter looks like the globe, or a clock, whose hands are the figure's arms, and behind its 'bars', the woman appears to be imprisoned. Has the world of objects turned against us? A crucial question in 1940.

Contrasting with this somewhat bleak statement, the object she made that year, *The Muse Listening* (illus. 86), testifies to both the hope and the expectancy the artist feels in spite of the situation. The shape of a lyre – Apollo's instrument played to the nine Muses – soon proves to be a heart, a musical heart with its two sides decorated with clefs and its top surmounted by an object, the head of a woman on the body of a bird, like the figurehead at the prow of an imaginary ship. Édouard Jaguer, the leader of the Phases group in France and the organizer of the 1982 'Children of Alice' exhibition at Galerie 1900–2000, saw it resembling bellows, adding 'the bellows of the mind', an object for kindling inspiration. Is the Muse actually listening to the artist's plea, to the music he will no doubt play? – a most musical Muse! The multiple layers of meaning one may detect in the object are in themselves a superimposition of potentialities open to the future, open to artists waiting for their muses' visit! Here again is revealed the bewitching contradiction which sums up Agar's approach: everything seems to be so natural and, at the same time, nothing seems to be more unexpected – the very spirit of *play*, a spirit one may also find in one of the photographs she took that year, *Haystack*. It is indeed an object lesson in the sense that objects, when juxtaposed, modify our vision and make us see something other than those objects. The structure of the photo and the angle of the shot are agents of de-realization.

Above: 86 Eileen Agar, The Muse Listening, *1940, mixed media.*

Opposite: 87 Eileen Agar, The Politician, *1942 (subsequently destroyed).*

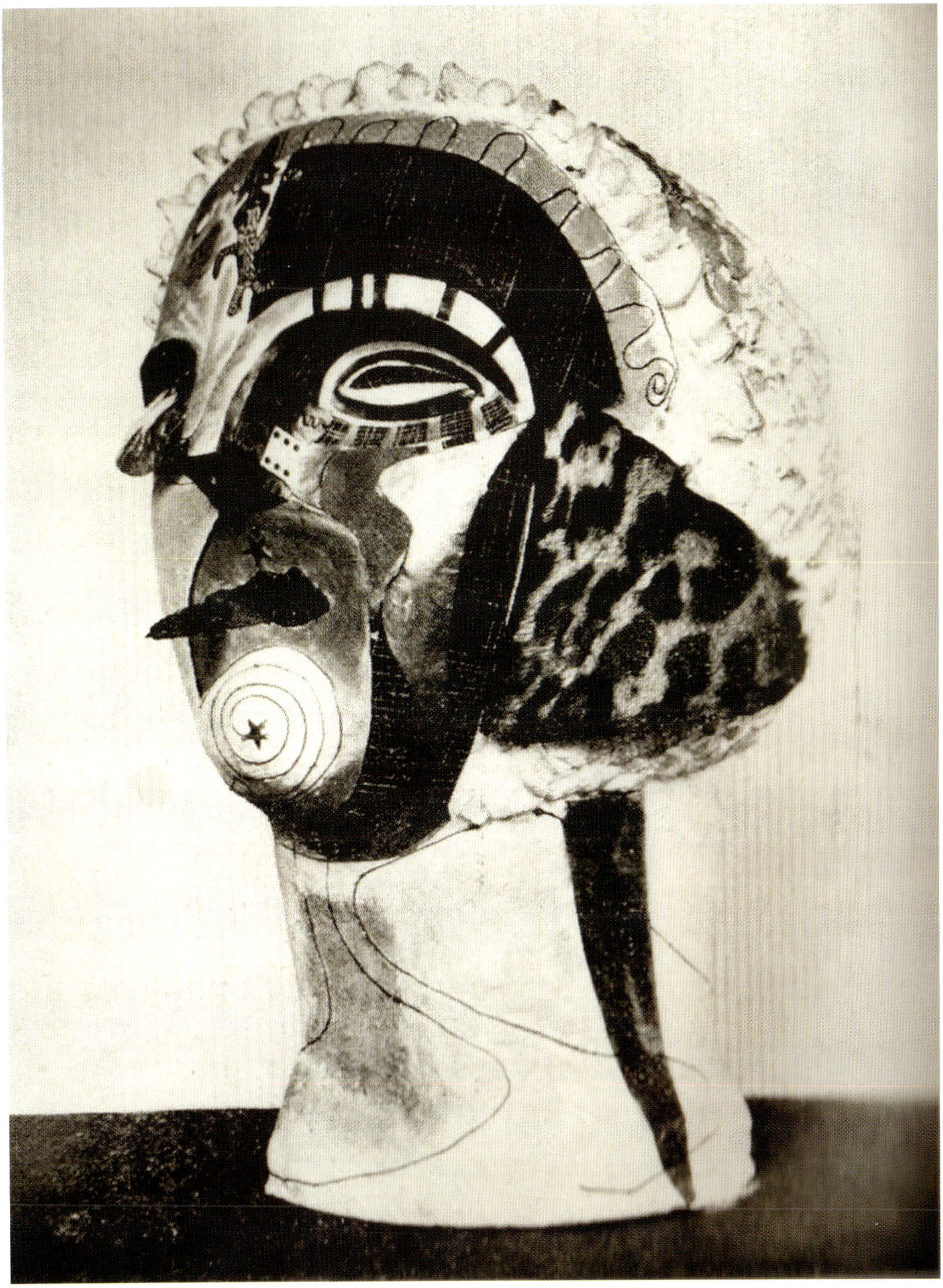

Apart from the London Group's exhibitions in which she regularly participated – almost every year – but refusing to sit on the London Group Committee so as not to have to pass judgement on other artists, Agar held three other exhibitions. One of these was the 'Imaginative Art since the War' exhibition at the Leicester Galleries, in which she exhibited *Honeymoon* (1941), next to Surrealist works by Toni del Renzio, John Melville and Paul Nash in May 1942. Another one was the presentation of 24 collages arranged by Rex Nan Kivell, one of the directors, at the Redfern Gallery from 30 April to 23 May 1942. Nash wrote the foreword for the catalogue: 'There is evidence of a skilful hand, creating sometimes with abrupt, alarming results but as often with a delicate, persuasive magic. Either seems to bring about a vivid efflorescence.' He continues with an oft-quoted lyrical statement: 'This bouquet of flowers is an explosion of fireworks, this explosion of flowers is a bouquet in the sky; the echoing detonation is a carillon of silence.' Perhaps less poetical but more 'technical', he ends by stressing a key factor in Agar's art, that 'throughout the exhibition an element of poetic mystery rises here and there . . . We find it again in states of paradox and enigma and especially in the huge collages of leaves.' These last words, 'mystery', 'paradox' and 'enigma', point to the core of Agar's imaginative approach of the real. The 'carillon of silence' is the voice of her mythopoetic mind. This kind of joyful, enthusiastic estrangement from the situation in which England was finding itself in those days is not alien to the general attitude of Surrealists, for whom the war was by definition something which they should not feel concerned about, as was emblematized by the move many Surrealists took by emigrating to the United States at the outset of the war – as did Samuel Haile, Gordon Onslow Ford or S.W. Hayter, not to mention the majority of the French Surrealists – in order to flee the alienating madness of politicians and other warmongers.

Next, in 1942, Agar participated in the 'New Movements in Art' exhibition at the London Museum and the same year, in November, in the exhibition entitled 'Surrealism' organized at the International Art Centre by Toni del Renzio. Del Renzio had taken refuge in England, travelling from Italy through France at the outbreak of the war in 1940. When circumstances forced the group to disperse, he set out to create a forum of ideas to keep the Surrealist flag flying at all costs. In March 1942, with the financial help of Kenneth Clark, he had launched *Arson*, 'a spectral review . . . a testimony of a vital life lived among the ruins not only of bombed houses, but of exploited people', to which Agar contributed with the reproduction of *The Politician* (illus. 87), an object which was another plaster cast reminding us of *Rococo Cocotte* and very similar to *The Angel of Mercy*. The division of the face into two coloured areas, one white, one black, takes on another meaning, no

88 Eileen Agar, Erotic Landscape, *1942, mixed media and collage on paper.*

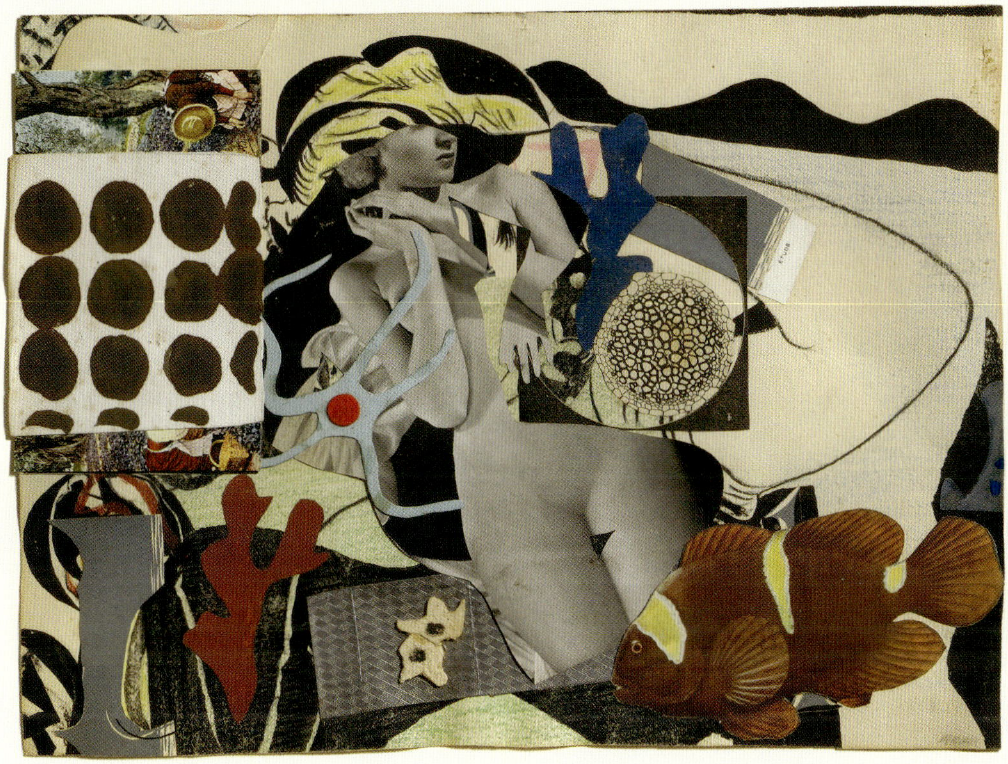

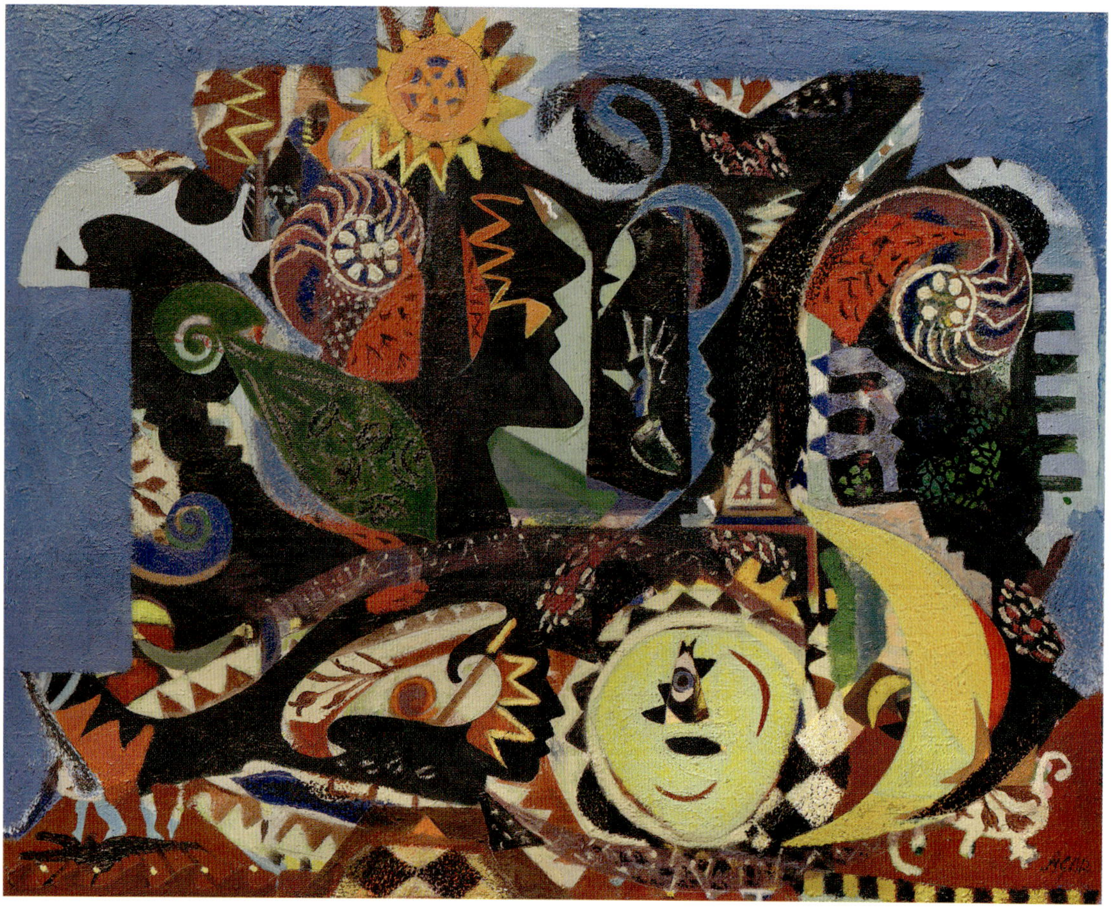

longer Janus but rather the unreliability and fickleness of politicians, thus bringing to the surface the hidden meaning and deep subversive nature of the two objects. A note on 'our collaborators' at the end of *Arson* said of her that she has 'a foreign eye but an English finger and is Irish'.

Two works from those years indicate the fundamentally Surrealist defiance she felt towards the intellectual and aesthetic acceptance of the world's situation there and then. *Erotic Landscape* (illus. 88), based on its central motif, the cut-out photograph of a feminine nude, is a choreography of vegetable and marine life arranged in a circular rhythm, as underlined by the semicircle on the right and the starfish-like shape on the left of the body. Fish fins, sea plants and leaves, the fragment of a postcard showing women picking up lavender, and circular shapes, create a dense fluidity imbued with the violence of desire. Eros – inseparable from the various

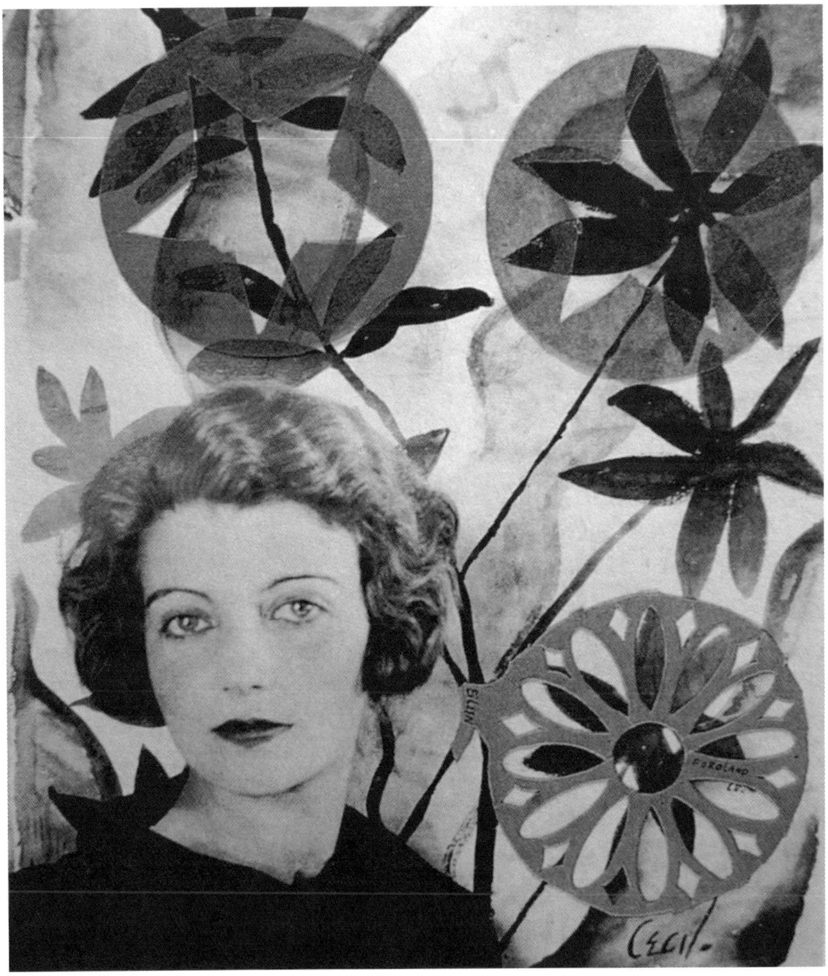

Opposite: 89 Eileen Agar, Abundance, *1942, oil on canvas.*

Left: 90 Eileen Agar, Untitled, *1943, collage on photograph.*

manifestations of natural life – as against Thanatos. Another work, an oil painting ironically entitled *Abundance* (illus. 89), painted at a time of dearth when oil and canvas were hard to get, is a literal act of resistance in the sense that the proliferation of forms and the lavishness and richness of colours are indicative of an optimistic and subversive spirit which refuses the situation as it is and warns us against accepting it uncritically. Egg shapes, sea-shells, bird shapes, flowers blooming and leaves unfurling, stars and wheels and moon crescents, all on board a drakkar-like vessel, create a profuse, festive celebration of energy, variety and the plenitude of life, increased by the domination of green, blue and orangey colours, whose complementary quality suffices to build the intensity of the painting. It is impossible not to associate *Abundance* with *Aurora* (which featured in the Redfern Gallery exhibition and was reproduced and mentioned by Paul Nash in his foreword to the catalogue), another defiance to the war, an unleashing of life-forms, vegetable and animal, with the introduction of spiral shapes reminiscent of ammonite fossils, the explosion of flowers, butterflies, birds and tree forms, out of which there rises an imposing, towering goddess-like feminine head, as if she were the one generating and orchestrating such a proliferation of births. The same atmosphere prevails over *Untitled* (illus. 90) from 1943 (the year of her mother's death), a collage of floral stems and a photograph of herself taken by Lee Miller. The collage is made up of four circles, one of them a rosace – the geometrical mind; two of them circles with leaves – the vegetable world; and the fourth Agar's own face, another autobiographical treatment of the blending of the three worlds which keep on haunting her inspiration into repeated wheels of life – the shape of the leaves and of the rosace petals echoing that of the artist's eyes.

In November that year, the fifth wartime exhibition of the London Group took place with Jacob Epstein, Ivor Hitchens, Augustus John, Duncan Grant, Matthew Smith, Graham Sutherland, and also the Surrealists Henry Moore, John Tunnard and Agar, the latter being called 'non-representationalist'. In January 1943, the third United Artists' exhibition was held at Burlington House, organized by the Royal Academy, in collaboration with 26 other art societies – the epitome of a whole nation's resistance in the face of war. The exhibition, to which Agar contributed *Robe of an Angel*, went to Stockport in May. Six months later, the same work was shown at the Alfred East Gallery in Kettering.

In 1942, Joseph Bard, who had just had his ironic radio play *Nietszche* broadcast on the BBC Home Service, became a Fellow of the Royal Society of Literature and in 1944 a member of the RSL Council. He participated in a few publications and broadcasts to the United States. A close friend of Mesens, the French Surrealist filmmaker and poet Jacques B. Brunius, a broadcaster for the Free French Forces at the BBC, made a brief stay at their flat – long enough to make Horace Kesteven's daughter Mary fall in love with him and marry him. The impenetrable ways of Surrealism!

In 1944, Bard and Agar went on holiday to the Lake District and then Edinburgh, followed in 1945 by a holiday in Cornwall and in June to July 1946 in Ireland. Those three years were moments when, as Agar says herself in her autobiography, she was 'losing naturalness and spontaneity even if [she] was gaining in technical expertise'. What is certain, however, is that she was no longer thinking of her different techniques, collages, paintings or objects as distinguishable, but as inseparably operative to the same end. They all became for her equivalent, similar ways of letting her imagination and subconscious speak.

Acknowledgement of her resilient Surrealist spirit came from E.L.T. Mesens himself, still the leader of the English Surrealist group, who dedicated a poem to her in his bilingual *Troisième Front* (*Third Front*) published by London Gallery Editions in 1944, entitled 'Seen in a Sketch by Eileen Agar'.

> The trestles are set up on lake surrounded by autumn tinted woods. Two or three trees with their foliage hold up the scenery. The scene represents – what? – a white screen heavily daubed with paint. The footlights are not lit: why should they be since the performance is given by daylight.
> It is here that she appears,
> Stars of day with wasp-waist,
> Star-flower in a locked dress,
> Star-flower of day with a bodice that sings,
> Star with the long feet of Little Tich hidden by her train . . .
> She throws her black heart in the stalls.
> But where indeed are her eyes? One is on the prompt-side and the other off-prompt. Her eyes – red violets – scarlet scarlet red – violets never seen – turn.

Mesens's text is clearly a homage to the oneiric theatricality of Agar's 'staging' of botanic, animal and metaphorical encounters, but also to her all-seeing, ever-wandering eyes, which embrace the interior as well as the exterior worlds. Her paintings and collages are plays, performances which dovetail day and night, comedy ('Little Tich') and tragedy ('her black heart') on the timeless stage of the world – a vibrant acknowledgement of her Surrealist vision of reality.

Overleaf left: 91 Eileen Agar, Bread Basket, *1943, collage on paper.*

Overleaf right: 92 Eileen Agar, Caliban, *1945, oil on canvas.*

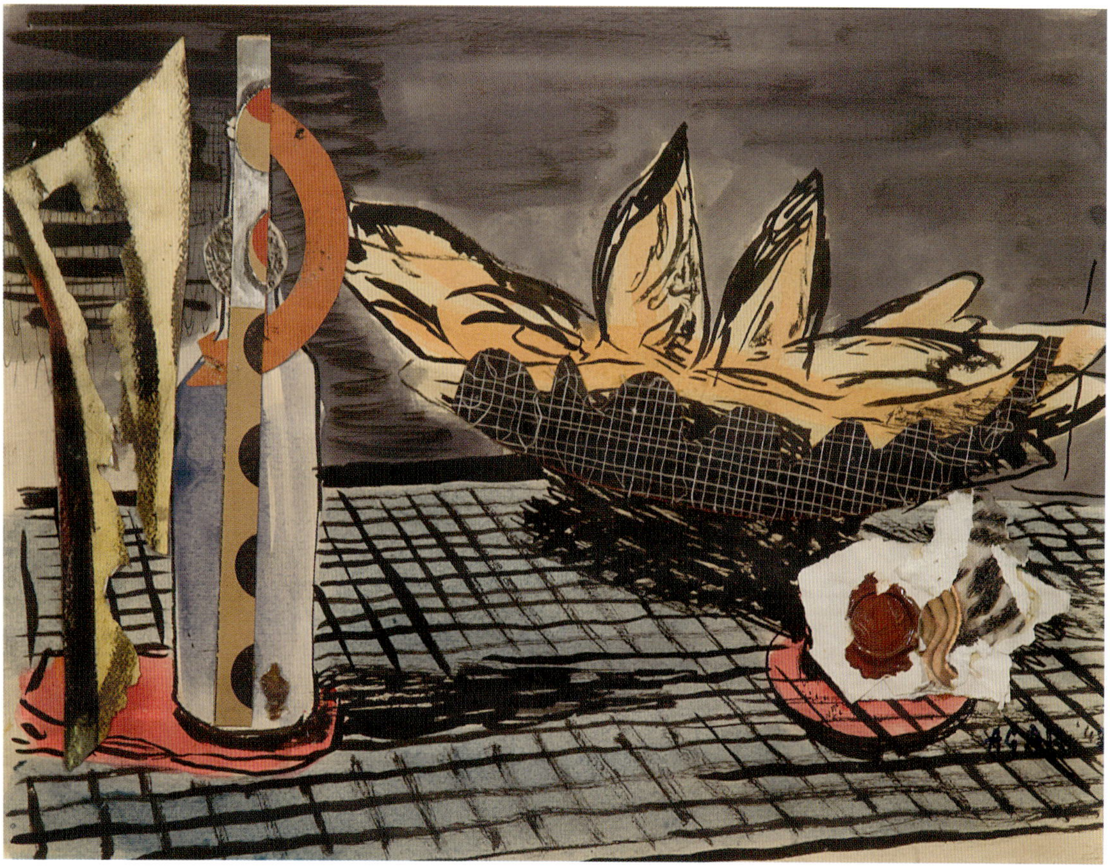

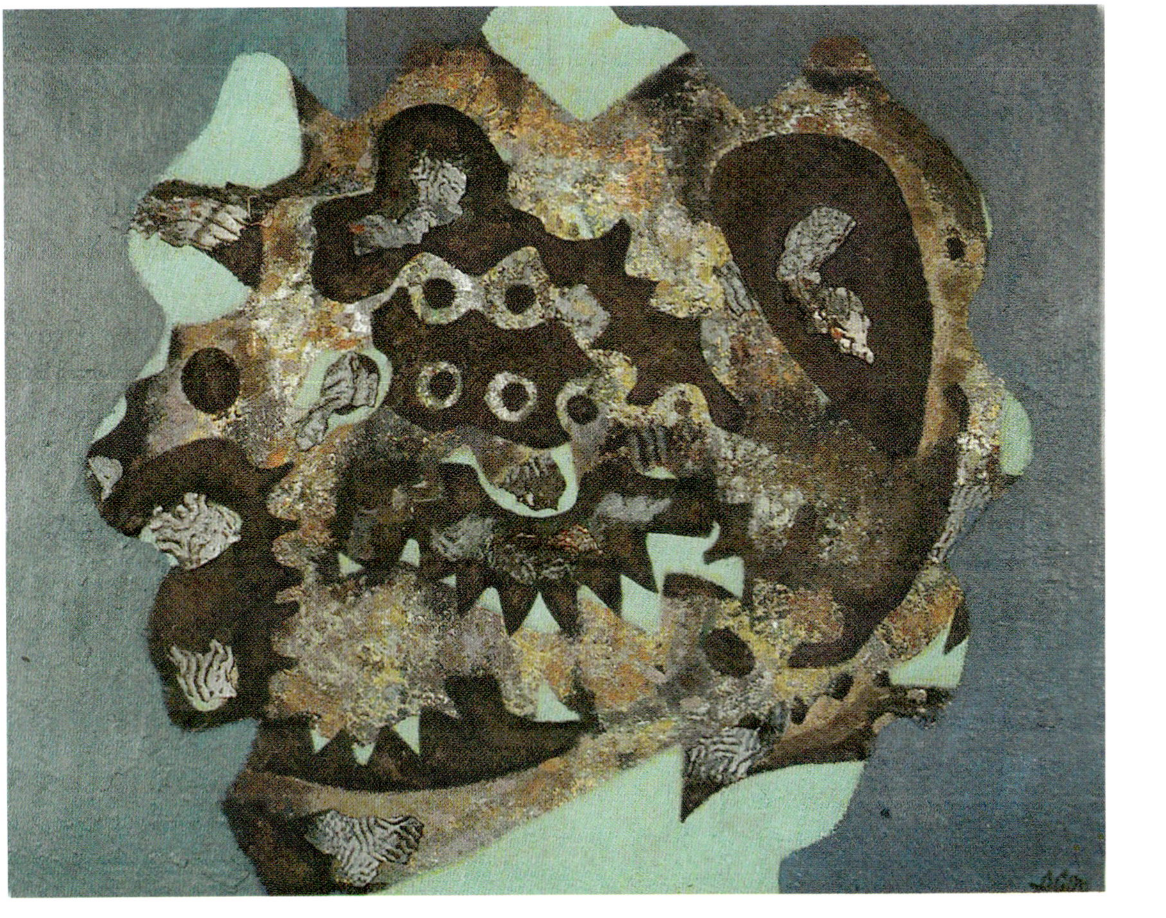

No work produced during those years actually refers to the war directly – that would go against the Surrealist spirit of resilience founded on the powerful independence of the imagination from the world of calculation and compromise. In 1943, *Bread Basket* (illus. 91) may ironically refer to those years of desperation and rationing, a rather sinister, dark grey and ochre-ish still-life with a bowl out of which huge corn ears seem to rise, an inverted echo, one might say, of *Abundance* from the previous year. This, as well as her return to favourite themes, such as the world of insects and butterflies (*Bug of Genius*, 1943) almost appear as attempts to step away from focusing on mankind as such and take refuge in nature – an across-the-board statement against the feeling that man is a wolf to man. Finding respite and solace in her successive holidays away from London, she brought back a series of lyrical oils and watercolours from Lake Buttermere in the Lake District, which she exhibited at the Redfern Gallery in December 1944. The critic Terence Dennis wrote in the *New English Weekly*: 'She makes the landscapes yield everything they are capable of – no mystery – sharp as a kitchen knife.' The clear and happy figurativeness of her watercolours indicated a newly gained serenity, a moment of repose in which to relish the tranquil but strange beauty of both thought and vision in this highly charged landscape of Wordsworth and Coleridge.

In my opinion, the painting fundamental to this immediate post-war period is no doubt *Caliban* (1945, illus. 92), an ironical comment on the state of mankind and the civilization that man's primitive instinct of war had brought to the brink of disintegration. In a reassessment of the Shakespearean character, the poet-cum-artist-cum-magician Agar-Prospero sees Caliban as embodying the chthonic forces of vegetation, growth and earthliness. He is turned into an emblem of man, a blending of animal, vegetable and human forces; the dominant browns and greens of the figure are significant of this blending, a blending of heaviness and lightness, of materiality and immateriality, a kind of spiritualizing of matter and of the chthonic forces. Agar plays with the concrete materiality of the pigment to make the figure a mythical one telling us of our predicament. Clearly, Prospero couldn't but spare Caliban's life, could he? Caliban, the indestructible and obscure cursed part of ourselves.

Two years later, *Garden of Time* (illus. 93) makes a similar point. The painting is based on a gradual, almost majestic spiralling movement of fragments. From bottom to top, one can identify the skeleton of a hand and two femora, ascending towards an opening corncob and a huge water-lily leaf, unless it is that of a rubber tree. This movement upwards embraces the figure of a lizard or chameleon, and reaches a cat's skull at the top, while the eye is

93 Eileen Agar, Garden of Time, *1947, oil on paper.*

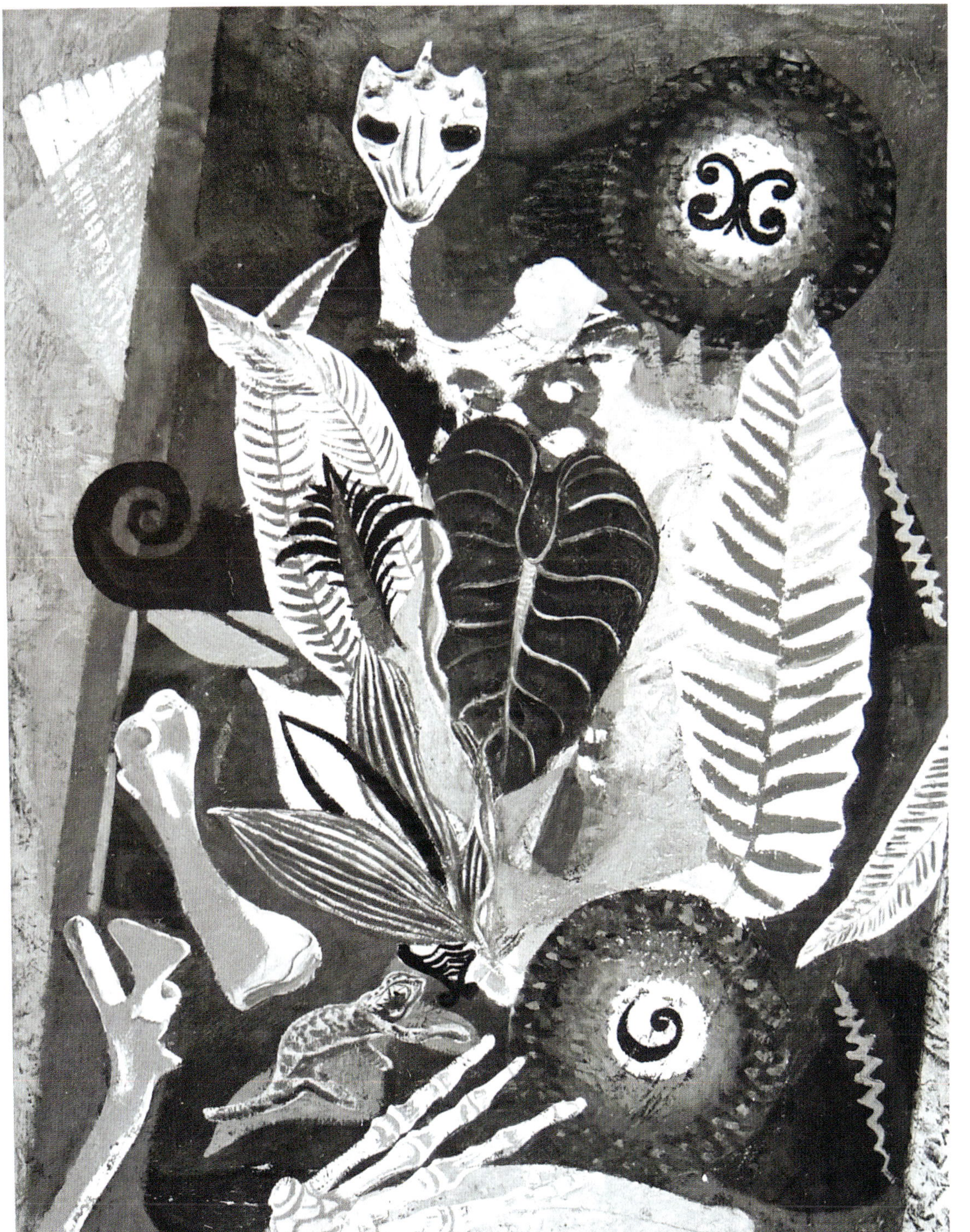

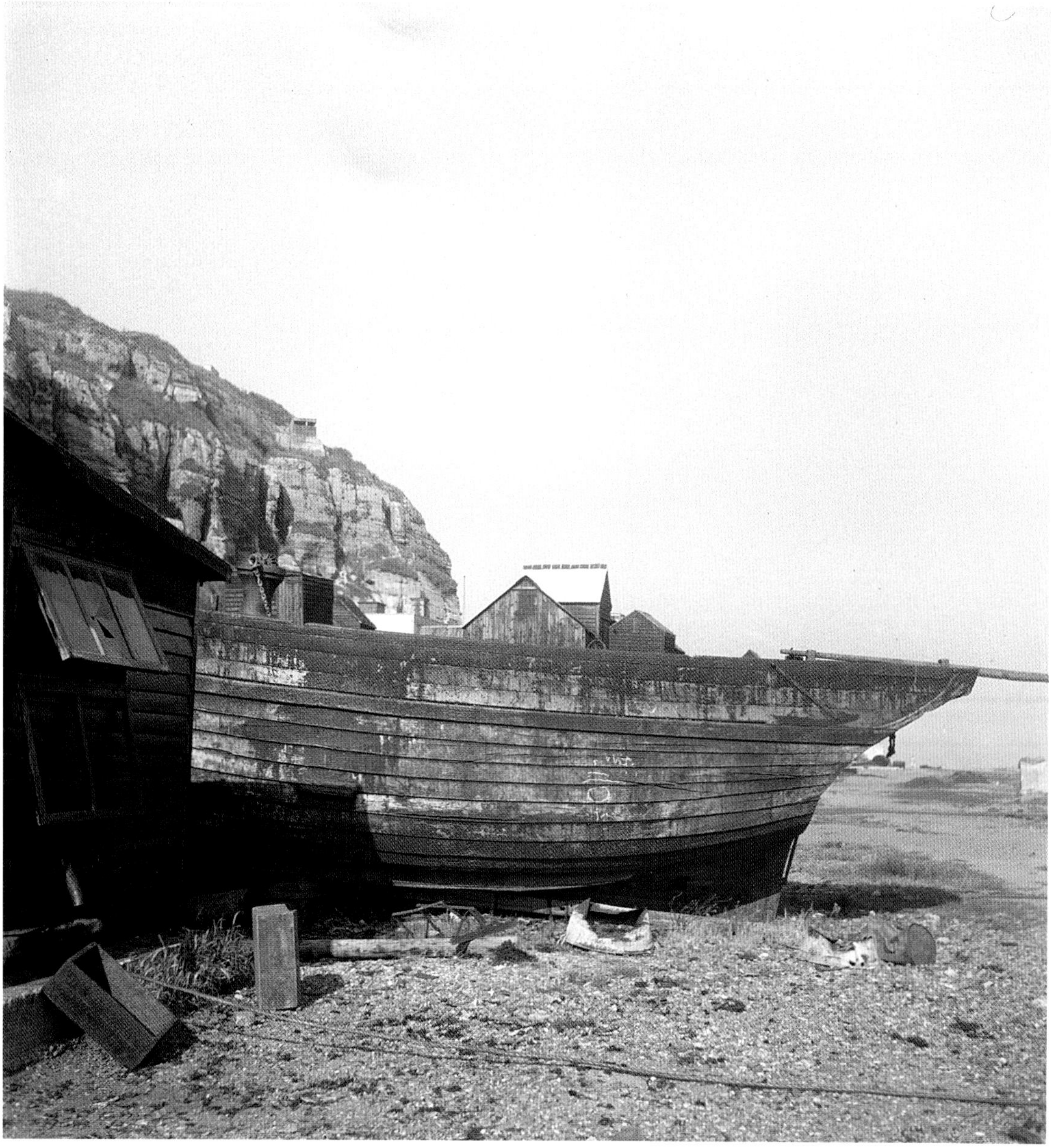

arrested by three geometrical shapes which form a triangle emphasizing the general movement – two spirals and one 'x' held up within circles and linked by huge fern leaves. We thus travel through time, through vertebrates and invertebrates, natural and lifeless forms, zoological and botanical presences; through musical and mathematical symbols; through the mystery of life and death, grasped in a garden, the garden of Eden, of course – that is, before time was chronological time, indeed the place of timeless growth. In her autobiography, she described the creative, mythopoetic process in almost Keatsian terms:

> You see the shape of a tree, the way a pebble falls or is formed, and you are astounded to discover that dumb nature makes an effort to speak to you, to give you a sign, to warn you, to symbolize your innermost thoughts. I am a secret painter, painting for me is a vey private occupation . . . it is something that germinates like a seed; in the dark soil and recesses of the living coral of the mind . . . They grow like a plant, slowly putting out shoots, they need pruning, meditating on, while the roots grow in the dark.

In the midst of several unconnected statements in her diaries, she scribbled: 'Painting is like gardening.'

On 11 July 1946, Agar, back from her holiday in Ireland with Bard, was buying some paint in a tiny shop on the Earl's Court Road, when the attendant there told her he had heard news over the radio of Paul Nash's death in Boscombe. Her affair with Nash, which had torn her heart away from Bard, thus came mournfully to an end. Agar had met Nash in the spring of 1935 and both had fallen in love with each other. Nash had guided her through the pebbles and driftwood of Swanage beaches and the dead tree trunks and fossil stones of the surrounding fields and a deep, heartfelt complicity had developed between them, blooming into a passion unabated by time, although discreetly, if not clandestinely, expressed. From August 1935, when he sent her a poem ('You broke on me waves no heavier than dust / you broke over my heart / my stone heart that was a lake water lapping with love – I hear it in the heart's deep cave'), to July 1936, when Agar realized their liaison was an emotional dead end, the situation grew more and more desperate. In October 1936, Nash admitted to the unavoidable break-up but the painfulness of the situation lasted until July 1937 when it had become obvious that a new liaison had taken place between Agar and the French Surrealist Paul Éluard. (Nash wrote: 'I could share you with Joseph because there was something you gave me which

94 Eileen Agar, photograph of boat and cliff, 1947, photograph.

was not for him. But I cannot share you with Éluard because you gave him what was mine.') The reference to her new deep aesthetic complicity with the Surrealist poet – however brief that was – was too much for Nash, and they kept apart. Still, their intellectual proximity remained solid and developed into 'moments we snatched together', as she recalls in her autobiography. It was very difficult for them to keep on seeing each other even occasionally, not only with Margaret Nash's formidable presence, strong character and the constant help she was bringing to Nash, who was suffering from severe asthma, but also with Bard's diminishing tolerance and jealous patience, nourished as it was by his deep love for Agar. During the war, when Agar was working in the Savile Row canteen, she and Nash would meet at Newman's paint shop in Kensington Church Street, at the Café Royal in Piccadilly or in a flat Nash had rented near Euston Station. The aesthetic and intellectual 'elective affinity' between them was complete and, in a way, *ideal*, and its influence can be sensed as the source of the inspiration behind many, if not most, of Agar's works.

In the period immediately following the war, Agar had many exhibitions in London, which helped her to re-emerge: at the Leger Gallery in Old Bond Street in January 1947, at the Hanover Gallery in spring 1949 and in 1951, then at the Obelisk Gallery in 1958. She also appeared in a television programme in 1948, 'The Eye of the Artist', invited by the writer and fashion journalist James Laver, who interviewed her about her work. On that occasion, she displayed her *Ceremonial Hat for Eating Bouillabaisse* (illus. 95), a fantastical object: a cork basket picked up in St Tropez, painted blue and covered with fishnet, a lobster's tail, starfish and other marine objects – Arcimboldesque headgear, as it were, that she had devised in 1936. The work was essentially a lesson in Surrealism: how a hat loses its obvious only utilitarian meaning – that is, to be worn for protection or fashionable appearance – or rather how a hat subordinates that meaning to what one eats ('I'll eat my hat'!), thus proclaiming in a sense its impossible but wished-for edibility; in other words, how reality can be exceeded by itself and deprived of its conventional limits through processes of accretion, contradiction and condensation. This period of intense and fecund painting starting in the early 1950s would not abate until her very last day.

95 The artist wearing her Ceremonial Hat for Eating Bouillabaisse, *1938–9, cork, paint, lobster shell, fish bones, artificial flowers, with the* Hand of Fate, *photograph.*

In 1948, friendship with Ezra Pound was reaffirmed at a distance, when both Bard and Agar were mentioned in Pound's *Pisan Cantos*, the former for his remark on the fact that even poor French people use a language not devoid of a sophisticated literariness and the latter for her 'sunlight qualities'. The lines on Joseph Bard, from Canto LXXVI, read:

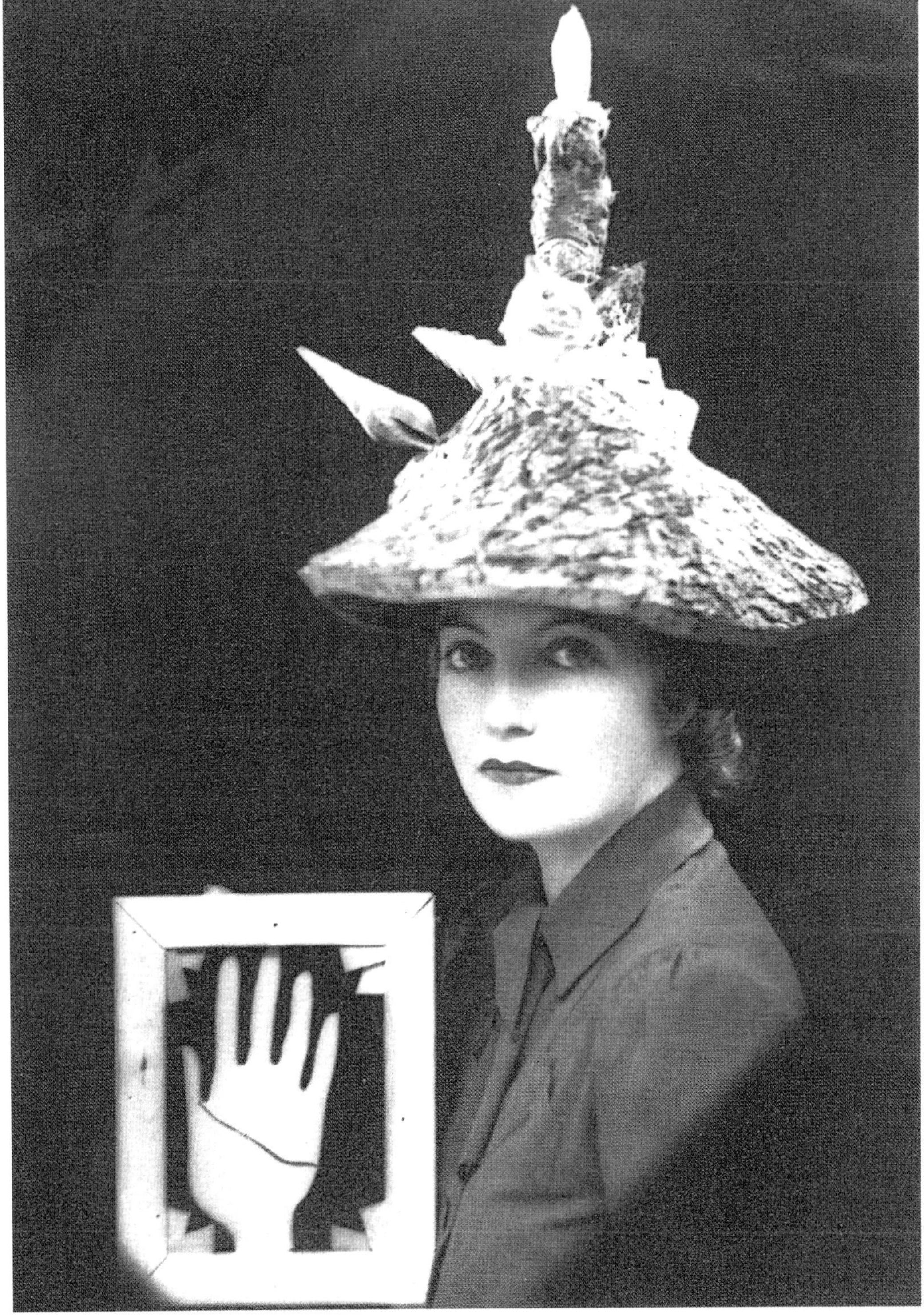

> Or as Jo Bard says: they never speak to each other, if it is baker and concierge visibly
>
> It is La Rochefoucauld and de Maintenon audibly

On Eileen Agar, the line, from Canto LXXXI, read:

> But Eileen's trick sunlight softens London's November

A similar experience took place when they visited Venice in autumn 1949 on the occasion of the PEN Club Congress – Bard was a member – and met with old friends like Nancy Cunard, Stephen Spender, Cyril Connolly, W. H. Auden, Cecil Day-Lewis, Pamela Travers and, not least, Peggy Guggenheim. They toured Umbria, Tuscany and Rome, a moment which was like plunging into one of Agar's canvasses – at the limits of consciousness and reality, moments of different visions and fragrances, a trip into the ancient past, into timelessness, as she liked to say. The year after, they travelled to Aix-en-Provence to visit Cézanne's studio and then walk in the steps of Van Gogh at Arles and Saint-Rémy-de-Provence.

As a result, couldn't we see *Demeter* (illus. 96), painted in 1949, as the emblematic work of this period, a painting which means both the end of a grave, tense period and the beginning of a more serene one? For the ambivalence of the mythological meaning of the goddess lends itself to a kind of double meaning, bringing together summer and winter in a synthetic, non-contradictory vision of life. The story is well known. Demeter is Mother Earth. Her daughter, Persephone, had been abducted by Hades, the sovereign of the dead, who made her his wife. Having eaten six pips from the pomegranate Hades had given her, Persephone could no longer leave the empire of the dead and her mother did not manage to retrieve her. Only Zeus could do something and he made Hades meet her halfway; Persephone was allowed to spend the winter with her husband and leave him to spend the rest of the year with her mother in the world above. For Greek mythology, Demeter is thus at the origin of the cycle of the seasons, teaching mankind how to cultivate the earth, ploughing and sowing, so that summer became the season of plenty. Here, Demeter is, in a way, revisited by Agar, seen in profile and looking at us – the movement of her veil shows she has just turned around from winter to the abundance of summer, symbolized by her suddenly revealed 'ample' buttocks and by the flowery shapes and bright colours proliferating all around.

96 Eileen Agar, Demeter, 1949, mixed media on panel.

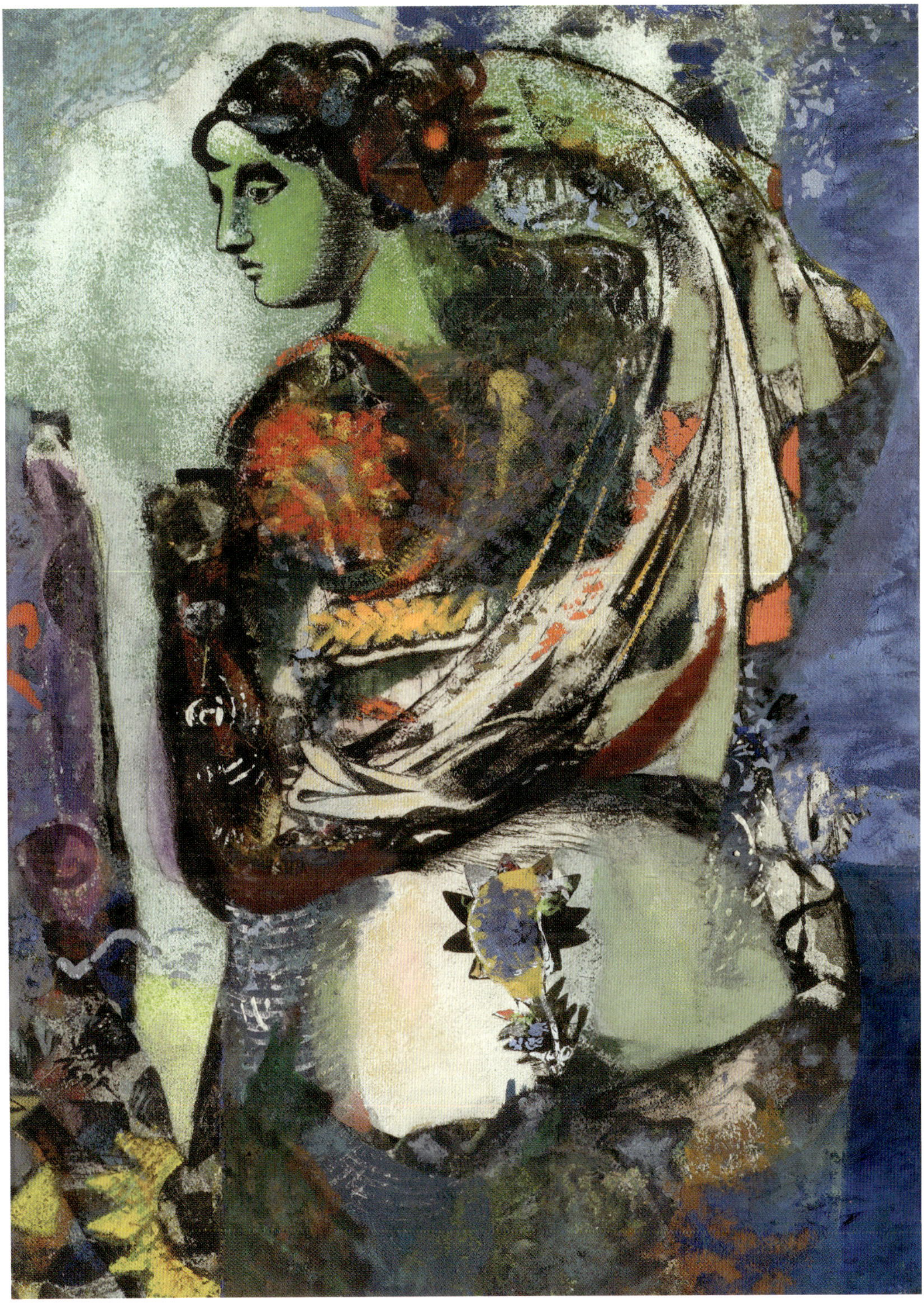

5 Dreaming oneself awake, 1953–91

'Take a minute to think about it, and then guess,' said the Red Queen. 'Meanwhile we'll all drink your health – Queen Alice's health!'

Lewis Carroll, *Through the Looking-Glass, and What Alice Found There* (1871)

Almost as a crystallization of these journeys, renewal of activity and inspiration was given another decisive boost in the winter of 1952–3 when Agar travelled with Joseph Bard to the island of Tenerife and holidayed there in Puerto de la Cruz, repeating their visit every winter from 1954 to 1957 (illus. 97). The island had attracted the Surrealists in the 1930s, especially as a Surrealist group had been formed there in 1934. In 1935, on his visit to the island, André Breton had issued a solemn declaration in an interview for the magazine *Indice*, in which he insisted on the political attitude a Surrealist should adopt – a statement fundamental to the understanding of Surrealism's political position and certainly not contradicted by Agar. To the question 'Confronted by an immediate social action, can art put itself into the service of a definite political idea?', Breton answered in these terms:

> It must unreservedly put itself into the service of the idea during the period in which the idea is transformed into action; and this action, to achieve full success, must be exalted in every way. It is indispensable, however, that art regain its independence if the artist wishes to escape serious contradictions objectively harmful even to the idea which he wishes to serve (as in the suicide of Mayakovsky).

The group had been formed in Tenerife around the poet and essayist Eduardo Westerdahl. Back in 1932 he had founded the review *Gaceta de Arte*, to which the main currents of the 'intellectual left' in Europe at the time contributed, from Brecht and Kandinsky, to Picasso and Bertrand Russell. On 11 May 1935, the review instigated the 'First International Surrealist

97 Eileen Agar, Tenerife, *c. 1952, mixed media on paper.*

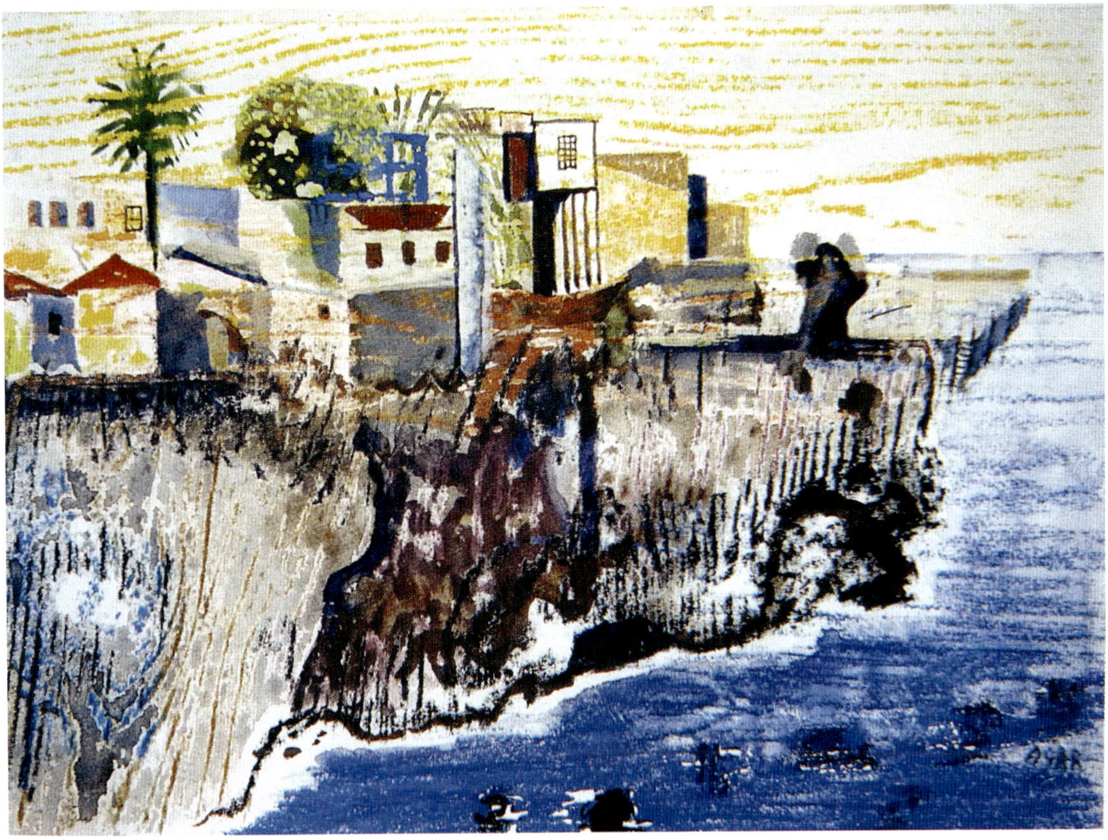

Exhibition' in Sainte-Croix-de-Tenerife in the presence of Jacqueline and André Breton (Breton was to devote some most admirable pages to the magic of the island and its natural environment in *L'Amour fou* in 1937). Then, Westerdahl published the first issue of the bilingual *Bulletin international du surréalisme*, in which French and Canarian Surrealists reaffirmed their opposition to fascism and Stalinism. One understands why Agar was so thrilled to meet Westerdahl, and this must have lingered at the back of her mind for quite a while (illus. 98). But the point was essentially to go to Tenerife in order to find new inspiration and it is true that 'the colour and the light brought a new sense of joy to [her] paintings', as she remembers in her autobiography, adding that what worked on her was the contrast between the abundant sub-tropical vegetation of the north of the island

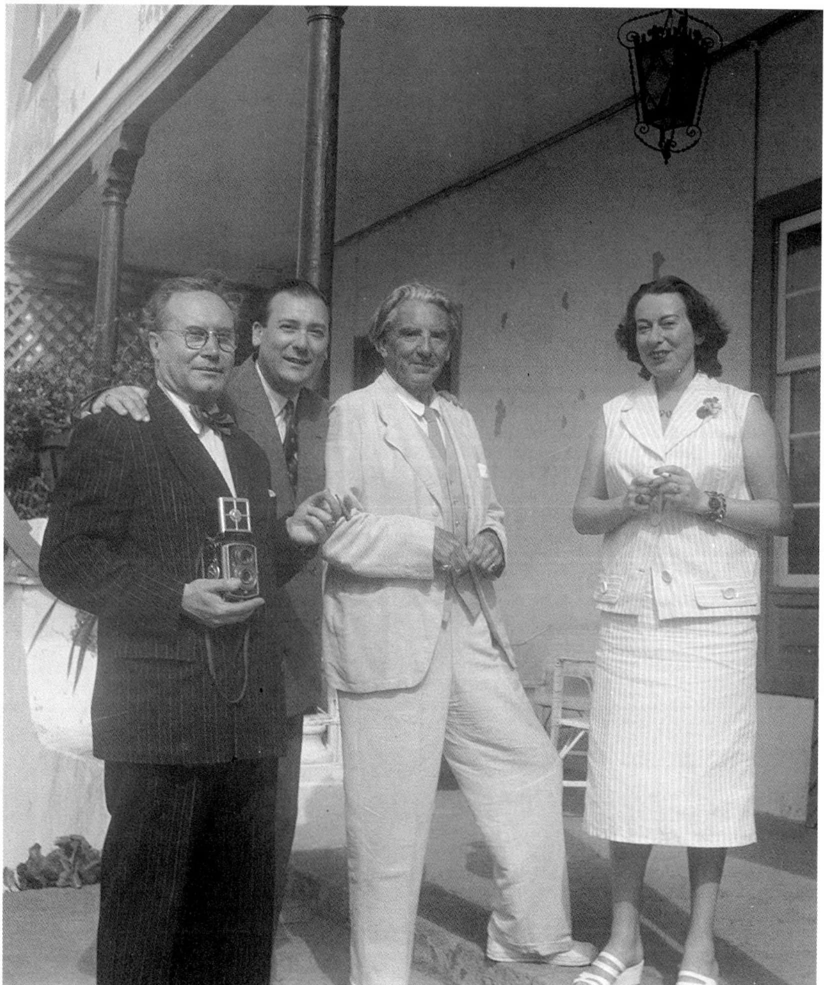

Right: 98 Eileen Agar, from left to right: Eduardo Westerdahl, Antonio Ruiz, Joseph Bard and Maud Westerdahl in Puerto de la Cruz, Tenerife, 1952–6.

Opposite: 99 Eileen Agar, The Birth of Christopher Columbus, *1950, wood and metal.*

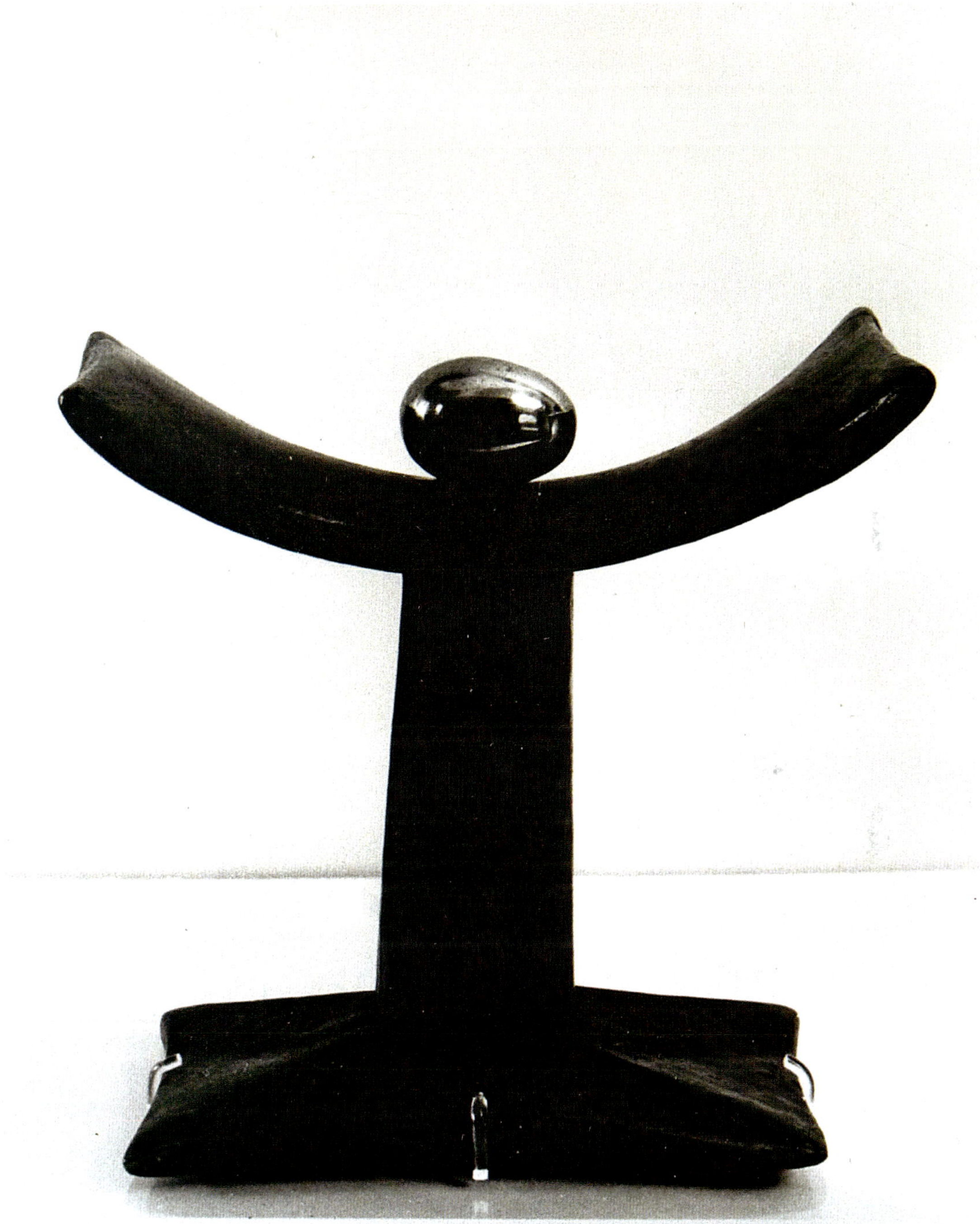

and the drier, more arid, desert-like southern part, a contrast rendered by lavish colours and the use of frottage – which Penrose had developed so extensively in the late 1920s and '30s following Max Ernst's example. Indeed, frottage is a way to catch the evanescent traces of reality, while vivid colours remind us of the permanence and resilience of life, which defies the transience of reality. This experience exacerbated Agar's sensitivity to the colour of the volcanic soil and the exoticism of the vegetation, a kind of love-match between sea and fire. There, in the Puerto de la Cruz gallery, Agar put on an exhibition for which Westerdahl wrote a review in the island newspaper, *La Tarde*.

Was this aesthetic adventure on the margins of the Western world at the origin of the name she gave to the object she made in 1950, *The Birth of Christopher Columbus* (illus. 99)? The object indeed shows how her creativity implied versatility and a whirling concatenation of meanings. The object is so different from the 'collage' which all her other objects result from, that it takes us aback on account of its Brancusi-like aspect. The bare slickness of the stand, the purity of the metal egg poised in the middle of a semicircle, the shine of the metal and the polish of the wood – all this creates an impression of hieratic power *and* fragility, a most appropriate and successful attempt to render the solemnity of the historical episode referred to in the multi-meaning title. The egg not only indicates the actual, physiological birth of the great discoverer but it is also the object which, according to an anecdote – however apocryphal that might be – helped Columbus emphasize the importance of his discovery of the New World by one of the simplest gestures. Indeed it is said that in the course of a meal Columbus had been invited to, one of the guests wanted to minimize the importance of his discovery. To reply to such provocation, Columbus challenged all the guests by asking them to make a hard-boiled egg stand on its end. Everyone failed. Columbus then slightly tapped the larger end of the egg and stood it on the table. Agar requalified the anecdote by integrating it into a larger, almost cosmic reference. Indeed, the semicircle on which it is poised is, of course, the table on which the egg was made to stand in the anecdote, but also the womb and the world, both spheres where creation takes place. A perfect Surrealist object, needless to say, in the sense that its general form is *also* that of a human figure, the egg being its head, the spring of creation, the figure thus extending its arms to welcome the whole world he is about to remap.

Other evidence of Agar's Surrealist permanent alertness is provided by the photo she took in 1952, *Bird in a Cage*, also entitled *Caged Bird* (illus. 100). A typically Surrealist photograph – Magrittian one could say – it presents us with a cage hanging from a dead tree, inside which

100 Eileen Agar, Bird in a Cage, *1952, photograph.*

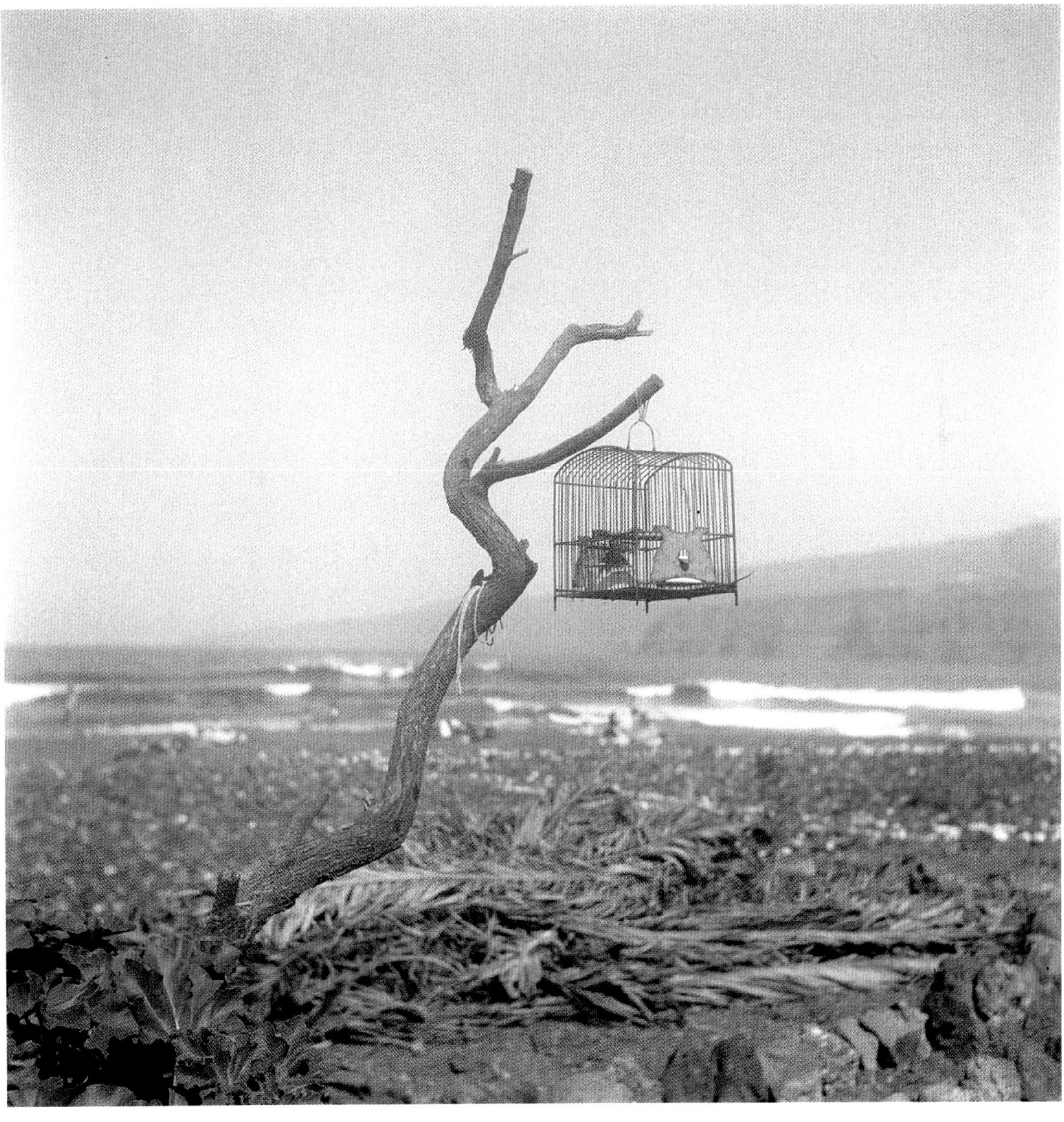

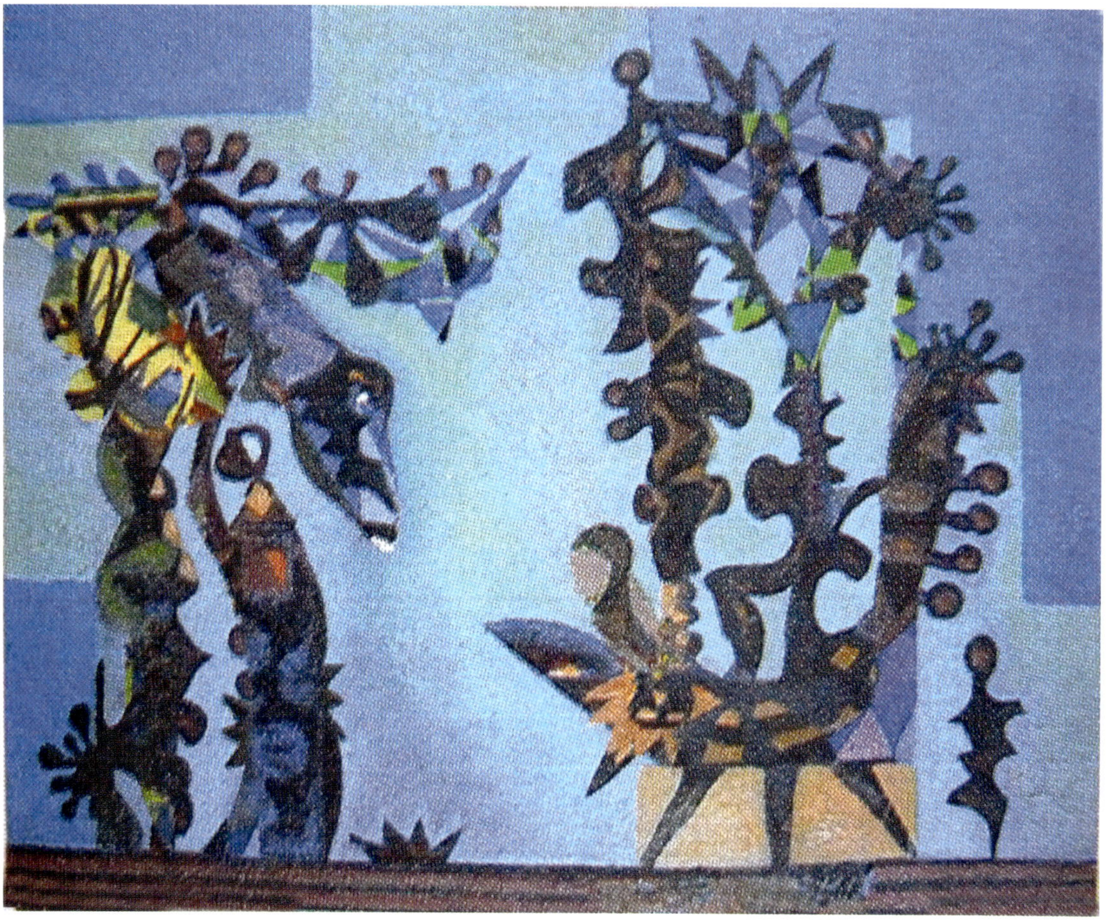

there is a bird, and behind, a vast open desert-like field. The photo is thus based on a series of interacting oxymorons, telescoping in superimposed layers of meaning the closed space of the cage and the vastness of the landscape, the dead tree and the living bird, the loss of freedom and unbounded freedom, the finite and the infinite. Probably influenced by her several stays in Tenerife, an oil on canvas titled *Musical Garden* is one of the rare oils of that period, dominated as it was by the production of watercolours (illus. 101). Contrary to many paintings of gardens in her work, it is a rather sober composition simply based on two standing figures on a blue background formed with three large squares in darker blue. The figures are two erect, thin, jagged, serrated bodies, each one being turned into ribbons of musical notes liberated from their staves, and parts of musical instruments, dancing with the other in a festive choreography.

Fisherman (illus. 102), painted in 1957, displays a renewal of inspiration in the Arcimboldesque vein. Here, the head of the fisherman is made of fishing net and fish forms. The fish-net pattern – which looks like the reproduction of the creased or crumpled surface of a leather garment, especially at the bottom and on the left-hand side of the collage – acts as a kind of frame to the proliferation of fish forms, one falling from the top right and the seven or eight others packing together while the red and blue profile seems to be taken aback by the miraculous catch.

This inexhaustible renewal of inspiration becomes blatant in a painting of 1958, *The Artist* (illus. 103), which, like all self-portraits, appears to be a summary of the various technical processes Agar had hitherto developed. A series of overlapping planes, three rectangles, one green, one pink and one red – complementary colours – whose surface is perturbed by circular and semicircular shapes, create a triangular rhythm, top right, side left and bottom right. A series of lines, the result of dripping paint at random, criss-cross the surface over them in an apparently automatic, haphazard way – Pollock-like. But what gives the painting its deep sense is a human figure, the artist of the title, drawn in outline right at the centre of the painting, as well as a closed door, also drawn in outline, next to the standing figure. What comes out, then, is first the idea that at the back of every work there is the artist, hiding and only appearing, literally, as a watermark. Exactly like the door, his art opens into the surface of the canvas or, rather, the board. But the work is also the epitome of the different techniques at the artist's disposal, drawing, painting and using automatism, both the artist's – Eileen Agar's – consciousness of structure (the rectangles) *and* the artist's spontaneous outburst of emotion (the drippings), the blending of oil and enamel echoing this ambivalence.

Opposite: 101 Eileen Agar, Musical Garden, *1950, oil on canvas.*

Overleaf left: 102 Eileen Agar, Fisherman, *1957, crayon on paper with collage.*

Overleaf right: 103 Eileen Agar, The Artist, *1958, enamel and oil on board.*

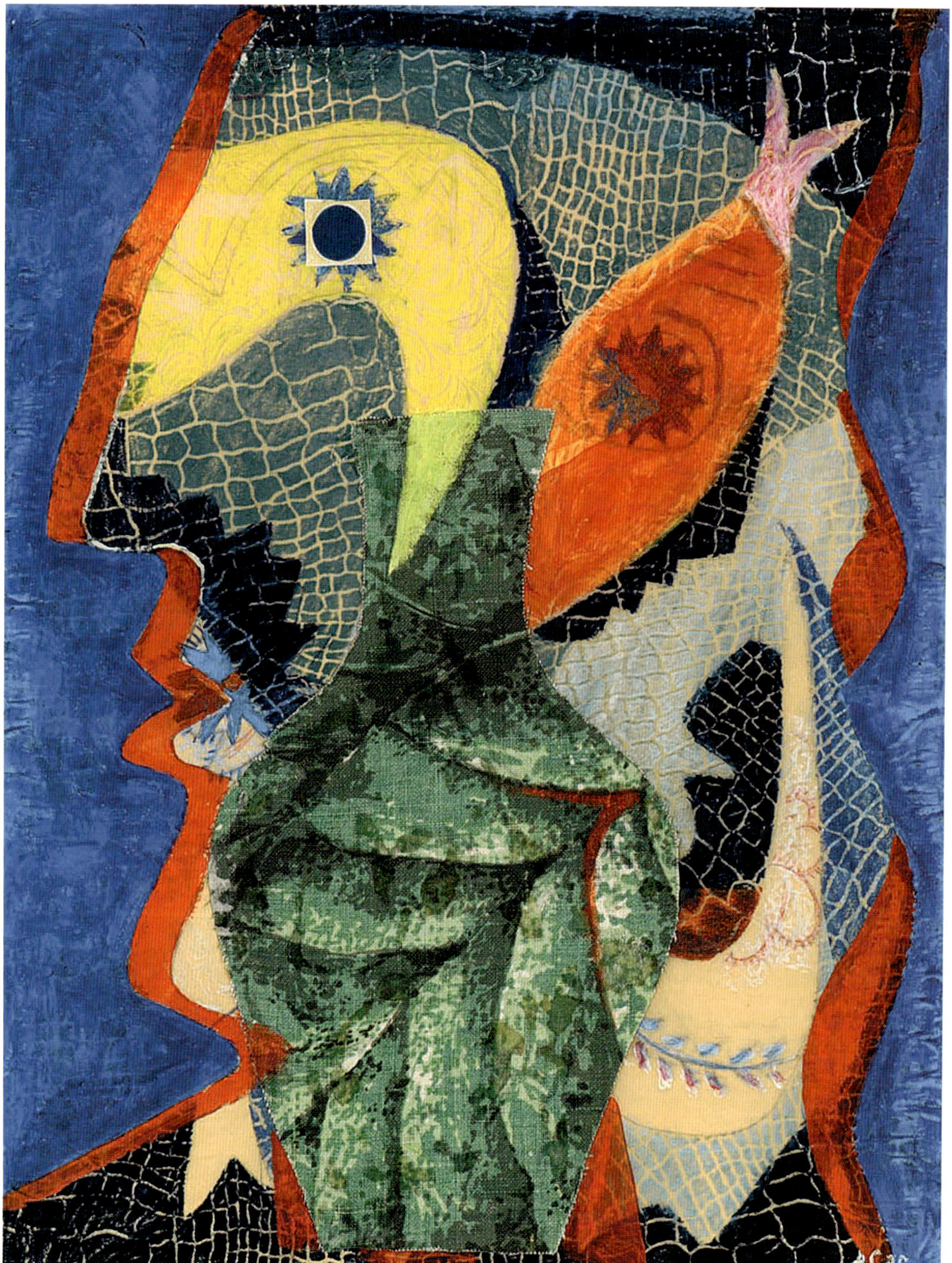
AGAR

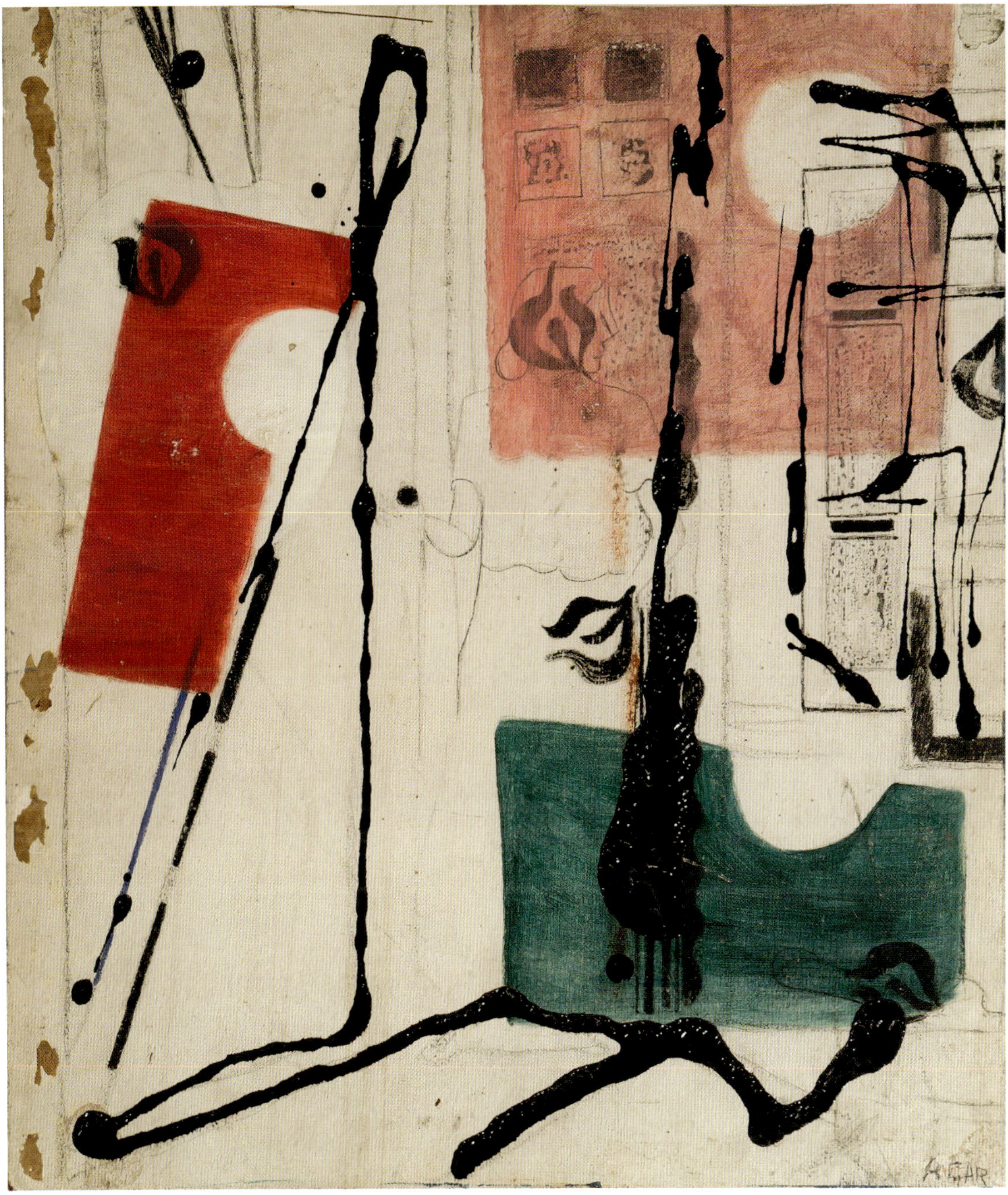
AGAR

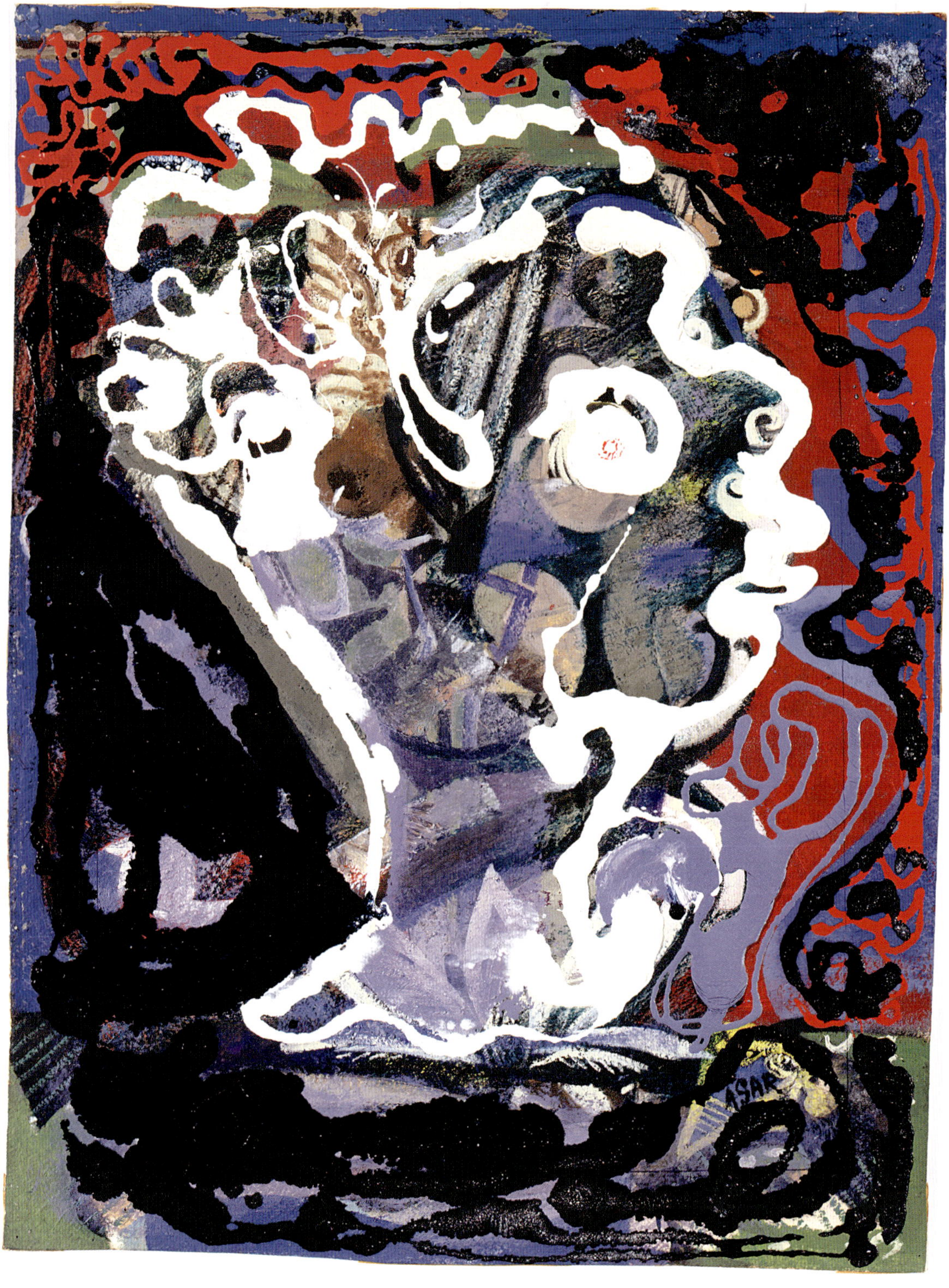
ASAR

This period was like a watershed in Agar's life. It not only confirmed the sense of joy one continually feels in her works but helped her develop into a renewed conscious and energetic attempt to privilege ambiguity as part of her modus operandi, so that the observer would be turned into an active witness of, and participant in, the workings of the imagination. In order to achieve this self-questioning commitment of the observer, she created effects which were more powerful and striking than the construction or the composition itself – or rather the latter had to be exceeded, as it were, by the former, which seemed superimposed upon it. Such a technical choice was greatly helped by her use, from the late 1950s onwards, of acrylic paint and the hard shiny glaze it gives to the representation of objects – an emphasis laid on their presence.

This is exactly what she tried in *Head of Dylan Thomas* (1960–62, illus. 104), which, as the note in the Scottish National Gallery catalogue says, is one of her experiments with automatism. Let us remember that the post-war years were marked by the development of Abstract Expressionism, as in Pollock's paintings, and the irruption on the European scene of the Cobra movement, which gave priority to the automatic gestures of the artist, independently of any rational control. In this work, Agar dribbled paint, oil and Valspar lacquer from above the board – a technique Max Ernst had actually pioneered – and then applied thick lines of paint, a singularly appropriate technique to evoke the thick-lipped, chubby-faced, 'magnificently bibulous, blasphemous and bardic' Dylan Thomas, whose profile is shown in thick white paint on a background of confused dark-coloured lines. The whole painting – the result of using lightning sketches she had made back in the 1930s when she met Dylan Thomas for the first time – gives the impression of a ghost-like, aura-like, spiritual emanation out of the entangled meshes of reality. Dylan Thomas had died in 1954 and this is a moving homage to the life-loving poet.

The same technique was used for *Apocalyptic Head* (illus. 105), painted after John F. Kennedy's assassination in 1963. The head, surrounded by subdued shapes typical of Agar's works – festooned triangles, leaves, shell-like forms – stands out staring at us, a Janus-like, double face, one half white, the other half darker, with disturbed features – an icon of the chaos that the face – our face? – is confronted with. Nineteen sixty-three was the year following the climax reached in the Cold War between the USA and USSR, and for once Agar was yielding to the zeitgeist.

In 1961, Agar was invited to exhibit in William C. Seitz's enormous gathering of artists in the Museum of Modern Art's 'The Art of Assemblage' with *Woman Reading*. That year, she also exhibited at the Brook Street Gallery in February and at the Contemporary Portrait Society at Wildenstein's, and

104 Eileen Agar, Head of Dylan Thomas, *1960–62, oil and acrylic on board.*

in October and November 1963, she had a retrospective show at the Brook Street Gallery again with a small catalogue containing a preface by Herbert Read, in which he defined her charm: 'Charm is not one of the surrealist virtues . . . But by dislocating charm, by fragmenting it and converting it into barbaric jewels, Eileen Agar deprives charm of its sentimentality.'

The production of canvases was phenomenal through the 1960s, '70s and '80s. It is true that the developing use of acrylic – which Agar discovered in 1965 – was a decisive factor in the sense, as she remarked, that 'acrylic, a water-based polymer emulsion paint, will not crack when the canvas is rolled up . . . It is very versatile, can be used as impasto, with palette knife, or a thin wash (which) gives wonderful glazes.'

In April 1958, Bard and Agar had moved to a new flat and a larger studio, West House in Melbury Road, Kensington. She had new premises to herself – the whole of the top floor – and could feel free to paint large canvases, which definitely exerted an influence on the development of her 'style'. Her work evolved towards more 'mystery' in meaning, more secret or complex symbolism and more celebratory disruption of reality, the reason being that she could go into more experimental combinations of forms and colours in a larger space. What she was developing then was the introduction of a new time dimension to her images, as well as a series of cultural cross-references and the creation of ambiguous and paradoxical paintings with no main 'theme' but from which the spectator, once drawn into them, may extract his own images; in other words the institution of a dialogue between nature and the intellect. At that time, she renewed links with Julian Trevelyan, F. E. McWilliam, Ceri Richards and Roland Penrose, the pioneers of Surrealism in England, rekindling old friendships. Julian Trevelyan and Mary Fedden, his second wife, had renewed their pre-war habit of holding parties every year at their place on Durham Wharf on Boat Race day. Friends would flock to their small garden overlooking the Thames in Chiswick Mall, a most festive occasion. This new development was brilliantly revealed at Agar's huge retrospective exhibition of 76 works at the Commonwealth Institute in 1971, hailed by Penrose, who saw in these 'sensations of time and space . . . where sharply delineated forms hover in darkness so that the blackness that surrounds them is alive in its own right and others where transparent forms with softer edges merge together creating new volumes and a magic sense of depth.' This repeated process, which consists in merging shapes and making other shapes emerge, is an obvious tribute to Surrealism – we think of Dalí, Brauner, Bellmer and Dominguez.

105 Eileen Agar, Apocalyptic Head, *1963, oil and lacquer on paper.*

One could thus consider together on a par the works *A Desert Island* (1960), *Portrait of My Mother* (1960), *Woman Bearing Fruit* (1962), *Harlequin*

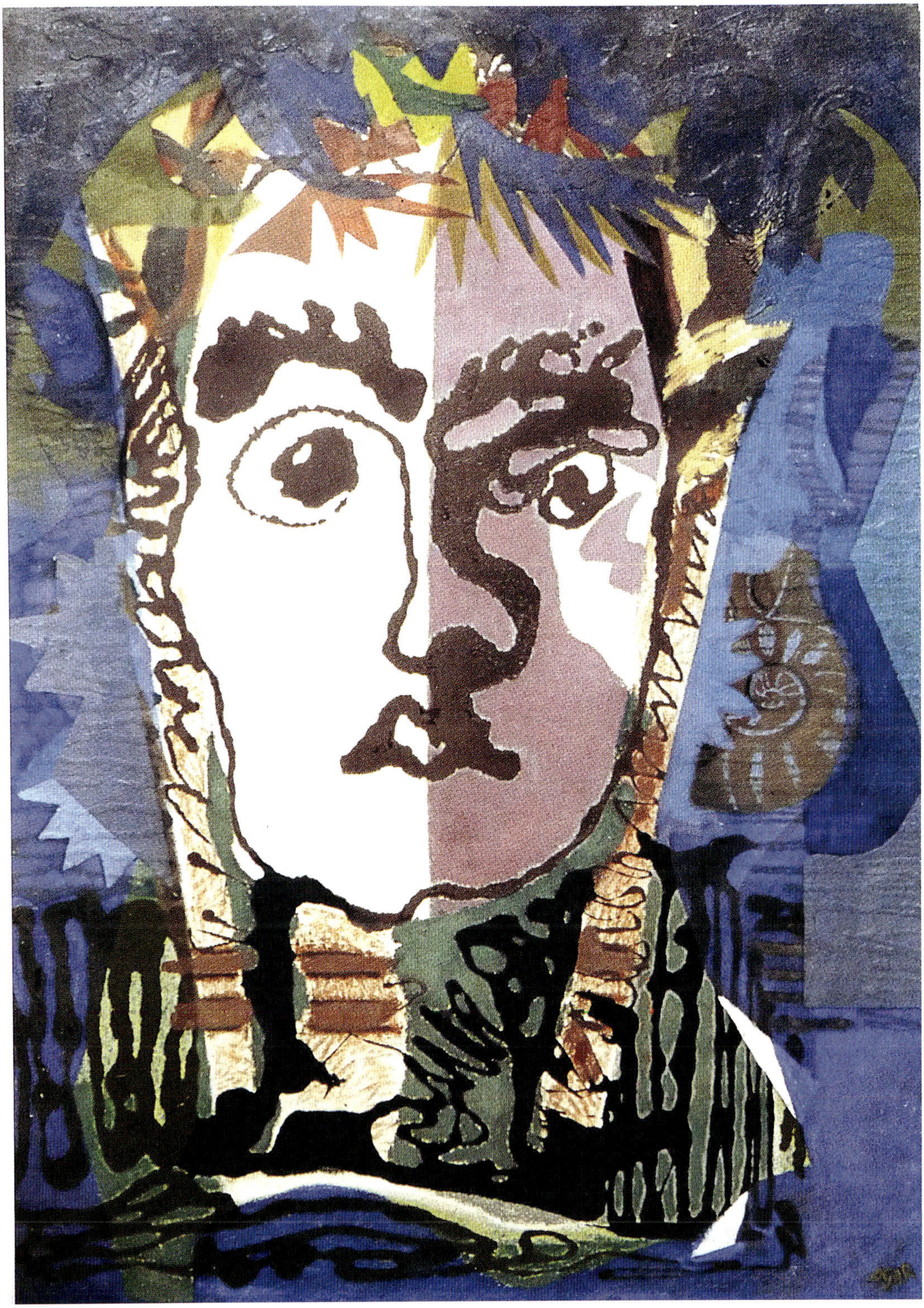

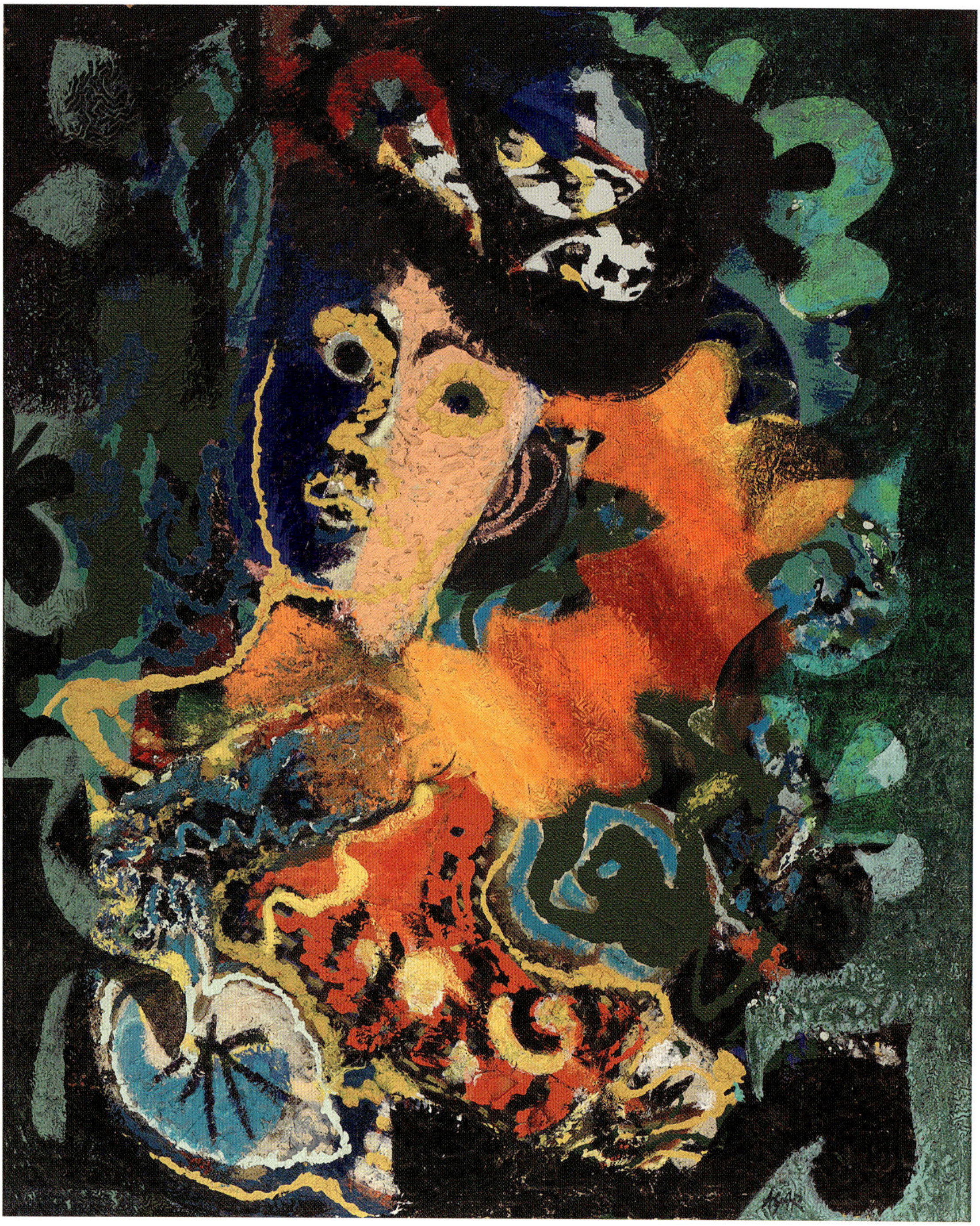

(1968), *The Bird* (1969) and *Slow Movement* (1970). They all testify to the stunning creativeness, energy and wealth of Agar's imagination. In *A Desert Island*, a most ironic title, profuse colours and shapes, here again both geometric and vegetable, dovetail into each other to make a figure emerge who proves to be an anthropomorphic, animal creature by the mere 'trick' of adding to a protuberance one little circle, which thus becomes an eye on a face profile. The figure is standing and wondering at huge bulbous forms, at the encounter of leaves, stems and a starfish on a uniform background – rather rare in Agar's works. Is this the landing of a man on a desert island, confronted with its exotic plants and himself turning into them? *Portrait of My Mother* (illus. 106) follows the process of condensation, as in dream work: the elaborateness of the hat worn by Agar's mother is echoed throughout the whole painting in a process of accretion, shedding leaves, flowers, feathers and various ornaments, as well as all kinds of colours in a whirling movement, and contrasts with a certain 'vacantness' in the eyes, another portrait from beyond death. As the note in the Scottish National Gallery of Modern Art catalogue specifies: 'Eileen's mother was a lady of many hats and would not dream of going away to the seaside without some forty hats.' They were 'enormous constructions of straw, velvet and fur like frigates under sail or birds on the wing', and it is true that hats often recur in Agar's own photographs. One can recall the Schiaparelli hat she wore at the opening of the 'International Surrealist Exhibition' in London in 1936, and which looked exactly like a shoe upturned, or the hat covered with overlapping Schiaparelli gloves which she wore at the opening of the 'Surrealist Objects and Poems' exhibition in November 1937 – a pun on the expression 'to touch one's hat'? – and the 'hat for eating bouillabaisse', covered with sea-shells, starfish and seaweed, which she wore for the James Laver TV programme in 1948.

Woman Bearing Fruit (illus. 107) is another dovetailing of two contrasting elements, the figure of a woman and the shape of a vase with a handle, one being indistinguishable from the other. The vase is the body of the woman, its swelling forms her womb – womb-magic here again, but made material and figurative. An arabesque, like a cast-iron decoration, forms the eyes – another metamorphosis of the mineral into the anthropomorphic, echoing the femininity of both the vase and the figure. The vase has become like a keyhole for the viewer, through which the woman can be seen together with what the vase is supposed to bear – so much so that the fertility of the woman turns into, and is inseparable from, the fertility the viewer's eyes are now endowed with.

Is it possible to see *The Bird* (1969, illus. 108) as Agar's most emblematic, symbolical work? Even if the symbol is simple and straightforward – the bird

106 Eileen Agar, Portrait of My Mother, *1960, oil on board.*

laying eggs which in turn give birth to the bird which has laid the eggs – it is the process of superimposition which is intriguing, because the eggs, which partially 'contain' the bird, are also depositories of other forms and colours, a festival of creation and a celebration of the alchemical operation. Indeed, the painting brings together the vessel-like shape of the bird, floating on the chessboard of the world through the dark forest of the mind. The magical eggs which hold the birth of the future are visited and 'reviewed' by the bird, the Supreme Being of Creation, a material *and* immaterial entity wearing both translucent and solid colours. *Slow Movement*, in spite of its title, hints at a deep, unstoppable movement of the two twin forms, trembling, so to speak, at the limit of their immobility, one about to touch and embrace the other and probably couple with it, shapes attracting shapes in their similarity – an elegant gesture which the observer's eye is tempted to develop and make complete. As a note appended to the painting reveals, it comes from one of Agar's memories of a work she had seen in the Musée des Thermes in Rome, *The Throne of Ludoviso*, representing two women raising Aphrodite from the sea. The doubleness and symmetry which fuse into a subtle circularity, the two hands on the right and on the left, the head shape in the middle, all seem to spell out the slow ascending movement mentioned in her declaration about the work: 'Although the painting is far removed, I was interested in the movement of the arms above the head (mine being almost abstract) and the circular movement of the whole.' Indeed, a most hieratic choreography, a magical dance.

As a kind of rest from the intricate entanglements and overlappings of forms, Agar made an object, *Spear Plant* (illus. 109), in 1965, emblematic of the simplest and least elaborated process at the heart of the Surrealist object – an object just found at first, then given an interpretation. The initial object, a spear with a handle, is simply planted in an earthenware flower pot and that is all, an object-collage in a way, a most minimal bringing together of two distant realities, never meant to meet – in the way Picasso would turn a bicycle handle into a bull's head. From two realities, *Spear Plant* creates a third reality, conjured up by the imaginative powers of the mind – the sign of a radical rebellion against what reality imposes upon us. The Surrealist object, let us remember, is somehow flipped away from the world it belongs to, and handed over to a new, indefinite process of re-identification.

The same symmetry found in *Slow Movement* haunts *Figures in a Garden*, first painted in 1970 under the title *October 70* but added to and modified in 1979 and given a new title. The two figures, strictly parallel with each other, both holding similar colours in their hands and with the same head shapes, identically crowned, are made transparent to nature.

107 Eileen Agar, Woman Bearing Fruit, *1962, acrylic on canvas.*

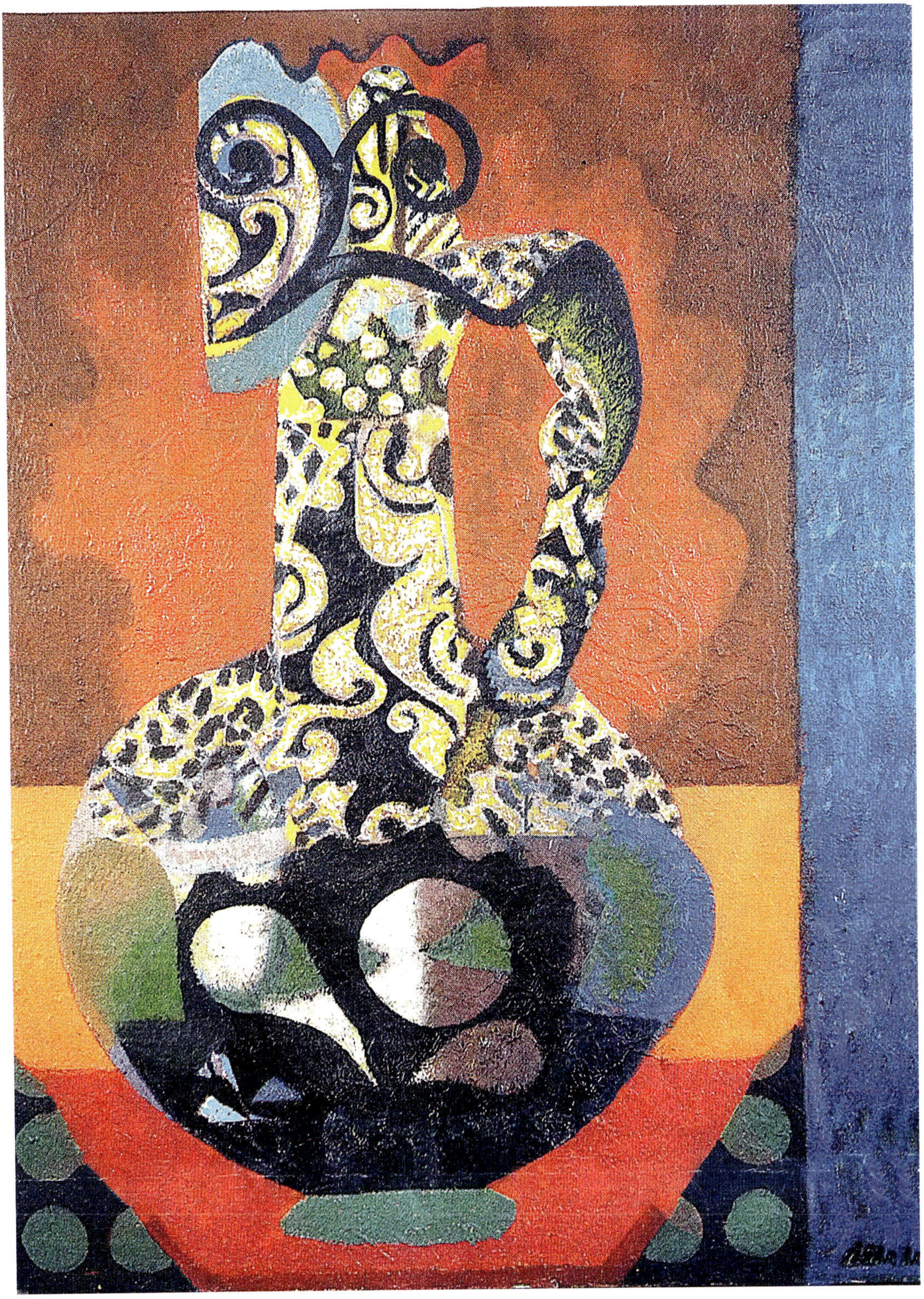

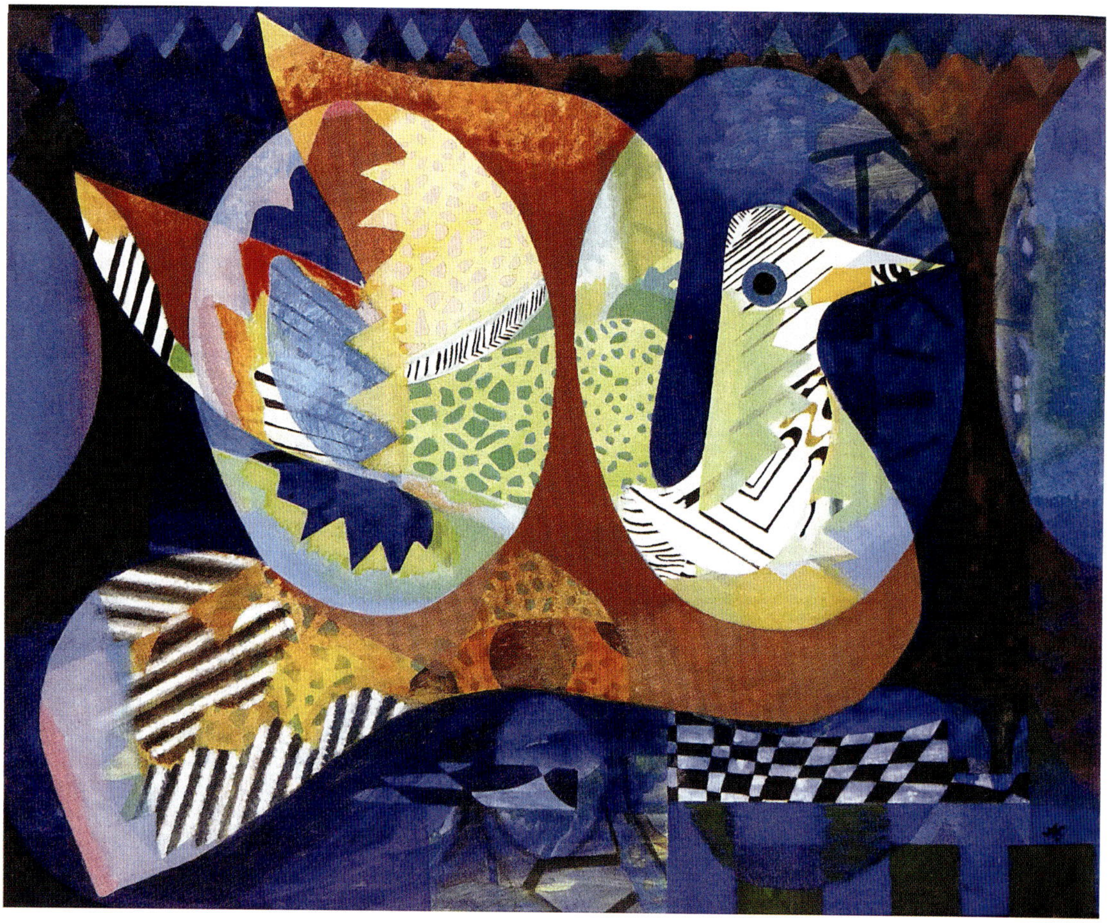

Their bodies are hidden and covered in various places as if they were passing behind plants, bushes or trees and were partially absorbed, eaten away and hollowed out – probably Agar's own phantasmatic wish to fuse with nature and its forces of transformation. A painting of the same fruitful year, *Muscles of the Imagination* (illus. 110), illustrates this passionate fusion between the artist and her work, as if the painting were the very photograph of the workings of her own mind. Should we here remember André Breton's definition of automatism as the 'dictation of the subconscious'? Indeed, *Muscles of the Imagination* appears as a kind of X-ray of the forces at work in the brain. Long tongues of colours with prehensile hands or tentacles form a kind of dervish dance, interacting with, and overlapping each other in, a flourishing outburst of hearts, star shapes and eye-like circles – a powerful jigsaw puzzle, the perfect representation of the unrepresentable forces of the imagination – Éluard's 'fertile hands', full of tension and almost magnetic attraction, stretching out towards the inner reality of the mind.

Laocoon (1972, illus. 111) is a collage which distances itself from the classical representation of the visionary seer seen in the coils of snakes, in the sense that it represents an interiorization of the struggle between Laocoon and the snake – a kind of reversal, or rather a negative, of the famous mythological episode as described by Virgil in the *Aeneid*. The original sculpture by three artists from Rhodes in the first century BC was dug out in Rome and is now in the Vatican Museum, which Agar must have known, if not seen. Laocoon, a Trojan priest, had warned his compatriots against the wooden horse outside their walls but no one listened to him, and then two serpents emerged from the sea and killed his two sons. In her collage, Agar appropriately emphasized the meaning of the episode by showing Laocoon struggling with himself and his various 'colourful' visions – he who held the truth of his visions was not trusted. The joyful rainbow colours inside Laocoon are indeed superseded by the twisting brown shapes of the interior demons. Compared to Leon Underwood's *Laocoons*, the oil painting from 1955 and the sculpture made in 1962, which represent in a very figurative way Laocoon and his two sons struggling with the snakes, Agar's *Laocoon* – a deliberate or unconscious answer to Underwood's? – is clearly a visionary, almost psychological, interpretation of the metaphysical dilemma and physical struggle which tore Laocoon's mind and body apart, and, as a consequence, a kind of 'eternalization' of the Trojan priest's dilemma: never will he be liberated from an eternally suspended time; the snakes will always be his future.

Dance of the Minerals (illus. 112), painted a little later, in 1973, conveys the same interiorization and sense of deep convoluted rhythm which Agar raised to being *the* principle which underlies natural forms. Here the

108 Eileen Agar, The Bird, *1969, acrylic on canvas.*

playfulness of the minerals is pushed to extremes: precious or semi-precious stones, agate-looking or diamond-like, with their many reflections, as if they received different kinds of light simultaneously, are involved in an ascending and descending rhythm, creating a circulation of gems together with other favourite shapes of hers – a chequer-board, stripes which reappear here and there to form an underlying backcloth, winding bands and eyes, angular and circular forms, an alternation of light and dark colours – a festival for the eye, again, a celebration of the aerial, prolific invention of the imagination which, actually, *sees* human minerals.

A similar confusion of categories haunts *Apollo's Lyre* in 1973 (illus. 113), a collage which requires at least a secondary reading into the work. Indeed, the collage suggests the stylized representation of the two hemispheres of the brain – an anatomical diagram whose scientific origin is emphasized by the numbers which it bears, since it was probably cut out from some plate illustrating the natural sciences. The space between the two slightly opened hemispheres – like a door ajar – reveals the drawing of a human figure behind, likely to be the owner of the brain, while the title estranges us from whatever we see. Indeed, one of the two hemispheres is 'opened out' to reveal the stem of a plant with leaves growing on it and the general shape can only be what the title says. Here, the content (the brain) reveals the container (the human figure) while opening on to another realm – the vegetable kingdom. At the centre, five lines may refer to the original five chords of the Greek lyre and the two hemispheres of the brain may also remind one of an upturned tortoise shell, the original resonance chamber created by Hermes and given to his brother Apollo. Let us remember that Joseph Bard was a great Greek classicist.

The same year, *A Vase Awakened by Music* (illus. 114) coalesces the themes of woman and music. The womb-like shape of the vase is brought in to another life by the collage of three triangles – geometric as well as musical connotations – and by anthropomorphic attributes. The vase is fragmented and a series of five strings seems to transform it into a guitar-shaped instrument, smiling at us, the whole composition echoing the face of a jester, huge eyes like musical notes dancing round, the top of the face reminiscent of a jester's hat with its bells. Is there any hint at Orpheus, who could raise emotions in inanimate creatures, or at Amphion, who could move stones to the sound of his music? In any case, the status of the object, its stability, its identity, are jocularly but subtly questioned.

Throughout that period, Surrealism was constitutively present in Agar's mind and vision, whether she accepted the idea consciously or not – one can hardly trust her repeated unilateral declaration of independence

Opposite: 109 Eileen Agar, Spear Plant, *1965, metal, plastic and wood.*

Overleaf left: 110 Eileen Agar, Muscles of the Imagination, *1969, acrylic on canvas.*

Overleaf right: 111 Eileen Agar, Laocoon, *1972, oil on canvas.*

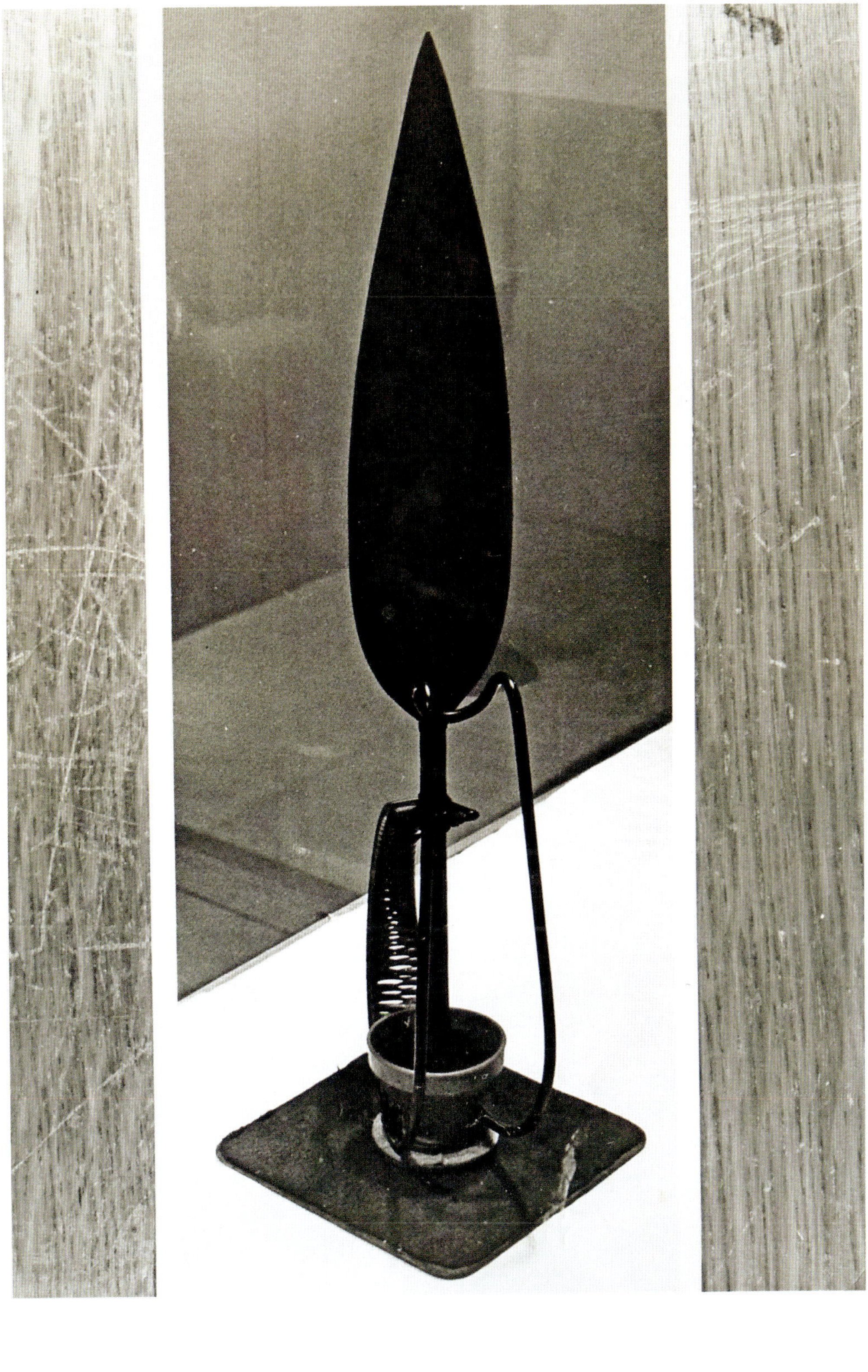

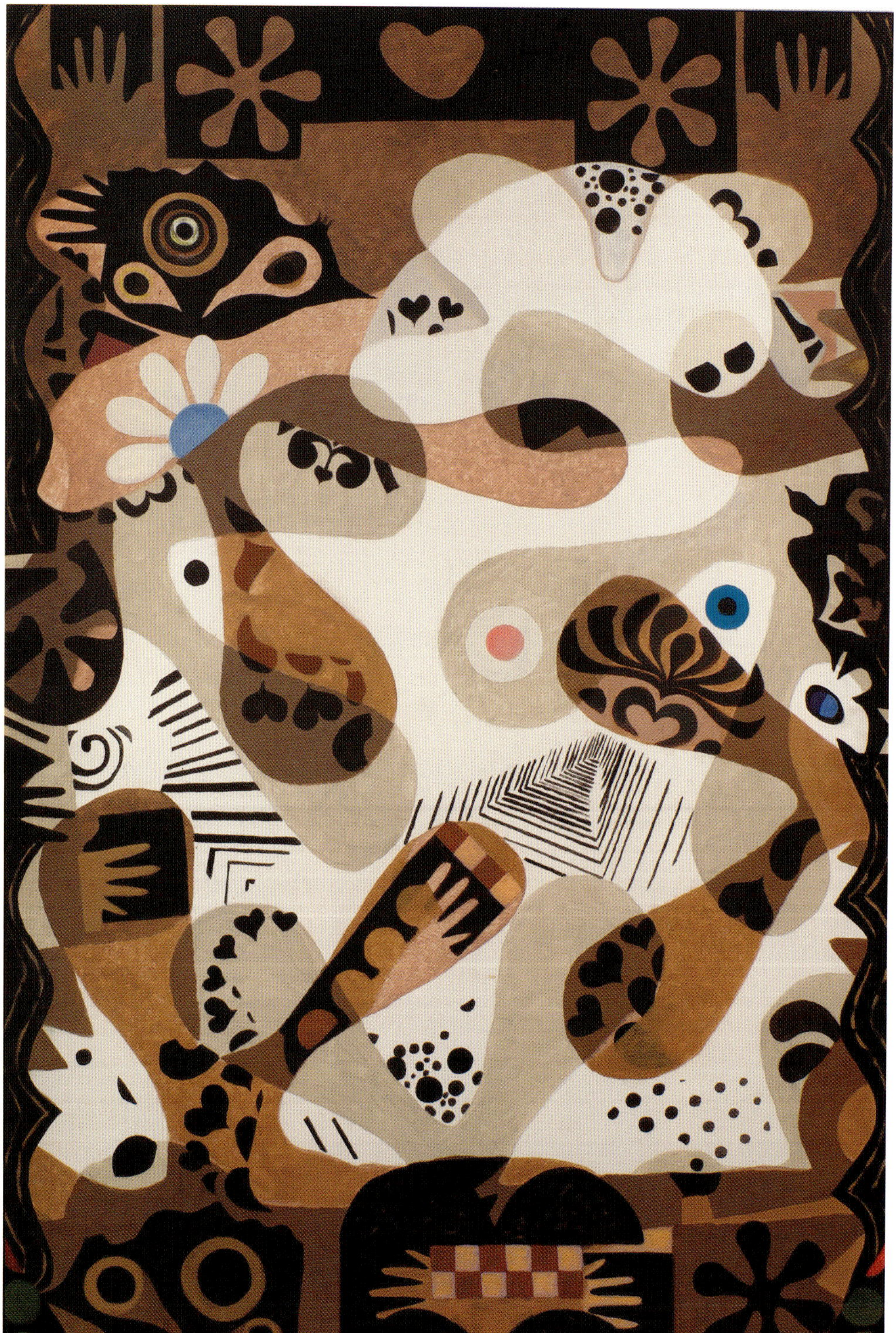

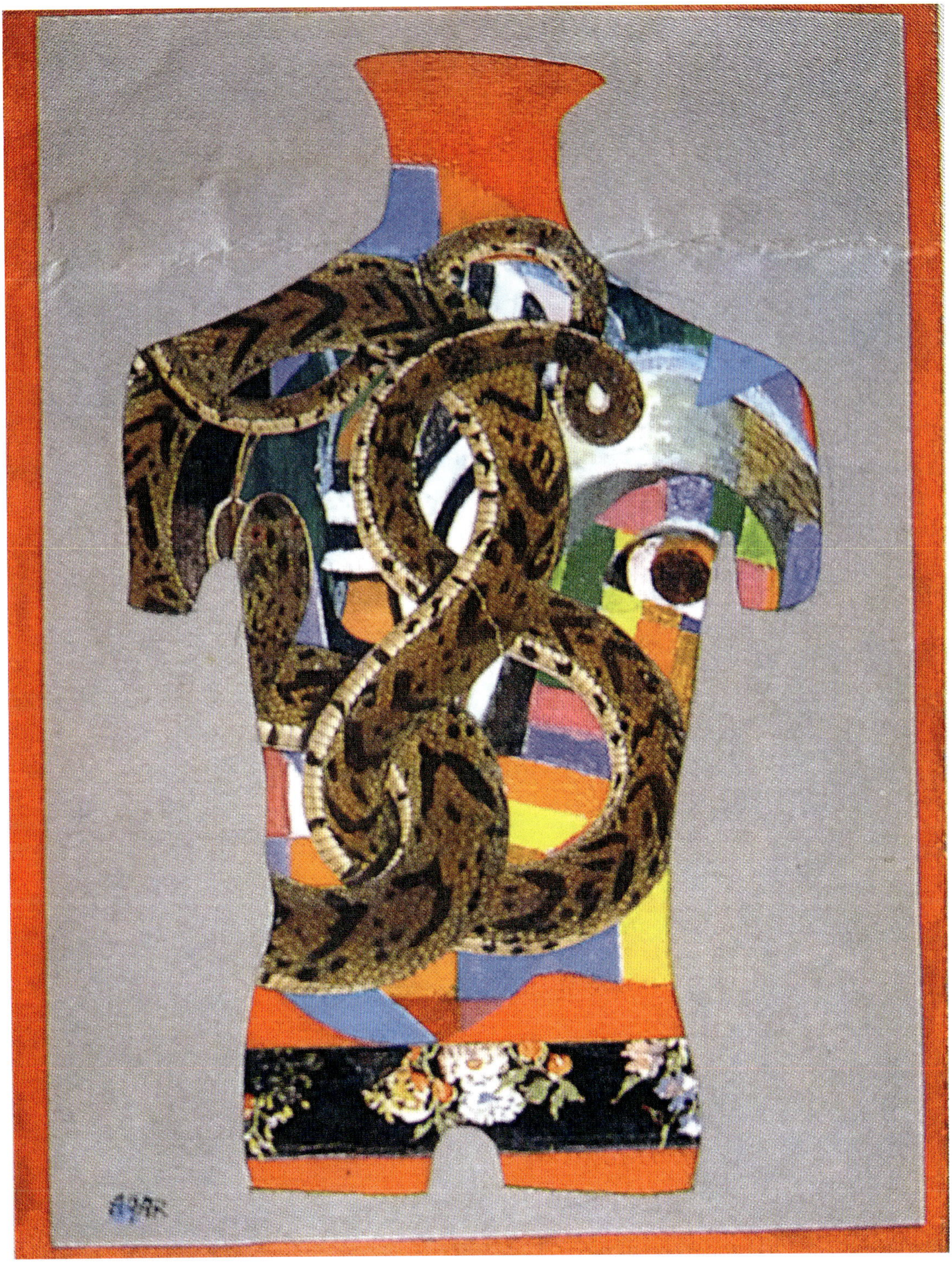

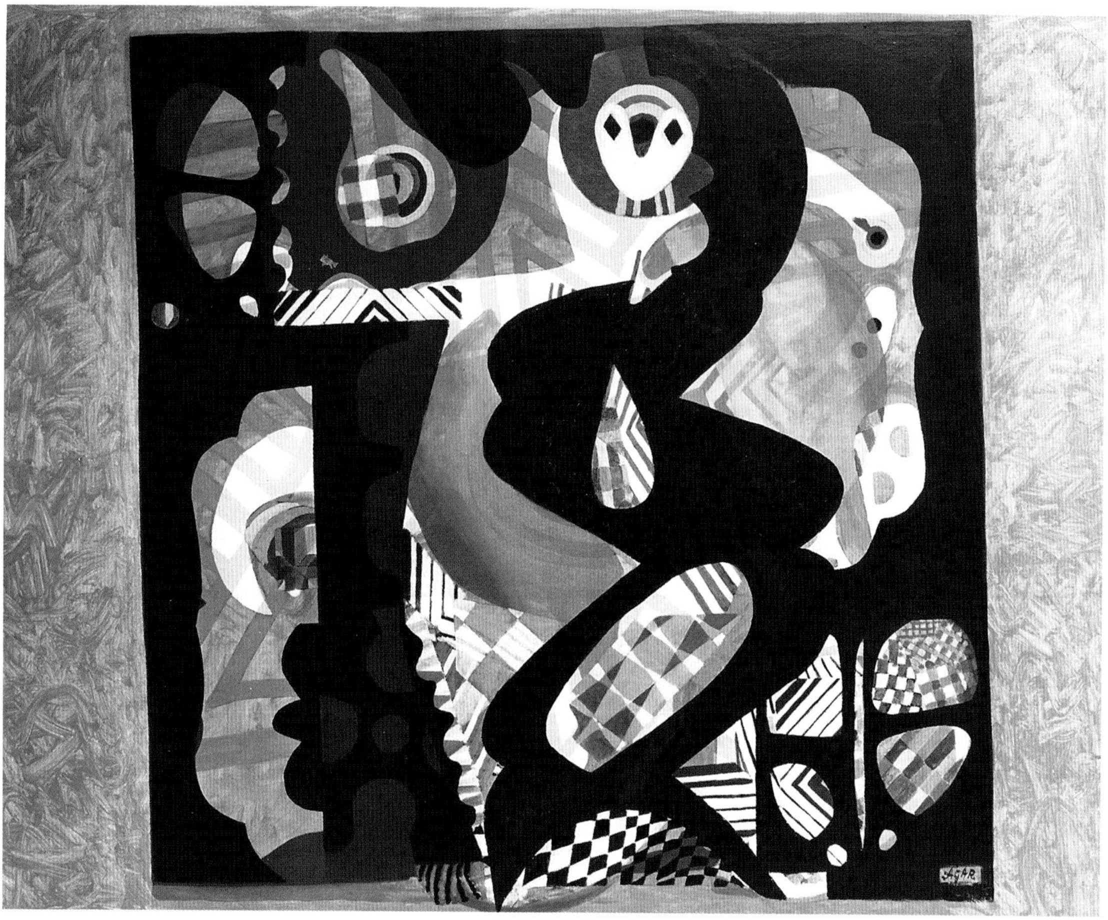

from the movement! Indeed, Surrealism was back on the agenda starting in 1967, from 24 April to 20 May, when E.L.T. Mesens, Conroy Maddox, Roland Penrose and John Lyle – a courageous bookseller thoroughly devoted to Surrealism in Exeter, who was to inspire British Surrealism to return to the art scene for the next twenty years or so – staged the formidable gathering of Surrealists in the 'Enchanted Domain' exhibition held at Exeter City Gallery and Exe Gallery. The exhibition also featured lectures, film shows, discussions, plays, teach-ins and readings, with the participation of many prominent post-war French Surrealists (Breton had died the year before in September 1966). In his preface to the catalogue, George Melly pointed out that 'surrealism was not confined to its own time' and was able 'to place itself historically and recognize its own ancestors', thus emphasizing Surrealism's timeless validity in its urge to 'exteriorize one's vision of a counter-reality based on our "inscape", our dreams, our real nature', and seeing Surrealism as a kind of axis between the past and the future, the visible and the invisible, a constantly moving axis. Agar was obviously invited to exhibit, and among the 125 works selected, she displayed two oil paintings (*Sphinges* from 1936 and *Seek and Hide* from 1960), one object, *The Muse Listening* (although the work reproduced in the catalogue was *Mate in Two Moods*) and two collages (*Three Archons* from 1965 and *Katchina* from 1967). The welcome extended to a new generation of Surrealists, like Anthony Earnshaw and Patrick Hughes, who were to contribute to the development of the movement, thus indicating its permanence.

From 3 to 27 November 1971, the Hamet Gallery in Cork Street, London, staged an exhibition of 115 works which represented British Surrealism at its best and most forceful. Helped by Penrose and George Melly, the directors of the gallery managed to attract into the exhibition 27 of the 'historical' Surrealists: those who had exhibited at the New Burlington Galleries in 1936, even those who left the group soon after, and two or three fellow-travellers like John Lake, Victor Reinganum and Edward Wadsworth, who were rather 'magic realists' than pure Surrealists. Agar exhibited five of her most epoch-making works – *Muse of Construction* (1939), three collages, *Possessed* (1939), *Parcel Post* (1942) and an untitled one from 1939, and a *Portrait* from 1934. It was the occasion to renew friendship with the pioneers of the heroic days – Roland Penrose, F. E. McWilliam, Julian Trevelyan, John Banting, John Melville, Conroy Maddox and others. A photograph showing Trevelyan, Banting, Melville, Maddox, Merlyn Evans, Emmy Bridgwater and Edith Rimmington boarding a bus specially hired for the occasion shows them all together (illus. 115). The re-emergence and permanence of the

112 Eileen Agar, Dance of the Minerals, *1973, acrylic on canvas.*

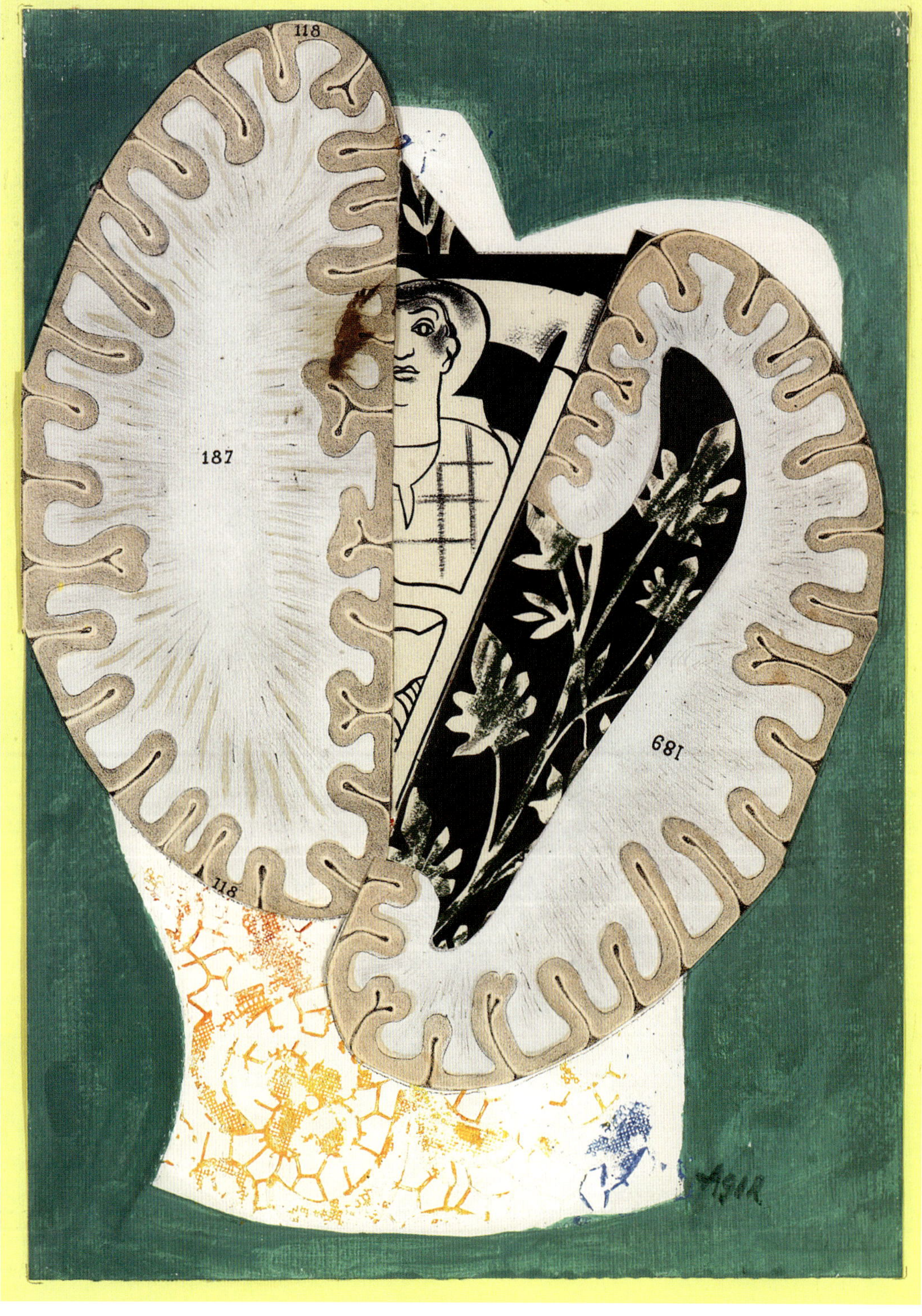
118
187
118
189

Surrealist spirit, four years after the Exeter show, was confirmed, and reaffirmed Agar's central presence within the ranks of British Surrealists.

There is no doubt that the formidable bout of creation in the 1960s and early '70s helped her to assuage and mask the deep personal pain she felt at the breakdowns and eventual demise of her beloved husband Joseph Bard on 26 July 1975, the sudden interruption of a fifty-year solid and fully reciprocal faithful relationship, whatever the vicissitudes of life. Bard had been ill for about fifteen years and the last years had been miserable for both. For one thing, Bard couldn't stop being depressed at the thought of having not completed his memoirs and his other many projects. A fundamentally European mind, a personality open to all new ideas and averse to the restraint and restrictiveness of English intellectual life, eager to live and love life, he couldn't but be disappointed by the zeitgeist, as he said, and disillusioned at the advent of cold, impersonal times. For him, Europe was losing, had lost, even, its vitality and all its promises by 'allowing' dictatorships and their bloodbaths. His appetites were too plain and too large. 'The leopard could not suddenly put on a tiger skin' is the way Agar summed up the dead end he eventually found himself in, for all that he resisted it. In her autobiography, she lucidly explains: 'distrustful [as he was] of psychiatric therapy', and getting more and more worried about his own financial situation and, more generally, about what the future held in stock, beset by age and illness, subject to hallucinations, he spent his last years in Agar's care and attention. Those years were occasionally brightened by his election as vice-president of the Royal Society of Literature (at Cecil Day-Lewis's instigation), and by his sustained enjoyment of reading and collecting gems and by a few, but rarer and rarer, social events at their flat. Bard was the one who had introduced Agar not only to luminaries of the time, including Ezra Pound, but to classical lore, art and literature, and to the treasures disclosed in intellectual exchanges and conversations.

Life for Agar throughout the 1970s and '80s was the life of a 'celebrity', a life of intense, prolific work as well as a busy social and intellectual life, entertaining close friends, scholars and critics at her home, going out to the theatre, the opera, the cinema, and to private views with friends like Annette Armstrong. This is revealed by her carefully kept diaries. A few telling examples from the 1980s will suffice. In 1980, on the occasion of the 'Abstraction: Towards a New Art' exhibition at the Tate Gallery, she noted her thoughts on Terry Frost ('effect very invigorating'); later, on Dalí ('very influenced by Max Ernst but not such an artist'), and on Penrose, on the occasion of his eightieth birthday exhibition at the ICA in September ('extremely imaginative and poetic'). In a 1981 note, she records going to

113 Eileen Agar, Apollo's Lyre, *1973, collage.*

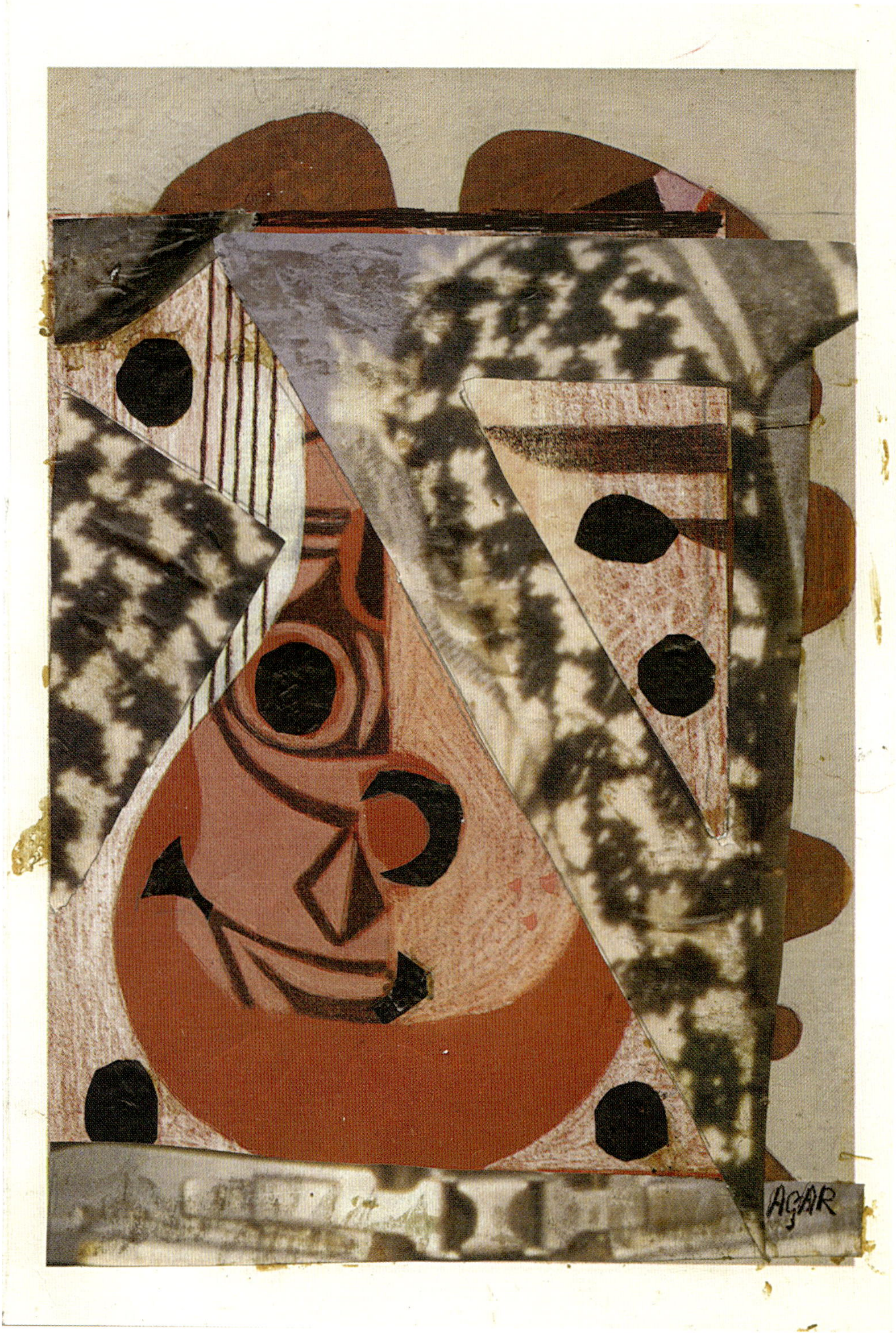
AGAR

Sadler's Wells to see *Così fan Tutte*; in July, she confided that Diana's wedding dress 'made her look like a pudding and the train too long didn't match the dress', adding: 'She has a lovely figure, so why hide it?' Parallel to this she shared her thoughts on Heidegger and Existentialism, on Wittgenstein and the *Tractatus*, and on Chomsky, too. In March 1983, on listening to A. J. Ayer at Eton, she agreed with his atheism, adding that, for her, 'God is a work of art created by Man through literature, the building of cathedrals and painting of holy pictures . . . Man's emotional needs reaching out to an idealized version of himself, woman and child, making God and religion a sort of universal art form.' In another entry in 1985, she focused on the philosophy of language as 'positing the world of reality and language as a subjective performance',

Opposite: 114 Eileen Agar, Vase Awakened by Music, *1973, collage.*

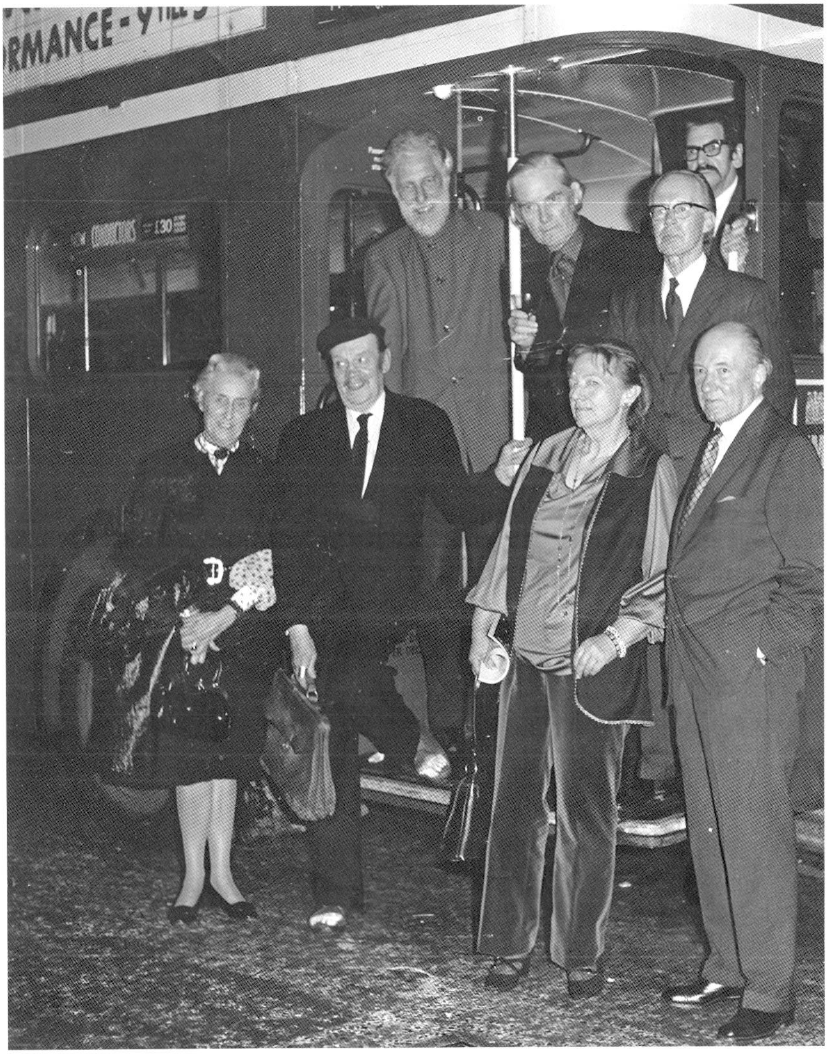

Below: 115 Eileen Agar, photograph of members of the Surrealist group at the opening of 'Britain's Contribution to Surrealism of the '30s and '40s' at the Hamet Gallery, London, November 1971. Back row, left to right: Julian Trevelyan, Merlyn Evans, John Melville, Conroy Maddox. Front Row: Edith Rimmington, John Banting, Emmy Bridgwater, ?.

and wondered 'why the surrealists were more influenced by Freud than by Jung and his theory that shared unconscious images modify the collective experience of the world', this being closer, she added, to the Surrealists' interest in myths and legends. She also loved ballet, such as *Coppélia*, 'because it comes nearest to flying and I have always desired wings.' Besides, every summer, she never missed going to Cornwall for her holidays, staying at St Ives (where she met Patrick Heron), St Mawes and St Austell. It was a life full of eclectic interests and receding horizons spent far from any ivory tower in the permanent search for the marvellous.

In 1975, she chose the New Art Centre as the gallery which would act as her agent. She was not to leave it until ten years later and in 1976 a large exhibition of her recent works was held there. In a preface to the catalogue of the show, 'A Decade of Discoveries', consisting of about forty works – collages, oil paintings and photographs – Roland Penrose celebrated the way 'stones became her children, the sky and the sea her intimate friends, leaves became her clothing and with sensitive love she learnt to create new symbols and transform by magic objects that had formerly passed unnoticed', able as she is now, he concluded, 'to add personal significance to all that she had learnt from surrealism' when, earlier on, she had been struck by 'the brilliance of the paintings of Max Ernst, Miró, Picasso' and had been 'highly susceptible to the inspiration that came from poets such as Breton and Éluard'. Who better than Roland Penrose could describe the 'ascendancy' of Agar's artistic imagination in 1976?

Is there any trace of almost autobiographical self-irony in *The Sorcerer's Apprentice*, painted in 1976? Against a background of night, perturbed by a drizzle of red rain, there appear grey, greyish and white forms, as if a magic wand had struck a flat earth-like, or epiderm-like base. Circles, spikes, biomorphic shapes are liberated, as well as groups of parallel string-like lines creating distant symmetries and rhythms. A background of strange apparitions can be entered by breaking through the screen of darkness – the main form reminding us of a soaring bird or bat, unless it be the spread-out robe of the sorcerer's apprentice as he opens his arms and reveals his tricks. This is one of the rare examples of totally unidentifiable forms seen at their emergence from the alchemical *terra nigra*. Had Agar seen Walt Disney's *Fantasia* or read Goethe's poem about the young boy who tried to imitate his master, the Great Wizard, but was defeated by the magic he had raised?

116 Eileen Agar, The Sleepwalkers, *1980, acrylic on canvas.*

The following year, in late 1977, Conroy Maddox, the spirit at the back of the resurgence of Surrealist activity in London in the wake of the 'Enchanted Domain' exhibition in Exeter, organized a meeting of Surrealists at the Barcelona restaurant in Beak Street where E.L.T. Mesens had held

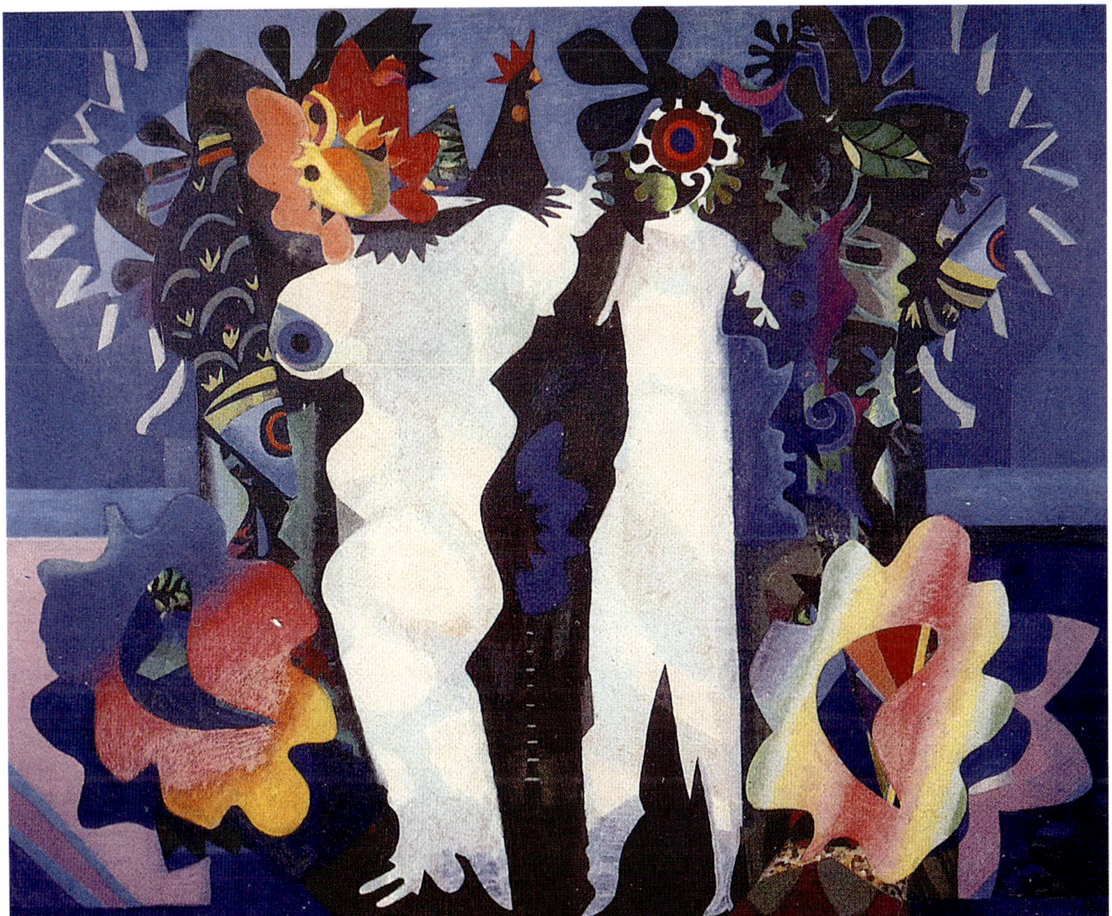

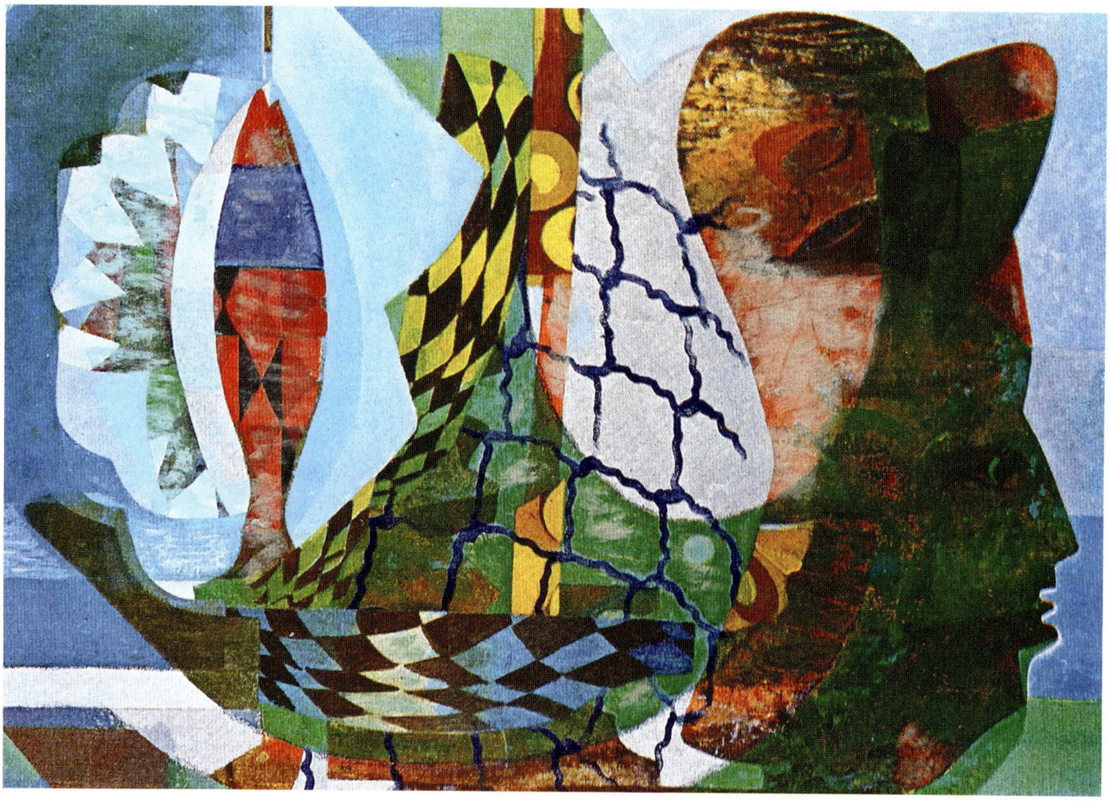

meetings of the group at the beginning and end of the war. Agar, George Melly, Robert Melville, Roland Penrose, Feyyaz Fergar (who had edited *Fulcrum*, a one-issue publication of Surrealist poems in 1944) and Conroy Maddox were filmed for television and Melly, as Agar recalls in her autobiography, recited a poem in which it rained knives and forks, and, actually doing what he was saying, he threw the knives and forks of the restaurant into the air, which led to the dismissal of the Surrealist gang immediately. This, among other things, tightened her relationship with Conroy Maddox, who would visit her rather frequently until her demise.

From January to March 1978 Conroy Maddox organized a formidable gathering of Surrealists from all countries in the world, entitled 'Surrealism Unlimited', at the Camden Arts Centre in London. One hundred and eighty-three works were brought together by 91 artists from France (Édouard Jaguer, the leader of the Phases movement – and continuator of Breton's role in post-war France – lent his hand and brought over no fewer than 29 artists), Canada, the USA, Czechoslovakia and Romania, among other countries. Agar exhibited four works – *Muscles of the Imagination* (1969), *The Sorcerer's Apprentice* (1976), *Vase Awakened by Music* and a collage of 1973. Evidently the exhibition was devoted exclusively to post-1968 Surrealism. The underlying idea was that the enormous 'Dada and Surrealism Reviewed' retrospective organized at exactly the same time at the Hayward Gallery by David Sylvester and Dawn Ades had limited the activity of Surrealism in England to around 1940 – a choice erroneously defended by David Sylvester – and had omitted so many 'historical' British Surrealists (such as Grace W. Pailthorpe, Edith Rimmington or Emmy Bridgwater), that the fundamental, *unlimitable* permanence of the Surrealist spirit was somehow betrayed. In reaction, Maddox conceived the Camden Arts Centre exhibition as a protest against the academic conservatism of the Hayward Gallery's truncated collection and wanted, by contrast, to emphasize the continuing life of Surrealism across the world there and then, and the necessity of reacting against any undertaking which might fossilize the movement. Agar was in total favour of this standpoint, even if she also exhibited at the Hayward Gallery with works from the past.

This being said, one must stress the historical interest of the Hayward exhibition, which was articulated around the main successive reviews, magazines and bulletins published by and with Surrealists in many countries since the days of Dada. Under the section given the title 'London Bulletin', Agar showed *Quadriga* (1935), lent by Roland Penrose, *Battle Years* (1939), lent by Gordon Onslow Ford, and two iconic objects from her studio, *The Angel of Anarchy* (1940) and *Marine Object* (1939).

117 Eileen Agar, Bride of the Sea, *1981, acrylic on canvas.*

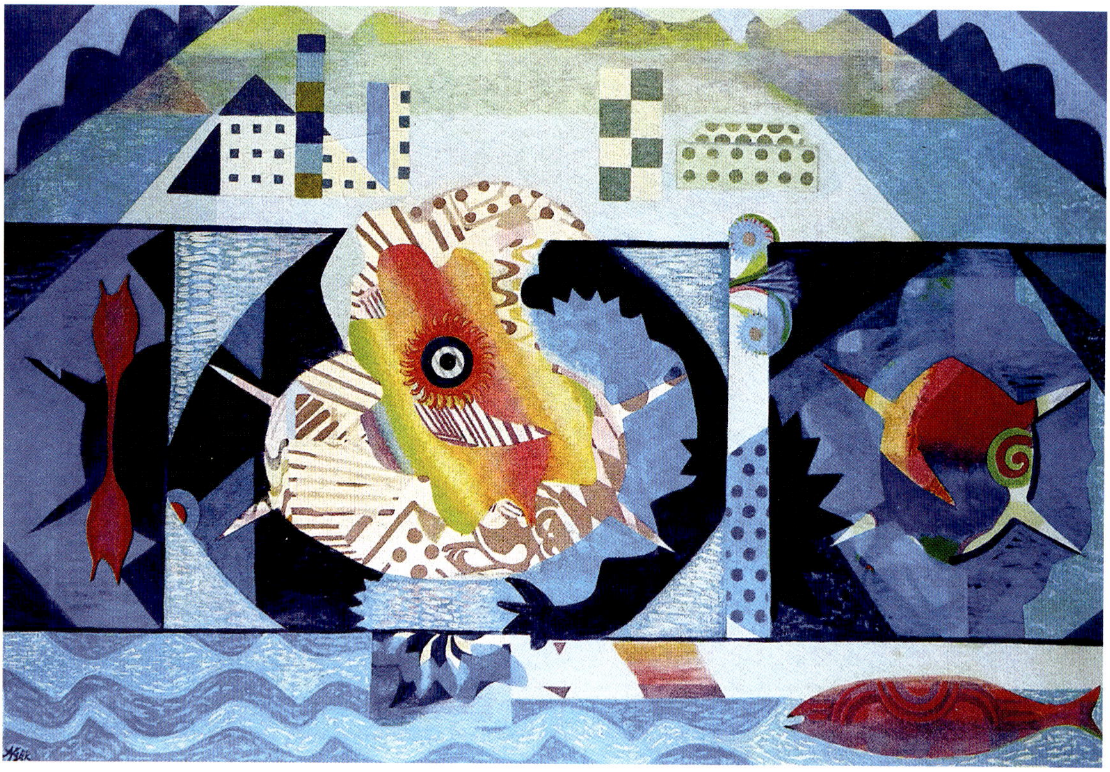

In October 1981, Agar's exhibition at the New Art Centre superlatively emphasized her 'highly sensitive imagination, her feminine clairvoyance and her sensitive love' with which 'she learnt to create new symbols and transform by magic objects that had formerly passed unnoticed', as Roland Penrose wrote in the preface to the catalogue. The exhibition featured a painting which bore some resemblance to *Figures in a Garden* and linked her undeniably to one of the main preoccupations of Surrealism – the world of dreams. In *The Sleepwalkers* (1980, illus. 116), two white spectral figures are caught strolling through a forest of fiery flowery shapes and dark trees with fish's eyes strewn in their foliage. According to Agar, 'it recalls the moment when all conscious control is gone, but when we are also rich with fantasy and unrestricted imagination. This, too, is terrifying, yet imagination is also our greatest strength.' Is it a dream or a nightmare? Are we those sleepwalkers, blind to the violence around us? Or should we allow our imagination to balance waking life with these imaginary adventures through the forest of the mind? Nobody will be able to tell, since it is during the artist's *and* the observer's descent into their own undecipherable mind, where they walk in another state, that the answer may be approached unawares. Let us be precise: the logic of the dream is articulated not by a binary opposition of contraries but by a kind of refusal of that binariness, thanks to which contraries are made to coincide and dovetail into each other – a credo which never left Agar's compositions.

In an article on the exhibition, the critic John Russell Taylor underlined in *The Times* the artistic debt Agar owed to Surrealism:

> I imagine we are not supposed to seek any too definable programmatic significance but just let the half-apprehended shapes and rich tint and textures work on our unconscious minds. To that extent, Agar is a surrealist still . . . the freedom and the life are still there: the pleasure principle rules.

Opposite: 118
Eileen Agar, Creatures of the Sea, *1981, acrylic on canvas.*

Oswell Blakeston, on 9 October, wrote about the same exhibition: 'She juggles with shapes and sings with colour' – noted down by Agar in her diary without precise reference to the newspaper in question.

Overleaf left: 119
Eileen Agar, Serenade for Spring, *1981, acrylic on canvas.*

Overleaf right: 120
Eileen Agar, Points of View, *1981, acrylic on canvas.*

The War Bride (1978–9), by contrast with another bride, *Bride of the Sea* (1979), both on show at this exhibition, stages a feminine figure's fluid, vegetal forms, encountering and struggling with all the violent forces of a mechanized, masculine world, a world made of angles, squares, straight lines, triangles and wheels which attack the lithe body of the bride. She proves to be the victim of the assault of rationality and the grinding emblems of machines. Indeed, *Bride*

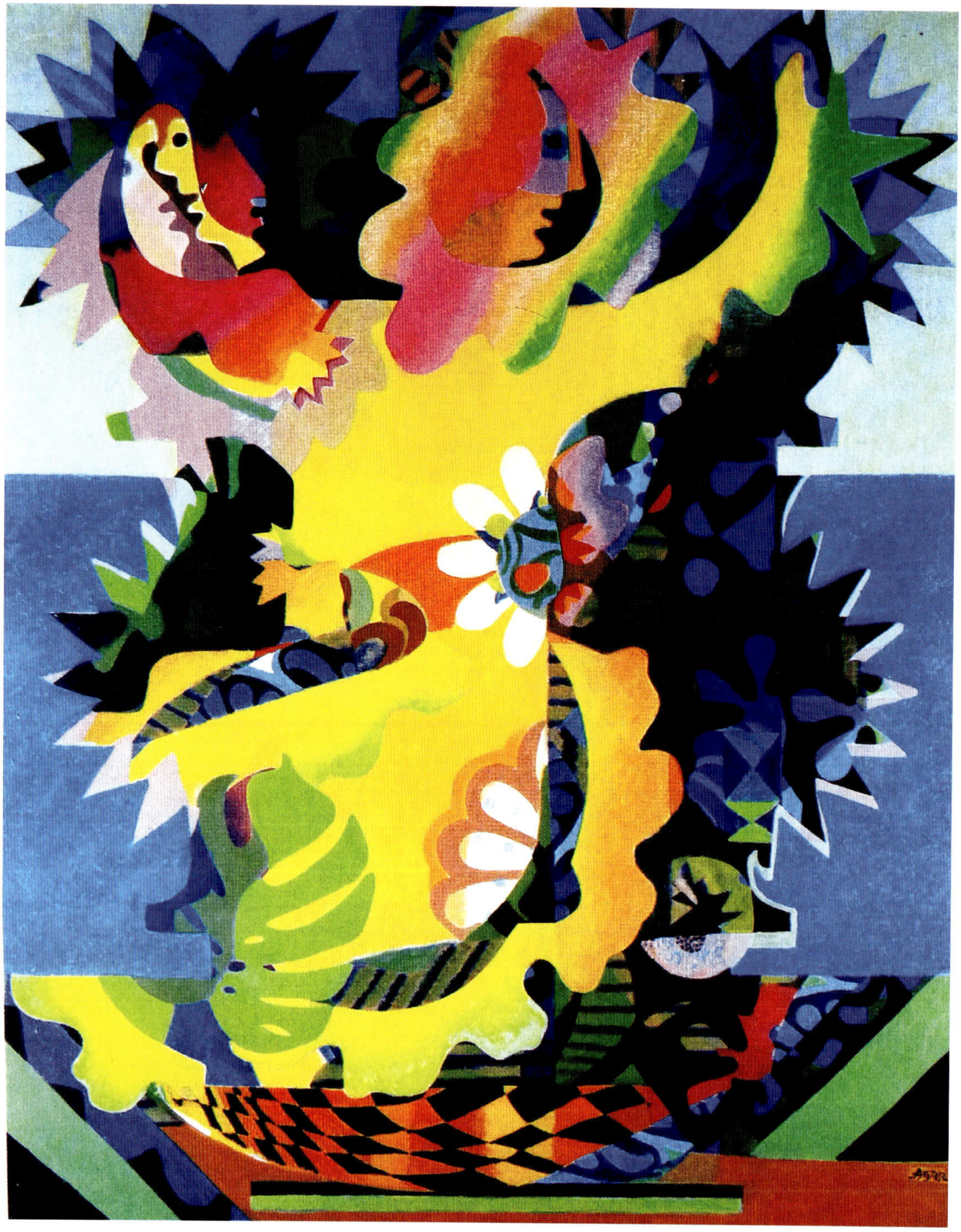

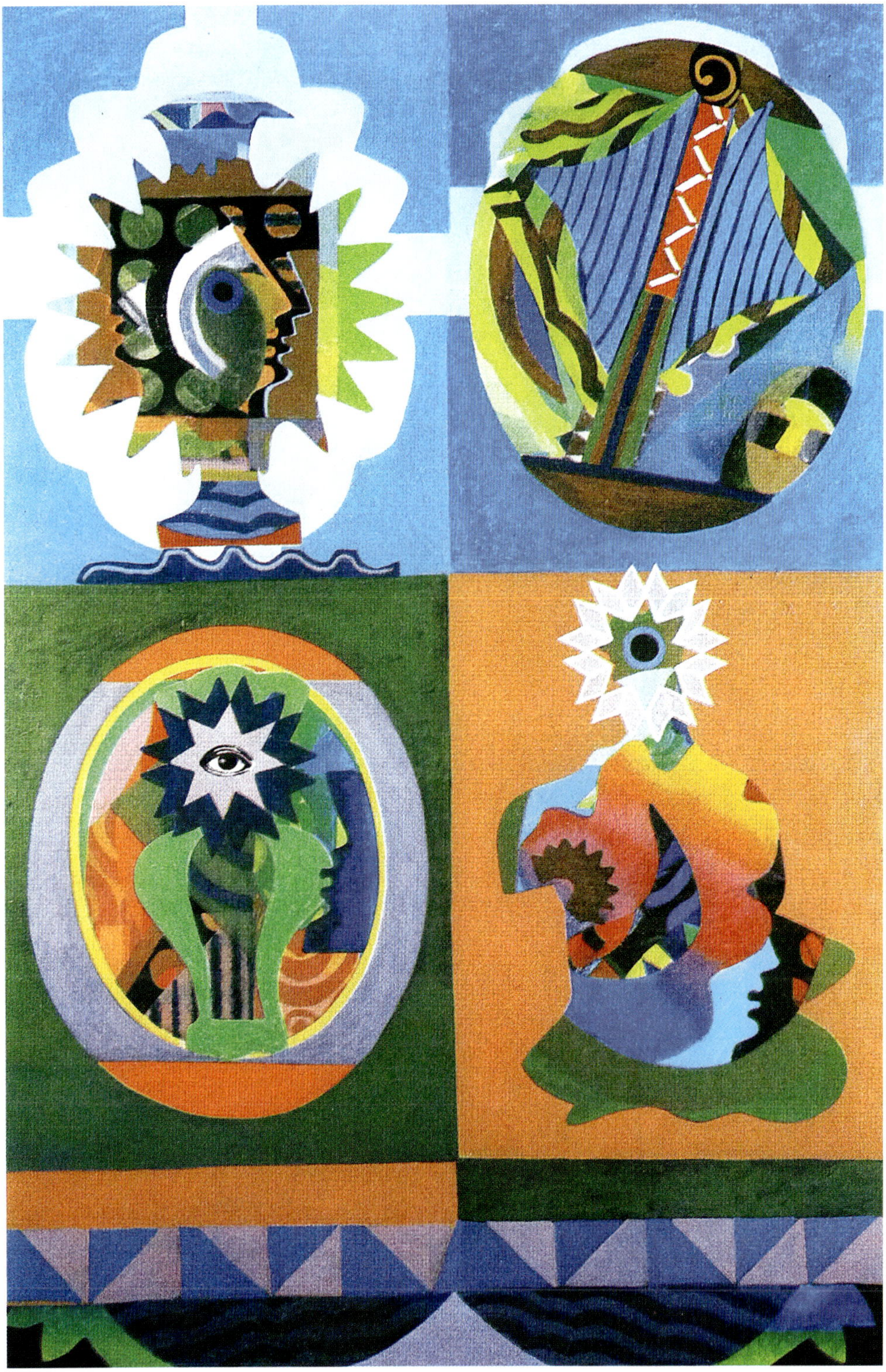

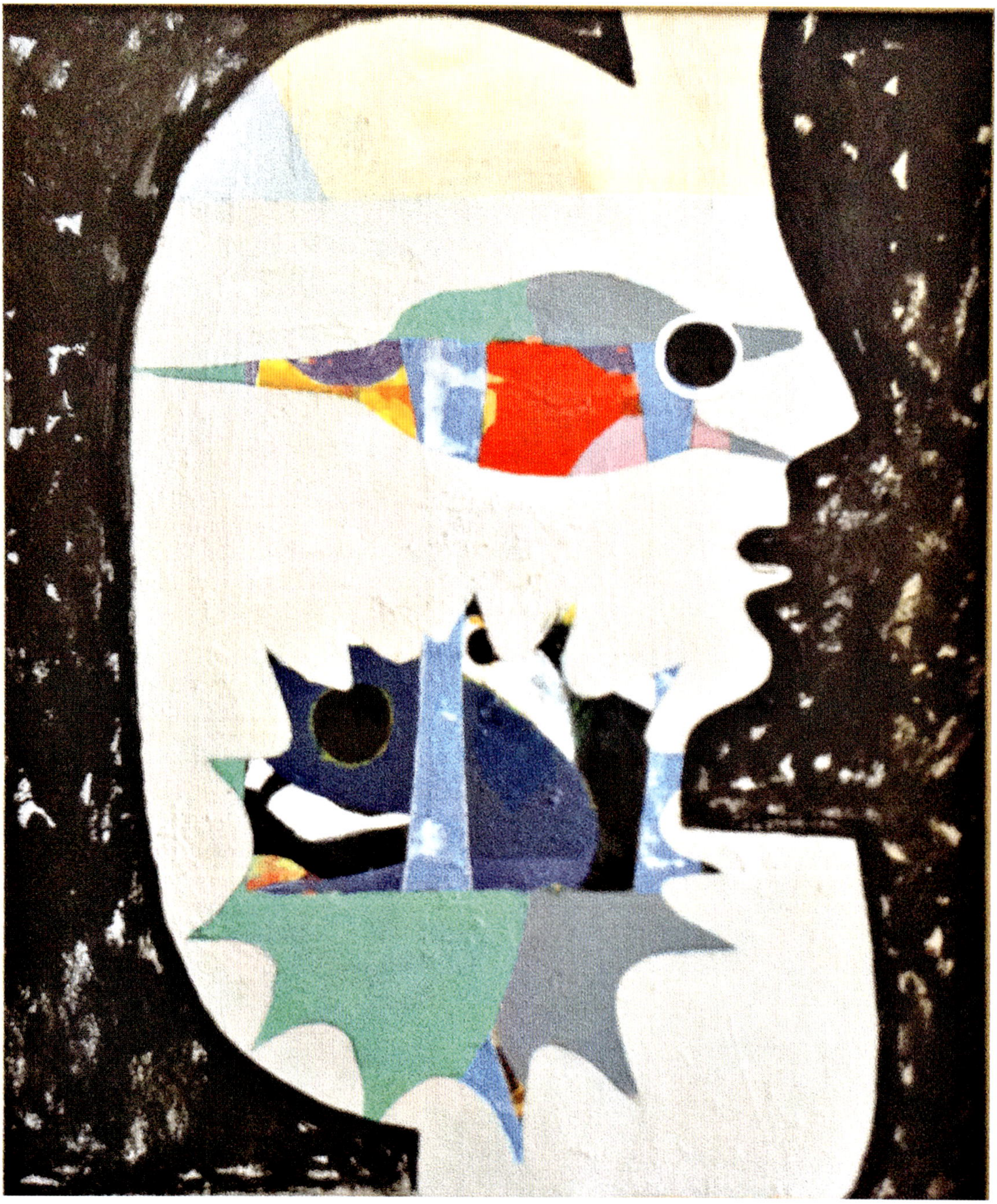

of the Sea (1981, illus. 117) is different and offers us the reading into the head of woman as the materialized spirit of the sea. But there is no metaphysics in this, only the concrete, material components of what the sea carries and conveys: the whole shape of the bride's head is that of a ship or galley with the typical feminine figure at its prow, sailing through what constitutes the idea of the sea – the ship and her mast, swollen sails made of fishnet, a fish and the blue horizon of the expanse of water. This is again given a rhythm with the chequer-board pattern which balances the whole composition and brightens it up. The bride is in a way fecundated by what she carries along with her, with a domination of blues and greens, which, like the various shapes, are juxtaposed, overlapping and fused together. *Creatures of the Sea* (1981, illus. 118), made at the same time and also exhibited at the New Art Centre, rather follows the basic structure of *The Autobiography of an Embryo*, in the sense that it asks us to read 'panels' from left to right as if we saw the depths of the sea through rectangular portholes, scenes which glide past us between a geometrical set of urban buildings above, and waves below. The form in the middle is a kind of madrepore, the emblem of monstrous unidentifiable sea creatures, and echoed on the right and left, imaginary fish and mollusc forms. The depths of the ocean – the subconscious, as we know – are inaccessible to our knowledge and hold unsolvable secrets.

Agar's faith in the restorative forces of nature is again expressed in *Serenade for Spring* (1981, illus. 119), the celebration of the love of man for woman, of the love of man for nature, and of the intimacy between them. Rising from a typical Agaresque chequer-board recipient, a huge feminine shape literally *embodies* the profusion and proliferation of natural forms, faces, hands, arms entangled into one another, exploding with the usual blue and green crests of pointed triangles which contrast with the fluid meanderings of yellow and orange garlands – against the background of a seascape. The rhythm of the forms, the harmony of colours, broken here and there by darker tones, definitely endow this composition with a deep musical quality which turns any evening on which a serenade is supposed to be performed into an everlasting bright day – and who are the performers if not Agar herself and, by way of consequence, the viewer of the painting?

The epitome of Agar's quest not for solutions but for the dissolution of our certainties, is most brilliantly represented by *Points of View* (1981, illus. 120), which uses the same structure as *Marine Collage* of 1939 and whose ancestor is *Quadriga* – a structure based on the slipping of our eyes from one square to the next in a four-square structure. During this process of accretion, we are confronted with similarities and differences so that the eye has constantly to change its focus. Three squares contain oval shapes whose

121 Eileen Agar, The Dreamer, *1979, oil on canvas.*

colourful interior is revealed and opened to the surface, while three squares – not exactly the same – are linked by containing a similar star-shaped head. Two of the squares only contain profiles, two others are perfectly formed eggs, another two contain vase forms, while colours recur in different tonalities and quantities from one square to another. Restlessness and change of focus and 'spirit' haunt our 'reading' while we feel that what is permanent in this composition is its impermanence – all the squares share a common feature: the opening of the surface of reality onto its constitutive variability. Two years before, Agar had tackled the same deep process in the mind when she painted *The Dreamer* (1979, illus. 121). The painting suggests the same revelation of the secrets which are conjured up in dreams – a kind of laying bare of the double operation of displacement and condensation at work in sleep, when the face slips away and opens itself to dovetailing images of hitherto unidentified shapes, star shapes, fish shapes, literally exploding at the back of the mind. The painting, here, deepens the meaning of the face profile, a recurrent motif in Agar's oeuvre, and exposes it as a perfect reminder of the impenetrability and inexhaustibility of the mind. The painting, just like the mind it 'represents', actually *dreams itself dreaming*.

Frances Spalding's comment on Agar's New Art Centre exhibition in 1981 throws precious light on the painter's creative process in her discussion of the painting entitled *The Bomber* (illus. 122):

> A memory [of her holidays in the Canaries] has resurfaced in the painting *The Bomber*. Over the cheerful, Klee-like landscape hovers a menacing spectre, half bird, half machine. Looked at again, it becomes a helmeted head. This element of horror creates a note of dissonance in an otherwise harmonious tapestry of colour. It is not necessary to know that the painting is based on actual experience, that while playing tennis in Tenerife Eileen Agar watched the ball-girl run screaming from the court as a jet passed overhead.

Opposite: 122 Eileen Agar, The Bomber, *1979-80, acrylic on canvas.*

Overleaf left: 123 Eileen Agar, Spider Woman, *1983, crayon and collage on paper.*

Overleaf right: 124 Eileen Agar, Metamorphosis, *1979, gouache on paper.*

Such a comment may not be 'necessary' but it is extremely enlightening in the sense that it informs us of the deep telescoping process, the blending of images and movements and the spontaneous condensing dynamism of her compositions – a typical Surrealist self-surrendering to the exterior world immediately brought in and turned into a 'third multifold reality'. This almost infinite, boundless creativity is possibly emblematized by *Spider Woman* (illus. 123), a work of crayon and collage on paper. A feminine torso with fluid, organic contours is seen floating on a stylized vivid green vegetable landscape, symbolized by a tree on an orange ground. From the

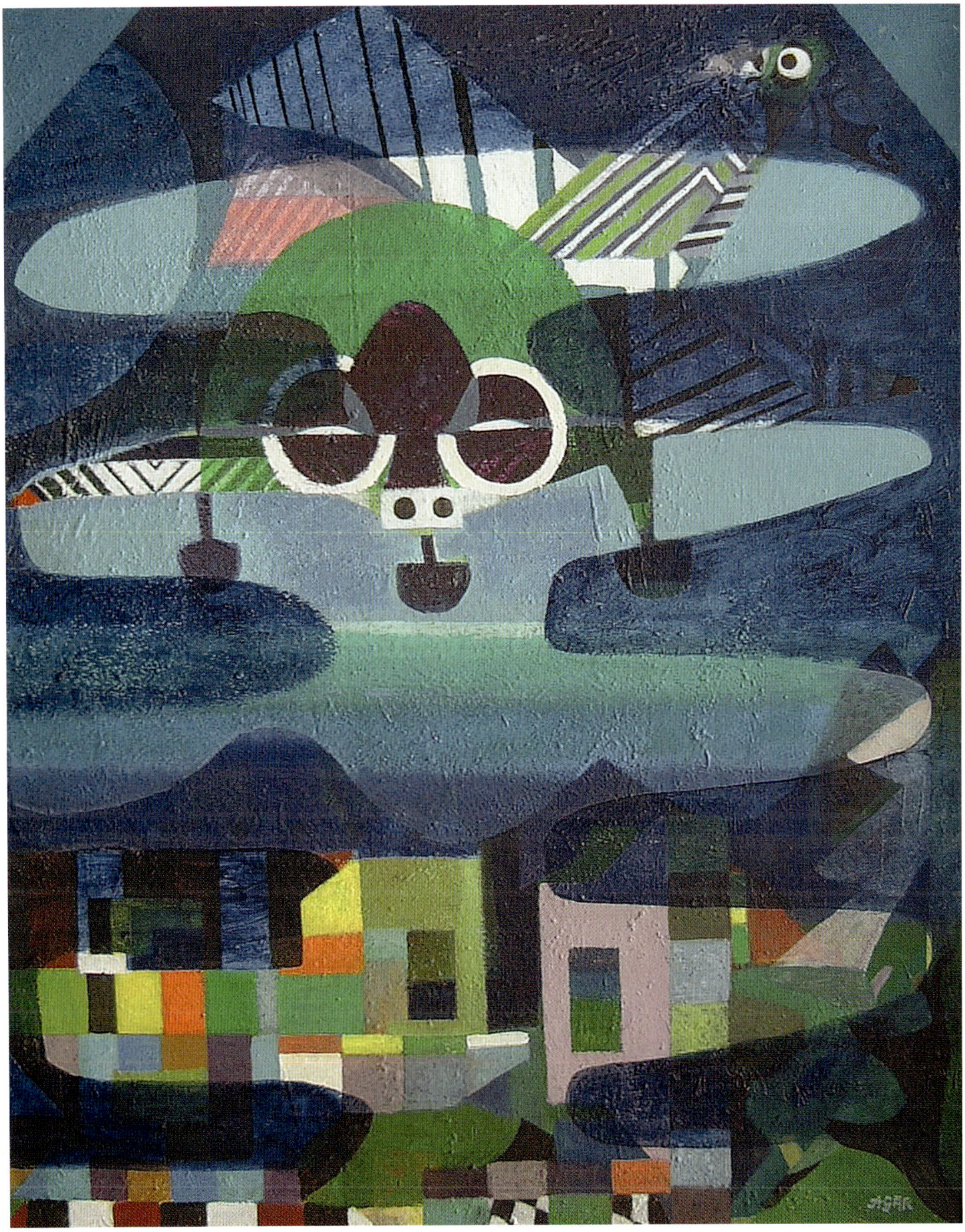
AGAR

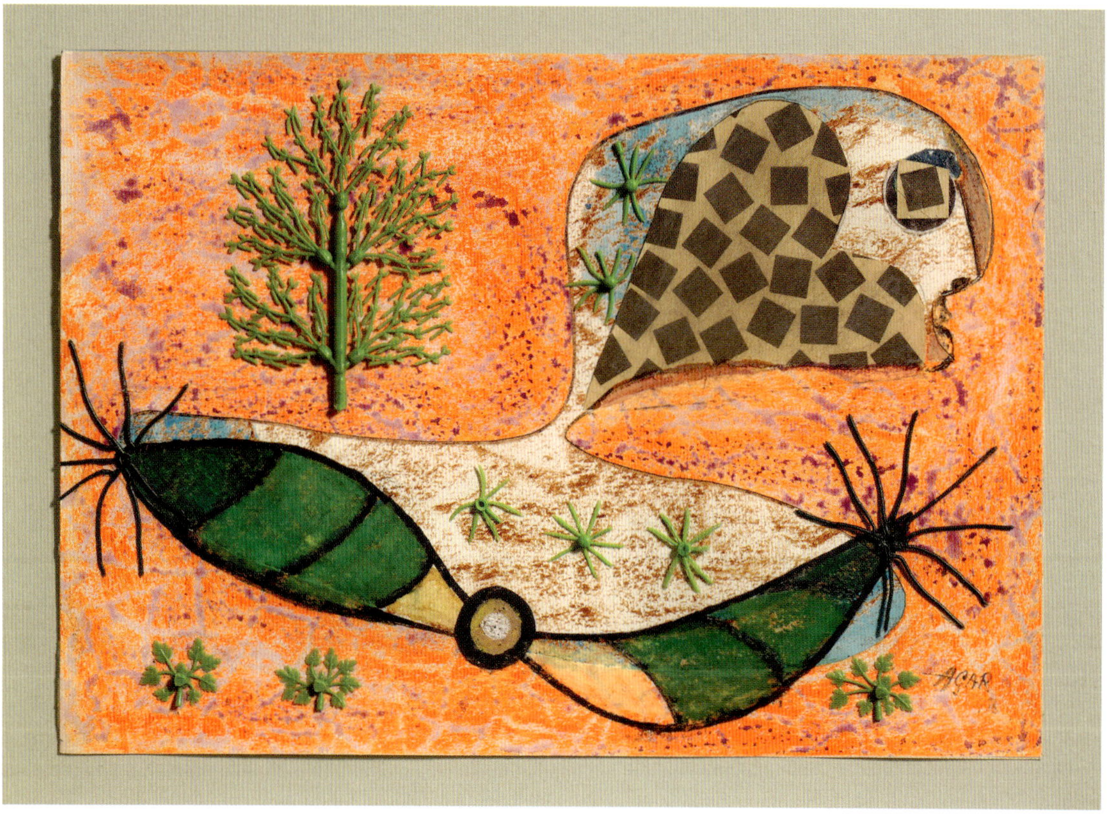

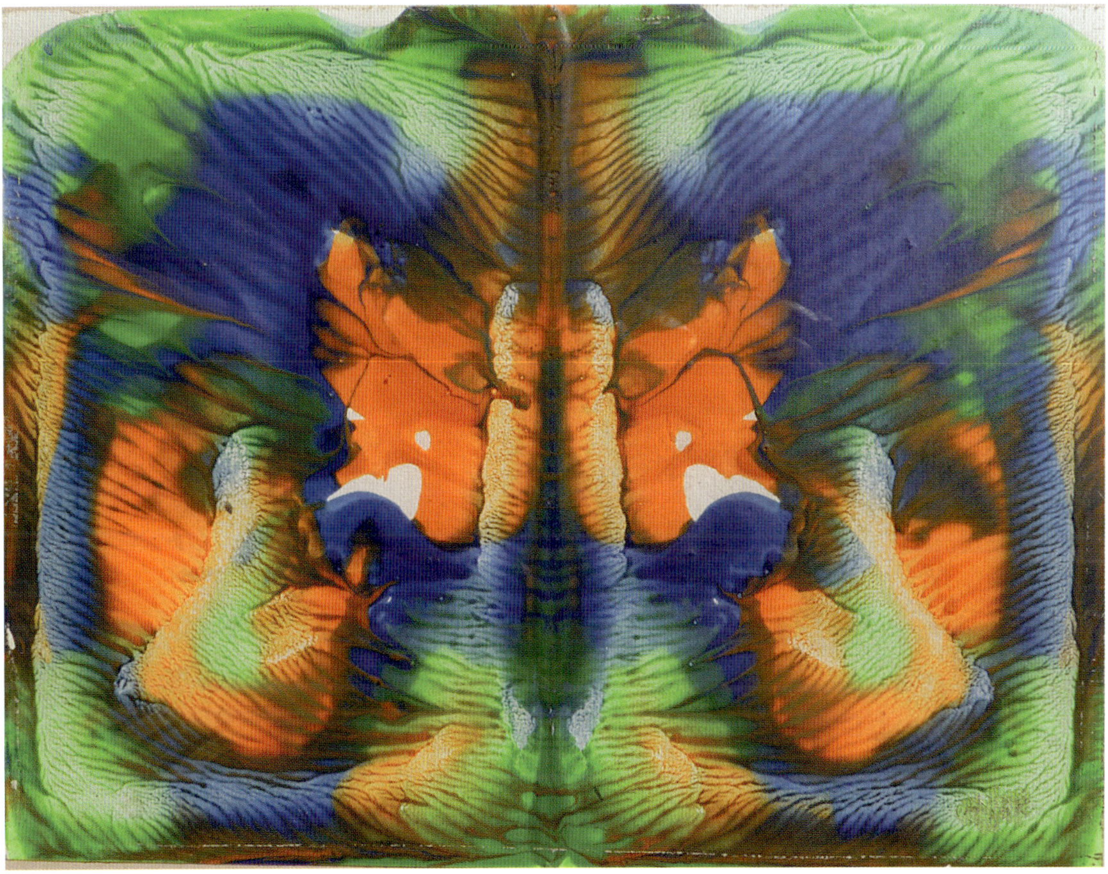

nipples of her breasts, unless it be the upper part of a dress or robe, there grow short black lines in a fan-like shape resembling spiders' legs. This pattern of lines is repeated three times at the base of her neck and twice at the back of her head. The face stretches toward the right in search of its prey but its movement is balanced by the symmetry of the breasts and the tree on the left, one balancing the other – a remarkably poised structure, its colour partly blending with and absorbed by that of the background. Femininity and predatoriness are made to blend as the emblem of the artist.

Self-questioning and boundless exploration are also to be seen, not without a sense of wonderment, in the series of *Butterflies* which she started to paint in the late 1970s and early '80s. A simple use of the decalcomania technique, unavoidably comparable to Rorschach tests, ties in with her favourite theme of the butterfly, which she is likely to have thought of as the 'embodiment' of the psyche, if one refers to Greek mythology, which Agar was well aware of. *Metamorphosis* (1979, illus. 124) is a case in point, with the bright colours turning into wings, ready to take their flight out of the green and blue forest around them. The technique seems to be simple and even childish, but the point is to prepare half the sheet of paper so that by pressing that half on the other white empty one, one obtains a perfect double shape – in other words one has to guide, and be guided by, chance.

In 1984, unable to escape from the grip of Surrealism, Agar featured in the Oliver Bradbury and James Birch exhibition 'In the Spirit of Surrealism', together with the new generation of English Surrealists gathered around Conroy Maddox, Anthony Earnshaw, Les Coleman, John Welson, Dezz Mogg, Patrick Hughes and Paul Hammond. In the foreword to the catalogue, George Melly pays homage to her by stressing how 'Eileen Agar offers Surrealism gaiety and elegance as spontaneous as a dreamer's smile.'

Opposite: 125 Eileen Agar, Ploumanac'h Rocks, Stone 3, *1985, felt-tip pen and pastel on paper.*

Overleaf left: 126 Eileen Agar, Ploumanac'h Rocks, *1984, felt-tip pen, pastel on paper.*

Overleaf right: 127 Eileen Agar, Brittany Rocks, *1983, felt-tip pen, oil pastel and biro on paper.*

In 1985, a new outburst of inspiration took hold of Agar with a return to the photographs of rocks in Brittany, which she had discovered and photographed with Joseph Bard when holidaying in Ploumanac'h (illus. 125–7). In her diary on 26 February 1985, she wrote that she has decided 'to combine photography and imagination in a new way'. Obsessed with rocks, she resolved to 'change them into fantastic shapes and colour'. In her notebook she added:

> Paintings of immense convoluted rocks: images so strong that they imprinted themselves on my unconscious to be awakened decades later from their slumbers and appear in paint, resurrected by the womb of time and the oceans of the moon onto the grassy plains of Ploumanac'h.

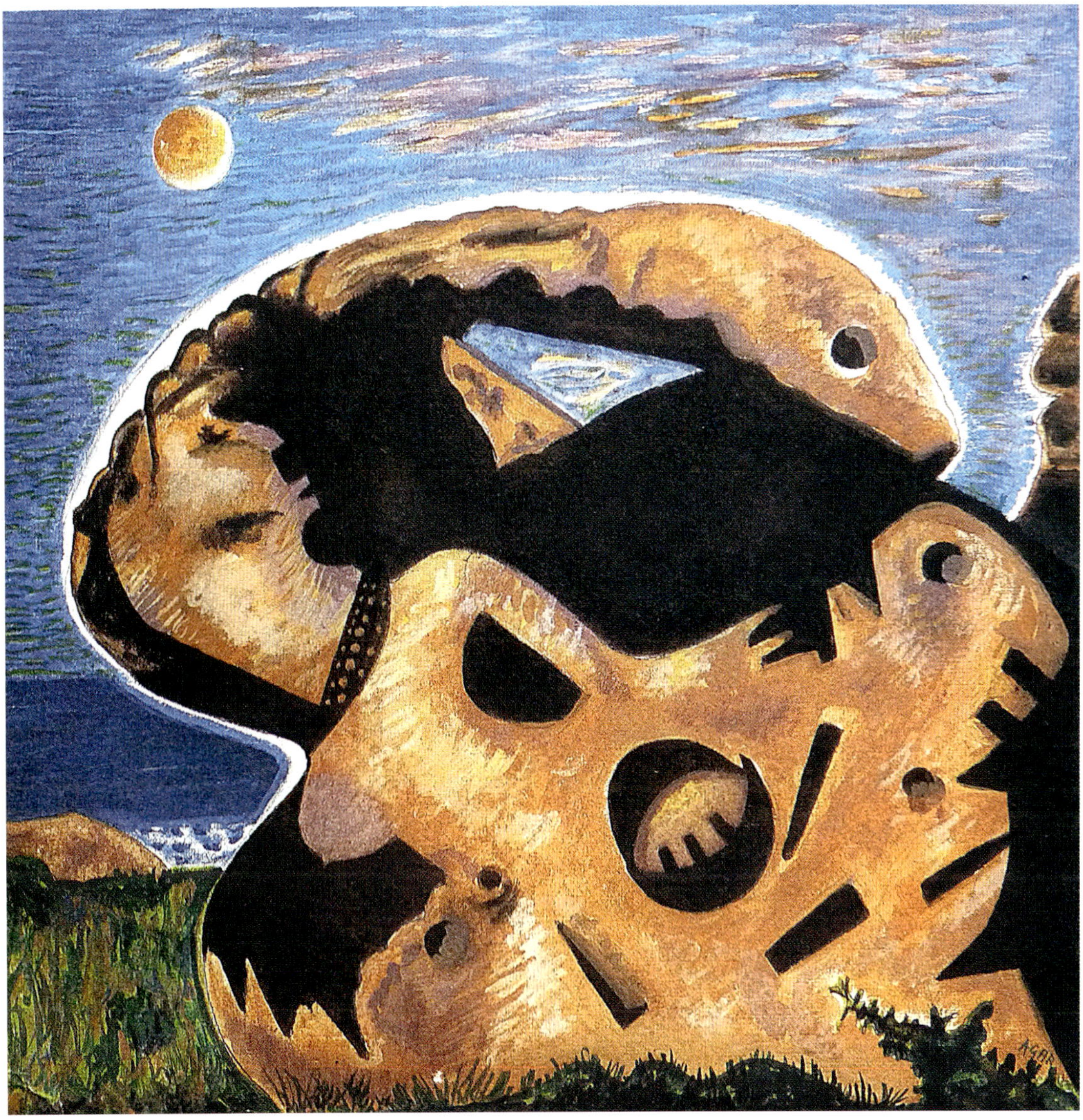

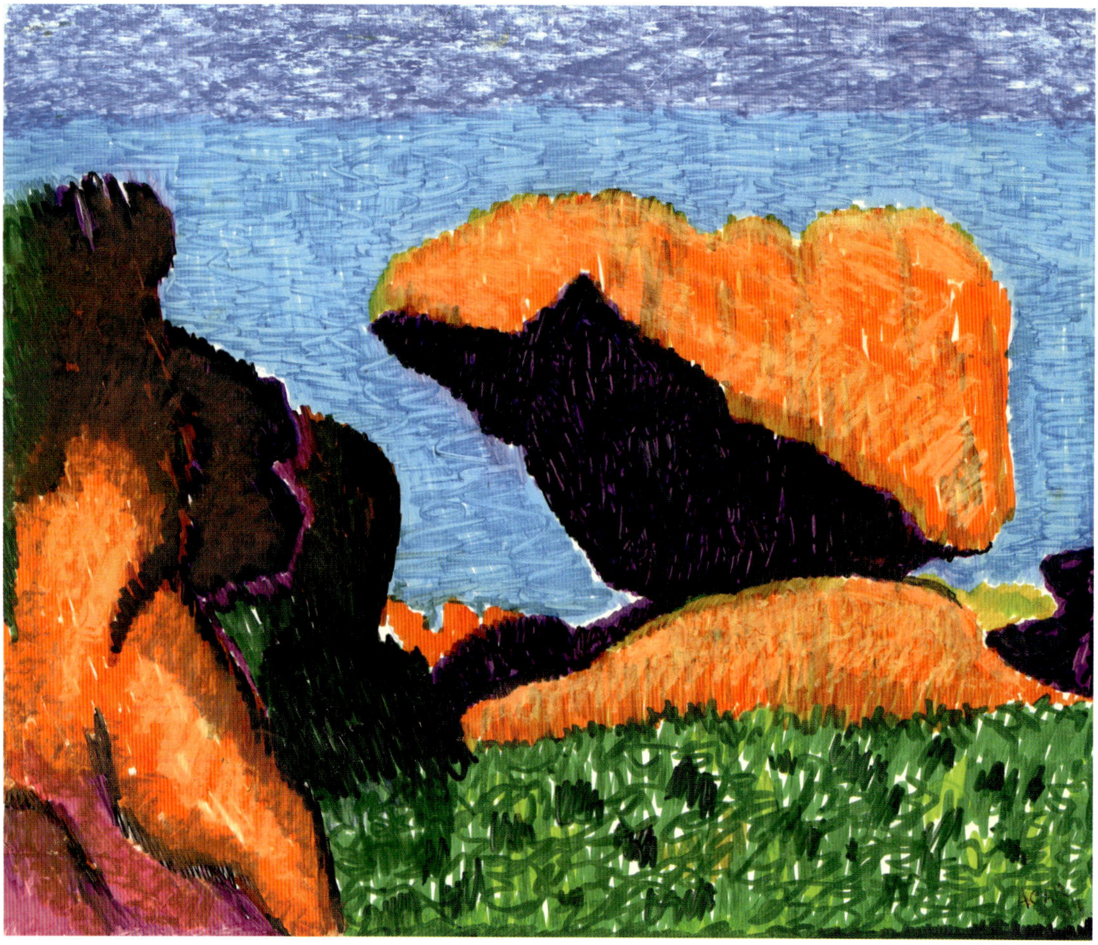

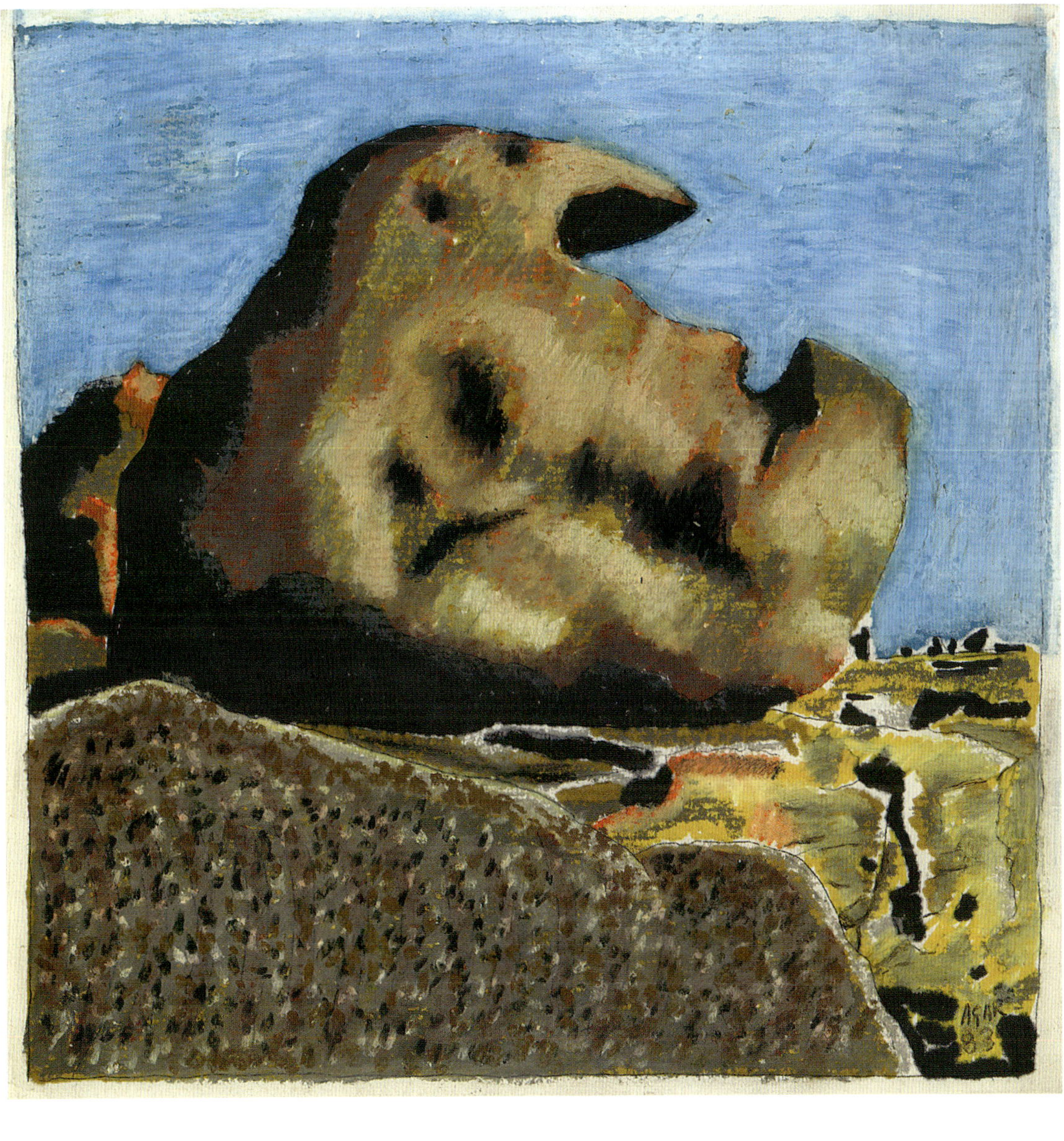
AGAR
83

She went back to them out of nostalgia – a kind of pilgrimage in search of the past or in quest of the essence of things in such a way as to challenge their evanescence and endow them, as in most of her paintings, with the dimension of myth. So she made a series of paintings of the photographed rocks, projecting them into another dimension, almost hallucinatory in the sense that some of the shapes are emphasized at the cost of others and magnified; some of them are anthropomorphized, as if they were 'read' anew and interpreted in the light of the magical transformation which takes place in all her works – thus partaking of the endless process of the mind's forceful appropriation of reality. The result was coldly received by the critics, probably on account of the particularly garish colours used. They are rocks revisited by the colours of Agar's dream, as if they were appearing in a half-trance-like, half-visionary state of mind. Quite evidently, Agar had managed to destabilize the critics by taking them aback with a technique they had not expected from an 85-year-old artist!

Early in 1986 Agar was photographed by Lord Snowdon, wearing clothes designed by the Japanese couturier Issey Miyake, whom she was modelling for – an experience she relished 'for the Miyake designs were like new masks, which released the wearer from him or herself.' Snowdon took photographs of her sitting cross-legged on an upturned waste-paper basket, and standing; she had become the object of an artist, covered with someone else's creations and being played with after playing with her own creations. Indeed, a leading thread which runs through all she did, is in her autobiography:

> To play is to yield oneself to a kind of magic, and to give the lie to the inconvenient world of fact and the hideous edifice of unrelieved utility. In play the mind is prepared to accept the unimagined and the incredible, to enter a world where different laws apply, to be free, unfettered, and approach the divine.

Playing with life, but also playing with death – the latter being the consequence of the former. In 1986, eleven years after Joseph Bard's death, she paid him a wonderfully bucolic and time-defying homage by going back to, and using, a 1937 photograph she had taken of him seated in the nude in a wickerwork armchair, as the motif of a watercolour (illus. 128–9). In this, the body is painted with the stripes of a vest – which repeat the wickerwork pattern and tend to flatten the drawing and make it look like the negative of a photo, almost 'eternalizing' the subject. Next to the body, the bright colours of a summer's day – blue, green and yellow, the colours which Agar probably remembered from when she took the photo of Bard in Mougins in

128 Eileen Agar, Joseph Bard nude on Picasso's balcony at Hotel Vaste Horizon, Mougins, 1937, photograph.

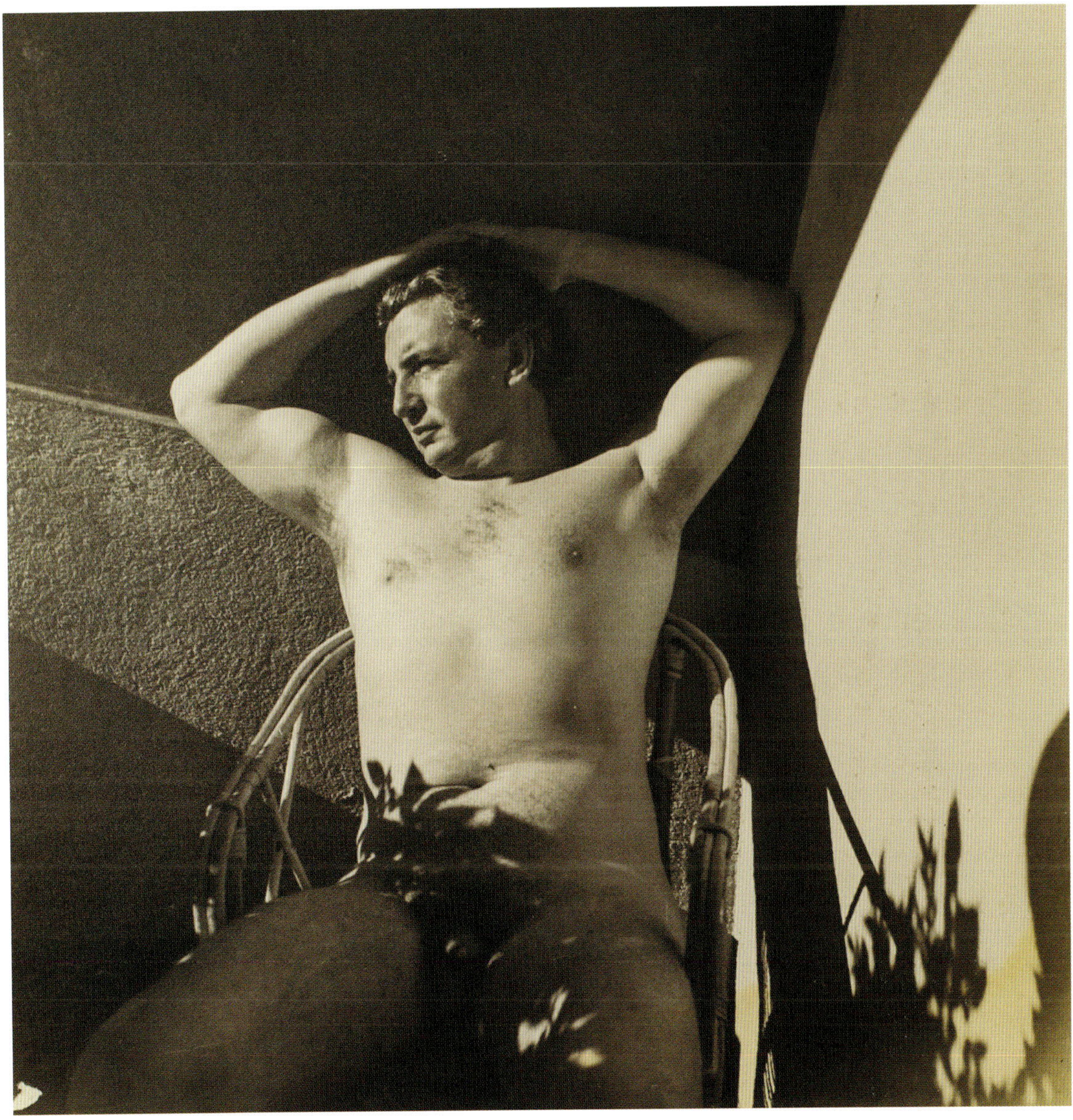

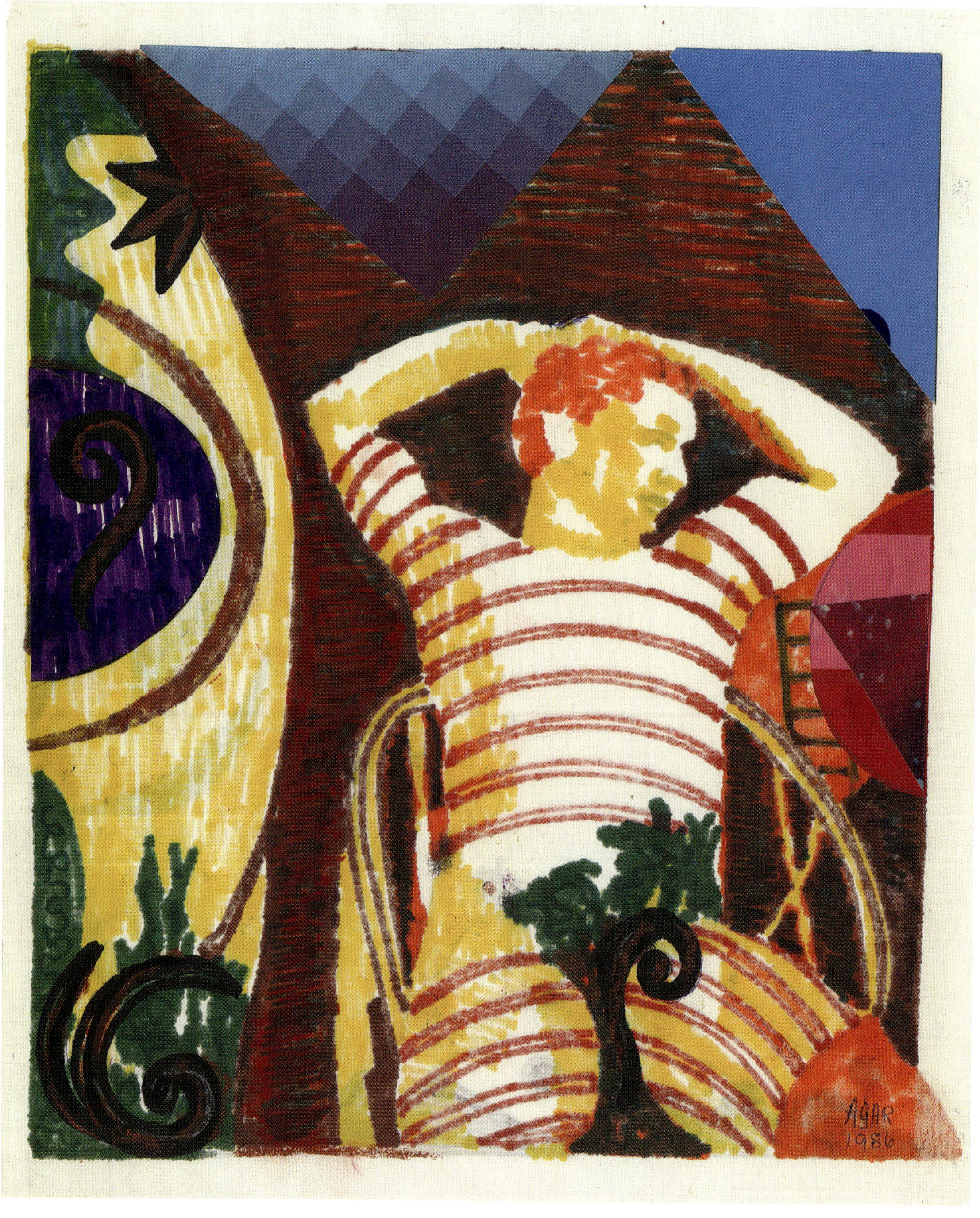
AGAR
1986

August 1937 – literally explode, while a flower stem in the shape of a crook grows erect from his crotch, a solemn and joyous defiance of death and a celebration of healthy sexuality and undying love. Behind him there rises a pyramid, the symbol of ancient art, and a reference to Bard's own classical erudition, thus joining the past with the timelessness of nature. The unveiling of a ghost in the bright light of summer – Bard died on a summer day in July – this is the materialization of the secret wish for eternal love in the splendour of masculine force. Revisiting, in a way, her previous life with Bard and reaffirming her love of him in this vegetable reincarnation, is emblematic of her belief in the eternal return of the cycle of nature, Demeter-like, a belief which underpins her whole outlook on life. An undated poem Bard wrote and Agar illustrated testifies to this 'eternal passion' (illus. 130).

The year 1986 was, more than anything else, the year of the 'national' celebration of the fiftieth anniversary of the epoch-making 'International Surrealist Exhibition' in London. Following upon a choice selection of English Surrealist works by Andrew Murray at the Mayor Gallery, an exhibition entitled 'British Surrealism Fifty Years On', which then travelled to Middlesborough Art Gallery and displayed ten of Agar's works (including *The Unnatural Child*, *Philemon and Baucis*, *Family Trio* as a woodcut, and photographs of rocks), another exhibition bringing together 116 works by every single actor of British Surrealism in England from 1936 to 1947, travelled from the Herbert Read Gallery in Canterbury to the National Museum of Wales in Cardiff and the Laing Art Gallery in Newcastle. At the official grand opening in Canterbury on 19 May, organized by Duncan Scott and Roger Cardinal (the latter then belonged to the short-lived Surrealist Melmoth Group around Conroy Maddox in London), Agar was asked to speak and declare the exhibition open. Her speech, short but powerful in its images, was a vibrant tribute to the movement she had never disowned, stressing – were it only in the mode of address – the sense of community which still bound its protagonists together:

> Dear Bretheren [sic].
> We are gathered together this evening to do hommage to the idea of Surrealism. What is surrealism? For me it is the mood to divine buried treasure, it is a fishy-figure phantom that lives in a looking glass world, while dreaming of dead men's bones. It is a natural break in dull routine. It is the Holy emanation of an explosive and creative capacity Brooding over this shrinking and destructive world.
> And so I have much pleasure in declaring this exhibition open – (illus. 131).

Opposite: 129 Eileen Agar, Man Reclining *(drawing of Joseph Bard), 1986, felt-tip pen, pastel and collage on paper.*

Overleaf left: 130 Poem by Joseph Bard illustrated by Eileen Agar, watercolour and gouache.

Overleaf right: 131 Eileen Agar's declaration on the opening of the 'Surrealism in England, 1936 and After' exhibition in Canterbury (1986).

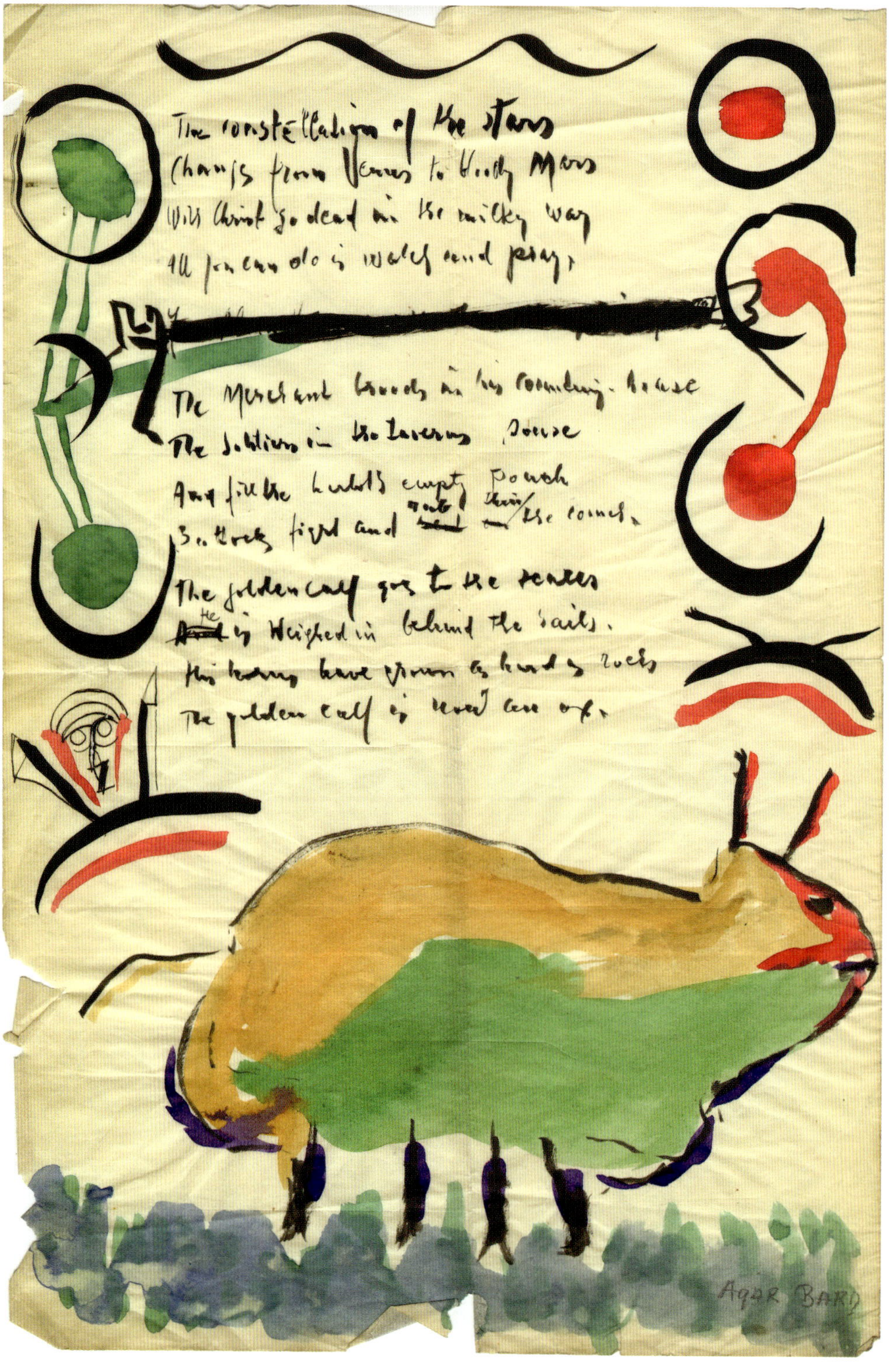
The constellation of the stars
Changes from Venus to bloody Mars
With Christ gone dead in the milky way
All you can do is watch and pray.
The Merchant broods in his counting-house
The soldiers in the taverns souse
And fill the harlot's empty pouch
Brothers fight and ~~[illegible]~~ wait ~~on~~ their the couch.
The golden calf goes to the scales
~~[illegible]~~ He is Weighed in behind the sails.
His horns have grown as hard as rocks
The golden calf is need care of.
AGAR BARD

Dear Bretheren.

We are gathered together this evening to do Hommage to the idea of Surrealism – What is Surrealism? For me it is the mood to divine buried treasure, it is a Fishy-Figure Phantom that lives in a looking glass world, (it* is a natural break in dull routine) while dreaming of DEAD Men's Bones*. It is the Holy emanation of an Explosive & creative Capacity Brooding over this SHRINKING & destructive world.

And so I have much pleasure in declaring this exhibition open –

The same year she participated in a programme about Picasso, broadcast by the BBC World Service, and in October another important exhibition showing two hundred works was organized in Leeds by Alex Robertson, 'Surrealism in Britain in the Thirties: Angels of Anarchy and Machines for Making Clouds', in which Agar's *Angel* was given pride of place together with her *Marine Object* of 1939, in a fascinating confrontation of British Surrealists and 'Continental' Surrealists, not necessarily to the advantage of the latter, as the received opinion of many critics would have it.

These exhibitions definitely brought back to public notice the immense output of British Surrealist artists, Agar herself ranking first. After the 1986 celebrations, not a year passed without an exhibition of British Surrealism being held in both large and small venues. The Mayor Gallery, Blond Fine Art, John Bonham and Murray Feely Fine Art, England and Co, the Whitworth Art Gallery, Bradbury Gallery and Birch and Conran Gallery all contributed to the discovery of powerfully intriguing works often hidden away and almost forgotten. Not to mention international exhibitions, among which, 'I Surrealisti' in Milan, organized by Arturo Schwarz in 1989, which travelled to the Schirn Kunsthalle in Frankfurt in 1990, 'Anxious Visions' at Berkeley University Art Museum in 1990, and 'Revolution by Night' at the National Gallery of Australia in Canberra in 1993. The list is almost endless.

On 11 April 1988 Agar was invited to speak to George Melly on Surrealism on the Third Ear programme on BBC Radio 4, and in 1989 a huge retrospective was organized at Birch and Conran, 40 Dean Street, London. An *Art Line* magazine special supplement was edited on the occasion, in which she appeared very lively, vivacious, even slightly impish in the photograph showing her wearing the famous glove-covered hat and a colourful knitted cardigan with geometrical blue and light-brown patterns, and standing below *The Bird* – a kind of thoughtful magician ready to do a trick (illus. 133). Andrew Wilson wrote a biographical text and Mike von Joel conducted an interview with her in which she declared: 'I always have loved surprises and my idea of surrealism was surprise. You do a drawing then you change it a bit and turn a female into a horse.' As a matter of fact, surprises may lead to upheavals and Agar's artistic process may well unwillingly illustrate the chaos theory!

132 Eileen Agar, L'Horloge de la Femme, *1989, collage on paper.*

Late in 1989, on the occasion of the forthcoming birth of my own daughter, Agar composed a collage entitled *L'Horloge de la femme* (*Woman's Clock*) (illus. 132). Using a postcard representing Magritte's

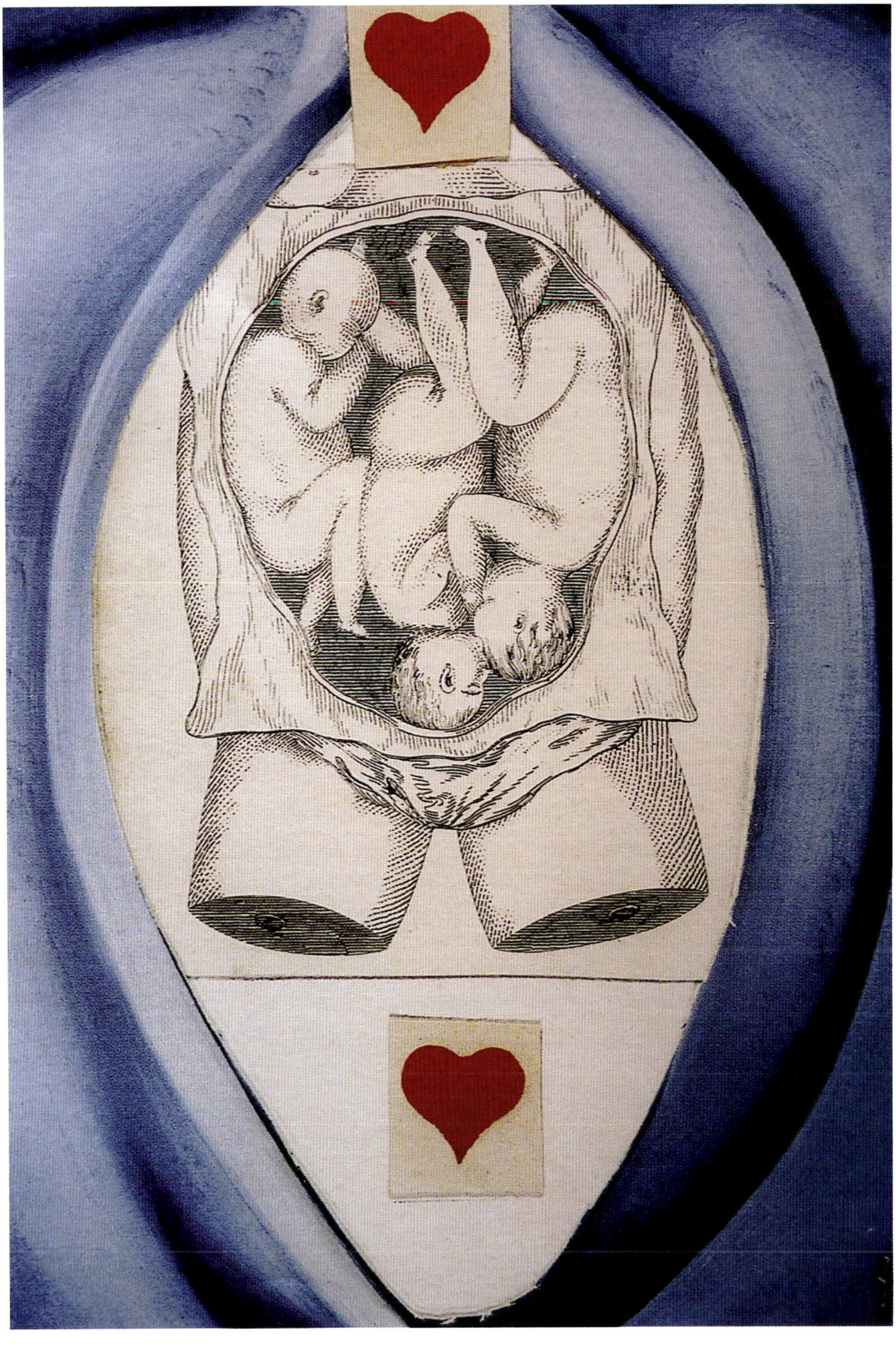

painting *The False Mirror* (1929), she cut out the inside of the eye on the card and turned it round so that it was seen vertically, making it look exactly like a woman's vulva. Inside, she stuck right at the top a drawing of a uterus containing three foetuses clinging together. The whole composition has the exact appearance of a grandfather clock with the triplets in the place of the pendulum, which one can see through the glass aperture. Two red hearts – one at the top, the other at the bottom – frame the 'pendulum' and create an axis of symmetry, the joint symbols of love and blood. In this perfectly Surrealist composition, Agar telescopes the eye, the woman's vagina and the emblem of time in a multilayered series of simultaneous meanings – not so different from, for example, Magritte's own *Rape*, in which one is asked to see a woman's torso *and* her face in a totally double, simultaneous vision. Not to mention the celebration, which the collage also constitutes, of woman as the one who marks, punctuates and in a way creates time by giving birth.

'In play the mind is prepared to accept the unimagined and the incredible, to enter a world where different laws apply, to be free, unfettered, and approach the divine', as we have already referenced from Agar's autobiography. If Agar imagined the unimagined and made us believe in the unbelievable, did she approach the divine? Except for its last word, the above statement would not have been refused or criticized by André Breton. The last word is precisely what may be seen as making the difference between staunch supporters and defenders of Surrealism and Eileen Agar, who did not literally claim she belonged to the movement but did not really refuse anyone's affirmation that she belonged to it. Although she never really confided what she believed in theologically, it is most likely that the divine for her was another word for the magic, or rather the marvellous, in the Surrealist sense – that is, the sudden awareness that conscience is being exceeded by what is seen. What she did was to explore all the possibilities of appealing to the marvellous and to make the observer *actively* see the surreal in the real.

133 John Glynn, Eileen Agar under The Bird *and with her* Glove Hat *on, 1989, photograph.*

When Agar died on 17 November 1991, the world of art mourned the muse and magician she never stopped being. If one were to imagine an epitaph for her, it might be a paraphrase of the inscription on Breton's own grave: she 'seeks the gold of Time', nuggets of which have been bequeathed to us as long as we *realize* them.

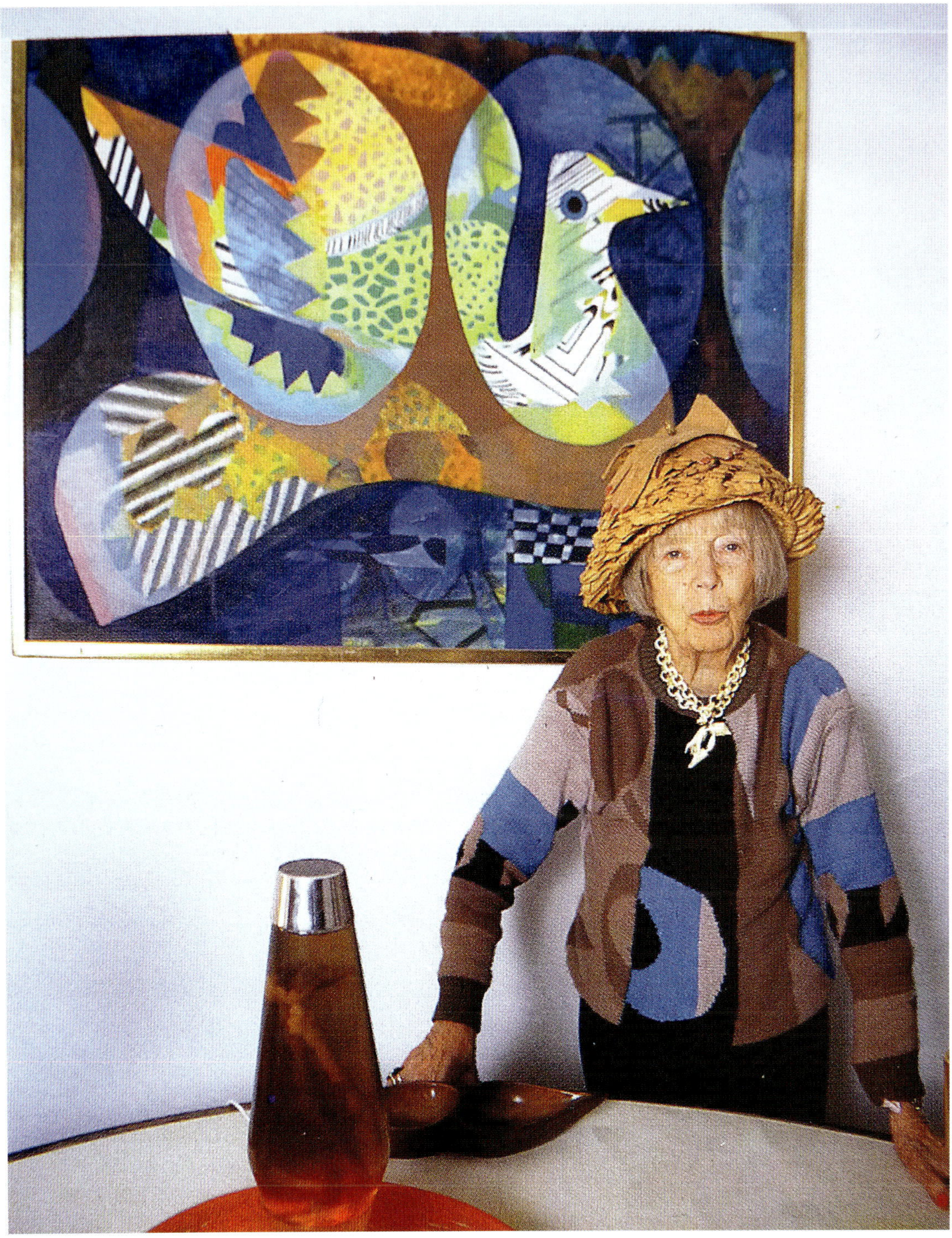

Conclusion

'Now Kitty, let's consider who it was that dreamed it all . . . You see, Kitty, it *must* have been either me or the Red King. He was part of my dream, of course – but then I was part of his dream, too!'

Lewis Carroll, *Through the Looking-Glass, and What Alice Found There* (1871)

The marvellous, which emanates from and pervades all the objects, collages and paintings of Eileen Agar's oeuvre, means the access to a dimension which raises the viewer above the prosaic and flat banality of the socialized real. The marvellous manifests itself from the depths of the subconscious by short-circuiting all dualities and all well-defined categories. In his *Second Manifesto*, André Breton declares that the marvellous is 'the ideal moment when man, seized by a particular emotion', suddenly feels he is in the hands of something larger and stronger than he can conceive. In other words, the real is de-realized through the subversion of the habitual relationships between the subject and the moral and social world, a sublimation seen as the expansion of the mind. The marvellous, like Hermes, acts as a messenger between man and the surreal. Indeed, the Surrealist marvellous (different from the religious kind of marvellous) is clothed in concrete, material, obvious forms – a face, a hand, a flower, a shell – but also possesses a certain obscurity which requires man to develop his visionary and magical faculties in order to go beyond temporal and spatial contingencies. It is thus linked to a kind of hermeticism which founds and furthers the passage between man and the universe, thus enabling the former to interpret and recreate the latter. The marvellous is to be found in this very movement, in this very dynamism – a kind of dialectics but with an inaccessible synthesis. Lastly, it is obvious that, in the course of this rising from the subconscious and from timeless archetypal regions of the mind, the marvellous will activate myths and mythopoetic processes, blending the past and the present and the future, the masculine and the feminine, the ephemeral and the permanent, the subjective and the collective – both a revolt against the established order, here and now, and a determination to create the conditions for a new myth. 'The marvellous is everywhere, ready to explode like a time-bomb,' said Benjamin Péret. The marvellous is the matrix of myths.

As a matter of fact, Breton's own statement at the beginning of the *Second Manifesto*, written in 1929, that 'There is every reason to believe that there exists a certain point in the mind at which life and death, real and imaginary, past and future, communicable and incommunicable, high and low, cease to be perceived in terms of contradiction,' emblematizes the very conditions for the emergence of a 'mythology' analogous to, and consubstantial with, the feeling of the quotidian marvellous to take place: the suspension of time, the suspension of moral imperatives, the liberation of a mental flux which connects man to the deepest areas of his inherited mental images and the steadfast refusal of the total control of consciousness. Louis Aragon brought together those conditions in *Paris Peasant*, just as Breton did in *Nadja* and *L'Amour fou*, and, in England, Humphrey Jennings in his poems and Roland Penrose in his *The Road is Wider than Long*.

The marvellous, in its challenge to dualism, is of course the lodestar of Surrealist strategies and, indeed, the quest for the marvellous lies at the core of Agar's works. This, clearly, raises the issue of whether she is a Surrealist or not. The reader will be left to decide for himself, but let us, at this final stage, give elements for an answer.

In one of her diaries, in which she tries to epitomize her own ideological development, she jotted down in 1986:

> If cubism is the mechanizing of forms, surrealism means the de-mechanizing of it. There is nothing surprising about the surrealist's primary aim: search for content. Surprise is in their utter overthrow of what the cubists fought so hard to attain – the rebirth of construction. What they aimed for is the rebirth of content.

In other words, the rebirth of myth-making, the retrieval of a lost content, that is man's myth-making activity at the core of his subconscious. Agar progressively understood that Surrealism was not merely a 'mechanizing' technique but that it was a state of mind to which corresponded a new mode of thinking, a way of creating which refuted the exclusive control of logic and reason but also any kind of 'technique'. This is why the lack of obvious automatism in her works cannot be evidence of her having drifted away from Surrealism's principles. If automatism was hailed as a liberating process in André Breton and Philippe Soupault's *The Magnetic Fields* in 1919, it was also deemed to be 'the history of a continuous misfortune', as Breton realized in December 1933, admitting its limitations and the perversion to which it could be prone. As a result, automatism has to be considered solely and essentially as one of the most efficient ways of short-circuiting logic, no more, no less – a way of accessing the world of hitherto unsuspected relationships between objects taking place in the subconscious and surfacing into the conscious mind. Eileen Agar is a Surrealist, there is no doubt about it, and her automatism simply and genuinely lies in her surrendering to chance encounters taking place between cut-outs, photographs, bits and pieces found in nature – leaves, shells, stones – lying there on her desk and in her studio, or shapes, lines and geometric figures lying in her mind. She leaves them to act on, and in, her imagination.

But there is more concerning her Surrealist commitment. This determination to help man retrieve his pristine mythopoetic powers and recreate, refresh and revitalize his own world permanently, thanks to the marvellous, is central to the Surrealist undertaking and is expatiated on 'theoretically' by Agar as early as 1928. I have already referred abundantly to her diaries and notebooks in which she jotted down her most urgent and pressing thoughts, but it is appropriate to recall them since they will most clearly establish her position. First her belief is strongly affirmed and reaffirmed, in the endless process of transformation at work in nature, in man and in the whole of reality. Starting with the idea of the 'likeness in build of the giant reptiles and the modern trains, the modern aeroplanes and immense dragon flies that existed in Paleozoic and Jurassic times', she concludes on this glorious vision:

> In a sublimated and harmless way we still live with all these strange wonderful creatures around us, among us, beautiful because death has removed their poison fangs and left us the miracle of their memory. Death has sublimated them and yet not a leaf of their tree is lost, any more than a leaf of the coal forests, for in us is Eternity.

Now, a myth is a narrative which aims at retelling the creation of the world and of man, and at giving clues to approach an explanation of the unexplainable. Here is how Agar put into words the myth she was elaborating as the driving force of her inspiration:

> Things do not seem to go on everlastingly transforming for no reason but nothing lives eternally without transformation until it has reached this stage of fusion of 'frozen life' into its form. Thus once the amber has gone through its rounds of transformation and become perfect amber, it remains static and does not transform again into something else. It is a living example of Life in Death. How would I have you believe that mind-types go through this same process before they can achieve crystallization, the European mind-type can only achieve this through the Female because the European Male has gone through this process of transforming and gestation and when the moment arrives the crystallization takes place in the Female, and the mind becomes real, and that is a type and frozen in its form as the amber.

This radical evolutionary, almost Darwinian, principle, fundamental in Agar's work, is developed in another brief paragraph in the same 1928 diary:

> In every case the Coal becomes the Form and the Tree Life history the content, the Woman the Form, European Male history the Content, the Flint the Form and the animal the Content. In every case, the Form hints at the next approaching the Man that follows the Animal.

And immediately afterwards, she adds:

> Nature takes millions of years to gestate and turn out something more solid than a passion tree, European Man takes less time, 2,000 years to turn out a mind-type which will last once crystallized. For the Force left Nature and moved with Man, always leaving behind great ideals and from man the force left and moved into Woman, again leaving behind the ideal man, the Jew, the perfect crystal male intellect.

It almost seems a pity that these rambling notes jotted down in a precipitate, quick, rushing way of writing – indicating their imperative quality – should not have been given more form and order, but again, they were given, maybe not order, but form, in each and every one of her works. In point of fact, the same transformation process is what she conceives the imagination to be the seat of:

> Imagination is by no means the faculty of the Unreal, fantastic and fanciful, it is the stripping of the actual to lay bare the essence. The life-giving spirit which informs the object with meaning and sense by glorifying that which it has been through, by penetrating to its history and revealing the content of its form. Mind-types are created in the same way that continents were formed in geological times.

Not only Darwin, but also Lyell! The materialization of these conceptualizing statements is obviously found in many of her works, most centrally in *Family Trio*, which was discussed at length earlier.

Regarding the status of the artist, as a kind of logical outcome of these reflections – in other words, regarding her own status and development – she defined it in such a firm, solid and clear-sighted way in her notebooks in 1985 and '86, when she could envision the whole of her artistic itinerary, that we now understand the constancy and coherence of inspiration in her works:

> The artist is an artist only on condition that he or she is double, and that no aspect of this duality should be neglected. I am so double that I have two names, two bank accounts, two doctors, two desires and two friends. I always buy two of everything and live in the twentieth century. My interest is in two movements, abstract art and surrealism, the word 'cubism' is a spatial concept, the word 'futurism' a concept of time and the word 'surrealism' is a concept of space-time.

The attraction towards binary and ternary enumerations which we notice in practically all her works – or as juxtapositions in her collages – is indicative of the challenge Agar never ceased to take up when testing the limits of dualistic or dialectical relationships. This almost naturally ties in with the more or less avowed belief that a definitive synthesis is forever unreachable. Indeed, in all the preceding statements, Agar's obsession is clearly with the unending process of the transformation of reality the mind is grappling with – the inexhaustibility of meaning, the cross-fertilization, if not mutual metamorphosis, of both external reality and the internal workings of the mind and the imagination. Obviously, here, we cannot but evoke André Breton's positing of the famous 'supreme point' at the beginning of the *Second Manifesto*, the famous point at which all oppositions 'cease to be perceived in terms of contradiction' and which he saw as the goal which Surrealists had to reach – bearing in mind, however, that it is an ever-vanishing point and that what essentially matters is the actual search for it, however unfindable it eventually is. This irreducible search for the 'supreme point', the endless endeavour to indicate the direction towards that point, is what defines Surrealist activity and explains the coherence and consistency of each and every one of Agar's works throughout the eighty or so years of her career as a painter. In direct relation to this, Agar added in the same notebook dated 1985:

> The moral code of surrealist artists is the code of science, the disinterested attitude of research. The work of art is a 'communicating vessel' of spiritual values and has also become a scientific mirror held up to nature in the contemporary world, where we may see if we do not yet recognize a secret process which only comes fleetingly into focus with the spotlight of commonplace reality.

134 Eileen Agar, Christmas card, 1985, felt-tip pen and biro.

The sense of an unending and secret process – instilled, as well, almost unawares, into the viewer the moment he is confronted with her collages and paintings – is the cornerstone of her artistic approach and is

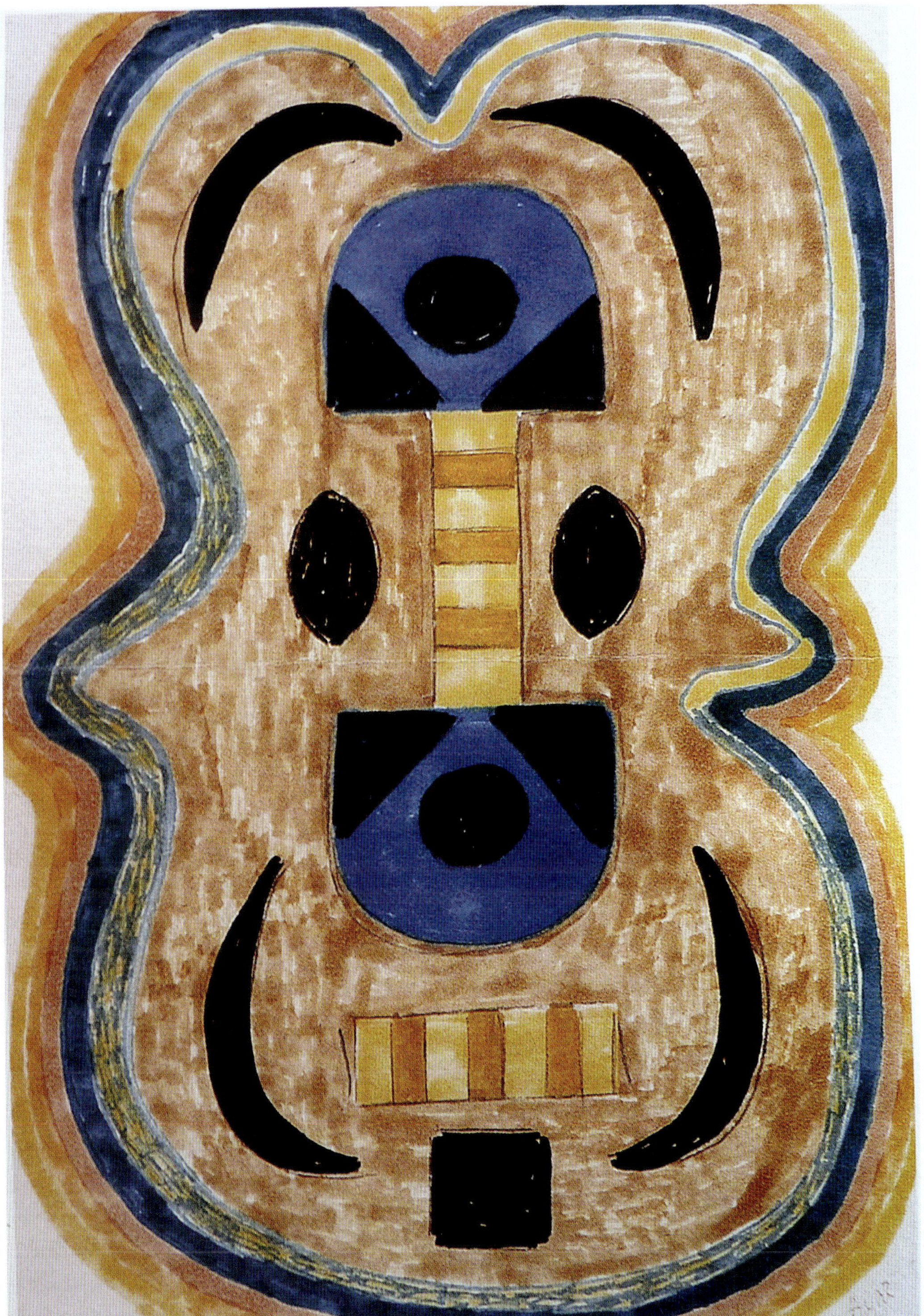

also found in her own idea of Freudianism, tinted with the Hegelianism she had undoubtedly inherited from Joseph Bard and the Surrealists:

> The Freudian notion of fragments does not presuppose the breaking of an image or a totality, but the dialectical multiplicity of a process . . . It is not the clash between contradictory fragments that counts but the movement between such fragments.

We now understand why the myth which forms the subtext of her works cannot be the alleged, but all too limited myth of the feminine, or of woman, as many critics, especially American, have tried to reduce her work to, but a more inclusive, all-encompassing myth. Indeed, the image of woman or the notion of femininity, which are so obvious when one deals with her works, should not be the tree that hides the forest. Of course, there are many 'feminine archetypes', such as eggs, shells, flowers and leaves, and psychoanalysis could find more, but Agar's works cannot be reduced to merely one of the two elements of such a simplistic dichotomy as the masculine/feminine opposition. Inseparable from each other are Demeter and Caliban, Pamela Travers and Dylan Thomas, Spider Woman and Fisherman, just like Philemon and Baucis. Agar never ceased to rise above artificial, theoretical or intellectual divisions that aim to create categories – and this also applies to her discreet, non-committal silence regarding her own politics. The myth she constantly revisits is the timeless, universal myth of Creation.

As a conclusive synthesis and desperate attempt at seizing the elusive magic of Eileen Agar's work, one feels prompted to refer to her photograph, found in the heaps of photos which she left. *Somebody Eating a Poached Egg* (illus. 135) gathers the gist of all the preceding pages: her flirtation with Cubism, her life-long precipitation of the viewer into an inextricably oneiric space and her tongue-in-cheek humour – not inseparable from the subtle, almost unconscious, hint at the symbol of eternal creation lurking through the triviality of the title. The photograph, left undated in the archives, is the perfect coda to this homage to her.

All in all, Agar's concern is with the emancipation of the mind, as such – man's and woman's – not only, as we have seen, through the blending, juxtaposing and overlapping of elements stolen from a reality whose permanence is radically denied, but mainly through the challenge and subversive energy awakened in the viewer's eye and mind. Yes, Agar has an 'eye for collage' – to refer to the title given by Andrew Lambirth to a recent exhibition – but also an eye for the eye of the viewer. For it is

135 Eileen Agar, Somebody Eating a Poached Egg, *n.d., photograph.*

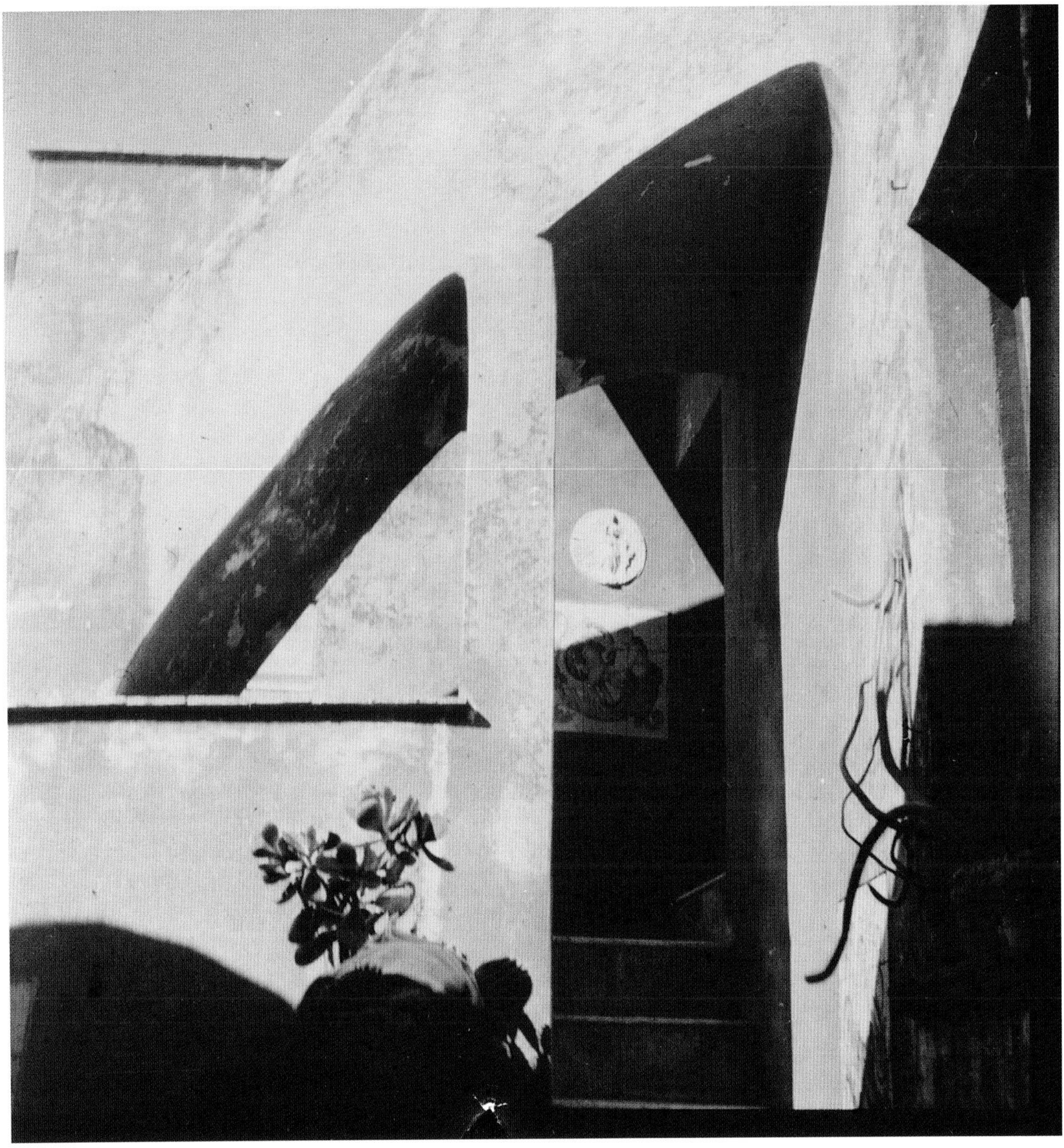

in the viewer's eye, and in no other place, that she knows that the idea of the myth actually turns into a mythopoetic process, endless, irreducible, dovetailing the individual and the collective.

Agar's principles are the result of an unbounded curiosity, an amazing capacity to seize hold of whatever makes the limits of the mind and the imagination recede, a thirst for exploration and discovery and above all for self-questioning. More concretely, these were the results of the relationships she entertained with the artistic and literary world. She absorbed all she could from Joseph Bard, in the first place, as well as from all her teachers, who saw in her the potentialities of a rebellious spirit, but mainly she drew on what her own experience had taught her with the Surrealists, Paul Nash and Roland Penrose in England, Pablo Picasso, Paul Éluard, Man Ray and Max Ernst in France. None of them revealed anything to her; they revealed her to herself: 'I am in a sense a constructivist, but not purely of angles and squares, a constructed harmony of ideas and images, would perhaps be a better description.'

'The world is a cryptogram which requires deciphering', wrote Breton. Agar, a microcosm at the heart of the macrocosm, is one of the decipherers who testifies to the possible union of matter and spirit, materialism and idealism – a magical, almost alchemical, union. The legacy left by Eileen Agar is that of a personal, powerful, all-embracing poetics, making the internal external, nature thought, and thought nature. Based on the refusal of categories and preconceived divisions, her poetics involves and questions the pure functioning of thought. It also challenges and questions the fundaments of the culture and society of man – mankind seen as a mere part of reality – by returning him to the imaginative forces deep in him and constantly under threat of being lost. Painting, for Agar, was a mode of thinking, a process of unhinging the process of thought, and as such it interrogates the boundaries and explores the crossings between the philosophical, the literary, the moral and the artistic. In her paintings, her objects, her photographs and her collages, she has shaped, developed, altered and reoriented – disoriented also – our traditional conceptions of the ancient question of what is art, to which Surrealism answered that 'it is what will be.'

Appendix

Because Eileen Agar's unique contribution to *The Island* is little known and almost inaccessible, except from the Victoria and Albert Museum Archives, it seemed appropriate to print it in this appendix. With all our thanks to the V&A Library Department.

Eileen Agar
Religion and the artistic imagination

The Island, I/4 (15 December 1931), p. 102

As an artist, the Earth, the Sun and the Moon have a greater significance for me than the highly rarefied idea of the Holy Trinity. For natural symbolism has a greater emotional appeal to a woman than has religious mysticism. Measured by the artists' sensitiveness Christianity appears to undergo profound changes resulting in a new and more naturalistic mythology in Europe, Russia and America.

In Europe the importance of the subconscious in all forms of Literature and Art establishes the dominance of a feminine type of imagination over the classical and more masculine order. Apart from rampant and hysterical militarism, there is no male element left in Europe for the intellectual and rational conception of life has given way to a more miraculous creative interpretation, and artistic and imaginative life is under the sway of womb-magic. The Sun is an increasingly important symbol in the new mythology of Europe. Turner, Van Gogh, Monet among others, have helped just as much to realize the plastic nature of this pre-eminently European symbol as any fifteenth century painter of the Christian tradition.

Russia obviously repudiates Christianity and the female concept as a form of life, and as a logical conclusion of their programme of social reconstruction they are bound to do away with all forms of imaginative life. This extreme rationalism will give a Jewish character to their outlook and therefore, their emotional life is bound to be nourished from Jewish sources. The new Russian form of life is already near to earth. They are the only people in the world to build up images tied directly to the earth, pictures of fertility and fecund life, no sharp-shadowed moon-like landscapes as in America, for under the hammer and sickle grow waving seas of corn. The Jewish race alone has this same quality of virile earth-nearness, expressed not in terms of the peasant but in terms of the intellectual. For having been forbidden the worship of graven images, the mainstream of Jewish creative life has flowed in the direction of the written word. The centre of energy in Russian life will be essentially Jewish.

Only in the child-like emotional veracity of the negro can America find its creative fulfilment, for, excepting the Indian tradition, there is no other cultural background to the present day amorphous civilization of America. The negro's emotional life is moon-hit, in him life is the most primeval, what is before sex is also capable of sublimation into something beyond sex. Music carries this undifferentiated quality. It is essentially an art of the night. Negro music is at present but a note in the desert, a plaintive, new-born cry, a note nevertheless taken up by the whole of America, distorted into a syncopated, savage, sexless roar. The emergence of this new form in America lies much more in the distant future, than the immediate epoch we face in Europe and Russia, for the two latter are bound to exert a cultural influence long before the American life-form has taken shape.

Thus a woman finds these three forms of vitality important, because they are the only crystallizations of emotional integrity in the world today. For only by reaching back to the deepest and simplest emotional sources native to a particular life-form can a creative harmony be projected into the world. Expressed in the symbolism of the Earth, the Sun and the Moon, the Holy Trinity of Christianity is realized and surpassed by these three emergent cultures in Russia, Europe and America.

Chronology

1899 Born 1 December in Buenos Aires

1906–17 Comes to England. Educated at Canford Cliffs, Dorset; Heathfield, near Ascot; Tudor Hall in Kent, and Byam Shaw School of Art in London

1920 Returns to Argentina for twenty-first birthday party

1920–22 Taught watercolour painting by Georges William Thornley who takes her to see the murals by Puvis de Chavannes at the Pantheon in Paris and to Rodin's studio. Attends Leon Underwood's Brook Green School

1921–4 Attends the Slade part-time. Taught by Henry Tonks. Visits Paris and Spain with Robin Bartlett

1925 Marries Robin Bartlett, a Slade student. Father dies. Moves to Varengéville in France with Bartlett

1926 Meets Joseph Bard. Separates from Bartlett

1927 Settles with Bard in Fitzroy Square

1928 Spends winter 1927/8 in Rapallo with Ezra Pound. Photographed by Cecil Beaton. Bard publishes *Shipwreck in Europe*. They move to Paris and live on the rue Schoelcher. Meets André Breton who introduces her to Paul Éluard. Works under Czech painter Foltýn. Meets Brancusi

1929 Spends the spring in Basque country and the summer at Bandol and Menton with Foltýn

1930 Goes to Cap Martin. Starts to paint abstract works. Back in London, moves to Bramham Gardens. Rodney Thomas designs her bathroom and interior

1931 Publication of *The Island* magazine (ed. Joseph Bard and Leon Underwood)

1933 First solo exhibition at Bloomsbury Gallery. Joins the London Group at Henry Moore's suggestion

1934 Meets Dylan Thomas and David Gascoyne. Becomes friends with Ben Nicholson, Jacob Epstein and Alexander Calder in Hampstead

1935 Meets Paul Nash in Swanage through Ashley Havinden. Starts an affair with Nash, which is to last until 1944

1936 Participates in the 'International Surrealist Exhibition' in London (11 June–4 July). In the summer goes to Brittany. Buys a Rolleiflex and takes many photographs of the Ploumanac'h rocks. A member of the Surrealist Group in England, she signs the fourth Bulletin International du Surréalisme

1937 Features in Alfred Barr's 'Fantastic Art, Dada and Surrealism' exhibition at MOMA in New York. Signs the English Surrealist Group's declaration 'We Ask Your Attention' on the occasion of the AIA exhibition 'For Peace, Democracy and Cultural Development'. Spends the summer with Roland Penrose, Lee Miller, Paul and Nusch Éluard in Devon. Then they all go to Mougins to join Picasso and Man Ray. Participates in the 'Surrealist Objects and Poems' exhibition at the London Gallery in November. Also exhibits with the London Group. Participates in the 'International Surrealist Exhibition' in Tokyo

1938 Participates in the 'International Surrealist Exhibition' at the Galerie des Beaux-Arts in Paris and in the following one at Gallerie Robert in Amsterdam. Also participates in several Surrealist exhibitions organized by Mesens in England (Gloucester and Liverpool)

1939 Spends holidays in Toulon. Gives a Surrealist party for artist refugees from Central Europe (Gropius, Breuer, Moholy-Nagy, Kokoschka). Exhibits works at the 'Living Art in England' Surrealist and Constructivist exhibition at the London Gallery

1940 Participates in the 'Surrealism Today' exhibition at the Zwemmer Gallery in London. Contributes to the *London Bulletin 18–20* published in June. Works in a canteen in Savile Row as part of her war duty. Marries Joseph Bard

1941 Exhibits with the London Group

1942 Contributes to Toni del Renzio's Surrealist publication *Arson*. Solo exhibition at the Redfern Gallery

1943 Mother dies on 13 April

1944 Spends the summer in the Lake District and paints watercolour landscapes

1945 War ends. Visits Cornwall with Bard

1946 Paul Nash dies

1948 Appears on the TV programme 'The Eye of the Artist' and on a programme introduced by James Laver on 'Hats'

1949	Meets Peggy Guggenheim in Venice on the occasion of the PEN Club meeting
1952–3	Spends the winter in Tenerife. Meets Eduardo Westerdahl. Makes watercolours, collages and frottages. Goes back every year until 1957
1958	Moves to West House, Melbury Road, Kensington
1960–66	Visits Cornwall
1965	Discovers acrylic paints
1971	Participates in the 'Britain's Contribution to Surrealism of the '30s and '40s' exhibition at the Hamet Gallery in London. Full-scale retrospective of her works at the Commonwealth Institute
1975	Joseph Bard dies on 26 July
1977	TV reconstruction of a Barcelona meeting of the British Surrealists with Conroy Maddox, George Melly, Roland Penrose and Robert Melville
1985	Begins a series of paintings based on her 1936 photographs of Ploumanac'h rocks
1986	Photographed by Lord Snowdon modelling clothes by Issey Miyake. Her works are featured in all the exhibitions celebrating the fiftieth anniversary of the London 'International Surrealist Exhibition' of 1936 (in Canterbury, Newcastle, Leeds and Bristol)
1987	Moves to a smaller flat in Melbury Road
1988	Publishes *A Look at My Life*, her autobiography, written with Andrew Lambirth
1990	Huge retrospective exhibition of her works at Birch and Conran. Elected Academician of the Royal Academy
1991	Dies in London on 17 November

Selected exhibitions

Solo exhibitions

1933 Bloomsbury Gallery, London
1942 The Redfern Gallery, London
1947 The Léger Gallery, London
1949 'Recent Paintings', The Hanover Gallery, London
1951 The Hanover Gallery, London
1957 The Obelisk Gallery, London
1962 Brook Street Gallery, London
1963 Bilico Gallery, Rome
1964 'Retrospective Exhibition of Paintings and Collages, 1930–64', Brook Street Gallery, London
1965 Moyan Gallery 2, Manchester
1971 'Retrospective Exhibition', Commonwealth Art Gallery, London
1975 New Art Centre, London
1976 'A Decade of Discoveries', New Art Centre, London
1978 New Art Centre, London
1980 Clementi House, London
1981 'Paintings and Drawings', New Art Centre, London
1983 New Art Centre, London
1984 New Art Centre, London
1985 'Objects from a Landscape: Ploumanac'h and Port-Cros', New Art Centre, London
1990 'Retrospective Exhibition', Birch and Conran Gallery, London
1999 'Eileen Agar, 1899–1991: A Centenary Exhibition', Scottish National Gallery of Modern Art, Edinburgh, and Leeds City Art Gallery, Leeds
2000 'A Centenary Exhibition', The Redfern Gallery, London
2004 'Eileen Agar: An Imaginative Playfulness', The Redfern Gallery, London
2008 'Eileen Agar: An Eye for Collage', Pallant House Gallery, Chichester

Group exhibitions

1936 'International Exhibition of Surrealism', New Burlington Galleries, London
'Fantastic Art, Dada and Surrealism', Museum of Modern Art, New York

1937 Artists' International Association, 'Unity of Artists for Peace, Democracy and Cultural Development', Grosvenor Gallery, London
'38 Surrealist Objects and Poems', London Gallery, London
'Exposition Internationale du Surréalisme', Nippon Salon, Tokyo, Japan

1938 'Exposition Internationale du Surréalisme', Galerie des Beaux-Arts, Paris
'Exposition Internationale du Surréalisme', Galerie Robert, Amsterdam
'Pictures on the Staircase', London Gallery, London

1939 'Living Art in England', London Gallery, London
'British Surrealists and Abstract Paintings', Northampton Art Gallery, Northampton
Artists' International Association, 'Artists for Peace, Democracy and Cultural Development', Whitechapel Art Gallery, London

1940 'Surrealist Work: Artists' International Association', Whitechapel Art Gallery, London
'Surrealism Today', Zwemmer Gallery, London

1942 'New Movements in Contemporary Art: Contemporary Work in England', London Museum, London

1945 'Works by Eminent British Artists', Russell-Cotes Gallery, Bournemouth

1951 'London Group', New Burlington Galleries, London

1952 'The Mirror and the Square', New Burlington Galleries, London

1956 'Modern Trends in Watercolour Painting', Cumberland House, Museum and Art Gallery, Portsmouth

1961 'John Moore's Exhibition', Walker Art Gallery, Liverpool
'The Art of Assemblage', Museum of Modern Art, New York

1964 'Fifty Years of British Art, 1914–64', London Group Jubilee Exhibition, Tate Gallery, London

1965 'Art in Britain, 1930–40', Marlborough Gallery, London

1967 'The Enchanted Domain, Surrealist Art', The City Gallery, Exeter

1969 'John Moore's Exhibition', Walker Art Gallery, Liverpool

1971 'Britain's Contribution to Surrealism of the '30s and '40s', Hamet Gallery, London

1973 'The Illusion of Reality and the Reality of Illusion', McRobert Centre, Stirling University

1974 'British Painting 1974', Hayward Gallery, London
'Hampstead in the Thirties: A Committed Decade', Camden Arts Centre, London

1976 'Leon Underwood and 12 Girdler's Road', New Art Centre, London
'British Painting, 1900–1960', Sheffield City Art Gallery, Sheffield

1978 'Dada and Surrealism Reviewed', Hayward Gallery, London
'Surrealism Unlimited', Camden Arts Centre, London

1979 'International Exhibition of Soft Art', Kunsthaus, Zurich
'Thirties: British Art and Design Before the War', Hayward Gallery, London

1980 'The Other Face of the Avant-Garde, 1910–1940', Palazzo Reale, Milan and Stockholm
'Photographic Surrealism' (travelling exhibition), New York, Cleveland and elsewhere

1981 'Image and Form: British Sculpture in the 20th Century, 1901–1950', Whitechapel Art Gallery, London
'The First Fifty Years: British Art in the Twentieth Century', National Art Gallery, Wellington, New Zealand

1982 'The Women's Art Show, 1950–1970', Nottingham City Museum and Art Gallery, Nottingham
'Les Enfants d'Alice, la peinture surréaliste en Angleterre, 1930–1960', Galerie 1900–2000, Paris

1983 'The Story of the Artists' International Association, 1933–1953', Museum of Modern Art, Oxford (and touring)

1984 'In the Spirit of Surrealism', Oliver Bradbury and James Birch Fine Art, London

1985 'British Women Surrealists', Blond Fine Art, London
'A Salute to British Surrealism, 1930–1950', The Minories, Colchester; Blond Fine Art, London; Ferens Art Gallery, Hull
'Je ne comprends pas la raison', James Birch Fine Art, London
'La Planète affolée: surréalisme, dispersion et influences 1938–1947', La Vieille Charité, Musées de Marseille, Marseilles

1986 ‘British Surrealism: Fifty Years On’, The Mayor Gallery, London
‘Surrealism in England: 1936 and After’, Canterbury College of Art, Herbert Read Gallery, Canterbury (and touring)
‘Angels of Anarchy and Machines for Making Clouds: Surrealism in Britain in the Thirties’, Leeds City Art Galleries, Leeds
‘Women Artists of the Surrealist Movement’, Baruch College Gallery, New York
‘1936 Surrealism: Photographs, Collages, Documents’, Zabriskie Gallery, New York

1987 ‘La Femme et le Surréalisme’, Musée Cantonal des Beaux-Arts, Lausanne
‘Surrealismi Retretti’, Art Centre Suomi, Finland

1988 ‘The Surrealist Spirit in England’, Whitford and Hughes, London

1989 ‘British Surrealism’, Blond Fine Art, London
‘I Surrealisti’, Palazzo Reale e Arengario, Milan
‘Die Surrealisten’, Schirn Kunsthalle, Frankfurt

1990 ‘Collages Surréalistes’, Galerie Zabriskie, Paris

1992 ‘Ten Decades: Careers of Ten Women Artists Born 1897–1906’, Norwich Gallery, Norfolk Institute of Art and Design, Norfolk

1996 ‘In the Mind’s Eye: Surrealist Works on Paper’, Whitworth Art Gallery, Manchester

1997 ‘El Objecto Surrealista’, IVAM Centre Julio Gonzalez, Valencia, Spain

2000 ‘Inaugural Exhibition’, Tate Modern, London (and subsequent displays)

2008 ‘British Surrealism and Other Realities’, The Sherwin Collection, Middlesbrough Institute of Modern Art, Middlesbrough

Bibliography

On Eileen Agar

Ades, Dawn, 'Notes on Two Women Surrealist Painters', *Oxford Art Journal*, III/1 (April 1980), pp. 36–43
Agar, Eileen, with Andrew Lambirth, *A Look at My Life* (London, 1988)
Byatt, A. S., 'An Imaginative Playfulness', foreword to *An Imaginative Playfulness: Eileen Agar, Paintings and Works on Paper*, exh. cat., London, The Redfern Gallery (2004)
Jaguer, Edouard, *Les Enfants d'Alice, Le Surréalisme en Angleterre 1930–1947*, exh. cat., Paris, Galerie 1900–2000 (1982), pp. 19–23
Lambirth, Andrew, ed., *Eileen Agar: An Eye for Collage*, exh. cat., Pallant House Gallery, Chichester (Chichester and Lausanne, 2009)
Penrose, Roland, 'A Decade of Discoveries', foreword to exhibition catalogue, London, New Art Centre (1976); also in *Eileen Agar, Paintings, Drawings*, exh. cat., London, New Art Centre (1981)
Remy, Michel, 'Eileen Agar', in *Ellebore* (Paris, 1981)
Simpson, Ann, ed., *Eileen Agar, 1899–1991*, exh. cat., Scottish National Gallery of Modern Art, Edinburgh (1999). With contributions by Ann Simpson, David Gascoyne and Andrew Lambirth.
Trevelyan, Julian, *Indigo Days* (London, 1957)
van Joel, Mike, 'A Twentieth Century Artist's Life: A Conversation with Eileen Agar', in *Eileen Agar at 90: A Special Presentation, Art Line*, special supplement (1989)
Walker, Ian, 'The Comic Sublime: Eileen Agar at Ploumanac'h', *Tate Papers*, 4 (Autumn 2005)
Wilson, Andrew, 'The Spirit of Surrealism', in *Eileen Agar at 90: A Special Presentation, Art Line*, special supplement (1989)
Young Mallin, Judith, 'Eileen Agar', in *Surrealism and Women*, ed. Mary Ann Caws, Rudolf Kuenzli and Gwen Raaberg (Cambridge, MA, 1991)
And exhibition catalogues from the Brook Street Gallery, the Hamet Gallery, Birch and Conran, John Bonham, Murray Feely Fine Art, the Commonwealth Art Gallery, the New Art Centre and the Redfern Gallery.

Miscellanies

Bard, Joseph (and Leon Underwood), *The Island*, I/1–4 (15 June 1931–15 December 1931)
Breton, André, Interview with Indice, Tenerife, Canary Islands (1935), in What is Surrealism?, ed. Franlin Rosemont (New York, 1978)
Buck, Louisa, *The Surrealist Spirit in Britain*, exh. cat., Whitford and Hughes, London (1988)
Chadwick, Whitney, *Women Artists and the Surrealist Movement* (London, 1981)
Mesens, E.L.T., ed., *London Bulletin*, 1–20 (April 1938–June 1940). Only the first issue bore the name *London Gallery Bulletin*
—, *Troisième Front / Third Front* (London, 1944)
Neve, Christopher, *Leon Underwood* (London, 1974)
Nevinson, R.W., 'The Adventure of Modern Art in England', *The Island*, I/4 (December 1931), pp. 112–14
Penrose, Antony, *Roland Penrose: The Friendly Surrealist* (Edinburgh, 2001)
Penrose, Roland, *Scrapbook* (London, 1982)
Read, Herbert, ed., *Surrealism* (London, 1936)
—, *The Philosophy of Anarchism* (London, 1940)
Remy, Michel, *Surrealism in Britain* (Aldershot, 1999)
Robertson, Alexander, Michel Remy and Mel Gooding, *Surrealism in Britain in the Thirties*, exh. cat., Leeds City Art Galleries (Leeds, 1986)
Roughton, Roger, ed., *Contemporary Poetry and Prose*, I/1–8 (May 1936–December 1936) and II/9–10 (Spring 1937–Autumn 1937)
Trevelyan, Julian, *Indigo Days* (London, 1957)

Acknowledgements

This book is dedicated to the memory of Eileen Agar, who was always prompt to welcome me and share memories in a hospitable and friendly atmosphere. I remember her with immense affection.

This book would never have been possible without the generous help of a large number of friends, artists and gallery owners, all enthusiasts of Surrealism. Among them I wish to acknowledge my debt to the Agar Estate and to Conor Mullan, one of the dynamic directors of the Redfern Gallery, and to all those who gave their disinterested permission for the reproduction of the works of Eileen Agar, especially James Birch of the Birch Gallery, James Mayor of the Mayor Gallery, James Gould of Offer and Waterman Gallery, Jessica Sutcliffe, Silvano Levy and Jeffrey Sherwin, who let me reproduce works which they own.

Special mention should be made of the invaluable assistance provided by India Lewis, then a MA student at the Courtauld Institute and now a research assistant at the Redfern Gallery, whose expertise was precious in the retrieval and digitization of Eileen Agar's works.

I am also deeply indebted to the Tate Gallery Archives and to the Archives at the V&A for letting me access their resources and, on a more personal level, to Andrew Lambirth, a close friend and biographer of Eileen Agar, and Simon Martin of the Pallant House Gallery in Chichester.

All my gratitude to Desmond Morris, John Welson, Dawn Ades and Silvano Levy, the torchbearers of living Surrealism in England, for their friendship and encouragement.

Obviously this project could not have been successfully completed without the enthusiasm and patient understanding of Michael Leaman, the director of Reaktion Books and of his assistants, especially Harry Gilonis, Vivian Constantinopoulos, Howard Trent and Martha Jay, who were generous to a fault with technical advice.

It also gives me special pleasure to thank Margaret Llasera, my dear friend and university colleague in Nice, my generous, indefatigable reader, and Guy Raybaud, a most efficient and dedicated computer graphic designer in Beuil who did not count the hours he spent scanning images and texts.

Finally I have a special grateful thought for my children, Nicolas and Lisa, and for Susie, my wife, who unflaggingly supported this project and patiently helped me bring it to fruition. She, too, dearly cherished Eileen Agar as an artist and friend.

This book has been selected for, and is supported by, a Publications Grant from the Paul Mellon Centre for Studies in British Art. May they be warmly thanked for their generosity and constant and often courageous support of studies in British Art.

Photographic acknowledgements

The author and publishers wish to express their thanks to the below sources of illustrative material and/or permission to reproduce it. Some locations of artworks are also given below, in the interests of brevity. Every effort has been made to contact copyright holders; should there be any we have been unable to reach or to whom inaccurate acknowledgements have been made please contact the publishers, and full adjustments will be made to any subsequent printings.

Collection of the author: 115; reproduced courtesy of Birch and Conran Fine Art, London: 11, 111, 133; reproduced courtesy of James Birch: 23; The British Museum, London: 62; © The Cecil Beaton Studio Archive at Sotheby's: 4; City Art Gallery, Leeds (courtesy Leeds Museum and Galleries): 44; from *Contemporary Poetry and Prose*, 3 (July 1936): 38; Eileen Agar Estate (reproduced courtesy of the Redfern Gallery, London): 30, 56, 57, 58, 59, 128; © Lee Miller Archives, 2016: 60, 61; The Mayor Gallery, London: 46, 77; photos Andrew Murray (reproduced courtesy the Murray Family Collection): 28, 34; National Art Gallery, Auckland, New Zealand: 45; National Portrait Gallery, London: 3; The Potteries Museum and Art Gallery, Stoke-on-Trent: 63; private collections: 2, 8, 12, 14, 20, 21, 22, 24, 27, 29, 32, 42, 43, 47, 48, 49, 50, 51, 69, 70, 71, 72, 75, 76, 78, 79, 86, 90, 92, 93, 97, 99, 101, 105, 107, 108, 109, 112, 116, 117, 119, 120, 121, 124, 125, 131, 132, 134; private collection and N.A.G. Leeds: 25; private collections (courtesy of the Redfern Gallery): 74, 88, 89, 91, 96, 106, 110, 113, 118, 122, 123; private collection (on loan to Southampton City Art Gallery): 85; private collection (courtesy Jessica Sutcliffe): 31 (and back cover); from Herbert Read, *Surrealist Objects and Poems* (London: London Gallery, 1937): 64; Redfern Gallery, London (photos

Redfern Gallery; reproduced courtesy of the Redfern Gallery): 5, 6, 9, 15, 16, 102, 103, 114, 126, 127, 129, 130; Scottish National Gallery of Modern Art, Edinburgh: front cover; Tate, London (photos © Tate, London 2016): 7, 19, 68, 84, 104; Tate Archive, London (photos © Tate, London 2016): 10, 17, 18, 26, 52, 53, 54, 55, 66, 67, 73, 94, 98, 100, 135; works known to have been destroyed: 39, 40, 41, 64, 65, 87.

Index